WITHDRAWN
UTSA Libraries

WORK AND FAMILY IN THE NEW ECONOMY

RESEARCH IN THE SOCIOLOGY OF WORK

Series Editor: Lisa Keister

Recent Volumes:

Volume 3:	Unemployment
Volume 4:	High Tech Work
Volume 5:	The Meaning of Work
Volume 6:	The Globalization of Work
Volume 7:	Work and Family
Volume 8:	Deviance in the Workplace
Volume 9:	Marginal Employment
Volume 10:	Transformation of Work
Volume 11:	Labor Revitalization: Global Perspectives and New Initiatives
Volume 12:	The Sociology of Job Training
Volume 13:	Globalism/Localism at Work
Volume 14:	Diversity in the Workforce
Volume 15:	Entrepreneurship
Volume 16:	Worker Participation: Current Research and Future Trends
Volume 17:	Work Place Temporalities
Volume 18:	Economic Sociology of Work
Volume 19:	Work and Organizations in China after Thirty Years of Transition
Volume 20:	Gender and Sexuality in the Workplace
Volume 21:	Institutions and Entrepreneurship
Volume 22:	Part 1: Comparing European Workers Part A: Experiences and Inequalities Part 2: Comparing European Workers Part B: Policies and Institutions
Volume 23:	Religion, Work, and Inequality
Volume 24:	Networks, Work and Inequality
Volume 25:	Adolescent Experiences and Adult Work Outcomes: Connections and Causes

RESEARCH IN THE SOCIOLOGY OF WORK VOLUME 26

WORK AND FAMILY IN THE NEW ECONOMY

EDITED BY

SAMANTHA K. AMMONS
University of Nebraska-Omaha

ERIN L. KELLY
University of Minnesota

United Kingdom – North America – Japan
India – Malaysia – China

Emerald Group Publishing Limited
Howard House, Wagon Lane, Bingley BD16 1WA, UK

First edition 2015

Copyright © 2015 Emerald Group Publishing Limited

Reprints and permissions service
Contact: permissions@emeraldinsight.com

No part of this book may be reproduced, stored in a retrieval system, transmitted in any form or by any means electronic, mechanical, photocopying, recording or otherwise without either the prior written permission of the publisher or a licence permitting restricted copying issued in the UK by The Copyright Licensing Agency and in the USA by The Copyright Clearance Center. Any opinions expressed in the chapters are those of the authors. Whilst Emerald makes every effort to ensure the quality and accuracy of its content, Emerald makes no representation implied or otherwise, as to the chapters' suitability and application and disclaims any warranties, express or implied, to their use.

British Library Cataloguing in Publication Data
A catalogue record for this book is available from the British Library

ISBN: 978-1-78441-630-0
ISSN: 0277-2833 (Series)

ISOQAR certified
Management System,
awarded to Emerald
for adherence to
Environmental
standard
ISO 14001:2004.

Certificate Number 1985
ISO 14001

INVESTOR IN PEOPLE

CONTENTS

LIST OF CONTRIBUTORS   vii

INTRODUCTION: WORK AND FAMILY IN THE
NEW ECONOMY   xi

ITALIAN PARENTS IN PRECARIOUS WORK:
HOW NORMATIVE BELIEFS AFFECT SOCIAL
UNDERSTANDINGS OF THE WORK–FAMILY
BOUNDARY
    Anna Carreri   *1*

THE SECOND SHIFT AND THE NONSTANDARD
SHIFT: HOW WORKING NONSTANDARD HOURS
AFFECTS THE RELATIONSHIP BETWEEN THE
DIVISION OF HOUSEHOLD LABOR AND WIVES'
FAIRNESS PERCEPTIONS
    Katie James and Jody Clay-Warner   *35*

TECHNOLOGY USE AND THE NEW ECONOMY:
WORK EXTENSION, NETWORK CONNECTIVITY,
AND EMPLOYEE DISTRESS AND PRODUCTIVITY
    Noelle Chesley and Britta E. Johnson   *61*

WHAT WOULD JESUS HAUL?: HOME, WORK, AND
THE POLITICS OF MASCULINITY AMONG
CHRISTIAN LONG-HAUL TRUCK DRIVERS
    Rebecca L. Upton   *101*

POLICING WORK AND FAMILY: HOW WORKERS
COPE WITH CONTRADICTIONS AND DILEMMAS OF
IMPLEMENTING WELFARE-TO-WORK
    Tiffany Taylor   *127*

WHEN WORK BECOMES FAMILY: THE CASE OF LOW-WAGE CAREGIVERS
Naomi Gerstel and Dan Clawson   151

IS WORK-FAMILY CONFLICT A MULTILEVEL STRESSOR LINKING JOB CONDITIONS TO MENTAL HEALTH? EVIDENCE FROM THE WORK, FAMILY AND HEALTH NETWORK
Phyllis Moen, Anne Kaduk, Ellen Ernst Kossek,   177
Leslie Hammer, Orfeu M. Buxton, Emily O'Donnell,
David Almeida, Kimberly Fox, Eric Tranby, J. Michael
Oakes and Lynne Casper

THE RELATIONSHIP OF WORK UNIT PRESSURE TO SATISFACTION WITH WORK–FAMILY BALANCE: A NEW TWIST ON NEGATIVE SPILLOVER?
Jacquelyn Boone James, Marcie Pitt-Catsouphes,   219
Tay K. McNamara, David L. Snow and
Patricia L. Johnson

GIVING CARE AND PERCEIVING DISCRIMINATION: THE SOCIAL AND ORGANIZATIONAL CONTEXT OF FAMILY RESPONSIBILITIES DISCRIMINATION
Lindsey Trimble O'Connor, Julie A. Kmec and   249
Elizabeth C. Harris

POLICY OR EMPOWERMENT? POLICY ENVIRONMENTS, POLITICAL EMPOWERMENT, AND WORK–FAMILY CONFLICT
Leah Ruppanner   277

DISCUSSING WORK-LIFE FIT: FACTORS THAT PREDICT MANAGERIAL PROMOTION OF FLEXIBLE WORK ARRANGEMENTS
Stephen Sweet, Jacquelyn Boone James and   301
Marcie Pitt-Catsouphes

IMPLEMENTING INSTITUTIONAL CHANGE: FLEXIBLE WORK AND TEAM PROCESSES IN A WHITE COLLAR ORGANIZATION
Kelly Chermack, Erin L. Kelly, Phyllis Moen and   331
Samantha K. Ammons

LIST OF CONTRIBUTORS

David Almeida	Pennsylvania State University, University Park, PA, USA
Samantha K. Ammons	Department of Sociology & Anthropology, University of Nebraska at Omaha, Omaha, NE, USA
Orfeu M. Buxton	Department of Biobehavioral Health, Pennsylvania State University, University Park, PA, USA; Division of Sleep Medicine, Harvard Medical School, Boston, MA, USA; Department of Medicine, Brigham and Women's Hospital, Boston, MA, USA; Department of Social and Behavioral Sciences, Harvard School of Public Health, Boston, MA, USA
Anna Carreri	Department of Sociology and Social Research, University of Trento, Trento, Italy
Lynne Casper	Department of Sociology, University of Southern California, Los Angeles, CA, USA
Kelly Chermack	Walden University, Minneapolis, MN, USA
Noelle Chesley	Department of Sociology, University of Wisconsin-Milwaukee, Milwaukee, WI, USA
Dan Clawson	Department of Sociology, University of Massachusetts, Amherst, MA, USA
Jody Clay-Warner	Department of Sociology, University of Georgia, Athens, GA, USA

Kimberly Fox	Department of Sociology, Bridgewater State University, Bridgewater, MA, USA
Naomi Gerstel	Department of Sociology, University of Massachusetts, Amherst, MA, USA
Leslie Hammer	Department of Psychology, Portland State University, Portland, OR, USA
Elizabeth C. Harris	Department of Sociology, Washington State University, Pullman, WA, USA
Jacquelyn Boone James	Sloan Center on Aging & Work, Boston College, Chestnut Hill, MA, USA
Katie James	Department of Sociology, University of Georgia, Athens, GA, USA
Britta E. Johnson	Department of Sociology, University of Wisconsin-Milwaukee, Milwaukee, WI, USA
Anne Kaduk	Department of Sociology, University of Minnesota, Minneapolis, MN, USA
Erin L. Kelly	Department of Sociology, University of Minnesota, Minneapolis, MN, USA
Julie A. Kmec	Department of Sociology, Washington State University, Pullman, WA, USA
Ellen Ernst Kossek	Krannert School of Management, Purdue University West Lafayette, IN, USA
Tay K. McNamara	Sloan Center on Aging & Work, Boston College, Chestnut Hill, MA, USA
Phyllis Moen	Department of Sociology, University of Minnesota, Minneapolis, MN, USA
J. Michael Oakes	Division of Epidemiology & Community Health, University of Minnesota, Minneapolis, MN, USA

List of Contributors

Lindsey Trimble O'Connor	Sociology & Anthropology Program, California State University Channel Islands, Camarillo, CA, USA
Emily O'Donnell	Harvard School of Public Health, Harvard University, Boston, MA, USA
Marcie Pitt-Catsouphes	Sloan Center on Aging & Work, Boston College, Chestnut Hill, MA, USA
Leah Ruppanner	University of Melbourne, Melbourne, Australia
David L. Snow	Department of Psychiatry, Yale University School of Medicine, New Haven, CT, USA
Stephen Sweet	Department of Sociology, Ithaca College, Ithaca, NY, USA
Tiffany Taylor	Department of Sociology, Kent State University, Kent, OH, USA
Eric Tranby	Department of Sociology and Criminal Justice, University of Delaware, Newark, DE, USA
Rebecca L. Upton	Department of Sociology & Anthropology, DePauw University, Greencastle, IN, USA

INTRODUCTION: WORK AND FAMILY IN THE NEW ECONOMY

ABSTRACT

This volume of Research in the Sociology of Work *brings together chapters that address the intersection of work and family in the new economy. In our introductory chapter, we provide a short overview of some characteristics associated with the current era, briefly introduce the other chapters in the volume, and explain the major themes that connect them. The chapters are diverse – ranging from how precarious employment influences the boundaries workers create between work and family, to how social environments present within work teams, organizations, or nations shape the work–family intersection, and workplace interventions that aim to create more flexibility in when, where, and how work is done. Collectively, these chapters reflect some of the breadth present in the growing work–family field. We conclude with our parting thoughts about the current state of work–family scholarship.*

Volume 26 of *Research in the sociology of work: Work and family in the new economy* provides a multi-faceted examination of how paid work intersects with family and personal life today. The 12 diverse and compelling chapters cluster around four themes: (1) how changing work conditions affect families and employees' health and well-being, (2) how work is understood and experienced by workers in specific occupations or social locations, (3) what we can learn by moving the analysis from individuals and couples to the social environment, including how teams, organizations, and public policies affect the work–family interface, and (4) analyses of new interventions that intend to ameliorate work–family conflict by changing public policy, workplace practices, or communities.

The common thread binding all the chapters together is the backdrop of the new economy, which we characterize as having rising income inequality, the continued rise of nonstandard work, further erosion of unions, technological advancements that encourage permeable boundaries between work and home, and the pressures of a global 24/7 economy. In this era, some workers have more stability than others and some workers put in long hours at work but have some control over when, where, and how they work. But many workers are poorly compensated and struggle with underemployment; have little say over their schedules; lack adequate benefits; and must cobble together several jobs and/or rely heavily on kinship networks to make ends meet (Jacobs & Gerson, 2004). The new economy generates an aura of insecurity for all (Hollister, 2011; Kalleberg, 2011; McCall & Percheski, 2010).

When we submitted our call for papers, we formulated a "dream list" of possible submissions that would help address what we saw as deficiencies or limitations in our interdisciplinary field of study. We hoped we would receive nuanced analyses that were sensitive to class variation in work conditions and to diverse family formations (such as the studies by Bianchi, 2011; Schieman & Glavin, 2011; Shows & Gerstel, 2009), and research that addresses how current work conditions are experienced in different life course stages and in different policy contexts. To a large extent, we succeeded. After profiling the merits of each chapter, we discuss what is missing from the volume and conclude with our parting thoughts about the current state of work–family scholarship.

PROGRESSION OF CHAPTERS

The volume begins with chapters that address the work conditions, arrangements, and technology that are a vital part of the new economy. The first two chapters discuss what happens to family lives when work schedules regularly deviate from 8am to 5pm or when there is no implicit or explicit understanding of long-term employment. Although many workers would prefer to have stable employment with fairly standard hours, contingent and nonstandard work schedules are likely to continue due to the demands of a 24/7 economy (McMenamin, 2007; United States Department of Labor, 2005). We have also seen a growth in the use of information and communication technology (such as mobile phones and email) for work and personal needs. The chapter by Chesley and Johnson investigates how technology use effects workers' sense of distress and productivity.

Introduction

In the chapter "Italian Parents in Precarious Work: How Normative Beliefs Affect Social Understandings of the Work−Family Boundary," Carreri explains how families with chronic job insecurity view their work and care responsibilities and craft work−family boundaries. Using interview data gathered from Italian parents working in contingent and temporary jobs, Carreri challenges separate spheres ideology and vividly illustrates that work and family were intertwined in respondent's narratives, but in unexpectedly gendered terms. Carreri's respondents were not able to invest in any one particular job long enough to feel a sense of belonging or achievement, which affected how they viewed and enacted their family roles. While fathers gained fulfillment through increased time with their children, these mothers thought unfulfilling work impeded their ability to be "good mothers." In support of work−family enrichment theory, feeling accomplished outside the home made them feel like better mothers to their children. This chapter is also a valuable addition to the small but growing scholarship on work−family boundaries. Not only does this chapter contextually ground boundary work processes within normative gender and cultural frameworks and institutional structures, but it provides a rare glimpse into how boundaries are understood and negotiated by couples. Carreri's chapter also offers readers an insightful gendered analysis of precarious work and its potential for constraining or freeing workers.

In the chapter "The Second Shift and the Nonstandard Shift: How Working Nonstandard Hours Affects the Relationship between the Division of Household Labor and Wives' Fairness Perceptions," James and Clay-Warner discuss how the timing of employment affects wives perceptions of fairness in the household division of labor. The authors use data from the National Survey of Families and Households, and compare married women who work primarily nonstandard hours to those with more standard schedules. Although wives reported spending close to four times the amount of time on housework as their husbands, they find that only a third thought their arrangement was unfair. Surprisingly, wives with standard hours were more likely to have an unfavorable view of chore imbalance than those with nonstandard hours. James and Clay-Warner make sense of this finding by considering who was doing routine "feminine" chores (such as preparing meals, washing dishes, and cleaning house). As the authors explain, wives with nonstandard hours thought their husbands participated in these types of chores to a greater extent than other husbands, and this mitigated their perceptions of unfairness. This chapter enriches our understanding of the interplay between work conditions, the gendered division of household labor, and couples' relationships − including the economy of gratitude (Hochschild, 1989) − in a new economy.

As Chesley and Johnson discuss in their chapter "Technology Use and the New Economy: Work Extension, Network Connectivity, and Employee Distress and Productivity," we do not have a good sense of how technology is being used or by whom, nor its perceived effects on workers. This chapter examines the prevalence of email, instant messaging, texting, cell phones, and use of social networking sites while at work, and assess whether these forms of technology are linked to self-reported distress and work productivity. The authors provide a useful descriptive analysis of who uses each form of technology, by individual, job, and organizational characteristics, and find that technology influences us in unexpected ways. Using nationally representative data collected in 2008, they find that the overwhelming majority of Americans use at least one form of information and communication technology (ICT) while at work. Most ICT users did not think that using these forms of technology had changed their overall work time, but half reported that they thought it expanded the number of people they communicated with and a sizable number did think that it affected their productivity and perceived distress. By offering new insights how technology shapes our lives, for better and for worse, Chesley and Johnson's chapter is invaluable to employers, scholars, and practitioners who seek to foster thriving workplaces.

Having set the stage with changing employment relations, technological tools, and family arrangements, the next three chapters describe how new economy conditions are experienced differently across groups. The chapters by Upton; Taylor; Gerstel and Clawson, respectively, address the work–family interface differs by occupation, and how gender influences and structures work experiences. The chapter by Gerstel and Clawson delves even further by investigating how gender, race, and class intersect and produce unique viewpoints and experiences among those in the similar fields.

The chapter "What Would Jesus Haul?: Home, Work, and the Politics of Masculinity among Christian Long-Haul Truck Drivers" by Upton contributes to two small but growing areas of work–family literature – research on fatherhood and masculinity construction (see Kimmel, 1996; Townsend, 2002; Williams, 2010) and studies of religious beliefs and practices affecting work and family decisions (see Ammons & Edgell, 2007; Aune, 2010; Wilcox, 2004). Using ethnographic data, Upton explores how religious beliefs shape what it means to be a good father, good husband, and good worker among Christian long-haul truck drivers. These men tempered and infused the rugged blue-collar masculinity associated with driving big rigs for days on end with provider and protector roles. One of the main contributions of this chapter is Upton's vivid portrayal of how these truckers sought to come across as "average joes," but also used their truck décor, behavior at truck stops, and clothing to redefine public images of Christian masculinity and truckers.

Likewise, the chapter "Policing Work and Family: How Workers Cope with Contradictions and Dilemmas of Implementing Welfare-to-Work" by Taylor addresses how workers construct identities as a good worker and a good person, but it focuses on job demands rather than personal beliefs. Taylor discusses the strategies that welfare-to-work caseworkers employ to find meaning in their work and cope with the requirements of the job. Building on Hochschild's "emotion labor" (1979, 1983), Taylor shows how these women justified sanctioning their clients (who were often mothers) and coaxed them to take the jobs commonly offered to those living at the economic margins of society – dead end jobs which are low in wages, status, and schedule control. The caseworkers framed these pressures as "helping" their clients and drew upon working class notions of femininity and motherhood that differ notably from middle class expectations of intensive mothering. In particular, Taylor demonstrates how caseworkers argue that good mothers were self-reliant, sacrificed their pride, and took care of their children by economically providing for them.

In the chapter "When Work Becomes Family: The Case of Low-Wage Caregivers," Gerstel and Clawson study certified nurse assistants (CNAs) and demonstrate that how these jobs operate as an escape from their family caregiving responsibilities. In a nuanced version of Hochschild's (1997) reversal model, they show us why recent scholars have failed to find support for one of the work–family strategies that Hochschild identified: we have simply not been looking in the right place. The authors briefly compare the feminized field of CNAs, which includes many women of color, to three other health-related occupations (doctors, nurses, and emergency medical technicians). Their analysis of gender, class, race, scheduling practices, and organizational context suggests that CNAs are especially prone to view work as an escape from home. This chapter demonstrates why we need detailed studies of occupations and comparative occupational analyses. As Gerstel and Clawson show, by attending to both the specifics of certain jobs and how the workers in different jobs occupy different social locations, we come away with a fuller understanding of the work–family intersection.

Moen, Kaduk, and their colleagues; James, Pitt-Catsouphes, McNamara, Snow, and Johnson; Trimble O'Connor, Kmec, and Harris; Ruppanner continue to examine how work and family are intertwined, but they emphasize the way these experiences differ across work teams, organizations, or nations. Collectively, these four chapters offer a greater understanding of how our social environments alter how we interpret the work−family intersection. In other words, they make the classic sociological move of looking at individuals embedded in a given social environment to argue that it is important to go beyond the individual level of analysis in order to understand individuals' experiences.

The chapter "Is Work-Family Conflict a Multilevel Stressor Linking Job Conditions to Mental Health? Evidence from the Work, Family and Health Network" by Moen, Kaduk, and their colleagues looks inside a work organization to investigate how particular work conditions affect the work−family conflict and mental health (including job satisfaction, emotional exhaustion, perceived stress, and psychological distress) of employees who report to the same manager and work together as a team. Moen, Kaduk, and their colleagues use clustered data from over 700 high-tech professionals to demonstrate that work conditions affect work−family conflict and mental health, as other research in sociology and health psychology has shown, *and* that these work conditions are shared appraisals that vary across work teams. Work-to-family conflict, they find, varies systematically across teams as does job satisfaction and emotional exhaustion or "burnout." This multi-level analysis considers how work conditions at the team level affect individuals' mental health, net of the individual's personal appraisals of their work situation and their own family status, gender, etc. For example, when there is a more supportive climate reported in a team, individuals report lower work-to-family conflict. Additionally, this chapter investigates work-to-family conflict as one mechanism through which work conditions affect mental health, suggesting that policies and initiatives that address the work−family interface will promote employees' mental health as well.

In the chapter "The Relationship of Work Unit Pressure to Satisfaction with Work−Family Balance: A New Twist on Negative Spillover?," James, Pitt-Catsouphes, McNamara, Snow, and Johnson investigate what leads employees of a large health care organization, who were mostly women, to have greater or lesser satisfaction with their work−family balance. In addition to studying factors such as hours worked, caregiving demands, pace of work, and schedule control, James et al. include an unusual variable in their study: budgetary pressures present within the work unit. With over a quarter of work units under-budget and half over-budget, they speculated that these environments might create different types of pressure on employees, which in turn influence how satisfied individuals are with their work−family balance. As expected, those with caregiving responsibilities, long work hours, and a hectic work pace had lower satisfaction, but being

Introduction

in an under-budget work unit also predicted lower levels of satisfaction. James et al. then investigated whether schedule control moderated these effects and found that high levels of schedule control tempered the negative relationship between caregiving responsibilities and satisfaction, and between being under-budget and satisfaction. One of the main contributions of this study is that it pushes scholars to think in innovative ways about how work−family resources, demands (including pressures to meet the budget that workers now feel directly), and workplace context intersect to shape perceptions.

In the chapter "Giving Care and Perceiving Discrimination: The Social and Organizational Context of Family Responsibilities Discrimination," Trimble O'Connor, Kmec, and Harris investigate who reports encountering workplace discrimination because of their caregiving responsibilities ("family responsibilities discrimination"). They use data from the 2008 National Survey of the Changing Workforce and assess how caregiving responsibilities and organizational contexts influence these perceptions. While only eight percent of respondents thought they had encountered family responsibilities discrimination, the authors speculate that the actual number may be much higher if it was assessed in a different way. Nevertheless, perceived family responsibilities discrimination was more prevalent in some contexts. For example, individuals juggling both childcare and eldercare, those with less schedule control, or respondents who did not think their supervisors supported their personal or family needs had higher levels of perceived discrimination. This study provides an important look at a new framing of work−family challenges as discrimination and points to new questions about how employees and others respond to claims of discrimination.

In the chapter "Policy or Empowerment? Policy Environments, Political Empowerment, and Work−Family Conflict," Ruppanner examines how structural conditions at the country level shape work-to-family and family-to-work conflict. This chapter builds on the long tradition of comparative social policy scholarship, including key work investigating how public policies affect women's employment and attainment. But Ruppanner's work is part of a newer stream of research that investigates cross-national variation in other relevant outcomes such as employers' work−family policies (Den Dulk, Groeneveld, Ollier-Malaterre, & Valcour, 2013) and the subjective experience of the work−family interface (see Lyness, Gornick, Stone, & Grotto, 2012; Ruppanner & Bostean, 2014). Using data from 29 nations, Ruppanner assesses how the percentage of female parliamentarians, the average number of children aged 3−6 enrolled in public childcare, and presence of affirmative action programs in each country (collectively, termed "gender and family-responsive environments") shaped how much work–family conflict was experienced by individuals, and whether the amount of conflict varies by parental status and gender. Ruppanner finds that levels of work–family conflict vary across nations, and within: mothers have higher levels of conflict than others. However, the expansiveness of public childcare enrollment and percentage of female parliamentarians in nations matters: high levels were associated with lower conflict, but not always in uniform ways across men, women, mothers, and fathers. Ruppanner's chapter illustrates why we must pay attention to cultural context and social structures if we want to understand how individuals experience work–family.

The last two chapters turn to workplace interventions to address work-life concerns. They reflect a growing interest in organizational changes — as opposed to individual and family coping strategies — that might facilitate the reconciliation of paid work and nonwork responsibilities. While "family-friendly policies" and benefits have long been studied, they have also been critiqued as limited in both their reach and their impact (e.g., Correll, Kelly, O'Connor, & Williams, 2014; Deitch & Huffman, 2001; Kelly & Moen, 2007). The studies included here investigate more innovative approaches to changing workplaces, highlighting initiatives that deliberately aim to make working flexibly more common and accepted.

In the chapter "Discussing Work-Life Fit: Factors that Predict Managerial Promotion of Flexible Work Arrangements," Sweet, James, and Pitt-Catsouphes examine the Supervisor-Promoted Flexibility (SPF) program implemented in a large financial organization. The authors note that many have called for expanded access to flexible work arrangements (FWA) but there have been few studies examining which managers allow these arrangements and even less research on initiatives to encourage managers to support and promote FWA (but see Hammer, Kossek, Anger, Bodner, & Zimmerman, 2011). Using longitudinal data, Sweet and colleagues analyze how many conversations managers have about potential use of FWA, whether they initiate those conversations (or employees do), and the approval rate once FWA are discussed. The authors find that the multifaceted SPF program increased access to FWA and conveyed the message that supervisors should actively facilitate FWA. Managers who participated in SPF training, those who had previous experience with employees using FWA, those with more subordinates, and those who believed supporting flexibility would affect their performance reviews positively engaged in more conversations about FWA. Participating in SPF training also significantly increased the likelihood that managers initiated FWA conversations. The study also includes a creative experiment, in which half of the managers received a personalized report comparing their early "performance" in FWA discussions with their peers; this too encouraged managers to actively pursue FWA conversations. Sweet and colleagues also provide new evidence that the gender of managers is *not* associated with FWA conversations in this sample and that older managers are initially as likely and then become more likely than younger managers to discuss FWA options with their subordinates. This study provides exciting avenues for future research on the social dynamics of FWA negotiations as well as concrete ideas for workplace interventions that aim to normalize and encourage workplace flexibility.

The final chapter in the volume is written by Chermack, Kelly, Moen, and Ammons. This chapter investigates how workplace initiatives that aim to create more flexibility in when, where, and how work is done are implemented in practice. Like the Sweet et al.'s chapter, this chapter begins by summarizing the limitations of flexible work policies as they are often implemented today. Then, using qualitative data from four work teams at Best Buy Co., Inc.'s corporate headquarters, Chermack and colleagues analyze how Results Only Work Environment (ROWE) changed the practices, processes, and expectations in some teams while only prompting minimal changes in others. ROWE attempted to challenge institutionalized expectations regarding who decides when, where, and how work is done and coordinated. Chermack and colleagues claim that deliberate institutional work is required to make that happen and they describe, in a grounded way from ethnographic observations and interviews, how that occurs — or is stymied — in different teams. One key argument is that managers with more task-specific knowledge, such as those who rose from the ranks to now manage work they had previously performed, feel more confident evaluating the "results" of their subordinates' work and so these managers find it easier to cede control and welcome the team's self-management of work processes, as ROWE suggests they do. This chapter provides insights into more participatory approaches to redesigning work practices and norms in ways that support family and personal life but also describes the challenges of making meaningful changes.

DIRECTIONS FOR FUTURE RESEARCH

While we are pleased with the content of this edited volume and each chapter pushes our knowledge of work and family forward, some gaps remain.

We share our reflections of these limitations in an effort to encourage further research on these questions.

First, we hoped the volume would address how working class and poor households manage and conceptualize work and family. "Balancing work and family" is often assumed to be a middle class or elite problem but the dilemmas faced by parents and caregivers with few economic resources need further explication. From our perspective, low or unstable wages that do not provide for your basic needs or the basic needs of dependents – that do not allow a worker to care for a family – are a work–family issue. In the research literature, though, there has historically been a divide between work–family research and studies of the work lives and survival strategies of poor women or poor families. Scholars, such as Henly and Lambert (2014), Williams (2010) and Dodson (2009), have begun addressing this divide. But, we need to continue to press for inclusion in both our theories of the work–family interface and deeper analysis of the work conditions of lower-wage workers. Such work might illustrate the real consequences of limited family-supportive public policies (and limited enforcement of existing labor standards) in the United States, particularly since organizational policies and benefits are much less likely to be available to less advantaged workers and their families. This work might also uncover and more systematically analyze the acute work–family conflicts for workers who are not concerned with moving up a career but are instead trying hard to keep a halfway-decent job while caring for family members on a shoestring budget. In their 2010 review of the field, Bianchi and Milkie push for this integration and we also believe more research that starts from that conceptualization will be valuable.

We had also hoped for more submissions that examined how multiple social locations produce new perspectives, particular privileges or challenges, and innovative ways to negotiate work and family at the individual, household, and community levels. While a discussion of gender was present in many of the chapters in this volume, only Gerson and Clawson's chapter adopted an intersectional approach. Despite a growing body of literature on how race/ethnicity shapes work and family experiences (see Browne & Misra, 2003; Garey, 1999; Gerstel & Sarkisian, 2005; Roehling, Jarvis, & Swope, 2005; Wingfield, 2013), and extensive theorizing about how race, class, and gender intersect (such as Anderson, 1996; Collins, 1994, 2000; Wingfield & Alston, 2012), much work remains to be done to empirically identify how race/ethnicity, gender, social class, and sexual orientation intertwine to produce different constraints and understandings of the work−family interface.

Third, there is limited attention to precarious work and how it influences the health and well-being of individuals and families. Within the volume, only one chapter out of 12 (Carreri) grapples with this topic. While we see some attention to job insecurity and job loss, especially among scholars who study the relationship between work−family conflict and health & well-being, we know less about the chronic strains caused by precarious employment and how it can spill over into families. Job insecurity research is thriving and often examines the health impacts of insecurity (e.g., Benach et al., 2014; Burgard, Brand, & House, 2009; Burgard, Kalousova, & Seefeldt, 2012), but fewer studies examine how the experience of precarious work affects family members or even discourages family formation. This insight comes through loud and clear in studies of working class young adults (e.g., Silva, 2013). We believe work−family scholarship should systematically take up these questions of how work − including a lack of steady work or good work as well as the need to devote oneself fully to long or unstable work schedules if one has landed in a decent job − affects personal relationships and young adults' experiences of forming families through childbearing, cohabitation, or marriage.

When Toby Parcel edited the last work and family volume in *Research in the Sociology of Work* in 1999, the field was just emerging and placing work−family articles in journals was sometimes difficult. Fifteen years later, we have seen a tremendous growth in work−family publications, the recent formation of an interdisciplinary professional association (the Work and Family Researchers' Network), and a journal dedicated explicitly to the work−family intersection (*Community, Work, and Family*). Work and family research has become more mainstream within sociology, though the field is explicitly interdisciplinary. With scholars from psychology, business, social work, family studies and human development, communications, economics, public policy, as well as sociology, the field is humming. The challenges of the current situation include corralling all that activity so that terminology and theories are consistently applied across disciplines. At a minimum, scholars should know what is going on in different disciplines and conversations so we can assess where frames and theories differ and engage in productive dialogues. In other words, tight coordination is probably not feasible and may be unwise but we believe scholars should work to stay abreast of new questions and claims so we can identify what we know and what we still need to explore. Certainly, the conversation pitch has risen to a steady roar, and it is an exciting time to be a work—family scholar. We look forward to seeing what the next 15 years will bring.

Samantha K. Ammons
Erin L. Kelly
Editors

REFERENCES

Ammons, S. K., & Edgell, P. (2007). Religious influences on work—family trade-offs. *Journal of Family Issues, 28*(6), 794—826.

Anderson, C. D. (1996). Understanding the inequality problematic: From scholarly rhetoric to theoretical reconstruction. *Gender & Society, 10*(6), 729—746.

Aune, K. (2010). Fatherhood in evangelical Christianity: Negotiating with mainstream culture. *Men and Masculinities, 13*(2), 168—189.

Benach, J., Vives, A., Amable, M., Vanroelen, C., Taraga, G., & Muntaner, C. (2014). Precarious employment: Understanding an emerging social determinant of health. *Annual Review of Public Health, 35*, 229—253.

Bianchi, S. M. (2011). Changing families, changing workplaces. *Future of Children, 21*, 15—36.

Bianchi, S. M., & Milkie, M. M. (2010). Work and family research in the first decade of the 21st century. *Journal of Marriage and Family, 72*, 705—725.

Browne, I., & Misra, J. (2003). The intersection of gender and race in the labor market. *Annual Review of Sociology, 29*, 487—513.

Burgard, S. A., Brand, J. E., & House, J. S. (2009). Perceived job insecurity and worker health in the United States. *Social Science & Medicine, 69*(5), 777—785.

Burgard, S. A., Kalousova, L., & Seefeldt, K. S. (2012). Perceived job insecurity and health: The Michigan recession and recovery study. *Journal of Occupational and Environmental Medicine, 54*(9), 1101—1106.

Collins, P. H. (1994). Shifting the center: Race, class, and feminist theorizing about motherhood. In E. N. Glenn, G. Chang, & L. R. Forcey (Eds.), *Mothering: Ideology, experience and agency* (pp. 45—65). New York, NY: Routledge.

Collins, P. H. (2000). *Black feminist thought: Knowledge, consciousness, and the politics of empowerment*. New York, NY: Routledge.

Correll, S. J., Kelly, E. L., O'Connor, L. T., & Williams, J. C. (2014). Redesigning, redefining work. *Work and Occupations, 41*(1), 3—17.

Deitch, C. H., & Huffman, M. L. (2001). Family responsive benefits and the two-tiered labor market. In R. Hertz & N. L. Marshall (Eds.), *Working families: The transformation of the American home* (pp. 103—130). Oakland, CA: University of California Press.

Den Dulk, L., Groeneveld, S., Ollier-Malaterre, A., & Valcour, M. (2013). National context in work-life research: A multi-level cross-national analysis of the adoption of workplace work-life arrangements in Europe. *European Management Journal, 31*(5), 478—494.

Dodson, L. (2009). *The moral underground: How ordinary Americans subvert an unfair economy*. New York, NY: New Press.

Garey, A. I. (1999). *Weaving work and motherhood*. Philadelphia, PA: Temple University Press.

Gerstel, N., & Sarkisian, N. (2005). Sociological perspectives on families and work: The import of gender, class, and race. In M. Pitt-Catsouphes, E. E. Kossek, & S. Sweet (Eds.), *The work and family handbook* (pp. 237−265). New York, NY: Psychology Press.

Hammer, L. B., Kossek, E. E., Anger, W. K., Bodner, T., & Zimmerman, K. L. (2011). Clarifying work−family intervention processes: The roles of work−family conflict and family-supportive supervisor behaviors. *Journal of Applied Psychology*, 96(1), 134.

Henly, J. R., & Lambert, S. (2014). Unpredictable work timing in retail jobs: Implications for employee work-life outcomes. *Industrial and Labor Relations Review*, 67(3), 986−1016.

Hochschild, A., & Machung, A. (1989). *The second shift: Working parents and the revolution at home* (pp. 463−481). New York, NY: Viking Penguin.

Hochschild, A. R. (1979). Emotion work, feeling rules, and social structure. *American Journal of Sociology*, 85(3), 551−575.

Hochschild, A. R. (1983). *Managed heart: Commercialization of human feeling*. Berkeley, CA: University of California Press.

Hochschild, A. R. (1997). *The time bind: When work becomes home and home becomes work*. New York, NY: Metropolitan Books.

Hollister, M. (2011). Employment stability in the US labor market: Rhetoric versus reality. *Annual Review of Sociology*, 37, 305−324.

Jacobs, J., & Gerson, K. (2004). *The time divide: Work, family, and gender inequality*. Cambridge, MA: Harvard University Press.

Kalleberg, A. L. (2011). *Good jobs, bad jobs: The rise of polarized and precarious employment systems in the United States, 1970s−2000s*. New York, NY: Russell Sage Foundation.

Kelly, E. L., & Moen, P. (2007). Rethinking the clockwork of work: Why schedule control may pay off at work and at home. *Advances in Developing Human Resources*, 9(4), 487−506.

Kimmel, M. (1996). *Manhood in America*. New York, NY: Free Press.

Lyness, K. S., Gornick, J. C., Stone, P., & Grotto, A. R. (2012). It's all about control: Worker control over schedule and hours in cross-national context. *American Sociological Review*, 77(6), 1023−1049.

McCall, L., & Percheski, C. (2010). Income inequality: New trends and research directions. *Annual Review of Sociology*, 36, 329−347.

McMenamin, T. M. (2007). A time to work: Recent trends in shift work and flexible schedules. *Monthly Labor Review*, 130(12), 3−15.

Roehling, P. V., Jarvis, L. H., & Swope, H. E. (2005). Variations in negative work-family spillover among White, Black, and Hispanic American men and women: Does ethnicity matter? *Journal of Family Issues*, 26(6), 840−865.

Ruppanner, L., & Bostean, G. (2014). Who cares? Caregiver well-being in Europe. *European Sociological Review*, 30(5), 655−669.

Schieman, S., & Glavin, P. (2011). Education and work-family conflict: Explanations, contingencies, and mental health consequences. *Social Forces*, 89, 1341−1362.

Shows, C., & Gerstel, N. (2009). Fathering, class, and gender: A comparison of physicians and emergency medical technicians. *Gender and Society*, 23, 161−187.

Silva, J. M. (2013). *Coming up short: Working-class adulthood in an age of insecurity*. New York, NY: Cambridge University Press.

Townsend, N. (2002). *The package deal: Marriage, work and fatherhood in men's lives*. Temple, PA: Temple University Press.

United States Department of Labor. (2005). *Contingent and alternative arrangements.* Retrieved from http://www.bls.gov/news.release/conemp.nr0.htm. Accessed in February.

Wilcox, W. B. (2004). *Soft patriarchs, new men: How Christianity shapes fathers and husbands.* Chicago, IL: University of Chicago Press.

Williams, J. (2010). *Reshaping the work-family debate: Why men and class matter.* Cambridge, MA: Harvard University Press.

Wingfield, A. H. (2013). *No more invisible man: Race and gender in men's work.* Philadelphia, PA: Temple University Press.

Wingfield, A. H., & Alston, R. S. (2012). The understudied case of Black professional men: Advocating an intersectional approach. *Sociology Compass, 10,* 728–739.

ITALIAN PARENTS IN PRECARIOUS WORK: HOW NORMATIVE BELIEFS AFFECT SOCIAL UNDERSTANDINGS OF THE WORK–FAMILY BOUNDARY

Anna Carreri

ABSTRACT

Purpose — *This chapter investigates how normative beliefs attributed to insecure paid work and care responsibilities affect social understandings of the work–family boundary, and either challenge or reinforce traditional links between gender and moral obligation.*

Methodology — *Within an interpretive approach and from a gender perspective, I present a discourse analysis of 41 interviews with Italian parents.*

Findings — *This chapter shows that women in the sample felt forced into blurred boundaries that did not suit their work–family normative beliefs. Men in the sample perceived that they had more boundary control, and they created boundaries that support an innovative fatherhood model. Unlike women, men's boundaries aligned with their desires.*

Research limitations − *The specific target of respondents prevents empirical comparisons between social classes. Moreover, the cross-level analysis presented is limited: in particular, further investigation is required at the level of organizational cultures.*

Originality − *The study suggests not only thinking in terms of work−family boundary segmentation and integration but also looking at the normative dimensions which can either enhance or exacerbate perceptions of the work−family interface. The value of the study also stems from its theoretically relevant target.*

Keywords: Work−family boundary; work−family normative beliefs; discourse; precarious work; parenthood

INTRODUCTION

It is in the double boundary − between productive and reproductive labor, on the one hand, and between male and female labor on the other − that we can trace the origins of the long-standing male breadwinner/female caregiver model. Contrary to the usual practice in contemporary sociological research, I want to direct attention to the fact that modern societies have resolved the dilemma between working and caring by dividing women and men into not only two different domains but also two different moral categories. Women and men have been differently expected to gain personal fulfillment, respectively by caring for children and husbands, and by sharing the rewards of their independent work achievements (Gerson, 2002). In this sense, the modern model of work−family articulation lasted so long because it was based not only on a social boundary, which operated at the institutional level, but also on a symbolic and ethical boundary that, in a gender-specific way, affected the individual as a cultural mandate.

Nevertheless, recent social changes − both in the organization of work and within the family − have challenged conceptual frameworks by unpacking taken-for-granted assumptions about work and family as two distinct spheres of activity (Houston, 2005), and they have produced new moral dilemmas and still unexplored sense-making processes regarding the meanings and significance of work and care. More specifically, the increased precariousness of work conditions, due to the spread of temporary contracts with lower employment and unemployment benefits, and the higher flexibility in work performance tend to confer greater responsibility upon individuals to negotiate the boundaries between work and family and to make sense of work and care activities. This is especially so in Italy, where parents in precarious work are left to cope on their own (Berton, Richiardi, & Sacchi, 2012). In this context, exploring people's margins of agency becomes of primary importance in shedding light on the micro-mechanisms through which actors constantly construct the work−family boundary. The family and the workplace are sites of ethical codes that are taken-for-granted frameworks for thinking, acting, and evaluating self and society (Blair-Loy, 2010). Examining them makes it possible, on the one hand, to adopt a subjective perspective in considering how the normative prescriptions of precarious work and those of care in the young family shape and may cross the work−family boundary, and on the other, to analyze how they forge the link between gender and moral obligation. To gain access to these dimensions, I integrate the interpretive approach with a gender perspective, and used the following conceptual tools: the concept of time as socially and culturally constructed (Daly, 1996), the concept of the boundary between work and family as located along the continuum from "integration" to "separation" (Nippert-Eng, 1996), and the concept of "ethical boundaries" with reference to definitions of "the right thing to do" regarding work and care demands. From a sociological perspective, the central fact is that this kind of analysis makes it possible not only to observe how the normative dimensions of precarious work and those of care enhance a certain symbolic and social order, but also to show that, in other respects, they challenge it in an innovative way, with the actors being aware of it or otherwise.

THEORETICAL FRAMEWORK

Between the Opposing Trends of the Decline and Persistence of the Ideology of Separate Spheres

During the Fordist era, employment become more stable and secure for many workers (Castel, 2007). The double separation between the public and private sphere and, within the latter, the division between paid and unpaid work according to gender, was the great mechanism of "conciliation" in industrial democratic societies, both at the micro-level of individuals and families and at the macro-level. These separations allowed not only the fulfillment of care and income needs but also the maintenance of separate areas of experiences, needs, values, and rhythms of time that were potentially in conflict. Of course, the male breadwinner/female caregiver model was never a reality because not everyone had access to it, but it worked precisely as an ideological template: that is, as a reference for both labor policies and corporate social policies and, more generally, people's cultural orientations (Moen & Roehling, 2005).

In recent decades a number of profound work and family changes have occurred in the Western world that have made the traditional male breadwinner/female caregiver model even more impracticable. More importantly, these changes have undermined the social, symbolic, and ethical boundaries between work and care, as well as the gender division of labor on which that model was based. Hence, interpretation of the current configuration of the work–family balance appears more difficult and controversial. In order to grasp the complex interdependencies between family and work, the following analysis considers the debates on employment and family changes simultaneously, rather than, as is more often the case, treating them as separate topic areas. The analysis of literature suggests that the ideology of separate spheres is eroding; however there are also very different interpretations of the phenomenon which all stress the continuing influence of this cultural model.

In regard to the former aspect, one finds, for example, an increased proportion of women, and particularly of mothers, in the labor market (Villa, 2010). Secondly, the deregulation of employment relationships, in the form of uncertainty and precariousness, affects family choices by encouraging their postponement because the conditions generally related to precarious employment do not guarantee the economic livelihood of a family, as was instead in the case of the male breadwinner model (Bertolini, 2011). Moreover, the deregulation of working hours in the form of flexibility alters the sharp distinction traditionally drawn between work time and other times of life by the ideology of separate spheres. This generates effects on the everyday organization of work and family whose interpretation is still very controversial (Blossfeld & Drobnic, 2001). Finally, signs of change are apparent in the behaviors, and especially in the attitudes, of men in regard to domestic work, and in particular, care work. There is evidence that fathers want more involvement and express greater dissatisfaction than mothers with current patterns of work–family balance (Gershuny, 2000; ISTAT, 2011).

On the other hand, confirming the hypothesis of the continuing influence of separate spheres ideology, it is often the woman in a heterosexual couple who has a flexible and precarious job; and it is usually also the woman who is employed on less protected and more discontinuous contractual bases (Villa, 2010). Secondly, the current models of motherhood, described in terms of "intensive motherhood" (Hays, 1996) or "family devotion schema" (Blair-Loy, 2003), are reformulations of the traditional ideology. Finally, the fact that job insecurity tends to exacerbate the work–family conflict for men but not for women seems to confirm the persistence of the division of responsibilities in the work–family system according to gender (Steiber, 2009).

The conceptualization of family and work in terms of separate spheres resulting from Fordist work culture has not only long justified a certain organization of the work–family system that today – at least for the younger generation undergoing the phases of family formation – competes with that of temporary and flexible work; it has also imbued the approach and theoretical frame through which work–family issues have been investigated (Wharton, 2006). Indeed, work–family studies lack – except in some rare cases (Becker & Moen, 1999; Berke, 2003; Blair-Loy, 2003; Townsend, 2002) – in-depth analysis of the micro-mechanisms underlying the construction of meanings, practices, and choices in the articulation of the work–family nexus, especially in relation to the new conditions of temporary employment. Because this study analyzes the emerging cultural models of the work–family boundary, it moves in this direction, and can therefore make an original contribution to the debate. Furthermore, as shown in the next section, Italy's labor market and policy context are particularly interesting in regard to precariousness.

Precariousness in Italy: Consequences on the Work–Family Boundary

In recent decades, the European labor market has experienced a significant growth of nonstandard work (Barbieri, 2009), but the Italian labor market is especially interesting because it is marked by a singular process of deregulation of the labor market which is called "partial and targeted de-regulation" (Esping-Andersen & Regini, 2000). This term refers to a set of important labor market reforms which since the mid-1990s have liberalized the use of fixed term contracts and externals collaborators, but affect only new entrants, specifically the younger cohorts and women, while leaving the legislation on insider workers and the terms and conditions of their open-end contracts largely unaltered.[1] Furthermore, these legislative changes have not been off-set by adjustment of the welfare system to the new social risks associated with flexibility. In Italy, therefore, for the majority of the workers involved, contractual flexibility tends to be tied to precariousness on several levels: temporary contracts, fewer employment benefits (training, holidays, career advancement, etc.), limited or no unemployment benefits, lower social security contributions, uncertainty of income, high flexibility in work performance, and limited organizational autonomy (Berton et al., 2012; Clark & Postel-Vinay, 2009). However, the risk of a temporary contract being linked to precarious conditions is significantly higher for women, because they are not only overrepresented in all types of temporary employment, but also more frequently have less protected and more discontinuous contracts (Villa, 2010), thus reproducing the asymmetry in the distribution of responsibilities between men and women.

In Italy, family policies are best characterized as "unsupported familialism" (Saraceno, 2010), where the dilemma of work *versus* family is still largely relegated to the private sphere while state involvement in this issue is missing and family (and the family network) is the main care and welfare provider. Reconciliation policy in Italy is also inadequate at company level, where "family-friendly" measures are not widespread and many employees are unable to take advantage of them (Den Dulk, 2001). Moreover, the childcare services are quite expensive and also scant in comparison to the demand (Saraceno, 2011). The consequence is that the male breadwinner family model is still the hegemonic cultural model in Italy, at least at the institutional level. Nevertheless, some findings suggest that the ideology of separate spheres is eroding: although female participation is still remarkably lower than the European average, dual-earner families prevail in the northern regions of the country, where 60—70 percent of mothers with very young children are employed (ISTAT, 2011), especially university-educated women (ISTAT, 2013).

Finally, although recent policies have seen the deregulation of the Italian labor market as facilitating conciliation of work and family demands, these policies underestimate the actual impact of precarious work on women and on the distribution of responsibilities within couples (Poggio, 2010). Precarious workers, especially if female, are excluded from almost all the work—family conciliation instruments provided by the Italian government or existing in business practices, despite the fact that these individuals may have the greatest need (Saraceno, 2005). In fact, some authors have noted that, for Italian couples consisting of young precarious workers, income uncertainty as well as the discontinuity and variability of working hours disrupt the work−family balance, so that such couples must constantly redefine the strategies they adopt (Salmieri, 2009).

Theoretical Perspectives and Conceptual Tools

In order to grasp the subjective and experiential dimensions of the lives of parents in precarious work, and to shed light on the micro-mechanisms underlying linkages between work and family, I have chosen to integrate an interpretive approach (Geertz, 1973; Schwandt, 2010) with a gender perspective. The interpretive approach makes it possible to investigate the attribution of moral responsibilities according to gender (Gerson, 2002), thus avoiding prescriptive use of the concept of gender and the public/ private dichotomy (Ferree, 1990). The symbolic order and moral commitments, often gendered, invade people's preconscious expectations in ways not captured by the work/family literature's language of individual "tradeoffs" and "strategies," and by narrow rational action assumptions (Blair-Loy, 2010). I thus employ two conceptual tools: the concept of time as socially and culturally constructed (Daly, 1996); and the concept of the boundary between work and family as located along the continuum from "integration" to "separation" (Nippert-Eng, 1996).

As regards the first aspect, this study considers the work−family articulation to extend beyond time use, the mere chronometric aspect of x hours for work and y hours for family life. Time is instead conceptualized as a socially and culturally constructed product (Brannen, 2002; Daly, 1996). In fact, the explanatory model of rational choice, to which refer the perspectives that interpret time in objective manner as uniform and standardized does not allow one to grasp the qualitative and subjective components of time (Brannen & Nilsen, 2002). In recent years, there has been a strong emphasis within work−family studies on the need to integrate the experiential and subjective dimension of time with the objective one in order to achieve more precise understanding of how time is experienced in the different domains of life, and of how the links between family and work are perceived by individuals (Dugan, Matthews, & Barnes-Farrell, 2012).

Secondly, my theoretical framework does not appeal to the dominant perspectives on how work and family domains conflict or enhance each another (Bellavia & Frone, 2005; Greenhaus & Powell, 2006); rather, it focuses on the concept of boundary between work and family. This concept is central in several recent studies (e.g., Ashforth, Kreiner, & Fugate, 2000;

Brannen, 2005; Clark, 2000; Kossek & Lautsch, 2008; Nippert-Eng, 1996), and it is analyzed along the continuum extending from "integration" to "separation" between these domains of life. Segmentation is the complete physical, behavioral, mental, and temporal separation of home and work so that all objects, people, and thoughts associated with one domain do not carry over into another. At the opposite end of the continuum is integration, where home and work domains are entirely blended. These poles are valid on a theoretical level: actually, most people fall in-between them due to context-specific structural constraints and social expectations associated with each domain (Kossek & Lautsch, 2008, 2012).

However, boundary work scholarship often emphasizes strategies, individual trade-offs, and coping practices rather than the substantive content of each domain in terms of social norms and moral prescriptions. These latter dimensions are crucial in our changing society because they redistribute constraints and resources among men and women which can either enhance or exacerbate perceptions of the work−family boundary. My aim in moving beyond the identification of an individual as a "segmenter" or an "integrator" is to understand the meanings of the work−family boundary in the context of respondents' lives. The same set of objective work−family demands may be viewed differently, by men and women for example, and result in different appraisals, depending on how they believe they should live their lives and how they perceive actually it is. I use the concept of "ethical boundaries" with reference to definitions of "the right thing to do" regarding work and care demands, which are understood as historically variable and affected by the social, economic, and historical context in which people live. "Ethical boundaries" are formed and shaped by the possibilities and constraints provided by an environmental context.[2] When people talk about their careers and family lives, they use repertoires which have been provided for them by a context-specific culture which supplies a range of ways to talk and think about an object or event (Gergen, 1991).

Finally, this framework makes it possible to show the permeability and flexibility between domains of life understood as sets of relationships, expectations, and meanings, and to understand how people build them and transit through them. Permeability (how some behaviors or emotions in one domain spillover into the other domain) and flexibility (role enactment in many different places or different times) are central concepts in work−family border theory (Clark, 2000) and boundary theory (Ashforth et al., 2000).

METHOD AND DATA

Sampling Strategy and Data Body

I conducted a discourse analysis on interview data because discursive and narrative practices are the privileged *loci* of sense-making. In this study, the questions and the theoretical framework directed the selection of interviewees. Subjects were identified by their theoretical significance and not because of their representativeness. My respondents were heterosexual couples in which both partners were precarious workers and had at least one child aged under 11: that is, the age at which most parents see children as old enough to be on their own at times (Ford, 1996). This specific target enabled me to observe what happens in the lives of people who have to balance the rigidity imposed by the times and needs of a child with the improvisation and adaptability that an unstable job necessarily entails.

Specifically, my definition of precarious workers, besides the area of temporary and part-time employment, which falls within unstable work by definition in all its contractual variants, included "occasional collaborators,"[3] "false self-employed workers,"[4] and members of cooperatives.[5] Although from the formal point of view these types of work fall outside the nonstandard area, from the substantive point of view they share the most important features of precarious workers (temporary employment, little or no level of protection and contractual social security, high flexibility in work performance, limited organizational autonomy, etc.). By contrast, I excluded traditional self-employed workers (such as entrepreneurs and freelancers) because they have a generally higher level of employment stability than do employees with permanent contracts (Barbieri & Scherer, 2009). The research also covered respondents transitioning between jobs and those looking for jobs, because these periods are unavoidable in a precarious worker's career, and especially so since the onset of the economic crisis (Murgia, Poggio, & Torchio, 2012).

In order to situate the narratives, I selected couples living in and around a city in Northeastern Italy. The couples were university-educated and consisted of people aged between 28 and 47. This specific target is particularly interesting because the traditional protection effect of higher education against the risks of unemployment and underemployment seems to have been eroded by the economic crisis (Lodovici & Semenza, 2012). The sample composition, moreover, reflected a recent national trend (Murgia et al., 2012).

Starting with a network of personal contacts and using the snowball sampling method, I interviewed parents separately in order to grasp differences between the partners and bring out their sense-making processes. Between April 2012 and April 2014 I contacted 23 couples but in five cases I was not able to interview both the partners for various reasons, such as permanent employment found in the meantime, moving abroad or to the south of Italy. This in fact was a sample of people who moved a great deal within Italy (and some abroad) and who worked in the service sector. Their families were often newly formed, mostly cohabiting, and contained few children (two-thirds of them had only one child) who were very young (the youngest child was seven months). The 41 home-based qualitative interviews lasted 1–2.30 hours, sometimes in the presence of children, and this facilitated a more thoughtful and confidential approach. At the time of the interview, the effects of the economic crisis were being strongly felt in Italy, and the unemployment rate was very high, especially among young people and women (ISTAT, 2013).

During the interviews, I asked respondents about their family situation, current job, work and care demands, the importance of work and family life, and their typical day in the past working week. I focused not only on the content and structure of the day and social interactions, but also on feelings at transitional moments in the day, especially when crossing the physical and mental boundaries between home and work. I encouraged the respondents to relate their responses to flexibility and work instability, giving space to their understanding of situations. All names are pseudonyms.

Analytical Strategy

The interviews were fully transcribed and analyzed using a qualitative analysis software, Atlas.ti. The linguistic dimensions that I primarily considered were interpretative repertoires, rhetorics, and accounting practices.

The concept of "interpretative repertoire" derives from the sociology of scientific knowledge (Gilbert & Mulkay, 1984) and refers to a cluster of terms, categories, and idioms that are closely conceptually organized and drawn upon to characterize and evaluate actions and events (Potter, 2012). In other words, they are relatively coherent ways of talking about objects and events, and part of any community's common sense. They provide a basis for shared and contested social understanding (Edley, 2001). In this sense, cultural repertoires, like discourse more in general, are both constructed and constructive (Potter, 2012).

The second analytical concept was that of "rhetoric" (Gherardi & Poggio, 2007). This peculiar analytical angle shows how people reset their inner coherence to themselves and to others and attribute a sense of order and meaning to their experiences.

The third analytical concept used to organize and analyze the data was derived from ethnomethodology. Harold Garfinkel (1967) introduced the concept of "accountability" in order to analyze practical reasoning processes. Accounts play a significant role in the management of relationships: our accounts usually develop on the basis of how we expect others to react and the consequences that we think may ensue.

Finally, I specify that the collection of interviews, systematization of the information, and analysis of the texts were closely intertwined, and not consecutive to one another (Charmaz, 2003).

RESULTS

Normative Dimensions Attached to Work in Conditions of Employment Instability

Analysis of the data showed no significant differences between men and women in the way that work time was experienced and interpreted. In most of the interviews collected, the specific content of the work was an important resource for personal identity. I found that in some respects the repertoires drew inspiration from the "work devotion schema" formulated by Blair-Loy (2003), which is a middle-class, traditionally masculine, twentieth-century model of devotion to a managerial career developed in part due to the pressures of late capitalism but it has a normative force of its own.

In line with the prescriptions of that cultural schema, apparent in the respondents' discourses was great devotion to work, and an emotional investment motivated by the content of the work and a passion for the profession. It is important to consider the particular composition of the respondents: they were young highly-qualified workers with a strong motivation to pursue their professional careers. Many respondents complained about a lack of fulfillment and attributed it to the temporariness and uncertainty of their employment contracts, which often did not allow them to see the results of their work. In the interviews collected, the lack of job satisfaction did not appear to be due to material and economic factors, but rather to the content and process of work, and it was indicative of great passion and devotion to the profession.

As Mattia, a 43-year-old teacher employed on a temporary contract and father of two children, said:

> I'd prefer to have a permanent contract, not so as to have a permanent job, but rather in order to have continuity with the activities I do at school. That is, I'd rather have the guarantee of remaining in the same school for a few years, in order to work better and make things better.

Nevertheless, the prescriptions of the work devotion schema were particularly severe, and they assumed different nuances for the precarious workers interviewed. I found that the major difference was the kind of loyalty that workers had to their employer. Whilst in the work devotion schema analyzed by Blair-Loy (2003) emotional allegiance to one's employer is explained by confidence in one's career advancement, in the case of the precarious workers interviewed this loyalty stemmed from the lack of future prospects that induced the respondents not only to build good relationships with employers but also constantly to broaden their networks in order to improve their chances of future employment. Indeed, the discontinuity of work and the lack of autonomy, stability, and family protection that distinguish precarious jobs force these workers to juggle multiple jobs in order to ensure reasonable economic security for themselves and, consequently, to achieve more confidence. This aspect was present in all the interviews, regardless of gender: indeed, the respondents felt compelled to keep other doors always open, never to refuse a job offer because *"opportunity knocks but once"* as many declared, and to invest in multiple jobs simultaneously because none was certain. I interpret these powerful normative prescriptions as an emerging variant of the work devotion schema (Blair-Loy, 2003).

For example, Elena, a working mother aged 30, said that she felt somehow obliged to invest in several jobs at once because she did not perceive her job at a child daycare center as her *"own job,"* but as replacement for a person on maternity leave. She perceived it as the job of another person, to whom she felt responsible, as if she was occupying a job on loan:

> It's a job that requires constancy, it requires application, and unfortunately, to be honest, sometimes I almost feel unable to commit enough, because in addition to thirty hours of work, I study, I have the internship, I have other activities that I must carry on because I don't perceive it as my own job, I mean the job I'll do all my life. (...) I'm forced to invest in other jobs ... to keep myself competitive even outside the daycare centre where I'm working.

Elena then went further in explaining the reasons why she felt compelled to invest in multiple jobs at once. In addition to doing her current work as best she could (hoping to be recalled in the future) she had constantly to seek a new job because de facto the contract would expire and she needed to ensure continuity of income for herself.

> Because if I devote myself fully to this work until September the thirtieth [*end date of the contract*], then what's left for me? The satisfaction of having worked well, but actually it's not my job, it belongs to another person! I'm trying, in all honesty, to do well because it's a job that I like and I'm emotionally attached to the guys I work with. But then when the contract expires, if I haven't invested in other jobs ... I won't know where to turn! (Elena, a 30-year-old mother working on temporary contracts)

Besides this norm, which prescribes maintaining multiple jobs at the same time, another element defines the culture of precarious work: being constantly available and never refusing a job offer. Hence, job precariousness makes blackmail by the employer more likely. The following extract gives a vivid image of this kind of availability. Bruno (a 40-year-old father working on temporary contracts) said that when they called him about a job involving handing out leaflets, he had to drop everything that he was doing because he had just enough time to get dressed and leave the house.

> Bruno: They call me the same day, at 10.30 am, or rather between 10.30 and 11.30 in the morning and they say: "Be there now." So if you have a plan, you have to give it up. You respond: "Okay, I'm going." Do you understand?
>
> Interviewer: So you have to give them your full availability?
>
> Bruno: Yeah, Yeah! Well, it's not that they have told you so, it's just obvious. At best, sometimes they tell me: "[...] Be there tomorrow. Be there tomorrow morning!"
>
> Interviewer: The best scenario is they warn you the day before.
>
> Bruno: Right. Yes, but this happens once out of ten calls. Most of the time they call you and you answer: "Okay." And they call at 11 on the same day! Watch out! You have just enough time to get dressed.

Normative Dimensions Attached to Care in Conditions of Employment Instability

From a gender perspective I found that respondents attached specific commitments to paternity and maternity, and crafted moral prescriptions that challenged traditional views of gender. In particular, men often viewed their relationship with their children as central to their personal development, and that this relationship required close emotional and educational involvement.

Francesco explicitly synthesized what made him feel a "good" father: being present as much as possible in the life of his daughter. He said:

> Knowing that I'm participating [in my daughter's life] helps me a lot, in feeling like a dad ... This is very important indeed. It helps me very much. [...] Sure, I hope to be successful one day, certainly to improve my economic situation, to make Emma (*his daughter*) and Luisa (*his wife*) peaceful, of course. But, really, for me it is essential in my opinion, more so nowadays, the presence of a parent ... I mean of both parents in a child's life, it is certainly important. I have seen many [family] situations where yes, there was great wealth, but in reality the child was happier with a little less but a bit more participating dad. The quality, as they say so often, the quality of time counts but also the amount does! (Francesco, a 34-year-old father working without contract)

This quote shows that men perceived economic contribution as a basic commitment but it played a minor role in their understanding of what makes a father a "good" father: time spent with children mattered more. This formulation challenges traditional views of paternity, and it is in accordance with the responsible fathering model (Doherty, Kouneski, & Erikson, 1998) which prescribes that the father be increasingly engaged in a nurturing role. Moreover, this understanding of fatherhood norms emphasizes the amount of time devoted to childcare.

As regards the parenting norms attributed to motherhood, I found that women respondents were searching for new ways to define their motherhood that did not force them to choose between devoting time to their children and professional fulfillment outside the family. This script is similar to the mother/worker integral model (Duncan, Edwards, Reynolds, & Alldred, 2003).

For example, Cristina, aged 41 and with a four-year-old son, who was working on a project contract, said:

> Cristina: It is very gratifying that I can do those two hours of work in the morning, that I must prepare for ... so I am very satisfied, and for this reason I feel better with my son, yes, yes.
>
> Interviewer: So the work can also help you feel good about Alessio (*her son*)?
>
> Cristina: Of course, indeed, I really felt bad when I didn't have work, I mean labor you love. If it was a job I didn't like, the matter would be different. I'm devoted to my son as other mothers are. But ... I'm here too. And in that I fulfilled myself! And I fulfill myself in work and with my son. I can. That is, if there was no work, it would not be the same thing.

Cristina considered her two hours of work per week to be essential because they enabled her to feel more serene as a mother. A similar experience was recounted by Barbara, who unlike Cristina, worked many hours a day (eight to ten hours in the office plus others at home in the evening when the children were asleep):

> I mean, I always comfort myself by saying that, in short, the children are happy if they see their mum happy with her work. Probably, if I gave up my work in order to spend more time with them, I don't think that I could give them all the excitement that I can now spread in those moments we spend together. Of course, I should try to spend quality time with them. This is often difficult because I'm tired, and this is something that stresses me very much. I say okay, because what little time I have I try to dedicate it completely to them. It is not that they mind their own business but you're there in the house; no, you listen to them, you're there with them, maybe they are just two hours, but those two hours, I mean, you're really there. Although it's difficult to do, it is very tiring ... (Barbara, a 35-year-old mother of two children and working on an annual research fellowship)

As with many of the other women interviewed, Barbara considered her work to be an essential resource for the full pursuit of motherhood, and ultimately for being a "good" mother. The women's ability to take care of their children and their partner depended not so much on the amount of time devoted to them, as on the quality of that time; that is, on how time was spent in the subjective terms of concentration, emotional involvement, and active listening. This kind of repertoire, central in the narratives of the women interviewed, seems to contradict the dominant theoretical perspective of work–family conflict (Greenhaus & Beutell, 1985) and instead supports "work–family enrichment theory" (Rothbard, 2001). Rather than time and energy being fixed and limited, mothers interpreted them as potentially expandable resources.

The Nexus between Precarious Work and Parenting: A Double Meaning

When considering the different moral commitments of men and women, job uncertainty assumed a double meaning when it was explicitly connected to parenthood. In the narratives of both men and women, for fathers job uncertainty was viewed as positive since it facilitated greater investment in the family in terms of identity, as well as time and energy, so that fathers could fulfill their paternal commitments. For example, Thomas, aged 41 and with a four-year-old son, who, at the time of the interview taught at a university on a project contract, said that he had always looked for a flexible job and avoided standard work, because among other advantages it gave him time to spend with his son:

> Again, there are many positive aspects, because I am at Alessio's (*his son*) disposal. Unfortunately, children often get sick when they are young and being at home has some advantages because I can give Cristina (*his partner*) a hand, so that Cristina, who is often at home, is not completely alone. If she had a husband who left home in the morning and returned in the evening ... But, if I'm here, nothing stops me from picking Alessio up from school ...

This reasoning, that precariousness allowed men greater flexibility and could therefore spend more time with their children, thus helping their wives, characterized the women's narratives as well when they talked of the impact that their partners' employment status had on the family domain. Claudia, a precarious worker and mother of a baby, said that her husband Paolo's job allowed him to be a more active and present father compared with other fathers in standard employment. At the same time it gave her a little more time to devote to activities outside the home:

> This is a good thing, compared to other dads, because he doesn't work from 8 a.m. to 8 p.m. every day, so maybe he is present all the morning, or all week, and then the week after he's totally absent. However, how can I say, it's more difficult to schedule things, but as far as the child rearing, in my opinion, it's easier because he has, all things considered, more time to be with him. Especially the time when he is awake. Whilst, for example, the problem I see with my sister is that her husband, who is a standard worker, sees his children only in the evening, when they go to sleep ... And this is also useful for me because if I have to study, he can be with Marco (*the son*). (Claudia, a 29-year-old mother working as an occasional collaborator)

By contrast, when job uncertainty concerned women it was because it hindered full accomplishment of the mother's role. However, women's sense-making processes did not appear related to the "ideology of intensive motherhood" (Hays, 1996) or to the "family devotion schema" (Blair-Loy, 2003), but rather to a new idea of motherhood that prescribed professional fulfillment outside the home if care activities were to be performed optimally. Care tended to be understood not only as an investment of time but also as the capacity to earn money and provide security for the family. This developmental view rejected the idea that individualism and commitment are in conflict by defining the search for independence as a necessary part of the process of becoming able to care for others, as has been found by other studies (Gerson, 2002). In most of the interviews, when precariousness concerned women, it caused a feeling of inadequacy with respect to the normative prescriptions on being a "good" mother and a sense of failure in achieving goals. This was most evident during periods of unemployment.

For example, the words of Mary (a 41-year-old mother of two children, looking for a job at the time of interview) expressed the need for complete economic independence in order to be happy and satisfied as a mother:

> Mary: Yesterday, for example, they (*the children*) didn't want to get up and it was a little hard ... They said to me: "Mom, why don't you go to work?" And I said: "Because I can't find a job, I can't go to work ...." How do I experience this situation? I mean, I need to be always mentally engaged, and a part of me is positive because I spend my time on myself: I read, I walk ... I do the things that I like. However, there comes a time in life when you say: "This is not possible!" I must do something, even for money reasons, but above all it is a question of the mind, because otherwise later you will not use your head well, so you should always work ...
>
> Interviewer: Would you feel even more satisfied?
>
> Mary: Yes, yes. I depend on somebody, and I don't like depending on anyone.

Mary, who was looking for work after losing her job because of her second pregnancy, recounted how she missed being committed on the professional level, certainly as a matter of economic independence, but above all, as she pointed out with strong emotional emphasis, as a matter of the "head"; that is, keeping her mind trained on various activities and being professionally updated and competitive. With a job, she would have felt fulfilled not only on an individual level as a person who had achieved her professional goals, but also on a family level as a mother whose children could feel proud of her (as they did of their father) and as a wife who actively contributed to the household expenses. In her husband's interview, precariousness assumed a double meaning: when speaking about himself, he emphasized the positive effects of employment on paternity, but he contrasted them with the consequences of uncertainty that affected his wife Mary. She had difficulty in finding a job that matched her qualifications and ambition, and this caused her frustration that inevitably impacted the family atmosphere.

> That is, I'd like Mary to find a job, in short, not a job that allows many other things (*in economic terms*), but a job that would give her a little satisfaction, her own. (...) So I'd be happy if there were, that is, if she could find a job that somehow gratified her. (Mattia, a 43-year-old teacher working on a temporary contract)

In these excerpts, as in most of the interviews collected, discourses about mothers and their family lives are not conveyed in factual terms by the respondents — as they were in the discourses about fathers — but in terms of how things should be. In the narratives of both men and women, women's aspirations were at odds with their lived work–family boundaries: the combination of precarious work and motherhood, the stage for increased work, economic stress, and feelings of inadequacy and subordination. Thus, the demands and moral prescriptions which derive from job insecurity (which are similar for men and women) and the emerging parenthood norms and social expectations (which are gender-specific) seem to be problematic only for women (Table 1).

To delve into this issue and to shed light on how the social consequences of job insecurity are differently incorporated into the discourses regarding men and women, we must think in terms of ethical boundaries as well as social boundaries. From a gender perspective, this means that attention should be paid to how gender is embedded in the individual, interactional, and institutional dimensions (Risman, 2004). In the next section I explore how these levels intersect and how the normative dimensions cut across the interactional and institutional levels. By looking across these levels, we can observe margins of agency that enhance or renew the traditional social order.

How Normative Dimensions Affected Experiences of the Work–Family Boundary

In this section, I discuss how the normative beliefs that respondents attached to work and care affected their work–family boundary crossing experiences. Useful for investigating this difficult issue was analysis of the rhetorics (Gherardi & Poggio, 2007) respondents used to justify their perceptions of the work–family boundary and the more or less explicit accounting practices (Garfinkel, 1967) referring to interactional and institutional levels.

Individual Level
At the individual level of the rhetorics (Gherardi & Poggio, 2007) used by respondents, I found significant differences between male and female texts. The men in the sample tended to present their work–family articulation in terms of a separation between the two domains of life. And even when their discourses showed visible features of interference (especially physical, temporal, and behavioral) between work and family, they said that they were able to handle the blurred boundaries since they resulted from personal and deliberate choices:

> Thomas: When they (*his wife and son*) return home at four p.m. ... it is perhaps the only time that's a bit more difficult for me because, not having a royal palace, I'm studying in his bedroom ... Anyway, he prefers to play in the living room, but you know, knowing that daddy is at home ... He understands that I'm working etc.,

Table 1. Normative Beliefs between Work and Care.

Gender Structures	Gender	Normative Dimensions		Appraisals
		Precarious work interpretative repertoires	Parenthood interpretative repertoires	Work–parenting nexus
No significant difference of gender	Men and women	Variant of "work devotion schema"		
The gender of who is speaking	Men		"Responsible father model" (stress on clock-time)	
	Women		"Mother/worker integral model" (stress on subjective time)	
The gender of the person being talked about	Men Women			Working well Problematic

however, it is more difficult. But thanks to Cristina (*his wife*), I can do it, well, I work. Then, I repeat, staying at home is a choice. I'm also happy.

Interviewer: Does it bother you that your son is knocking on the door while you work?

Thomas: No, no, no, not at all. Many times if he doesn't come, I come here (*the living room*) to call him, we have a fight. That is, in short, I mean ... it is fantastic! I'm crazy about him! (Thomas, a 41-year-old father working on a temporary contract at university)

Thomas, like many of the other men interviewed, did not have a specific work space in his own home. Because they were precarious workers, they were often unable to afford large homes and were compelled to live in small spaces. However, they preferred to take work home when they could, and to carry out their work in the living room (most often) or in the children's bedroom. They experienced this as a privilege, a sign of their freedom. They stressed that they could stop working whenever they wanted in order to play with their children or help their wives. However, they said that they could do work tasks requiring less concentration in the presence of noisy children, but they reserved the evenings, when the children were asleep, for activities that required more concentration in the living room. The men interviewed said that they had control over their time, which they said allowed them to cope well with the two life domains and not confuse them. There is a long line of research on the importance of perceived control for positive work−family outcomes (Karasek, 1979; Kossek & Lautsch, 2012; Kossek, Lautsch, & Eaton, 2006). In particular, my results exhibit similarities with Kossek and Lautsch (2012), who theorized that perceived control over boundary management style will help individuals enact their preferred boundary style and reduce levels of work−family conflict.

Greater difficulty, especially in terms of mental energy, was apparent in the narratives of the women who had more integrated work−family boundaries. Among the many possible examples, I report here that of Claudia, a mother of a ten-month-old baby, who at the time of interview had numerous jobs:

> Working hours are not so many ... More than anything else I feel the effort to focus on five different tasks in a single day! I can't knock off work, come here (*her home*) and take care of my son. I leave work, I come here and maybe I have to prepare something for my doctorate, prepare the lesson for the day, take care of my son, I have to go out again for another job ... so ... And ... it's very difficult to find time for myself. I mean, besides the work, besides my son, there should also be time to devote to myself, I don't know, reading a book, watching a movie ... and this wastes a great deal of energy, both in everyday life, and as ... energy invested in planning my life. (Claudia, a 29-year-old mother working as an occasional collaborator)

Whilst the interviews of precarious men did not reveal significant problems of interference between the work and family domains in terms of meanings, moral commitments and daily practices, and the dominant rhetoric was that of personal choice, the discourses of their female partners were very different. The ability to shift easily between domains was described in the women's discourses in strong terms of how their lives should be, rather than in factual terms. The women respondents said that they did not feel any conflict at the level of the ethical codes (beliefs about how the work−family nexus should be); on the contrary, as pointed out in the previous section, they described a reinforcement relationship: namely, work outside the home was an essential requirement for being a "good" mother. However, they complained about difficulties in handling work−family boundaries and managing everyday practices, because poor working conditions impacted negatively on their ability to tend to work and family (which, however, cannot be said of their male partners). The rhetoric that characterized most of the women's narratives was therefore that of *marginalization*. To understand what this means, we have to consider how individual-level boundary configurations intersect at the couple level, and take into account the possible social boundaries that operate at the institutional level.

Interactional Level
Not only did the parents interviewed have to fit their jobs into the hectic pace of daily life, but they also had to deal with the times, flexible and discontinuous, of their partners, who were precarious workers as well. Many of them talked of a miraculous interlocking when asked to describe their typical day in detail. Because there were children to look after, it was necessary for them to devise work time and family responsibilities, especially the care activities that infants required, and constantly adjust them depending on various contingencies.

However, most of the time these contingencies were strictly dependent on the father's job commitments, while the mother and children went along with him. For example, Carlo, a 35-year-old father of a 2-year-old child, was a sound technician and followed the various national and international tours some Italian musicians who commissioned his job. His job was completely unschedulable because it depended on artists' commissions, and whether the ongoing tour was successful or not. This meant that his readiness to follow the musicians (and to be away from home) was unlimited: tours could last longer than expected or several dates could be cancelled at the last minute.

> For ten years we had open calendar tours, meaning that in June we didn't have a calendar with the summer tour dates yet, but it usually got updated every two weeks. [...] In June you might have five dates confirmed, and in September you would find yourself having had twenty-five dates! Or you'd find yourself having had only seven dates if it was a tour that costs too much compared to revenues. In short, ability to predict: zero!

This job therefore did not allow family holiday planning. They managed to have a few days' vacation when his partner and their child joined Carlo in the city where he worked on his last tour date.

> Holidays are unfortunately not feasible for us as a family because the holiday season is when I work the most, the summer season is when there are more dates. Usually, if we try to have a week off together, we attach it to the last date of a tour. So Gabriella (*his partner*) and my son can join me if I'm in a beautiful location.

As well as the problem with family holidays, Carlo's job did not allow him to spend holidays with the family throughout the year. For example, Carlo had not celebrated New Year's Eve for almost 20 years. When I asked him what his partner thought about these working conditions he replied that the pay was double during the holidays and she was happy (she put up with it).

> New Year's Eve she (*his partner*) is with the family, with hers or mine. Therefore she isn't alone. But ... she is not with me. Not this .... I believe this partially weighs on her, even though it works okay for a number of reasons. We respect each other's jobs very much. And then, for example, New Year's Eve it's double wages, that is to say I take home in a day what she takes home in a month. So that's okay! New Year's day we celebrate and everyone's happy!

Such stories are quite frequent in the interviews collected. For example, Francesco, a 34-year-old father, remembered a specific situation he experienced when he worked as a set designer. He had planned a trip with his girlfriend, but on the same day he was called for an evening business meeting and he had to give up his plans. Francesco, who lived in Florence at that time, had joined Luisa (his current wife) in Rome and had planned – with some difficulty in "interlocking" each other's commitments – a trip to the beach to celebrate his birthday. Francesco said that he had no choice but to give up their trip. "It's a difficult thing to explain even to relatives. [...] In that situation, you cannot say no, because then you lose that job."

Here we can see how the effects of boundary permeability and flexibility work (Ashforth et al., 2000). They seem in contradiction with the men's rhetoric of personal choice and control over their management of the work–family boundary. However, when the analysis focused on the dynamics within the couple, I found that men could take advantage of the flexible and temporary nature of work because they were able to rely on the material and moral support of their partners. In fact, women in the sample took care of the children during the fathers' absences (which sometimes lasted several days), did most of the domestic work, and gave men support in terms of admiration and recognition as present and responsible fathers. Sometimes men also received economic support (e.g., in the few cases where the mother worked and the father was unemployed). Therefore, the perception of control was made possible by the fact that men knew they could always count on their partners. Thus, perceived control is influenced not only by a specific organizational climate but also – in the case of parenting responsibilities – by an "agreement" (in this case implicit) working at the couple level.

On the other hand, the experiences of female partners are very different. Within the household, women had a more restricted capacity than their partners to cope with the risks and unpredictability associated with precarious employment. Women did not seem able to enjoy the advantages of labor flexibility. I found that whilst the men's rhetoric of *personal choice* was based on accounts related to the interactional level, women tended to be silent on the dynamics within the couple. Since the absence of a relevant discourse ought to be taken as seriously as the presence of another discourse (Bernstein, 2000), I investigated the "silent" discourses further and found that the women interviewed either took for granted that they would do more of the childcare and housework than their partners, or they showed signs of gratitude toward their partners for doing tasks the women did not enjoy or did not have time to do themselves.

The following quote from Giada's interview most explicitly illustrates the first kind of "silences" where women viewed housework and childcare as "automatically" a woman's job. Usually the women interviewed were more subtle about being "in charge":

> Giada: Our house, well *I'm certainly more in charge of it* than my partner is. Actually he does help a little, but not with everything.
>
> Interviewer: What does your partner do, how does he help?
>
> Giada: Well, he does simple jobs, like he lays and clears the table, takes the rubbish out ... that sort of things. He doesn't do the ironing, the washing for example. What else does he do? The bed, of course. Quick jobs, anyway.
>
> Interviewer: Is it you guiding him or does he see himself what needs doing? For example, does he take the rubbish out on his own accord or is it you asking him to do it?
>
> Giada: He's quite independent on that front!
>
> Interviewer: He does do some things on his own, though ...
>
> Giada: Yes, that's right. If our child needs picking up from school or taking him somewhere he does that *if I'm away*, but I'm in charge of the relationship with the school. [...]
>
> Interviewer: I see. So you are in charge of the house and of your son ... but was this automatic or did you sit down and talk about it when you went to live together?
>
> Giada: We didn't talk about it. It was automatic. In the end the woman is in charge of these things.
>
> Interviewer: Are you happy with this arrangement or would you like him to help you a little more?
>
> Giada: I'm happy like this ... if he helped me a little more of course it would be wonderful, but *I'm used to it* by now ... for example sometimes he folds the clothes away but you can tell it was him folding them, but I think *it's normal*. (Giada, a 32-year-old mother working as a member of cooperative. Emphasis mine.)

In the second type of "silences," women praise their partners for doing specific chores. As we read:

> My husband does the cooking at home, so when we come home – *of course guys, I found the best on the market!* – he does the cooking. (Carlotta, a 33-year-old mother working on an annual fellowship at the university. Emphasis mine.)

> Bills and all of that ... Luca is in charge of that side; as far as cooking is concerned I do that, [...] also because I quite like that even if it's not a real passion. But when I'm very busy, like for example in the last few months when I've been writing my thesis, as he used to be on long lunch breaks, he would come home and cook something for the evening meal. *God bless Luca!* (Silvia, a 37-year-old unemployed mother. Emphasis mine.)

What these two patterns have in common is that the women interviewed did not problematize the unequal division of chores within the couple. The women were "silent" about this disparity and it was not part of the accounting practices which supported their rhetoric of boundary. Indeed, women's rhetoric of *marginalization* is better understood in light of their accounting practices at the institutional level.

Institutional Level
We can understand the rhetoric of *marginalization* by considering that women in Italy (as reflected by the sample) are more frequently employed on less protected and more discontinuous contractual forms. They were therefore forced to have more than one job at a time and to juggle different activities (Villa, 2010). Or, conversely they were not employed and constantly looking for a job, which was very stressful and frustrating. But the main obstacle identified by the female respondents consisted in social boundaries: when job instability combined with motherhood, they were doubly discriminated against and doubly exposed to the threat of losing their jobs. Moreover, the situation is made even more critical in Italy by the shortage of places at child daycare centers, and especially by a lack of affordable childcare (Saraceno, 2011). Indeed, many women are forced, after childbirth, to stay at home to look after their children because of the high costs of care services.

Although the women's narratives revealed difficulties handling symbolic boundaries, the women reported serious social boundary difficulties caused by unequal access to, and unequal distribution of, resources and social opportunities (Lamont & Molnàr, 2002). For example, several women in the sample said that because they had temporary contracts, they had lost their jobs when they became pregnant, and that they had also encountered many obstacles after childbirth. When Cristina (aged 41 with a four-year-old son and working on an occasional contract) recalled her experience, she explained how symbolic boundaries can become social boundaries: that is to say, real social barriers to the career advancement of women:

> There is attitude of thinking that if you're pregnant, it's a problem! No, it is not. (...) For that year I lost my job! For a year I didn't work. (...) Then, it is also difficult to find a job when they know you have a small child, I mean that after ... it's very difficult! Because it's a problem, it is always seen as a problem. You know you are qualified ... So why won't you take me? For them it is always a problem hiring a mother, because children tend to fall sick ... And you are not completely available, get it? And then you may have another baby, you may have another child later, so ... it's always a bit ... you're there, but there's a queue of other people ...

Therefore, the first and most significant obstacle was the traditional cultural model of work–family articulation, which is anchored to separate spheres ideology and deeply rooted in organizational cultures: the "ideal worker" should demonstrate total dedication to the company by working in the office for a long time (Moen & Roehling, 2005; Williams, 2000). In fact, "face time" (Fuchs Epstein, Carroll, Oglensky, & Saut, 1998) is feasible only for those who can rely on another person (usually female) to take care of almost all family commitments.

For example, Barbara (a 35-year-old university researcher with two children), under the threat of dismissal, decided to return to work long before the end of her maternity leave as established by law, and thus sacrificed the time with her children. Despite this demonstration of total devotion to work, the repercussions in terms of career were considerable. In Barbara's workplace, motherhood was seen as an impediment that not only slowed down career advancement but also hindered it in the long term (as in the previous case of Cristina). Added to this were the complications that an early return to work and a lack of early childhood services in the area entailed for the daily management of children.

> A mother who works as a university researcher must somehow accept it – which I find a little hard to do – she must accept that the years in which you raise children are not as productive as the other years of your like. I mean that you can't expect to get ahead in your career like, let's say, someone of your own age with the same experience who hasn't had children because, obviously, you've spent less time at work. So this is already a bit ... your own choice, and you have to be aware of it, so you know, you say, okay, okay: I'll delay my career a bit. Now I'm bringing up my children. But on the other hand, let's say, the work should meet your needs. It should allow you, put you in a condition, let's say, to do it without these enormous efforts that require you to manage it on your own. So, let's say, maybe you should have the right to switch to a part-time schedule ...[...] But this should be guaranteed by the system! Because you can't manage

Table 2. The Meaning of Work−Family Boundary.

Gender	Individual rhetorics	Interactional accounts	Institutional accounts
		Work−Family Boundary	
Men	Personal choice (flexibility is chosen)	Greater coping capacity without cultural penalties	"Silences" (unpronounced discourses)
Women	Marginalization (flexibility is constraining)	"Silences" (not challenged discourses)	Greater social boundaries for mothers

on your own. They're going to say: "Well, if you don't have enough publications, you're out! That's it." No one cares that you've had children, no one takes into account that you've been on maternity leave ... Then, it should be structured a little better ... and even encouraged, encouraged, also like ... I mean, if there were more places at nursery schools! Nurseries at the university don't take children until they are a year old. But you have maternity leave of five months, so how do you reconcile this? (Barbara, a 35-year-old mother of two children and working on an annual research fellowship)

The rhetoric that characterized most of the women's narratives was that of *marginalization*. There was no sign of this type of account in men's narratives. The female respondents were capable, high-qualified, and they wanted to contribute to society in terms of both production, by having access to proper paid work, and reproduction, by giving birth to children. Nevertheless, an analysis of their discourses reveal that Italian society is not yet able to meet these needs at the institutional or organizational level (Table 2).

DISCUSSION

In this chapter, I have illustrated how the social norms attached to precarious work and care affect and cross the work−family boundary among parents with young children, and how these boundaries forge a link between gender and moral obligation. Meanings and ethical codes attached to the family are affected by the instability of employment, specifically by the distinctive culture of work that it fosters. Precarious workers exhibited a new kind of "work devotion schema" (Blair-Loy, 2003) that had a strong emphasis on the content of work rather than on career advancement. This schema also entailed a different form of loyalty to the employer: workers must never refuse a job offer. At the same time, the assignment of moral commitments within the couples interviewed had a significant effect on the culture of work, and, especially on how the men and women respondents differently faced risks and opportunities related to precariousness.

Indeed, in light of the different moral commitments that induce fathers to emphasize the dimension of care, following the responsible father model (Doherty et al., 1998), and mothers to emphasize paid work outside the home, according to the mother/worker integral model (Duncan et al., 2003), it has been possible to clarify why job insecurity assumes a double meaning when it is explicitly connected to fatherhood or motherhood, and why it takes respectively a positive and a negative value. Whilst in the case of men, precariousness – and especially the flexibility often associated with it – facilitated the care practices expected of a "good" father, in the case of women it conversely hindered their pursuit of being "good" mothers because they tended to perceive risks rather than opportunities.

Social norms, moral prescriptions, and appraisals about the nexus between precarious work and parenting impact the rhetorics respondents used to justify their work–family boundary (Nippert-Eng, 1996). The analysis of rhetorics showed that men, without perceiving any contrasts, tend to depict their work–family articulation in terms of segmentation, even when there are visible signs of porosity between the two contexts. And, men often described the blurred boundaries between work and family life through the rhetoric of *personal choice*, especially in regard to temporal and spatial flexibility and permeability (Ashforth et al., 2000). This demonstrates the importance of how objective conditions shape individual interpretations of the work–family boundary: perceived control over the style of boundary management without facing cultural penalties played a fundamental role. In the precarious fathers' discourses there seemed to be no significant problems of interference between work and family domains in terms of meanings, moral commitments, and daily practices. However, men's rhetoric of *personal choice* was based on often taken-for-granted accounts (Garfinkel, 1967) related to the interactional level of the couple. The fathers interviewed showed a greater coping capacity in dealing with precariousness because they could also benefit from material help (especially in terms of women taking charge of the housework and childcare, but occasionally in economic terms as well), and moral support from their partners (in terms of admiration and recognition of father role).

By contrast, the women respondents complained of greater difficulties in handling symbolic boundaries, especially social boundaries (Lamont & Molnàr, 2002), with the result that the work–family boundary appeared more integrated. Whilst in the case of men the interpretation of porosity, permeability, and flexibility between domains of life was positive because it was mediated by the perception of control over their time and the rhetoric of *personal choice*, in the case of women the assessment was very different. Women in the sample were forced into a boundary arrangement that they felt did not suit their beliefs and aspirations. The dominant rhetoric was therefore that of *marginalization*, which emphasizes the constraints of precarious work rather than the benefits. The accounting practices (Garfinkel, 1967) in support of this rhetoric were not connected to micro-decisions within the couple but to the organizational level and institutional levels (here understood in a broad sense). The women recounted that they had suffered workplace discrimination, especially after childbirth, and had many difficulties managing work and family. In the case of women's texts, it was also challenging to explore the meanings of "silences" found in the couple-level accounts.

It should be borne in mind that dramatic changes in the organization of work and within the family had placed the couples at the intersection between contradictory sets of social structures, giving them unprecedented opportunities and greater risks. In order to face the new moral dilemmas, my respondents gave different interpretations to the work−family boundary and to the inherent contradiction between time in work and time devoted to care (Daly, 1996) by extending or transposing cultural repertoires to their situations. As they did so, the traditional micro-mechanisms, discourses, and practices that once created sharp markers between what was expected to be done and was worth doing at home and work faded. Indeed, the respondents, especially the young mothers, were searching for an innovative symbolic and ethical order so that they could reconcile work and family, public, and private.

CONCLUDING REMARKS

This study can stimulate future research in a number of ways. Firstly, the study suggests thinking not only in terms of work−family boundary segmentation and integration (Nippert-Eng, 1996) but also in normative terms. In this chapter, I investigated how the increasing demands of work (job insecurity and flexibility), as well as the emerging prescriptions of parenthood models, differently impact the men's and women's social understandings of work−family boundaries. Men had more control over their work–family boundary and some benefits from nonstandard working conditions, which gave them the opportunity to spend more time with children (in comparison to the male breadwinner model) so that they were able to follow their fatherhood model. In women's discourses, flexibility created a scenario where they felt forced to mix family and work against their aspirations, which were expressed in terms of what the work–family nexus should have been rather than actually it was. In particular, through in-depth analysis of people's interpretative repertoires (Potter, 2012), rhetorics (Gherardi & Poggio, 2007), and accounts (Garfinkel, 1967), I explored the work that actors perform in building and crossing work–family boundaries; showed how it related to their symbolic and ethical order; and how this reinforced or challenged the existing social order. The theoretical frame and the particular methodological approach adopted made it possible to overcome the tendency to assume that all workers regard the work–family overlap as problematic or idyllic. The same set of objective work–family arrangements may be evaluated differently by men and women according to the cultural model and their aspired boundary configuration.

Secondly, through the analysis of accounting practices (Garfinkel, 1967) used by respondents to make their rhetorics intelligible, I have shed light on some mechanisms operating at the couple level, organizational level, and institutional level; mechanisms and dynamics which were both ultimately rooted in the traditional boundary configuration based on separate spheres ideology. Nevertheless, this cross-level analysis is limited, and further investigation of the micro-decisions at the couples level and organizational culture levels is required.

Finally, this study was conducted on a very specific target of couples, which is theoretically significant but prevents empirical comparisons between social classes. We can only assume that the parenthood models and appraisals of the nexus between precarious work and parenting are class-based, similarly to what has been shown by other studies related to educational styles (Lareau, 2003). It would be very interesting to explore class variation and determine what kinds of work–family boundary social understandings are made available by the cultural repertoires and rhetorics of women and men with low-skilled profiles or from different social contexts.

NOTES

1. The main reforms were introduced with Law 335/1995 (extension of compulsory social security to independent workers performing tasks similar to those of

employees for private companies or in the public sector), Law 196/1997 (introduction of temporary agency work and incentives to part-time work), Law 368/2001 (liberalization of fixed-term contracts), and Law 30/2003 (introduction of other contractual forms to ease the hiring process for firms).

2. The term "ethical boundaries" is similar to "boundaries preferences" by Ammons (2013), but is preferred since it emphasizes normative boundary dimensions.

3. Collaborations are fixed-term contracts stipulated between a firm and a self-employed worker to perform a specific job/service for remuneration. These self-employed workers generally belong in the "semi-subordinate" area, which has characteristics midway between those of dependent employment and self-employment.

4. It is widely recognized that firms make growing use of false self-employment (also termed "dependent self-employment" or "economically dependent work") in order to attain flexibility at reduced labor costs and taxes. The position of these workers is practically the same as that of collaborators.

5. Social cooperatives are established with the aim of carrying out an economic activity using the labor of the members. In Italy cooperatives often work on commission and provide public services for reasons linked to greater flexibility in the management of work organization, and especially in the ability to reduce or terminate services and interventions with less difficulties. The employment relationship can be stipulated as for an employee or self-employed person or in the "semi-subordinate" area. However, the member of a cooperative often shares the business risks but does not take part in decision making.

ACKNOWLEDGMENTS

I am very grateful to Barbara Poggio, Barbara Risman, and Lea Sgier for their suggestions. I also thank Samantha K. Ammons and Erin L. Kelly for their useful comments. Finally, a special thanks to all people I interviewed for telling me their stories.

REFERENCES

Ammons, S. K. (2013). Work–family boundary strategies: Stability and alignment between preferred and enacted boundaries. *Journal of Vocational Behavior, 82*(1), 49–58.

Ashforth, B., Kreiner, G., & Fugate, M. (2000). All in a day's work: Boundaries and micro role transitions. *Academy of Management Review, 25*(3), 472–491.

Barbieri, P. (2009). Flexible employment and inequality in Europe. *European Sociological Review, 25*(6), 621–628.

Barbieri, P., & Scherer, S. (2009). Labour market flexibilisation and its consequences in Italy. *European Sociological Review, 25*(6), 677–692.

Becker, P. E., & Moen, P. (1999). Scaling back: Dual earner couples' work–family strategies. *Journal of Marriage and the Family*, *61*(4), 995–1007.
Bellavia, G. M., & Frone, M. R. (2005). Work–family conflict. In J. Barling, K. Kelloway, & M. R. Frone (Eds.), *Handbook of work stress* (pp. 113–147). Thousand Oaks, CA: Sage.
Berke, D. L. (2003). Coming home again: The challenges and rewards of home-based self-employment. *Journal of Family Issues*, *24*(4), 513–546.
Bernstein, B. (2000). *Pedagogy, symbolic control and identity: Theory, research, critique.* Lanham, MD: Rowman & Littlefield.
Bertolini, S. (2011). The heterogeneity of the impact of labour market flexibilization on the transition to adult life in Italy: When do young people leave the nest? In H. P. Blossfeld, D. Hofäcker, & S. Bertolini (Eds.), *Youth on globalised labour markets: Rising uncertainty and its effects on early employment and family lives in Europe* (pp. 163–187). Opladen: Budrich.
Berton, F., Richiardi, M., & Sacchi, S. (2012). *The political economy of work security and flexibility. Italy in comparative perspective.* Bristol: Policy Press, University of Bristol.
Blair-Loy, M. (2003). *Competing devotions: Career and family among women financial executives.* Cambridge, MA: Harvard University Press.
Blair-Loy, M. (2010). Moral dimensions of the work–family nexus. In S. Hitlin & S. Vaisey (Eds.), *Handbook of the sociology of morality* (pp. 439–453). New York, NY: Springer.
Blossfeld, H. P., & Drobnic, S. (2001). *Careers of couples in contemporary societies: From male breadwinner to dual-earner families.* Oxford: Oxford University Press.
Brannen, J. (2002). *Lives and time. A sociological journey.* London: Institute of Education.
Brannen, J. (2005). Time and negotiation of work–family boundaries. Autonomy or illusion? *Time & Society*, *14*(1), 113–131.
Brannen, J., & Nilsen, A. (2002). Young people's time perspectives: From youth to adulthood. *Sociology*, *36*(3), 513–539.
Castel, R. (2007). *Le metamorfosi della questione sociale. Una cronaca del salariato.* Avellino, Sellino.
Charmaz, K. (2003). Grounded theory. In S. N. Hesse-Biber & P. Leavy (Eds.), *Approaches to qualitative research* (pp. 496–521). Oxford: Oxford University Press.
Clark, A., & Postel-Vinay, F. (2009). Job security and job protection. *Oxford Economic Papers*, *61*(2), 207–239.
Clark, S. C. (2000). Work/family border theory. A new theory of work/family balance. *Human Relations*, *53*(6), 747–770.
Daly, J. (1996). *Families and time: Keeping pace in a hurried culture.* Thousand Oaks, CA: Sage.
Den Dulk, L. (2001). *Work–family arrangements in organisations. A cross-national study in the Netherlands, Italy, the United Kingdom and Sweden.* Amsterdam: Rozenberg Publishers.
Doherty, W. J., Kouneski, E. F., & Erikson, M. F. (1998). Responsible fathering: An overview and conceptual framework. *Journal of Marriage and Family*, *60*(2), 277–292.
Dugan, A. G., Matthews, R. A., & Barnes-Farrell, J. L. (2012). Understanding the roles of subjective and objective aspects of time in the work–family interface. *Community, Work & Family*, *15*(2), 149–172.
Duncan, S., Edwards, R., Reynolds, T., & Alldred, P. (2003). Motherhood, paid work and partnering: Values and theories. *Work, Employment and Society*, *17*(2), 309–330.

Edley, N. (2001). Analysing masculinity: Interpretative repertoires, ideological dilemmas and subject positions. In M. Wetherell, S. Taylor, & S. J. Yates (Eds.), *Discourse ad data. A guide for analysis* (pp. 189–228). London: Sage/Open University.
Esping-Andersen, G., & Regini, M. (2000). *Why deregulate labour markets?* Oxford: Oxford University Press.
Ferree, M. M. (1990). Beyond separate spheres: Feminism and family research. *Journal of Marriage and Family, 52*(4), 866–884.
Ford, R. (1996). *Childcare in the balance: How lone parents make decisions about paid work.* London: Policy Studies Institute.
Fuchs Epstein, S., Carroll, C., Oglensky, B., & Saut, R. (1998). *The part-time paradox: Time norms, professional life, family and gender.* New York, NY: Routledge.
Garfinkel, H. (1967). *Studies in ethnomethodology.* Englewood Cliffs, NJ: Prentice Hall.
Geertz, C. (1973). *The interpretation of cultures.* New York, NY: Basic Books.
Gergen, K. J. (1991). *The saturated self. Dilemmas of identity in contemporary life.* New York, NY: Basic Books.
Gershuny, J. (2000). *Changing times: Work and leisure in post-industrial society.* Oxford: Oxford University Press.
Gerson, K. (2002). Moral dilemmas, moral strategies, and the transformation of gender. Lessons from two generations of work and family change. *Gender & Society, 16*(1), 8–28.
Gherardi, S., & Poggio, B. (2007). *Gendertelling in organizations: Narratives from male-dominated environments.* Stockholm: Malmö, Liber.
Gilbert, G. N., & Mulkay, M. (1984). *Opening Pandora's box: A sociological analysis of scientists' discourse.* Cambridge: Cambridge University Press.
Greenhaus, J., & Beutell, N. (1985). Sources of conflict between work and family roles. *Academy of Management Review, 10*(1), 76–88.
Greenhaus, J. H., & Powell, G. N. (2006). When work and family are allies: A theory of work–family enrichment. *Academy of Management Review, 31*(1), 72–92.
Hays, S. (1996). *The cultural contradictions of motherhood.* London: Yale University Press.
Houston, D. M. (2005). *Work–life balance in the 21st century.* Basingstoke: Palgrave Macmillan.
ISTAT. (2011). *La conciliazione famiglia e lavoro.* Retrieved from http://www.istat.it/it/archivio/48912
ISTAT. (2013). *Rapporto annuale.* Retrieved from http:www.istat.it/it/files/2013/05/Rapporto_annuale_2013.pdf
Karasek, R. (1979). Job demands, job decision latitude and mental strain: Implications for job redesign. *Administrative Science Quarterly, 24*(2), 285–311.
Kossek, E. E., & Lautsch, B. A. (2008). *CEO of me: Creating a life that works in the flexible job age.* Upper Saddle River, NJ: Pearson.
Kossek, E. E., & Lautsch, B. A. (2012). Work–family boundary management styles in organizations: A cross-level model. *Organizational Psychology Review, 2*(2), 152–171.
Kossek, E. E., Lautsch, B. A., & Eaton, S. C. (2006). Telecommuting, control and boundary management: Correlates of policy use and practice, job control, and work–family effectiveness. *Journal of Vocational Behavior, 68*(2), 347–367.
Lamont, M., & Molnàr, V. (2002). The study of boundaries in the social sciences. *Annual Review of Sociology, 28*, 167–195.

Lareau, A. (2003). *Unequal childhoods: Class, race, and family life*. Berkeley, CA: University of California Press.
Lodovici, M. S., & Semenza, R. (2012). *Precarious work and high-skilled youth in Europe*. Milano: Franco Angeli.
Moen, P., & Roehling, P. (2005). *The career mystique. Cracks in the American dream*. Oxford: Rowman & Littlefield.
Murgia, A., Poggio, B., & Torchio, N. (2012). Italy: Precariousness and skill mismatch. In *Precarious work and high-skilled youth in Europe* (pp. 71–111). Milano: Franco Angeli.
Nippert-Eng, C. (1996). *Home and work: Negotiating boundaries through everyday life*. Chicago, IL: University of Chicago Press.
Poggio, B. (2010). Pragmatica della conciliazione: Opportunità, ambivalenze e trappole. *Sociologia del lavoro, 119*, 65–77.
Potter, J. (2012). Discourse analysis and discursive psychology. In H. Cooper (Ed.), *APA handbook of research methods in psychology* (Vol. 2, pp. 111–130). Washington, DC: American Psychological Association Press.
Risman, B. J. (2004). Gender as a social structure: Theory wrestling with activism. *Gender and Society, 18*(4), 429–450.
Rothbard, N. P. (2001). Enriching or depleting? The dynamics of engagement in work and family roles. *Administrative Science Quarterly, 46*(4), 655–684.
Salmieri, L. (2009). Job insecurity, flexibility and home-work balance for Italian couples in non-standard work: The effect of social class. *European Review, 17*(1), 93–120.
Saraceno, C. (2005). Le differenze che contano tra i lavoratori atipici. In S. Bertolini & R. Rizza (Eds.), *Atipici?* (pp. 15–24). Bologna: Franco Angeli.
Saraceno, C. (2010). Social inequalities in facing old-age dependency: A bi-generational perspective. *Journal of European Social Policy, 20*(1), 32–44.
Saraceno, C. (2011). Childcare needs and childcare policies. A multidimensional issue. *Current Sociology, 59*(1), 78–96.
Schwandt, T. A. (2010). Three epistemological stances for qualitative inquiry: Interpretivism, hermeneutics, and social constructionism. In M. Bevir (Ed.), *Interpretive political science* (Vol. 1, pp. 35–68). Los Angeles, CA: Sage.
Steiber, N. (2009). Reported levels of time-based and strain-based conflict between work and family roles in Europe: A multilevel approach. *Social Indicators Research, 93*(3), 469–488.
Townsend, N. (2002). *The package deal: Marriage, work and fatherhood in men's lives*. Philadelphia, PA: Temple University Press.
Villa, P. (2010). La crescita dell'occupazione femminile: La polarizzazione tra stabilità e precarietà. *Lavoro e diritto, anno, 24*(3), 341–358.
Wharton, A. S. (2006). Understanding diversity of work in the 21st century and its impact on the work–family area of study. In M. Pitt-Catsouphes, E. E. Kossek, & S. Sweet (Eds.), *The work and family handbook. Multi-disciplinary perspectives and approaches* (pp. 17–39). Mahwah, NJ: Erlbaum.
Williams, J. C. (2000). *Unbending gender*. New York, NY: Oxford University Press.

THE SECOND SHIFT AND THE NONSTANDARD SHIFT: HOW WORKING NONSTANDARD HOURS AFFECTS THE RELATIONSHIP BETWEEN THE DIVISION OF HOUSEHOLD LABOR AND WIVES' FAIRNESS PERCEPTIONS

Katie James and Jody Clay-Warner

ABSTRACT

Purpose − Research has not yet examined how paid labor performed at nontraditional hours may factor into women's perceptions of the fairness of the division of household labor. Here we specifically examine how being employed during nonstandard hours alters the relationship between the division of household labor and wives' perceptions of the fairness of this division of labor.

Methodology/approach — *We analyze data from the National Survey of Families and Households using multinomial logistic regression.*

Findings — *We find that over-work in household labor has a weaker effect on perceptions of unfairness for wives who work nonstandard hours than for wives who work standard hours. This interaction effect, however, is partially mediated by husbands' time in feminine-type chores.*

Research limitations/implications — *The cross-sectional design does not allow us to draw causal conclusions. Future research would benefit by considering how movement in and out and nonstandard work affects perceptions of fairness of household labor.*

Originality/value of the chapter — *Our findings suggest that one way that the gender revolution has stalled is through women's participation in the service economy since this participation is positively associated with their husbands' hours in routine chores, which women particularly value. Thus, women may continue to perceive fairness in the home, despite objective inequality, because their husbands are spending more time in feminine-type chores, as necessitated by women's participation in work at nonstandard times.*

Keywords: Household labor; gender; nonstandard work; justice; fairness perceptions

Studies consistently show that wives often view the division of household labor as fair, despite the fact that they perform more housework than do their husbands (Barnett & Baruch, 1987; Benin & Agostinelli, 1988; Berk, 1985; Bianchi, Milkie, Sayer, & Robinson, 2000; Hill & Scanzoni, 1982; Pleck, 1985; Rosen, 1990; Yogev, 1981). This pattern is largely consistent through time and across many cultures (Davis & Greenstein, 2004; Greenstein, 2009). A number of individual- and couple-level factors have been suggested to account for this paradox, including gender ideology and husband's appreciation for wife's household labor (e.g., Blair & Johnson, 1992; Braun, Lewin-Epstein, Stier, & Baumgärtner, 2008). Women who are highly involved in paid labor, have nontraditional gender ideologies, or are not highly dependent on their spouses' economic resources are the most likely to perceive inequities in their divisions of household labor as unfair (see Coltrane, 2000, for a review). Perceived unfairness in the division of household labor is associated with lower levels of psychological well-being

(Claffey & Mickelson, 2009), as well as lower levels of marital quality (Claffey & Mickelson, 2009; Frisco & Williams, 2003; Grote & Clark, 2001).

Recent changes in the U.S. workforce, however, call attention to the ways in which the structure of paid work, itself, may affect wives' perceptions of inequitable divisions of household labor. The number of people employed outside of the standard 8–5 workday has swelled in response both to the global economy and increased demands in the service sector. As a result of this expansion of the service economy, there is a disproportionate number of women working nonstandard hours (i.e., evenings, nights, weekend work, and variable work schedules), and this trend is expected to continue (Presser, 2003a). When women work nonstandard hours, they are less available to perform chores traditionally done by women, such as routine cooking and cleaning. Because these chores are time-sensitive, couples may rearrange the division of household labor when women are unavailable to perform these chores. In fact, Presser (1994) found a positive relationship between the number of hours each day in which wives were employed but husbands were not and husbands' share of traditionally female household chores. Since research demonstrates that men's engagement in feminine chores reduces wives' perceptions of inequity (Blair & Johnson, 1992), it is possible that wives who work nonstandard hours are less likely than other wives to view inequitable divisions of household labor as unfair (Presser, 1994). Alternatively, women who work during nonstandard hours may be *more* resentful of an inequitable division of labor, given the additional strains they face due to their work hours.

The purpose of this chapter is to examine how working nonstandard hours alters the relationship between the relative amount of household labor that wives perform and their fairness perceptions. We focus on wives' perceptions because historically it has been women whose fairness perceptions have been incongruent with the division of household labor. In doing so, we implicitly examine whether nonstandard work schedules, which are increasingly common with the shift toward a 24/7 economy, encourage fairness perceptions that are more congruent with women's greater housework or whether women continue accepting inequity in the division of household labor even in these conditions. In order to answer this question, we perform multinomial logistic regression analyses on data from the second wave of the National Study of Families and Households. We begin by reviewing trends in divisions of household labor and nonstandard work hours in the United States. We then develop theoretical arguments and predictions before presenting statistical analyses.

GENDERED DIVISIONS OF HOUSEHOLD LABOR

Although there have been changes in the labor market, imbalances between men and women's time in housework have persisted over time. There is consistent evidence that women do more housework than men. Blair and Lichter (1991) found that in the 1980s women performed an average of 33 hours of housework per week, compared to 14 hours averaged by men. Estimates show that in the 1980s men performed between 20% (Robinson, 1988) and 35% (Presser, 1994) of the total household labor. According to 2011 data from the Bureau of Labor Statistics, gendered imbalances in household labor continue. On an average day 85% of women and 67% of men reported spending time in household labor. Women spent an average of 2.6 hours a day on housework, while men spent an average of 2.0 hours per day (United States Department of Labor, 2011). Additionally, though current research shows that men's contribution to household labor has increased slightly over time, Bianchi et al. (2000) argue that this increase can be attributed to the fact that women are doing less housework, not that men today are doing much more than men in the past. Notably, however, Sayer (2005) shows that the ratio of women's and men's time in childcare has declined significantly and this is due entirely to men's increased time in childcare, indicating that men seem to be more willing to participate in domestic labor in terms of children but not in terms of housework. These statistics are consistent with Hochschild and Machung's (1989) conceptualization of the "stalled revolution," whereby women have entered the workforce but still do not experience equality at all levels. One reason for this stalled revolution may be that for many women, household labor reaffirms femininity. That is, household labor becomes a way that women "do gender" (West & Zimmerman, 1987). Completing chores that are typically designated as feminine (i.e., cooking, cleaning) may be a way for women to affirm the cultural meanings that are attached to their identities as women (Kroska, 1997). Thus, women may be unwilling to relinquish tasks they perceive to be inherent to their gender identities.

Though women continue to perform more household labor than do men, the service economy has changed the amount of work women do. For example, Bianchi et al. (2000) found that women both in and outside of the paid labor force have reduced the hours they spend on household labor by half since the 1960s. One reason that women have been able to reduce their hours is the increased availability of market services that allow people to outsource household labor. An aspect of service work that has particularly affected household labor, however, is the increasing number of jobs that require work to be performed during nonstandard hours.

NONSTANDARD WORK HOURS AND THEIR CONSEQUENCES

Since the 1950s, the United States has seen significant changes in both the economy and in the demographic composition of the workforce. These changes, coupled with advances in technology, have resulted in what Presser (2003b) terms the "24/7" economy. In the "24/7" economy, jobs that provide services to customers have largely replaced manufacturing jobs. Many workers in the service industry are now expected to be available to work at any time, thereby increasing the prevalence of work at nonstandard times. Nonstandard work schedules include work during the evening, at night, on a rotational basis, or on the weekend. Based on data from the Current Population Survey and the National Survey of Families and Households (NSFH), by the 1990s, over two-fifths of Americans worked during nonstandard times (Presser, 2003b). This trend has continued, with 20% of employed Americans now estimated to work *more hours* during nonstandard times than they do during typical working hours (Enchautegui, 2013).

Several demographic characteristics increase one's likelihood of working nonstandard schedules. Overall, men are slightly more likely than women to work during nonstandard hours, but there are gender differences in the likelihood of choosing specific types of nonstandard work schedules. For example, men are more likely than women to work fixed night and rotating schedules. Women, in turn, are more likely than men to work other nonstandard schedules such as fixed evening and irregular day schedules. Minorities are more likely to work nonstandard shifts than non-Hispanic whites. Education and age have negative effects on one's likelihood of working nonstandard schedules (Presser, 1995, 2003b).

Nonstandard work hours affect workers' mental and physical health. People who work at nonstandard times are more likely than those who work during standard hours to report job burnout, emotional exhaustion, and job stress. Those who work during nonstandard times also report higher instances of psychosomatic health problems such as headaches, inability to sleep, fatigue, and inability to relax (Jamal, 2004). Additionally, people who work at nonstandard times suffer more than those who work at standard times from gastrointestinal disorders, breast cancer, miscarriage, giving birth prematurely, and having babies with low birth weights (Knutsson, 2003; Schernhammer et al., 2001; United States Congress, 1991; Wedderburn, 2000). Rates of cardiovascular disease are 40% greater for shift workers than nonshift workers (Bøggild & Knutsson, 1999). Recently, the medical profession has pathologized the link between nonstandard work hours and negative health outcomes as "shift work disorder," a condition that has far-reaching consequences for workers' family lives (see Culpepper, 2010; Drake, 2010; Thorpy, 2010).

Nonstandard work hours also affect marital quality and children's well-being. Among dual-earner couples, when both spouses work nonday shifts, they both report lower levels of marital quality than do either single-earner couples or dual-earner couples who work only day shifts (Presser, 2003b). Parents who work nonstandard hours also report that their families are less well-functioning and that their children have more social and emotional difficulties compared to parents who work standard weekday times (Strazdins, Clements, Korda, Broom, & D'Souza, 2006). Additionally, nonstandard work schedules can increase the likelihood of divorce or separation (Presser, 2000). Thus, for many families, the presence of nonstandard work hours represents a strain in family well-being.

WHAT HAPPENS WHEN WOMEN WORK NONSTANDARD HOURS: THE DIVISION OF HOUSEHOLD LABOR AND FAIRNESS PERCEPTIONS

Nonstandard work hours also affect the family by changing the division of household labor. Traditionally, "routine chores," such as cooking, washing dishes, washing and ironing clothes, and cleaning the house have been performed by women. Among dual-income couples, the more hours that wives participate in the paid labor force while husbands are not at work, the more time that husbands spend on these traditionally female household chores (Presser, 1994). This occurs because these chores must be completed in a timely manner in order for the household to function properly. Thus, these routine chores often fall to the spouse who is at home when these tasks present themselves. As a result, even though these chores have traditionally been performed by women, when women work nonstandard hours their husbands often take on the responsibility of feminine-type chores.

While nonstandard work hours clearly affect divisions of household labor, it is not yet clear how work hours may alter the relationship between the relative amount of household labor that women perform and their fairness perceptions. There are two competing possibilities. First, women who work nonstandard hours may be more likely than other women to perceive an unequal division of household labor as fair because they have greater need for assistance with household labor than do women who work standard hours. Alternatively, women who work nonstandard hours may be less likely to view unequal divisions of household labor as unfair because they value the additional time that their husbands spend in feminine-type chores. To some degree, both predictions reflect a needs-based perspective on relationship equity, though the source of need varies, as explained in the section below.

PERSONAL NEEDS VERSUS RELATIONSHIP NEEDS

First, we consider the possibility that women who work nonstandard hours will be more resentful of an unfair division of labor than women who work primarily during traditional hours. As was demonstrated in the previous section, working nonstandard hours can negatively affect mental and physical health (e.g., United States Congress, 1991; Wedderburn, 2000). As a result, people with nonstandard work hours have different needs than people with standard work hours, such as the need for sleep at nontraditional times, as well as the need for exercise and social activities during hours in which those who work standard hours might be doing housework.

Married people who work nonstandard hours might logically look to a spouse to help meet these needs, as helping one's partner is seen as a normal and necessary part of a marital relationship. In fact, research has shown that when one partner has a particular need, the other partner is likely to put more in the relationship but not perceive unfairness. For example, Kuijer, Buunk, and Ybema (2001) find that partners of cancer patients do not feel unfairly treated in their relationships relative to partners of healthy people, despite the fact that they are contributing more to the relationship than are their partners. Such research suggests that people take their partners' needs into account when making decisions regarding relationship fairness. What is not known is whether women consider their *own* needs associated with working nonstandard hours when making fairness judgments.

If women do take their own needs into account, then an unfavorable division of labor will have an even stronger effect on fairness judgments when women work nonstandard hours than when they work standard hours. Using this "personal need" argument, it would be difficult for a woman who works nonstandard hours to justify the fact that she is performing a lion's share of the housework given the personal difficulties associated with working nonstandard hours. As a result, women who work nonstandard hours would more readily recognize the unequal distribution as unfair. If this is the case, the relationship between the division of household labor and wives' perceptions of unfairness to self will be stronger for wives who work nonstandard hours than for wives who work standard hours.

An alternative argument is that women who work nonstandard hours are *less* likely than other women to view an unequal division of household labor as unfair. Gender norms dictate that women should spend more time in household labor than do men. As a result, women value the time that men spend in household labor, causing women to be more likely than men to view unfavorable divisions of household labor as fair (Baxter, 2000). It is also true that wives particularly value men's time in traditionally feminine chores, such as routine cooking and cleaning and report higher levels of satisfaction when their husbands participate in conventionally feminine chores (Baxter & Western, 1998; Blair & Johnson, 1992; Sanchez & Kane, 1996). Additionally, men's involvement in these chores increases women's likelihood of perceiving fairness in their divisions of household labor, even when there is still an imbalance in actual hours performed (Baxter, 2000). The notion that women value men's time in routine chores suggests that women have been enculturated to believe that doing more household labor than their husbands is fair, and when their husbands participate in routine housework traditionally performed by women, they receive credit for both doing the housework and countering societal expectations. Men counter societal expectations when performing routine chores because doing so contradicts the ideals of hegemonic masculinity. Hegemonic masculinity (Connell, 1987) is the set of practices and expectations that promote men's dominance over women, thus defining the cultural "ideal" of what it means to be a man. Certainly, performing chores that are typically designated as "women's work" falls well outside of prescriptions of hegemonic masculinity.

Men's time in traditionally feminine chores is relevant here because women's nonstandard work hours may push men toward performing the types of household tasks that are typically performed by women. This could occur because the needs of the household require certain tasks to be performed at particular times, and the spouse who is available at those times is most likely to perform them. As a result, husbands of women who work nonstandard hours may take on more of the routine, feminine-type chores than do husbands of women who engage in paid labor during standard hours. Given that women value men's time in feminine-type chores, women who work nonstandard hours may be less likely than women who work standard hours to view over-work in household labor as unfair, as they give greater "credit" to men's time in such tasks. Thus, we offer the alternative suggestion that there is a *weaker* relationship between the division of household labor and women's fairness perceptions and propose that this interaction effect is driven by men's time in feminine-type chores. At its heart, this alternative argument suggests that the needs of the household require husbands whose wives work nonstandard hours to spend more time in feminine-type chores than is typical, which violates the norms surrounding hegemonic masculinity, and in turn alters wives' interpretation of the division of household labor.

Of course, it may also be the case that working nonstandard hours does not affect the relationship between the division of household labor and fairness perceptions. If so, then this would suggest that neither the additional needs of those who work nonstandard hours nor the types of work that men perform are taken into account in women's evaluations of the fairness of the division of household labor. Thus, we also recognize the possibility that the division of household labor may exert a constant effect on women's fairness perceptions, regardless of whether or not they work nonstandard hours.

Here we test for each of these possibilities in multivariate models using nationally representative data on working couples. We perform a multinomial logistic regression analysis on data from the second wave of the NSFH. In the following section, we briefly describe this dataset and explain the measures and analytic strategy used to obtain the results of this study.

METHODS

Data for this study are taken from the second wave of the NSFH, 1992–1994, which is the most recent national survey available that contains all of the variables necessary for our analyses.[1] The NSFH is a longitudinal, multistage area, probability sample. The NSFH is a rich dataset as it includes life-history data such as information regarding living arrangements, histories of marriage, cohabitation, education, fertility, and employment experience. African Americans, Puerto Ricans, Mexican Americans, single-parent families, families with stepchildren, cohabiting couples, and recently married couples were double sampled. The main interview response rate was 74.3% (Sweet, Bumpass, & Call, 1996). In this study, we include only married, employed female focal respondents ($N = 1,932$).[2] Following previous research on household labor (i.e., Blair & Johnson, 1992; Freudenthaler & Mikula, 1998; Gupta, 2007), we focus on data from women's interviews, as women have been historically disadvantaged in terms of gender inequality in the home.

Dependent Variable

The dependent variable is the *perception of fairness* regarding the division of household labor. This is measured with a single-item indicator: "How do you feel about the fairness of your relationship in household chores?" Respondents can answer that they perceive that their household labor arrangement is very unfair to them, somewhat unfair to them, fair to both partners, somewhat unfair to their partner, or very unfair to their partner. As others have noted, this is not an interval-level variable (Smith, Gager, & Morgan, 1998); therefore OLS regression methods are not appropriate (see Pampel, 2000). As a result, we collapse across responses to create a categorical outcome variable with the following response categories: somewhat or very unfair to respondent; fair to both partners; and somewhat or very unfair to the partner. This coding is consistent with previous research using this variable (i.e., Lively, Powell, Geist, & Steelman, 2008; Lively, Steelman, & Powell, 2010; Ward, 1993).

Independent Variables

The key independent variable is the *relative contribution to household labor*. Respondents were asked how many hours they spend as well as how many hours they perceive their partners to spend in a typical week on the following nine household chores: (1) preparing meals; (2) washing dishes and cleaning up after meals; (3) washing and ironing clothes; (4) cleaning house; (5) outdoor tasks/household maintenance; (6) automobile maintenance and repair; (7) shopping for groceries and other household items;

(8) paying bills; and (9) driving household members to various activities. To construct a measure of relative contributions to total household labor, we sum respondent's hours and partner's hours across these nine chores. Then, we create a ratio of respondent's hours to partner's hours. Values greater than 1 on this measure indicate that the respondent spends more hours in household labor than does her husband. Values of one indicate an even split of housework. Values less than one on this measure indicate that the respondent spends less time on housework than does her husband.

The next key independent variable is whether or not the *respondent [wife] works nonstandard hours*. This variable is dummy-coded to define someone who works 10 or more hours between 6:00 p.m. and 5:00 a.m. as having nonstandard work hours (1 = has nonstandard work hours, 0 = has standard work hours).[3] We chose these cut-off times because people who work 10 or more hours a week between 6:00 p.m. and 5:00 a.m. are likely working during times that are incongruent with routine activities in the family.

Following DeMaris and Longmore (1996), we also create measures for *husband's hours in routine housework*. This measure sums respondents' reports of the hours their husbands spend preparing meals, washing dishes and cleaning up after meals, washing and ironing clothes, and cleaning house. We shift from a relative measure of household labor to an absolute measure to capture the unique impact of hours of female-typed housework performed in addition to the relative amount of all housework that the chore ratio measures.

Control Variables

A number of factors have been found to affect perceptions of the fairness of the division of household labor. We incorporate measures of these factors in our models, along with appropriate demographic variables. These variables include: relative contributions to household income, hours worked in the paid labor force, ratio of wives'-to-husbands' hours worked in the paid labor force, gender ideology, length of marriage, age, number of children in the home, number of hours the respondent spends in childcare, physical or mental disability, race, and education.

First, we include relative contributions to income because the division of household earnings affects how couples divide household labor and their perceptions of the fairness of this division (Major, 1987; Thompson, 1991). That is, if a respondent does less housework than a partner but brings home more income, this arrangement may be seen as fair. We measured this variable as the proportion of household earnings contributed by the respondent.

Second, more household labor is typically completed by the spouse who has the most time available (Major, 1987; Thompson, 1991). Thus, we include a measure of how many hours the respondent spent in paid labor in the previous week. We also compare this to how much time husbands spend in paid labor by creating a ratio of the number of hours the respondent worked in paid labor compared to the number of hours her husband worked in paid labor.

Third, we estimate the effects of gender ideology on fairness perceptions. Past research has shown that the link between inequalities in divisions of household labor and perceptions of unfairness is weaker for women with a traditional gender ideology than for women who hold an egalitarian gender ideology (Greenstein, 1996). To control for *gender ideology*, we construct a scale ($\alpha = .61$) that sums responses on five statements, including items such as "it is much better for everyone if the man earns the main living and the woman takes care of the home and family" (item was reverse coded). Respondents were asked whether they strongly disagree (1), disagree (2), neither agree nor disagree (3), agree (4), or strongly agree (5). Higher values on the scale indicate an egalitarian gender ideology.

Finally, we include a number of relevant demographic variables. *Length of marriage* is measured in years and was calculated by subtracting the year of marriage from the year of the interview. Previous research finds that women with longer marriages are more likely to view their divisions of household labor as fair than women with shorter marriages (Greenstein, 1996).

Models include respondent's *age* because younger women tend to do less housework than older women. Additionally, younger women tend to share housework more equally with their husbands than do older women (Hersch & Stratton, 1994; Shelton & John, 1993; Van Der Lippe & Siegers, 1994).

We also controlled for the number of people in the household who are under age 18 and related to the respondent. Most of the youths are the respondents' children, but the measure also included any young siblings or other relatives for whom the respondent must perform additional household tasks or childcare. We will henceforth refer to this measure as *children*.

Hours spent in childcare is the number of hours in the past week that the respondent reported spending with her minor children in a variety of activities including leisure pursuits (picnics, movies, sports, etc.), at home working on a project or playing together, having private talks, helping with reading or homework, or watching television or videos. Respondents who did not have children, or those who had children but reported spending no time with them, were coded zero for this variable.

Disability is a dummy variable (1 = reports mental or physical disability, 0 = no reported disability) that measures whether the respondent reports having any long-term mental or physical condition or disability that limits what they are likely to do, or which is likely to limit what they might do in the future. *Race/ethnicity* was coded as non-Hispanic white, Black, Hispanic, or any other race/ethnicity; "Black" was the reference category. *Education* was coded as high school degree or less, having some college education (including an associate's degree), having a bachelor's degree, or having an advanced degree; "high school degree or less" is the reference category.

ANALYTIC STRATEGY

In order to answer the research questions presented above, we begin by presenting descriptive statistics of the sample (Table 1). Because our dependent variable is multidimensional (Smith et al., 1998), we use multinomial logistic regression analyses to test our arguments. This type of regression predicts the odds of membership in categories of the dependent variable compared to the reference category based on values of the independent variables (Pampel, 2000). In our analyses, "fair to both partners" is the reference category of the dependent variable.

We present three multinomial logistic regression models in Table 2. Model 1 shows the main effects of relative contributions to household labor and women's nonstandard work on women's perceptions of unfairness to self (as opposed to fair treatment). Model 2 adds an interaction term combining women's nonstandard work and their relative contributions to household labor. Finally, Model 3 includes all main effects, an interaction term for women's relative contribution to household labor and their nonstandard work hours and adds in husbands' time in routine chores. The models presented in Table 2 include only the coefficients that estimate the likelihood of perceiving unfairness to self as compared to perceptions of fairness. Also estimated as part of the multinomial logistic regression model were coefficients estimating the likelihood of perceiving unfairness to partner as compared to perceiving fairness. Because this chapter focuses on women's perceptions of unfairness – and due to the very small number of women reporting unfairness to partner – we do not present these results, but they are available by request from the first author.

Table 1. Descriptive Statistics.

Variables	Mean	Standard Deviation
Relative contributions to household labor	3.85	6.10
Husband's hours in routine chores	11.70	12.29
Relative contributions to household income	0.55	0.25
Respondent's work hours	23.32	20.18
Ratio of hours worked in paid labor	3.42	10.09
Gender ideology	2.95	0.70
Length of marriage	19.56	13.18
Age	43.55	13.14
Children	1.16	1.25
Hours in childcare	8.51	13.06
	N	Percentage
Perceptions of fairness of household labor		
Unfair to self	631	32.66%
Fair to both	1,186	61.40%
Unfair to husband	115	5.95%
Work hours		
Works standard hours	1,120	57.97%
Works nonstandard hours	812	42.03%
Has disability		
Yes	240	12.42%
No	1,692	87.58%
Race		
White	1,674	86.65%
Black	148	7.66%
Hispanic	88	4.55%
Other	22	1.14%
Education		
High school degree or less	972	50.31%
Some college	468	24.22%
College degree	334	17.29%
Advanced degree	158	8.18%

Note: Data are drawn from the second wave of the NFSH. Data presented above are from married, employed, female focal respondents ($n = 1,932$).

RESULTS

Descriptive Statistics

Descriptive statistics are presented in Table 1. On average, women in this sample perform almost four times as many hours of household labor as do

Table 2. Multinominal Logistic Regression Predicting Women's Perceptions of Under-Benefit in the Division of Household Labor.[a]

Variables	Model 1 Exp(β)	Model 2 Exp(β)	Model 3 Exp(β)
Chore ratio	1.05***	1.14***	1.09**
Nonstandard work	0.61**	0.88	0.81
Chore ratio × self's nonstandard work	–	0.91***	0.94**
Husband's routine chores	–	–	0.97***
Proportion of household income	0.78	0.80	0.82
Wife's work hours	1.00	1.00	1.00
Ratio of hours worked	1.00	1.00	1.01
Gender ideology	1.08	1.09	1.10
Length of marriage	1.00	1.00	1.00
Age	0.99**	0.98*	0.99
Children	1.11	1.10	1.11*
Hours in childcare	1.00	1.00	1.00
Disability	1.36	1.37	1.41*
Race/ethnicity[b]			
White	0.93	0.95	0.93
Hispanic	0.66	0.64	0.61
Other race	0.70	0.71	0.67
Education[c]			
Some college	1.12	1.13	1.11
College degree	1.27	1.33	1.26
Advanced degree	1.61*	1.69**	1.55*
N	1,932	1,932	1,932
Log-likelihood	−1,524.77	−1,514.89	−1,494.49

*$p < .05$, **$p < .01$, ***$p < .001$.
Note: Data are drawn from the second wave of the NFSH. Data presented above are from married, employed, female focal respondents ($n = 1,932$).
[a]The reference category is "fair to both." The results predicting "unfair to partner" are also estimated as part of the model, but the results are not shown here, as they are not relevant to theoretical predictions. They are available upon request from the corresponding author.
[b]For Race/Ethnicity, Black is the omitted reference category.
[c]For Education, high school degree or less is the omitted reference category.

their husbands (S.D. 6.10). The majority of women (61.40%), however, perceive their divisions of household labor to be fair. About a third of women (32.66%) perceive that their divisions of household labor are unfair to them, while less than 6% of women feel that these divisions are unfair to their husbands. On average, women report that their husbands spend 11.70 hours per week (S.D. 12.29) in routine chores like cooking and cleaning. Slightly less than half of the women in the sample (42.03%) work 10 or more hours per week between 6 p.m. and 5 a.m. The average age of the respondents is 43.55 (S.D. 13.14), and the average length of their marriage is 19.56 years (S.D. 13.18). The majority of the respondents are white (86.65%). Slightly over half of the respondents have a high school degree or less.

Multivariate Findings

Table 2 shows multivariate findings. As expected, Model 1 indicates that the reported ratio of household labor affects fairness perceptions. For a one-unit increase in relative contributions to household labor, women's likelihood of perceiving unfairness to self increases by 5% (O.R. = 1.05, $p < .001$). This finding does not negate the paradox of women and household labor described previously. As seen in Table 1, the majority of women perceive their household labor arrangements to be fair both to themselves and to their spouses. Logically, of course, as women do more of the relative share of household labor, the chance that women will perceive unfairness also increases. There are three other statistically significant variables in Model 1. First, women who work nonstandard hours are 39% less likely than women who work standard hours to perceive that they are unfairly treated in their divisions of household labor (O.R. = .61, $p < .01$). Second, for each one-year increase in age, the likelihood of perceiving unfairness decreases by 1% (O.R. = .99, $p < .01$). Third, women who have an advanced degree are 61% more likely than women with a high school degree or less to perceive to be unfairly treated in their divisions of household labor (O.R. = 1.61, $p < .05$).

To test whether working during nonstandard hours affects the relationship between relative contributions to household labor and fairness perceptions, we include an interaction term in Model 2 (Table 2). The interaction term is significant (O.R. = .91, $p < .001$). Because the multinomial logistic function is not linear, additional analysis is needed to interpret the interaction term. Jaccard (2001) suggests plotting predicted log odds, which we are able to do using Dawson's (2014) interactive tool that visually displays graphs of various forms of regression models that include interaction terms.[4] Thus, we calculated how the predicted probability of perceiving one's self to be unfairly treated varies depending upon both nonstandard work status and the reported division of household labor (see Fig. 1). As Fig. 1 shows, as the level of over-work in the division of household labor increases, the likelihood of perceiving unfairness to self increases only for

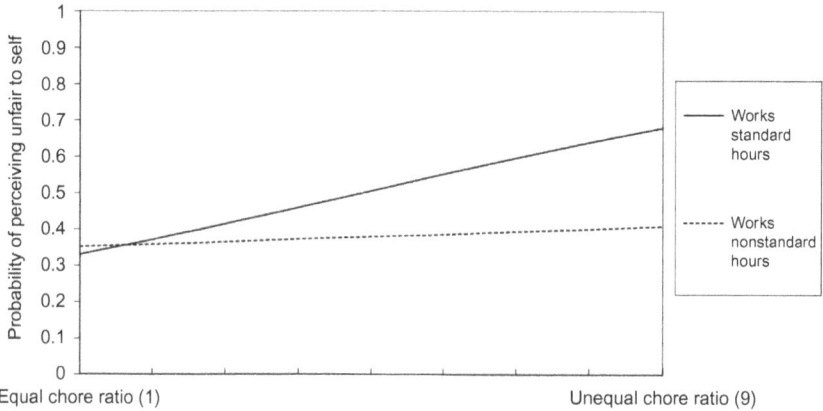

Fig. 1. Women's Predicted Probability of Perceiving Unfairness to Self by Chore Ratio and Work Hours.

women who work standard hours. When the chore ratio is equal, women's predicted probability of perceiving unfairness in their divisions of household labor is the same for women who work standard and nonstandard hours. However, as the chore ratio increases (indicating that women are performing more household labor relative to their husbands), the predicted probability that women will perceive unfairness increases for women who work standard hours but not for women who work nonstandard hours. Put differently, the slope for the effect of over-work is steeper for women who work standard hours than for women who work nonstandard hours. That is, the positive relationship between doing more household labor and perceiving unfairness to self is weaker for women who work nonstandard hours than for women who work standard hours. This finding refutes the "personal needs" argument that women who work nonstandard hours are *more* likely to view an unequal division of household labor as fair and instead supports the alternate "relationship needs" argument that these women are *less* likely than women who work standard hours to view unfavorable inequality in the home as unfair.

Model 3 tests whether the relationship between the interaction term (women's work hours and relative contributions to household labor) and perceptions of unfairness to self is mediated by men's hours in feminine-type chores. We find partial support for this, as the interaction term in Model 3 is reduced once men's hours in feminine-type chores are controlled. It is important to remember that Table 2 presents odds ratios, not coefficients. To derive coefficients from odds ratios, one must take the natural logarithm of the odds ratio. In doing so, the coefficient for the interaction term changes from −.04 in Model 2 to −.02 in Model 3, indicating that the coefficient for the interaction term between women's work hours and the chore ratio is weakened once men's hours in routine chores are added into the model. This supports the notion that men's time in feminine-type chores mediates the relationship between the interaction term and women's perceptions of unfairness to self. As the significance of the interaction term does not completely go away, however, men's time in feminine-type chores does not fully mediate the relationship between the interaction term and women's perceptions of fairness. Our results indicate that it is not simply nonstandard work hours that reduce the impact of the division of household labor on women's fairness perceptions. Instead, it is men's greater participation in feminine-type chores, necessitated by women's time in nonstandard work that is driving the moderating effect.

Due to the small number of women who work nonstandard hours and a potential for multicollinearity we also ran reduced models with only the main variables of interest (i.e., the chore ratio, women's nonstandard work, and husband's time in routine chores) and significant control variables (age and education). These models yield substantively similar results as the full models, which we describe above. In addition, we checked for multicollinearity by examining correlation coefficients of the independent variables.[5] The two variables that are most likely to be correlated are the chore ratio and husbands' hours in routine chores. The correlation coefficient for these two variables is −.29. This weak correlation suggests that there is not collinearity between these two variables. To verify that multicollinearity is not an issue, we examined variance inflation factors, which Allison (2012) suggests is an appropriate method to assess multicollinearity in logistic models. Typically, multicollinearity exists if the variance inflation factor for any variable is greater than five. None of our VIFs was greater than two.

DISCUSSION

The purpose of this chapter is to examine the effect of wives' nonstandard work hours on the relationship between over-work in household labor and perceptions of unfairness. Past research has revealed a paradox between over-work and perceptions of fairness. Women take on more household labor than their husbands but often do not view this relationship as unfair

(Barnett & Baruch, 1987; Benin & Agostinelli, 1988; Berk, 1985; Bianchi et al., 2000; Hill & Scanzoni, 1982; Pleck, 1985; Rosen, 1990; Yogev, 1981). We find, however, that women who work nonstandard hours are less likely than women who work standard hours to view over-work in household labor as unfair. This interaction, though, is partially mediated by men's time in feminine-type chores. It appears that women who work nonstandard hours may be less likely to perceive injustice due to their husbands' performance of feminine-type chores. These findings lend credibility to the idea that men's time in feminine-type chores is particularly valued by women, perhaps because performing these chores violates the norms of hegemonic masculinity. However, the valuation of men's time in feminine tasks represents only a slight shift in the metrics used to determine fairness, with women continuing to devalue their own time in routine and nonroutine household tasks. This speaks to the intractability of hegemonic masculinity.

These results also speak to the potential for broader shifts in the institution of marriage. The partially mediating effect of men's participation in feminine chores suggests that when women's paid work takes place outside of standard hours, couples renegotiate the division of household labor. This suggestion dovetails with findings by Estes, Noonan, and Maume (2007) who show that men who use family support policies at work (i.e., leave) perform a higher share of female-typed housework tasks than men who do not − indicating that the use of family support policies may compel couples to renegotiate their divisions of household labor. These two findings are consistent with Cherlin's (2004) argument that couples engage in active negotiation regarding distributions of labor when they deviate from societal norms (i.e., gay and lesbian couples, remarried couples) because they do not match the dominant cultural comparison referent. The ongoing need to perform paid labor during nonstandard hours may thus contribute to the deinstitutionalization of marriage, as it poses a challenge to the social norms surrounding marital behavior (see Cherlin, 2004). Yet, our research suggests that the end result reinforces women's subordinate position, as they continue to view doing more work in the house as fair.

This is the first study to our knowledge to examine the role of work hours in shaping perceptions of the fairness of the division of household labor. Thus, the results presented here not only provide information on this important topic but can be used to inform future research in this area. One limitation of this study, however, is the relatively small number of women in the NSFH who work primarily nonstandard hours. A second limitation is the age of the data, as our models are drawn from data gathered from

1992 to 1994. More recent surveys of workers, however, lack the variables necessary to test our arguments. We call for household labor researchers to collect new data that includes measures of self-reports of hours in both household labor and paid labor. Newer data would allow us to see the current impact of nonstandard work on perceptions of fairness of household labor. As a result of the limitations, it would be unwise to draw definitive conclusions from the research conducted to date. These limitations, however, are shared by the larger literature on household labor and nonstandard work, which also relies heavily on data from second wave of the NSFH (i.e., Presser, 2003b). Research on nonstandard work will be ever more relevant, however, as the 24/7 economy becomes more entrenched. Data from the 2010–2011 American Time Use Survey show that 20% of employed Americans worked most of their hours outside of 6:00 a.m. to 6:00 p.m. or on the weekends, and this trend has stayed roughly the same since the 1990s (Beers, 2000; Enchautegui, 2013; Hamermesh, 1999; McMenamin, 2007). Sixty-three percent of persons with nonstandard schedules are married, and certain occupations that employ nonstandard hours (i.e., registered nurses, personal care aides, and waiters/waitresses) are expected to experience growth by 2020 (Enchautegui, 2013). With such a sizeable portion of the married U.S. labor force working nonstandard hours, future research can benefit not only from increased sample size and more recent data but also from tracking how movement into and out of nonstandard work affects various aspects of family life.

Despite limitations, the results of our research have implications for understanding the role that nonstandard work hours play in shaping women's perceptions of the fairness of the division of household labor. As women's nonstandard work hours necessitate men completing chores that are incongruent with traditional gender roles, women do not seem to prioritize the needs that come with working nonstandard hours; instead, women privilege the needs of their husbands whom they feel may have their masculinity called into question by performing routine household chores. Therefore, these findings support the notion that women have been enculturated to privilege their husbands' needs above their own (Bem, 1993). Substantively, these findings suggest that future research in divisions of household labor must consider how the times that people work in paid labor influence not only the amount, but more importantly the *type* of household labor they perform. Our findings suggest that men need only contribute slightly to household labor in ways that are incongruent with traditional gender roles in order to increase the likelihood that women view their own over-work as fair. Provided that men spend time in chores in which they have not traditionally been held accountable, the 24/7 economy serves as a way for the paradox of women's lack of perceived injustice over inequitable divisions of household labor to persist. This provides further support for Hochschild and Machung's (1989) notion of the "stalled revolution." In order to jump start this revolution, women and men must continue to negotiate divisions of household labor but in ways that challenge hegemonic definitions of masculinity and femininity. Additionally, among dual-earner couples, men and women must use each other as comparison referents for performances of household labor. That is, rather than comparing themselves to their fathers or "average" men in their neighborhood, men must consider how much of the household labor they (and their wives) perform. Changing comparison referents and challenging hegemonic norms may help couples identify and rectify inequalities in their divisions of labor.

NOTES

1. There is a newer wave of the NSFH, but budget cuts restricted Wave 3 interviews to a nonrepresentative subsample of Wave 2 respondents. As a result, Wave 3 has a smaller sample size than Wave 2, and it is no longer nationally representative.
2. We focus on women because their perceptions of fairness of divisions of household labor have been shown to be incongruent with predictions posed by justice theories. Results for male respondents are available by request from the first author. These results show no significant interaction between nonstandard work and household labor.
3. We are indebted to Jeremy Reynolds for the code used to create these variables.
4. The website for this tool can be found at http://www.jeremydawson.co.uk/slopes.htm
5. The full correlation matrix is available upon request from the first author.

ACKNOWLEDGMENTS

The authors acknowledge support from National Science foundation grants SES 0966536 and BCS 0729396. An earlier draft of this chapter was presented at the 2010 Mid-South Sociological Association annual meeting and received the Association's Graduate Student "Paper of Distinction" Award.

REFERENCES

Allison, P. D. (2012). *Logistic regression using SAS: Theory and application*. Cary, NC: SAS Institute.

Barnett, R. C., & Baruch, G. K. (1987). Mothers' participation in childcare: Patterns and consequences. In F. Crosby (Ed.), *Spouse, parent, worker: On gender and multiple roles* (pp. 91–108). New Haven, CT: Yale University Press.

Baxter, J. (2000). The joys and justice of housework. *Sociology, 34*(4), 609–631.

Baxter, J., & Western, M. (1998). Satisfaction with housework: Examining the paradox. *Sociology, 32*(1), 101–120.

Beers, T. M. (2000). Flexible schedules and shift work: Replacing the "9-to-5" workday? *Monthly Labor Review, 123*(6), 33–40.

Bem, S. L. (1993). *The lenses of gender: Transforming the debate on sexual identity.* New Haven, CT: Yale University Press.

Benin, M. H., & Agostinelli, J. (1988). Husbands' and wives' satisfaction with the division of labor. *Journal of Marriage and the Family, 50,* 349–361.

Berk, S. F. (1985). *The gender factory: The apportionment of work in American households.* New York, NY: Plenum Press.

Bianchi, S. M., Milkie, M. A., Sayer, L. C., & Robinson, J. P. (2000). Is anyone doing the housework? Trends in the gender division of household labor. *Social Forces, 79*(1), 191–228.

Blair, S. L., & Johnson, M. P. (1992). Wives' perceptions of the fairness of the division of household labor: The intersection of housework and ideology. *Journal of Marriage and the Family, 54,* 570–581.

Blair, S. L., & Lichter, D. T. (1991). Measuring the division of household labor gender segregation of housework among American couples. *Journal of Family Issues, 12*(1), 91–113.

Bøggild, H., & Knutsson, A. (1999). Shift work, risk factors and cardiovascular disease. *Scandinavian Journal of Work, Environment & Health, 25*(2), 85–99.

Braun, M., Lewin-Epstein, N., Stier, H., & Baumgärtner, M. K. (2008). Perceived equity in the gendered division of household labor. *Journal of Marriage and Family, 70*(5), 1145–1156.

Cherlin, A. J. (2004). The deinstitutionalization of American marriage. *Journal of Marriage and Family, 66*(4), 848–861.

Claffey, S. T., & Mickelson, K. D. (2009). Division of household labor and distress: The role of perceived fairness for employed mothers. *Sex Roles, 60*(11), 819–831.

Coltrane, S. (2000). Research on household labor: Modeling and measuring the social embeddedness of routine family work. *Journal of Marriage and Family, 62*(4), 1208–1233. doi:10.1111/j.1741-3737.2000.01208.x

Connell, R. W. (1987). *Gender and power: Society, the person and sexual politics.* Palo Alto, CA: Stanford University Press.

Culpepper, L. (2010). The social and economic burden of shiftwork disorder. *The Journal of Family Practice, 59*(Suppl. 1), S3–S11.

Davis, S. N., & Greenstein, T. N. (2004). Cross-national variations in the division of household labor. *Journal of Marriage and Family, 66*(5), 1260–1271.

Dawson, J. F. (2014). Moderation in management research: What, why, when, and how. *Journal of Business and Psychology, 29*(1), 1–19.

DeMaris, A., & Longmore, M. A. (1996). Ideology, power, and equity: Testing competing explanations for the perception of fairness in household labor. *Social Forces, 74*(3), 1043–1071.
Drake, C. L. (2010). The characterization and pathology of circadian rhythm sleep disorders. *The Journal of Family Practice, 59*(Suppl. 1), S12–S17.
Enchautegui, M. E. (2013). Nonstandard work schedules and the well-being of low-income families. Urban Institute's Low-Income Working Families Project, paper 26.
Estes, S. B., Noonan, M. C., & Maume, D. J. (2007). Is work-family policy use related to the gendered division of housework? *Journal of Family and Economic Issues, 28*(4), 527–545.
Freudenthaler, H. H., & Mikula, G. (1998). From unfulfilled wants to the experience of injustice: Women's sense of injustice regarding the lopsided division of household labor. *Social Justice Research, 11*(3), 289–312.
Frisco, M. L., & Williams, K. (2003). Perceived housework equity, marital happiness, and divorce in dual-earner households. *Journal of Family Issues, 24*(1), 51–73.
Greenstein, T. N. (1996). Gender ideology and perceptions of the fairness of the division of household labor: Effects on marital quality. *Social Forces, 74*(3), 1029–1042.
Greenstein, T. N. (2009). National context, family satisfaction, and fairness in the division of household labor. *Journal of Marriage and Family, 71*(4), 1039–1051.
Grote, N. K., & Clark, M. S. (2001). Perceiving unfairness in the family: Cause or consequence of marital distress? *Journal of Personality and Social Psychology, 80*(2), 281–293.
Gupta, S. (2007). Autonomy, dependence, or display? The relationship between married women's earnings and housework. *Journal of Marriage and Family, 69*(2), 399–417.
Hamermesh, D. S. (1999). The timing of work over time. *Economic Journal, 109*(452), 37–66.
Hersch, J., & Stratton, L. S. (1994). Housework, wages, and the division of housework time for employed spouses. *The American Economic Review, 84*(2), 120–125.
Hill, W., & Scanzoni, J. (1982). An approach for assessing marital decision-making processes. *Journal of Marriage and the Family, 44*, 927–941.
Hochschild, A., & Machung, A. (1989). *The second shift: Working parents and the revolution at home*. New York, NY: Viking.
Jaccard, J. (2001). *Interaction effects in logistic regression* (Vol. 135). New York, NY: Sage.
Jamal, M. (2004). Burnout, stress and health of employees on non-standard work schedules: A study of Canadian workers. *Stress and Health, 20*(3), 113–119.
Knutsson, A. (2003). Health disorders of shift workers. *Occupational Medicine, 53*(2), 103–108.
Kroska, A. (1997). The division of labor in the home: A review and reconceptualization. *Social Psychology Quarterly, 60*(4), 304–322.
Kuijer, R. G., Buunk, B. P., & Ybema, J. F. (2001). Are equity concerns important in the intimate relationship when one partner of a couple has cancer? *Social Psychology Quarterly, 64*(3), 267–282.
Lively, K. J., Powell, B., Geist, C., & Steelman, L. C. (2008). Inequity among intimates: Applying equity theory to the family. *Advances in Group Processes, 25*, 87–115.
Lively, K. J., Steelman, L. C., & Powell, B. (2010). Equity, emotion, and household division of labor. *Social Psychology Quarterly, 73*(4), 358–379.
Major, B. (1987). Gender, justice, and the psychology of entitlement. In P. Shaver & C. Hendricks (Eds.), *Review of personality and social psychology* (pp. 124–140). Newbury Park, CA: Sage.

McMenamin, T. M. (2007). A time to work: Recent trends in shift work and flexible schedules. *Monthly Labor Review, 130*(12), 3–15.
Pampel, F. C. (2000). *Logistic regression: A primer* (Vol. 132). New York, NY: Sage.
Pleck, J. H. (1985). *Working wives, working husbands.* Beverly Hills, CA: Sage.
Presser, H. B. (1994). Employment schedules among dual-earner spouses and the division of household labor by gender. *American Sociological Review, 59*(3), 348–364.
Presser, H. B. (1995). Job, family, and gender: Determinants of nonstandard work schedules among employed Americans in 1991. *Demography, 32*(4), 577–598.
Presser, H. B. (2000). Nonstandard work schedules and marital instability. *Journal of Marriage and Family, 62*(1), 93–110.
Presser, H. B. (2003a). Race-ethnic and gender differences in nonstandard work shifts. *Work and Occupations, 30*(4), 412–439.
Presser, H. B. (2003b). *Working in a 24/7 economy: Challenges for American families.* New York, NY: Russell Sage Foundation.
Robinson, J. P. (1988). Who's doing the housework. *American Demographics, 10*(12), 24–28.
Rosen, E. I. (1990). *Bitter choices: Blue-collar women in and out of work.* Chicago, IL: University of Chicago Press.
Sanchez, L., & Kane, E. W. (1996). Women's and men's constructions of perceptions of housework fairness. *Journal of Family Issues, 17*(3), 358–387.
Sayer, L. C. (2005). Gender, time and inequality: Trends in women's and men's paid work, unpaid work and free time. *Social Forces, 84*(1), 285–303.
Schernhammer, E. S., Laden, F., Speizer, F. E., Willett, W. C., Hunter, D. J., Kawachi, I., & Colditz, G. A. (2001). Rotating night shifts and risk of breast cancer in women participating in the nurses' health study. *Journal of the National Cancer Institute, 93*(20), 1563–1568.
Shelton, B. A., & John, D. (1993). Does marital status make a difference? Housework among married and cohabiting men and women. *Journal of Family Issues, 14*(3), 401–420.
Smith, H. L., Gager, C. T., & Morgan, S. P. (1998). Identifying underlying dimensions in spouses' evaluations of fairness in the division of household labor. *Social Science Research, 27*(3), 305–327.
Strazdins, L., Clements, M. S., Korda, R. J., Broom, D. H., & D'Souza, R. M. (2006). Unsociable work? Nonstandard work schedules, family relationships, and children's well-being. *Journal of Marriage and Family, 68*(2), 394–410.
Sweet, J. A., Bumpass, L. L., & Call, V. R. (1996). *The National Survey of Families and Households − waves 1 and 2: Data description and documentation.* Madison, WI: Center for Demography and Ecology, University of Wisconsin-Madison.
Thompson, L. (1991). Family work women's sense of fairness. *Journal of Family Issues, 12*(2), 181–196.
Thorpy, M. J. (2010). Managing the patient with shift-work disorder. *The Journal of Family Practice, 59*(Suppl. 1), S24–S31.
United States Congress. (1991). *Biological rhythms: Implications for the worker.* Washington, DC: U.S. Government Printing Office.
United States Department of Labor. (2011). *American time use survey − 2011 results* (USDL-12-1246). Retrieved from http://www.bls.gov/news.release/pdf/atus.pdf
Van Der Lippe, T., & Siegers, J. J. (1994). Division of household and paid labour between partners: Effects of relative wage rates and social norms. *Kyklos, 47*(1), 109–136.

Ward, R. A. (1993). Marital happiness and household equity in later life. *Journal of Marriage and the Family, 55*(2), 427–438.
Wedderburn, A. (2000). *Shiftwork and health* (Vol. 1). Luxembourg: OOPEC.
West, C., & Zimmerman, D. H. (1987). Doing gender. *Gender & Society, 1*(2), 125–151.
Yogev, S. (1981). Do professional women have egalitarian marital relationships? *Journal of Marriage and the Family, 43*, 865–871.

TECHNOLOGY USE AND THE NEW ECONOMY: WORK EXTENSION, NETWORK CONNECTIVITY, AND EMPLOYEE DISTRESS AND PRODUCTIVITY

Noelle Chesley and Britta E. Johnson

ABSTRACT

Purpose — *To assess: (1) the prevalence of specific work practices that incorporate use of information and communication technology (ICT), (2) whether these practices are connected to employee distress or productivity via work extension or social network processes; (3) the implications of ICT-based work practices for the work/family interface.*

Design/methodology/approach — *We draw on the 2008 Pew Networked Workers data collected from a nationally representative sample of workers and use logistic regression methods to investigate links among use of specific ICT-based practices and increases in distress or productivity.*

Findings — *(1) Use of e-mail, instant messaging, texts, and social networking sites at work varies by demographic, organization, and job characteristics, and (2) ICT-based work extension, social network expansion, and connectivity to work colleagues are linked to increases in distress and productivity. Connecting with family or friends while at work can reduce the likelihood that an employee reports an increase in work stress.*

Research limitations/implications — *Limitations include a cross-sectional design, age of the data, missing data, and measurement issues. Even with these limitations, there are few investigations drawing from national samples of employees that can assess work-related ICT use with this level of depth.*

Originality/value — *Findings point to technological innovation as an important factor influencing work extension and social network processes and connect this to changes in employee distress and productivity. The focus on productivity is especially important given the emphasis that previous research has placed on linking ICT use and employee distress.*

Keywords: ICT; distress; productivity; work/family interface; work extension

A shifting technological landscape is arguably a critical element shaping contemporary employment experiences (Chesley, 2014; Duxbury, Towers, Higgins, & Thomas, 2006; Mano & Mesch, 2010; Perlow, 2012; Wajcman, 2006). Innovations in information and communication technology (ICT), the rise of mobile devices, and the advent of social networking applications are frequently highlighted as integral to the transition from an industrial to a knowledge economy (e.g., Castells, 2000; Rainie & Wellman, 2012). We know that the majority of employed Americans use ICT at work, and that work-related use often translates into use outside of work, as well (Madden & Jones, 2008). Technology use is also playing a role in blurring boundaries between paid work and personal life (Chesley, 2005; Duxbury et al., 2006). This is evident by research demonstrating that work-related ICT use can extend the reach of paid work into family life (Chesley, 2005; Duxbury et al., 2006). Further, personal forms of ICT use can affect work outcomes, like work strain and distress (Chesley, 2014). Thus, how employees use technology at and for work may have implications for understanding both employment and personal/family outcomes, making it a relevant area of inquiry for work/ family scholars.

Along with interest in understanding how individuals use ICT in a variety of contexts, like work, is interest in furthering understanding about how technology use might influence key employee outcomes. Work scholars have focused previous investigations on identifying links among ICT use, productivity, and employee well-being. Economic research does suggest a relationship among ICT adoption and broad workplace productivity gains (e.g., Baily, 2004; Brynjolfsson & Hitt, 2000, 2003; Stiroh & Botsch, 2007). While relatively little research has looked at how ICT use impacts individual levels of employee productivity (although see Mano & Mesch, 2010), a handful of studies link work-related ICT use to employee distress (Barley, Meyerson, & Grodal, 2011; Chesley, 2005, 2014; Mano & Mesch, 2010).

In spite of some excellent studies of ICT and work, a number of key questions about work-related ICT use are not sufficiently addressed in previous research. First, we do not know enough about how ICT is being used by employees drawing on population samples of workers. While qualitative and organizational studies have provided critical insights into the daily ICT-based work practices of very selective groups of employees, such as IT workers, consultants, or individuals in a single organization (Barley et al., 2011; Gonzalez & Mark, 2004; Mark, Gudith, & Klocke, 2008; Perlow, 2012; Wajcman & Rose, 2011), the few nationally representative survey studies available use very blunt or outdated measures of ICT use that tell us little about the prevalence of specific forms of technology use in today's workplaces (Chesley, 2014). Second, we have not done enough to understand whether specific work-related forms of ICT use may be influencing key individual outcomes that are salient to both employees and employers. What impact are different forms of use having, if any, on employee productivity or well-being? Understanding whether ICT practices influence such outcomes allows researchers, practitioners, and policy-makers to develop a broader understanding of the relevance of rapid technological innovation for employers, employees, and their families.

Thus, one goal of this chapter is to provide estimates of ICT use, drawing on measures that tap specific forms of use (e-mail, instant messaging (IM), texts, social networking applications), in order to broaden our understanding of how prevalent a range of specific ICT-based practices are in today's workplaces. We also investigate whether individual, organizational, or job factors vary by type of ICT use to better understand how individual and job characteristics may influence technology use. A second goal involves examining whether specific ICT-based practices — ICT-based work extension and network size and connectivity — influence two key employee outcomes: increases in self-reported distress or productivity. To accomplish these goals, we draw on survey data collected by the Pew Internet and American Life Project (*The 2008 Networked Workers Study* ($N = 1,000$)) from a nationally representative sample of workers. This survey incorporates a range of measures tapping how ICT is used in workplaces, as well as measures of employees' perceived distress and productivity. Although our investigation primarily informs research about the social forces shaping contemporary work, our focus on work extension and *both* work-related and personal forms of ICT use has clear implications for scholars who study the work/family interface.

LITERATURE REVIEW

Technology "Use" versus "Practice"

A large technology studies literature demonstrates that the process of technological innovation is, at root, a social process (Hackett, Amsterdamska, Lynch, & Wajcman, 2008; MacKenzie & Wajcman, 1999). Thus, technological innovation influences, and is influenced by, current social conditions in ways that can allow new practices to emerge or can reconfigure existing practices. We refer to "ICT-based work practices" to emphasize that ICTs are embedded in organizations with preexisting cultures, norms, and objectives, and technology, in combination with these features, can be used in ways that both reconfigure and reinforce current workplace conditions (Wajcman, 2006). While we may refer to "ICT use" for the sake of brevity, we always assume this use is grounded in social interaction.

Nationally representative data on the prevalence of ICT use among workers is limited. We are aware of only two sources of publicly available U.S. national data: (1) the National Study of the Changing Workforce (NSCW), which is conducted every five years and (2) the 2008 Networked Workers survey conducted by the Pew Internet and American Life Project, which is the focus of this chapter. The 2002 NSCW study asked about the frequency of computer use at work and documents that about 75% of employees use a computer at work once a month or more (67% are daily users; first author's estimates). While more recent NSCW data exist, the 2008 study asked only about personal technology use. The Pew 2008

Networked Workers survey indicates that 62% of U.S. employees use the Internet or e-mail at their workplace (Madden & Jones, 2008). Similar prevalence patterns at about the same time have been identified among Canadian employees (Desjardins Financial Security, 2006). While previous research recognizes the key role of ICT in organizations, past research often characterizes this use in very general terms, like overall frequency of computer or Internet use for work (e.g., Chesley, 2014). Our focus is not on very general forms of ICT use, but on ICT use as it is embedded in a series of work practices that were not possible or could not be performed on the same scale before the entrenchment of computers and mobile communications (Chesley & Johnson, 2010).

Previous research also provides some guidance on the individual and organizational factors that shape ICT use. Research examining the demographic factors shaping ICT use suggest that use is prevalent: 77% of all U.S. adults 18 and older use the Internet (Zickuhr & Smith, 2012). To the extent that there are demographic differences influencing access and use, these vary largely by age (those 65 and older use ICT less than younger people); levels of formal education (those without a high school degree use ICT less than those with more education), and low household income (those with incomes less than $20,000 use ICT less than those with higher incomes; Zickuhr & Smith, 2012). With respect to organizational factors that shape ICT use in national samples of employees, we know very little. Mano and Mesch (2010) draw on earlier 2002 Pew data measuring work-related e-mail use and find that older workers, full-time workers, those working in large organizations, as well as those working managerial jobs tend to send and receive more work-related (rather than personal) e-mails. In addition, individuals engaged in home-based work or in managerial jobs have higher overall volume of e-mail than others.

ICT-Based Practices and Work Extension

One way that ICT use can influence work experiences, and worker outcomes, is through technologically facilitated *work extension* (Duxbury et al., 2006). Work extension occurs when ICT use is incorporated into organizational practices that enable paid work to enter into nonwork time and space, making it difficult for employees to disengage from work (Chesley, Siibak, & Wajcman, 2013). Work extension is conceptually grounded in border and boundary theories (Ashforth, Kreiner, & Fugate, 2000; Clark, 2000; Desrochers & Sargent, 2003; Nippert-Eng, 1996).

Conceptually, boundaries are social constructions that use external and internal cues to demarcate key life domains. Nippert-Eng (1996) argued that boundary construction comes in four different forms – cognitive, physical, temporal, and behavioral – and showed how these different boundary constructions could be used, alone, or in combination, to create different degrees of segmentation or integration of work and family life.

A key feature of an entrenched technology infrastructure is the ease with which this infrastructure allows us to solidify or overcome both physical and temporal boundaries (Castells, 2000). For example, ongoing, technologically mediated communications can be asynchronous, widening the time frame for communication, and access to information can be obtained on the go through a mobile phone or tablet, overcoming the barriers of physical space. Thus, access to paid work, and, just as importantly, personal connections with family and friends, can be gained across both time and space among employees (Chesley et al., 2013). However, technology use can reinforce boundaries, as well, by allowing users to better control access to information and communications in ways that may further demarcate or separate social domains, as when employees use various features of ICT to limit personal communications at work (Rose, 2013).

There is evidence linking ICT-based practices to work extension experiences. Chesley (2005), drawing on a U.S. sample of dual-earner workers working at one of several organizations in New York State found that cell phone use was linked to increases in worker distress because it increased negative spillover from work into family life. Boswell and Olson-Buchanan (2007) draw on an organizational sample and also find that after hours ICT use is linked to higher levels of work–family conflict, a known antecedent of distress (Bellavia & Frone, 2005). Similar patterns are observed in research by Fenner and Renn (2010). Related to this, analysis of the 2002 NSCW by Schieman and Glavin (2008) shows that technologically facilitated contact with work outside of normal working hours is positively associated with higher levels of work/family conflict among workers with less job autonomy. In other work drawing on a different national sample of workers, these authors document that this form of ICT-based work extension is linked to increased distress in working women, primarily because of increased feelings of guilt (Glavin, Schieman, & Reid, 2011). As a whole, then, existing research suggests that ICT-based work extension will be positively associated with employee distress.

Another way ICT-based work extension may influence employee distress is by facilitating longer work hours (Barley et al., 2011; Towers, Duxbury, Higgins, & Thomas, 2006). Greater accessibility by employers to employees, and by employees to their work, may step up expectations of employers or employees to stay more fully engaged in their work responsibilities resulting in more work time. Mixed-methods research by Towers and colleagues (2006) documents exactly this process. In their study, employees who were engaged in ICT-based work extension practices also reported higher workloads and a longer work day. Given the cross-sectional nature of their data, they are careful to note that employees with higher workloads might turn to work extension practices to get their work done. However, their qualitative data indicate that many employees believed that their adoption of ICT-based practices shifted organizational expectations about both their accessibility and response time, thus lengthening their work day. Research by Barley and colleagues (2011) has also shown how e-mail use at work has shifted expectations toward faster response times in ways that many employees find stressful. Other work drawing on U.S. (Chesley, 2010) and Canadian (Duxbury et al., 2006) employee samples links work-related ICT use to worker perceptions of increased work demands. Thus, one of the mechanisms linking technologically based work-extension practices to greater employee distress may be increased work time.

Very little has been done to examine connections between the frequency of work-related ICT use and increased employee productivity via a work extension process. While Mano and Mesch (2010) do find positive associations between work-related e-mail use and self-assessed productivity, they are not able to investigate the process behind this association. There is some limited evidence that productivity gains may be connected to ICT-based work extension practices. For example, Duxbury et al. (2006) cite industry data (BlackBerry and Intel) reporting that users of notebook computers at home work an additional five hours per week, which results in an annual dollar benefit of $19,200 per employee for the organization (p. 11). In addition, Towers and colleagues (2006) find a positive relationship among frequency of ICT use outside of the office, total hours worked each week, and productivity ratings. These studies suggest that productivity gains may rely, in part, on ICT-based work practices that promote greater overall time in paid work activities.

The Networked Worker

Some scholars argue that our entrenched ICT infrastructure is supporting a new form of networked social connectedness that is infiltrating every social domain, including the workplace (Rainie & Wellman, 2012). New ICT-based practices support the creation of bigger, broader social networks and workers must now choose which networks to access, how to access them, and assess how to filter the vast amounts of information these networks will provide (Rainie & Wellman, 2012). Overall, empirical findings support this argument and document that ICT use is associated with larger and more diverse social networks (Hampton, Sessions, Her, & Rainie, 2009), as technologically mediated communication is used to augment and strengthen existing strong ties and facilitates access to greater numbers of weak social ties. Research drawing on a random sample of college students augments previous findings and indicates that using social networking tools helps to increase users' social capital and thus "could have strong payoffs in terms of jobs, internships, and other opportunities" (Ellison, Steinfield, & Lampe, 2007, p. 64). In fact, studies reveal that users of SNS with more "friends" are more likely to receive information about possible job openings than others (Rienties, Tempelaar, Pinckaers, Giesbers, & Lichel, 2010). Thus, much of this research emphasizes the potential for those with bigger social networks to have greater access to social support and information (Hampton et al., 2009). In a work context, the information and support provided by these expanded networks should enhance productivity.

However, a criticism of previous work is that it derives from studies of adults' friend and family networks, where personal discretion over when and how to communicate and respond to network requests should be relatively high. Indeed, qualitative work drawing on 27 workers employed in a telecommunications company suggests that ICT users employ specific ICT-based strategies to control personal access while they are at work (Rose, 2013). In contrast, studies of e-mail use for work suggest that the volume of work-related e-mail communication is positively related to employee distress (Barley et al., 2011; Mano & Mesch, 2010), with the work by Barley and colleagues indicating that organizational norms of responsiveness coupled with feelings of overload and loss of control related to e-mail use help explain this relationship. Mano and Mesch (2010) also link greater work-related e-mail use to higher productivity as well as distress, a pattern that mirrors findings in Chesley (2010) in which work-related computer/Internet use was positively associated with employee's assessments of their productivity and work demands. Previous research indicates, then, that ICT-expanded communication networks will be positively associated with both distress and productivity increases.

Because levels of discretion likely vary across the social domains of employment and personal life, Chesley (2010, 2014) has argued that we might see different well-being outcomes to be associated with work-related and personal ICT use. Indeed, recent work drawing on the 2002 NSCW demonstrates that while work-related ICT use contributes to work intensification processes that are associated with employee distress, personal ICT use can offset some of these effects (Chesley, 2014). Other work suggests positive links between personal forms of ICT use and enhanced self-reported productivity (Chesley, 2010).

Overall, a limited knowledge base points to connections among both work-related and personal forms of ICT use, work extension, changes in work time and social networks, and changes in the ways employees experience work, particularly in terms of distress and productivity. Investigating whether or not these connections are evident in a contemporary, national sample of workers is the goal of this chapter.

METHOD

Data

We use data from the 2008 *Networked Workers* survey conducted by the Pew Internet and American Life Project (www.pewinternet.org). The focus of the survey was to determine the amount, type, and influence of technology use drawing from a nationally representative sample of U.S. workers. This is an ideal dataset for examining the role that ICT-based work practices play in influencing levels of productivity and distress in employed U.S. adults because of the breadth of ICT-related topics it covers and because the data are drawn from a nationally representative sample of workers. While more recent data would be even better, we have been unable to identify other publicly available datasets that contain the breadth of information in this study.

Data were collected by phone in spring of 2008 from a sample designed to represent all continental U.S. telephone households. All individuals interviewed for this survey ($N=1,000$) self-identified as full-time or part-time workers. ICT use was defined as computer, Internet, e-mail, IM, or cell phone use. Our final sample includes all respondents who indicated that they use some form of ICT ($n=956$) and excludes cases with missing data ($n=150$, or 15.6%), resulting in an analytic sample of 806 workers.

The response rate for this survey was 24%, which may raise concerns about nonresponse bias. However, research suggests that there is not a consistent relationship between response rates and nonresponse bias. A recent meta-analysis (Groves, 2006) suggests that data drawn from probability-based samples with measures of key auxiliary variables (particularly gender and urban/rural address) on respondents and nonrespondents are best positioned to deal with issues of response bias. Our data are drawn from a probability-based sample with a clear sampling frame and Pew used auxiliary variables (including gender and region) to create a weight to correct for differential patterns of nonresponse. In our analyses we use this weight to correct for nonresponse bias and Taylor's linearization method is used to incorporate a design effect into the standard error estimates (following recommendations from Pew). Survey commands in STATA 12.0 (e.g., svy: logistic) were used to produce our estimates.

Measures

Dependent Variables
Both perceived *productivity* and *distress* are measured through a single question that asks respondents, "How much, if at all, have technologies such as the Internet, e-mail, cell phones, instant messaging: (1) improved your ability to do your job?" or (2) "increased stress in your job?" Responses range from 1 ("a lot") to 4 ("not at all"). The restricted measurement in the response scale coupled with inspection of each histogram lead us to recode both variables as dichotomies where 1 indicates an increase in productivity or distress (by "some," or "a lot") and 0 indicates little to no increase in productivity or distress.

ICT-facilitated work extension is measured using two indexes constructed from six items that, together, tap work extension via e-mail or phone use. Respondents were asked: "... Do you check your work-related e-mail (phone) on: (1) weekends; (2) vacations; (3) before work; (4) after work; (5) when you are sick; (6) when running errands?" Responses on these individual items range from 1 (often), to 4 (never) and were recoded so that higher numbers indicated greater frequency. We summed these recoded items together to form two different indexes tapping e-mail-based work extension and phone-based work extension (6 = no work extension; 24 = high levels of work extension).

ICT Use and Changes in Overall Work Time
We incorporate information about whether e-mail use has produced changes in overall work time in our analyses. Respondents were asked:

"Has using e-mail changed the amount of time you spend ... working overall." Responses are categorical and include (1) increased; (2) decreased; or (3) hasn't changed overall work time (comparison category in regression models).

ICT-based network expansion is measured using responses to a single item: "How much, if at all, have technologies such as the Internet, e-mail, cell phones, and instant messaging expanded the number of people you communicate with?" Responses range from 1 (not at all) to 4 (a lot). We treat this variable categorically, and compare those that experience some level of increase in their communications networks to those with no increase in regression models.

ICT Use at Work
To capture the variety of ICTs employees use while working, and reasons for use (for work or for personal/family reasons) we draw on a series of eight different measures. Respondents were asked: "While you are at work, how often do you: (1) check your personal e-mail; (2) check your work e-mail; (3) send instant messages to your colleagues at work; (4) send instant messages to friends or family; (5) send text messages to colleagues at work; (6) send text messages to friends or family; (7) communicate with your colleagues at work using social networking sites like MySpace or Facebook; (8) communicate with friends or family using social networking sites." Responses range from 1 (constantly) to 7 (never). With the exception of e-mail, most of these applications were not heavily used by employees and were lacking good variation in terms of use frequency, thus, we created a series of dichotomous variables that capture whether a respondent uses a particular technology or application with any frequency (1) versus no use (0).

Control Variables
A number of other characteristics are likely to influence employee perceptions of productivity and distress. Age, gender, race/ethnicity, education, and relationship status are factors known to influence job conditions at work, distress levels, and ICT use. We control for age (measured in years), gender (1 = female), and race/ethnicity. Although respondents were originally classified into four racial/ethnic categories (white, black, Hispanic, other), small cell sizes require us to collapse race into a dichotomy (1 = non-Hispanic white; 0 = otherwise). Education is also controlled and measured categorically; respondents fall into one of four categories: (1) less than high school; (2) high school graduate; (3) some college; (4) college or better (our comparison category in regression models). Relationship status

is measured categorically as (1) married, (2) cohabiting, or (3) single (our comparison category in regression models).

In addition, we control for a number of characteristics associated with a respondent's employment. To assess employment income, respondents were asked, "What was your wage last year (2007) before taxes?" The original variable had eight response categories, several with small cell sizes. As a result, we recoded this item into a four-category variable: (1) Less than $30,000; (2) $30,000–49,000; (3) $50,000–74,000; (4) $75,000 or more. We also control for organization type. There are seven response options: (1) large corporation; (2) medium-size company; (3) small business; (4) federal/state/local government; (5) school or educational institution; (6) nonprofit; (7) other. We combined "non-profit" and "other" into a single category because of small cell sizes and use this as our comparison in regression models.

We control for job type using a categorical measure based on the question, "What type of work do you do?" with possible responses: (1) professional: lawyer, doctor, teacher, nurse accountant; (2) clerical/office/sales: secretary, receptionist, sales clerk; (3) service work: waiter/waitress, hairstylist, police or fireman, janitor, nurses' aide, (4) skilled trades: electrician, plumber, carpenter; (5) manager, executive, or official: store manager, business executive; (6) semi-skilled trades: assembly line worker, truck driver, bus driver; (7) business owner; (8) other. There are very few business owners in the sample, so we collapsed "business owner" into the manager/executive category. We compare to "others" in regression models. We also control for self-employment using a binary measure (1 = self-employed; 0 = otherwise) and hours worked. To assess work hours, respondents were asked, "How many hours do you work in a typical week?" The responses ranged from 1 to 61 (Pew coded everyone working more than 60 hours per week as "61," thus this variable is truncated at the top end).

The remaining control variables assess a range of specific job characteristics known to be related to employee productivity and well-being, including perceptions of job satisfaction, autonomy, advancement opportunities, and job complexity. To measure *job satisfaction*, respondents were asked, "How satisfied are you with your job?" Responses ranged from 1 (completely satisfied) to 4 (completely dissatisfied) and were recoded to reflect those that are "completely" or "mostly" satisfied (1) versus those that are not (0) based on the distribution of the original variable. *Job autonomy* is measured with a single item which asks, "I have a lot to say about what happens in my job." *Job advancement* is also measured using a single item which asks "I have opportunities for advancement in my job." Responses for both items range from 1 (strongly disagree) to 5 (strongly agree) and were recoded such that higher numbers correspond to higher levels of agreement. *Job complexity* is a scale that combines responses to four individual items: (1) "My job requires a high level of skill," (2) "My job requires creativity," (3) "My job requires that I do the same thing over and over," and (4) "My job requires abstract knowledge about the ideas behind my work." Responses range from 1 (strongly disagree) to 5 (strongly agree) and were recoded so that higher numbers correspond to higher levels of agreement (except for the question that asks, "My job requires me to do the same thing over and over"). The final measure ranges from 4 (low job complexity) to 20 (high job complexity) and has an alpha = 0.613. Finally, we control for the frequency with which respondents work from home. Each was asked: "How often, if ever, do you work from home?" Responses range from 1 (everyday) to 6 (never) and were recoded so that higher numbers reflect greater frequency of work from home.

Analytic Strategy

We estimate a series of bivariate logistic regression equations to analyze the relationships among increases in perceived distress and productivity and (1) ICT-based work extension and changes in overall work time; (2) ICT use and changes in the size of communication networks; and (3) use of e-mail, IM, texts, and social networking applications for both work and personal reasons. These results are summarized in Tables 3−5.

Missing Data

Ninety-six respondents (10% of our analytic sample) did not report their income when completing the survey. Multivariate analyses of the patterns of missing income data indicate that age ($p < .001$) and education level ($p < .05$) are positively related to missing income reports (analyses not shown). An analysis of missing cases for all other variables in our analysis shows that these variables are missing substantially fewer cases (2% or less) than we see for income. We use multiple imputation procedures (*mi impute* command in STATA 12.1) to impute missing income data; however, because of the range of measurement of the variables in our analysis, and the small percentage of missing cases on the other variables, we do not impute missing data for the full dataset, following recommendations in the literature (StataCorp LP, 2013). Thus, the remaining dropped cases ($n = 150$ or 15.6% of the analytic sample) are dropped because of small amounts of missing data across a range of other variables. The multiple imputation procedures we employ here are frequently recommended as one of the best ways to impute missing information in survey data (Schafer & Graham, 2002).

After imputation, we are able to recover an additional 59 cases (61%) that were previously dropped because of missing income information. Imputation results indicate that the average relative inflation in variance of the estimates (RVI) caused by the missing values is very low (RVI < 0.01 across analyses). RVI close to zero is ideal (Acock, 2012), thus, our RVI estimates indicate that our imputed missing values are not inflating SEs much across the various descriptive and multivariate results. In addition, all analyses were conducted with and without imputed income with minimal differences. Thus, the patterns we report are robust to differences in sample size or the inclusion of cases with imputed income information.

RESULTS

Table 1 provides descriptive statistics for the full analytic sample. Average age for these employees is 40, 46% are female, and 78% are white. About 7% have no high school degree, 29% are high school graduates, 27% have some college, and 37% have a four-year college or advanced degree. A bit more than half of respondents are married (59%) and 36% are single. There is also variation in wage income, with about a third (34%) reporting annual wage income of less than $30,000, while 26% report earnings in the $30–49K range. The remaining 40% earned wages that were $50,000 or better. Employees work in a range of settings, with more than half the sample working for a large corporation (30%) or small business (28%). Fewer employees report working in a medium-sized business (16%), or government (9%), education (9%), or nonprofit (8%) sectors. Almost a quarter of the sample (23%) identifies as a "professional," while 20% report working in a clerical, office, or sales job. Thirty percent of employees are in service work (17%) or the skilled trades (13%). About 14% of the sample reports being self-employed, and average weekly work hours are full-time (41).

Most employees (90%) report being satisfied with their current job and also report average to higher job autonomy (3.7 on a five-point scale). On average, employees report some opportunities for job advancement (3.3 on a five-point scale), and middle-levels of job complexity (14 on a 4–20 scale). Frequency of working at home is one the low side (2.3 on a six-point

Table 1. Weighted Descriptive Statistics ($N = 806$).

	Mean	SE
Individual characteristics		
Age (years)	40.433	0.479
% Female	0.463	0.020
% White	0.777	0.018
Education		
% No HS degree	0.068	0.011
% HS degree	0.287	0.018
% Some college	0.274	0.018
% College/Advanced degree	0.371	0.018
Relationship status		
% Married	0.588	0.020
% Cohabiting	0.055	0.010
% Single	0.357	0.019
Income		
% Less than $30K	0.337	0.020
% $30–49K	0.258	0.017
% $50–74K	0.187	0.015
% $75K +	0.217	0.016
Organization and job characteristics		
Organization type		
% Large corporation	0.303	0.018
% Medium-sized business	0.162	0.015
% Small business	0.278	0.018
% Federal/State/Local government	0.094	0.011
% Education	0.085	0.010
% Nonprofit/Other	0.080	0.010
Job type		
% Professional	0.229	0.016
% Manager/Exec/Bus. owner	0.098	0.011
% Clerical/Office/Sales	0.199	0.016
% Service	0.170	0.016
% Skilled trades	0.125	0.013
% Semi-skilled trades	0.081	0.011
% Other	0.097	0.012
% Self-employed	0.136	0.013
Average weekly work hours	40.720	0.513
% Satisfied with job	0.900	0.012
Level of job autonomy (1 = low to 5 = high)	3.662	0.053
Potential for job advancement (1 = low to 5 = high)	3.333	0.055
Job complexity (4 = low to 20 = high)	13.824	0.143
Frequency works at home (1 = never to 6 = everyday)	2.333	0.068
ICT use		
ICT-based work extension		
E-mail work extension (6 = none to 24 = a lot)	10.207	0.211
Phone work extension (6 = none to 24 = a lot)	11.689	0.187

Table 1. (*Continued*)

	Mean	SE
ICT use and work time		
% Reporting increases in overall work time	0.149	0.014
% Reporting decreases in overall work time	0.056	0.009
% Reporting no change in overall work time	0.795	0.016
ICT use and communication network size		
% Expanded communication network none	0.176	0.015
% Expanded communication network only a little	0.137	0.014
% Expanded communication network some	0.206	0.016
% Expanded communication network a lot	0.482	0.020
Type of ICT use at work		
% Use e-mail to communicate at work	0.584	0.020
% Use e-mail at work for friends/family	0.432	0.019
% Use IM to communicate at work	0.170	0.015
% Use IM at work for friends/family	0.146	0.014
% Use texts to communicate at work	0.189	0.016
% Use texts at work for friends/family	0.322	0.019
% Use SNS to communicate at work	0.056	0.009
% Use SNS at work for friends/family	0.089	0.012
Outcomes: Productivity and distress		
% Increased productivity	0.685	0.019
% Increased distress	0.331	0.018

Source: 2008 Pew Networked Workers survey with imputed income.

scale). In terms of ICT-based work practices, levels of both e-mail and phone-based work extension appear relatively low, on average (10 and 12, respectively, on a 6−24 scale) and most employees (80%) report that ICT use has not changed their overall work time. However, among those that do report change in work time, it is more common to report that ICT use promotes *increased* work time (15%), than *decreased* work time (5%).

There is variation in experiences with ICT use and changes in the size of employees' communication networks, and the norm appears to be some level of expansion. Less than a fifth of employees (18%) report no change in the size of their communication networks, others report small levels of expansion (14%), "some" expansion (21%), or "a lot" of expansion (48%). We can also see that over half of employees use e-mail to communicate at work (59%), with 43% reporting personal e-mail use at work. It is much less common to use IM, texts, or SNS to communicate with work colleagues, although about a third (32%) of the sample reports sending personal texts while at work and all these applications are used at work for both work and personal reasons by some employees. Lastly, these statistics show that many employees (69%) in the sample report higher productivity levels that they attribute to ICT use, while a much smaller number (33%) report higher distress levels connected to ICT use.

Because so little is known about the individual, firm, and job characteristics associated with various types of work-related ICT use, we also provide descriptive breakdowns by employees who do or do not use e-mail, IM, texts, and SNS while at work in Table 2. The first thing to notice are the very different proportions of use across each ICT. Work-related e-mail use is prevalent, with 61% of all employees reporting e-mail use at work. Other ICT use at work is much less common. About 16% of employees report using IM or sending texts at work and just 5% report any form of SNS use while at work. Employees who report work-related e-mail use tend to be older than those that do not use e-mail at work and are also older than employees who report using other ICT-based applications at work, like IM, and, especially, texts or SNS. Gender also appears important in that a greater proportion of women report using e-mail at work than any other forms of ICT. In addition, a greater proportion of whites use e-mail or SNS at work than use IM or texts. Educational patterns for work-related use tend to match those for the general population in that greater proportions of highly educated employees use ICT at work than do not. There are not clear marital status patterns across ICTs. In general, it appears that greater proportions of married employees use e-mail than use other ICTs, while greater numbers of single employees use texts or SNS at work. Like education, patterns by income are generally consistent with overall use trends in the population in that individuals with higher incomes tend to be ICT users, although income differences are less pronounced among those employees that do or do not use texts or SNS at work.

Use patterns by organization type suggest that all forms of ICT use at work are more prevalent in private sector business, particularly large corporations, than in other sectors like government, education, or nonprofits. This is especially true for instant message technology, where 44% of all IM users report working for large corporations. Work-related e-mail use tends to be concentrated among professionals (32%) and clerical or sales staff (23%). Use of IM at work is also more common among professionals (30%), clerical/sales staff (23%), and managers/executives (13%) than other types of employees. With respect to sending texts or engaging with SNS while at work, professionals, clerical/sales staff, and managers/executives are also a common job type reporting use; we also see greater numbers of those in service work reporting this type of use at work.

Table 2. Weighted Descriptive Statistics by Type of Work-Related ICT Use (N = 806).

	E-mail				Instant Message (IM)				Texting				Social Networking Site (SNS)			
	Use (N=488)		No use (N=318)		Use (N=131)		No use (N=675)		Use (N=127)		No use (N=679)		Use (N=39)		No use (N=767)	
	Mean	SE	Mean	SE	Mean	SE	Mean	SE	Mean	SE	Mean	SE	Mean	SE	Mean	SE
Individual characteristics																
Age (years)	40.926	0.555	39.742	0.844	39.680	1.090	40.587	0.533	35.066	1.052	41.685	0.526	35.468	2.153	40.727	0.489
% Female	0.462	0.025	0.463	0.031	0.395	0.047	0.477	0.021	0.403	0.047	0.477	0.021	0.331	0.082	0.471	0.020
% White	0.784	0.023	0.768	0.028	0.599	0.050	0.814	0.018	0.611	0.049	0.816	0.018	0.825	0.069	0.774	0.018
Education																
% No HS degree	0.027	0.009	0.125	0.023	0.036	0.021	0.074	0.013	0.114	0.033	0.057	0.011	0.070	0.051	0.068	0.011
% HS degree	0.166	0.020	0.456	0.031	0.166	0.037	0.311	0.020	0.180	0.039	0.312	0.020	0.167	0.070	0.294	0.019
% Some college	0.272	0.023	0.277	0.028	0.268	0.044	0.276	0.019	0.315	0.046	0.265	0.019	0.247	0.074	0.276	0.018
% College/Advanced degree	0.535	0.025	0.141	0.019	0.529	0.049	0.339	0.019	0.391	0.046	0.366	0.020	0.516	0.089	0.362	0.019
Relationship status																
% Married	0.642	0.025	0.512	0.031	0.581	0.050	0.589	0.022	0.507	0.049	0.607	0.021	0.421	0.085	0.597	0.020
% Cohabiting	0.047	0.011	0.067	0.017	0.035	0.019	0.059	0.011	0.039	0.019	0.059	0.011	0.030	0.030	0.057	0.010
% Single	0.311	0.024	0.422	0.031	0.384	0.049	0.352	0.021	0.454	0.049	0.335	0.021	0.548	0.087	0.346	0.020
Income																
% Less than $30K	0.206	0.022	0.520	0.032	0.175	0.038	0.370	0.022	0.284	0.045	0.349	0.022	0.326	0.088	0.338	0.020
% $30–49K	0.254	0.022	0.264	0.028	0.227	0.041	0.265	0.019	0.218	0.041	0.268	0.019	0.222	0.075	0.261	0.018
% $50–74K	0.235	0.022	0.119	0.020	0.217	0.041	0.181	0.017	0.217	0.041	0.180	0.016	0.094	0.047	0.193	0.016
% $75K+	0.304	0.024	0.096	0.018	0.381	0.048	0.184	0.016	0.281	0.042	0.203	0.017	0.358	0.086	0.0209	0.016
Organization and job characteristics																
Organization type																
% Large corporation	0.293	0.023	0.317	0.030	0.440	0.049	0.274	0.020	0.337	0.046	0.295	0.020	0.278	0.081	0.304	0.019
% Medium-sized business	0.152	0.019	0.175	0.024	0.171	0.040	0.160	0.016	0.200	0.040	0.153	0.015	0.045	0.037	0.168	0.015
% Small business	0.249	0.022	0.318	0.029	0.252	0.042	0.283	0.019	0.257	0.042	0.282	0.019	0.366	0.085	0.272	0.018
% Federal/State/Local government	0.113	0.016	0.066	0.015	0.054	0.023	0.102	0.012	0.090	0.028	0.094	0.012	0.019	0.019	0.098	0.012
% Education	0.103	0.014	0.059	0.014	0.054	0.018	0.091	0.012	0.075	0.024	0.087	0.011	0.143	0.064	0.081	0.010
% Nonprofit/Other	0.091	0.014	0.065	0.016	0.029	0.014	0.090	0.012	0.040	0.016	0.089	0.012	0.149	0.061	0.076	0.010
Job type																
% Professional	0.318	0.023	0.105	0.018	0.299	0.043	0.215	0.017	0.218	0.039	0.232	0.017	0.259	0.074	0.227	0.016
% Manager/Exec/Bus. owner	0.145	0.018	0.032	0.009	0.134	0.035	0.091	0.011	0.118	0.030	0.093	0.012	0.161	0.065	0.094	0.011

% Clerical/Office/Sales	0.232	0.021	0.154	0.023	0.227	0.041	0.193	0.017	0.173	0.037	0.205	0.017	0.127	0.059	0.203	0.016
% Service	0.079	0.014	0.298	0.030	0.065	0.024	0.191	0.018	0.217	0.042	0.159	0.016	0.171	0.068	0.170	0.016
% Skilled trades	0.079	0.013	0.191	0.025	0.095	0.028	0.132	0.015	0.107	0.028	0.130	0.015	0.046	0.033	0.130	0.014
% Semi-skilled trades	0.030	0.009	0.153	0.022	0.030	0.017	0.092	0.012	0.075	0.028	0.083	0.011	0.065	0.045	0.082	0.011
% Other	0.118	0.017	0.068	0.016	0.149	0.038	0.087	0.012	0.091	0.029	0.098	0.013	0.171	0.071	0.093	0.012
% Self-employed	0.125	0.016	0.153	0.022	0.149	0.034	0.134	0.014	0.120	0.030	0.140	0.014	0.241	0.071	0.130	0.013
Average weekly work hours	43.078	0.590	37.413	0.871	43.548	1.260	40.141	0.558	42.600	1.303	40.281	0.554	40.664	2.746	40.723	0.519
% Satisfied with job	0.929	0.013	0.859	0.023	0.929	0.025	0.894	0.014	0.847	0.035	0.913	0.013	0.855	0.065	0.903	0.013
Level of job autonomy (1 = low to 5 = high)	3.755	0.065	3.533	0.088	3.848	0.119	3.624	0.058	3.718	0.123	3.649	0.058	3.992	0.224	3.643	0.054
Potential for job advancement (1 = low to 5 = high)	3.435	0.069	3.191	0.091	3.604	0.129	3.278	0.061	3.613	0.128	3.268	0.061	3.861	0.216	3.302	0.057
Job complexity (4 = low to 20 = high)	14.531	0.164	12.833	0.242	14.856	0.340	13.613	0.156	13.953	0.364	13.794	0.155	14.919	0.584	13.759	0.148
Frequency works at home (1 = never to 6 = everyday)	2.682	0.091	1.844	0.095	2.935	0.169	2.210	0.073	2.515	0.171	2.291	0.074	3.109	0.343	2.287	0.069
ICT use																
ICT-based work extension																
E-mail work extension (6 = none to 24 = a lot)	12.251	0.289	7.342	0.202	13.556	0.573	9.523	0.212	12.366	0.576	9.704	0.217	15.109	1.004	9.917	0.211
Phone work extension (6 = none to 24 = a lot)	12.537	0.240	10.500	0.282	13.295	0.452	11.360	0.203	13.253	0.487	11.324	0.199	14.404	0.807	11.528	0.191
ICT use and work time																
% Reporting increases in overall work time	0.232	0.021	0.033	0.011	0.232	0.045	0.122	0.014	0.222	0.040	0.132	0.014	0.230	0.067	0.145	0.014
% Reporting decreases in overall work time	0.084	0.014	0.016	0.008	0.081	0.026	0.050	0.009	0.083	0.028	0.049	0.009	0.127	0.053	0.051	0.009
% Reporting no change in overall work time	0.684	0.024	0.951	0.013	0.637	0.048	0.827	0.016	0.695	0.045	0.818	0.016	0.643	0.080	0.804	0.016
ICT use and communication network size																
% Expanded communication network none	0.078	0.014	0.314	0.029	0.036	0.019	0.205	0.018	0.090	0.027	0.196	0.017	0.105	0.058	0.180	0.016
% Expanded communication network only a little	0.096	0.015	0.194	0.024	0.108	0.030	0.143	0.015	0.099	0.029	0.145	0.015	0.028	0.028	0.143	0.014
% Expanded communication network some	0.194	0.019	0.223	0.026	0.158	0.033	0.215	0.017	0.154	0.035	0.218	0.017	0.222	0.075	0.205	0.016

Table 2. (Continued)

	E-mail				Instant Message (IM)				Texting				Social Networking Site (SNS)			
	Use (N=488)		No use (N=318)		Use (N=131)		No use (N=675)		Use (N=127)		No use (N=679)		Use (N=39)		No use (N=767)	
	Mean	SE	Mean	SE	Mean	SE	Mean	SE	Mean	SE	Mean	SE	Mean	SE	Mean	SE
% Expanded communication network a lot	0.633	0.024	0.270	0.028	0.698	0.044	0.437	0.021	0.658	0.046	0.441	0.021	0.645	0.086	0.472	0.020
Type of ICT use at work																	
% Use e-mail to communicate at work	—	—	—	—	0.900	0.028	0.519	0.021	0.674	0.046	0.563	0.021	0.767	0.079	0.573	0.020
% Use e-mail at work for friends/family	0.637	0.024	0.145	0.022	0.658	0.047	0.386	0.021	0.582	0.049	0.397	0.021	0.569	0.090	0.424	0.020
% Use IM to communicate at work	0.262	0.023	0.041	0.012	—	—	—	—	0.372	0.047	0.123	0.014	0.373	0.085	0.158	0.015
% Use IM at work for friends/family	0.216	0.022	0.048	0.014	0.547	0.049	0.064	0.011	0.381	0.048	0.091	0.013	0.266	0.077	0.139	0.015
% Use texts to communicate at work	0.218	0.022	0.148	0.024	0.414	0.049	0.143	0.016	—	—	—	—	0.480	0.089	0.172	0.016
% Use texts at work for friends/family	0.364	0.025	0.262	0.029	0.491	0.049	0.287	0.020	0.825	0.035	0.204	0.018	0.633	0.082	0.303	0.019
% Use SNS to communicate at work	0.073	0.014	0.031	0.012	0.123	0.033	0.042	0.009	0.142	0.034	0.036	0.008	—	—	—	—
% Use SNS at work for friends/family	0.131	0.019	0.029	0.009	0.171	0.039	0.072	0.012	0.188	0.039	0.066	0.011	0.650	0.085	0.055	0.010
Outcomes: Productivity and distress																	
% Increased productivity	0.851	0.019	0.452	0.031	0.906	0.030	0.640	0.021	0.733	0.044	0.674	0.020	0.822	0.074	0.677	0.019
% Increased distress	0.427	0.025	0.196	0.025	0.457	0.049	0.305	0.019	0.403	0.047	0.314	0.020	0.306	0.080	0.332	0.019

Source: 2008 Pew Networked Workers survey with imputed income.

The self-employed report relatively low proportions of ICT use across the board, although their use of SNS is a bit higher than other types of ICT. ICT users also tend to report working more hours than non-ICT users in general, although work hours are similar among SNS users versus nonusers. Slightly greater numbers of employees who use e-mail or IM at work also report being highly satisfied with their jobs; this pattern is reversed when comparing text and SNS users. ICT users tend to report higher levels of job autonomy, opportunities for advancement, and job complexity than nonusers. ICT users also report working at home more frequently than non-ICT users. Thus, there is some indication of a relationship between these broad individual and job characteristics and various forms of work-related ICT use.

It is also clear that work-related ICT use is connected to work extension in these descriptive data. Overall, ICT users report higher levels of both e-mail- and phone-based work extension. ICT users of all kinds are also more likely to report increases in overall work time than non-ICT users. In terms of the role of ICT in shaping expanded communication networks, the general pattern is that the vast majority of ICT users (about 90% across different types of use) believe some level of expansion has happened as a result of ICT use. Finally, the descriptive statistics outlining the type of ICT use at work shows that, among ICT users, use of a range of ICT at work for both work and personal reasons is typical, although this pattern is less pronounced among those that report work-related e-mail use. Thus, we might expect that there are more employees that only use e-mail at work, while employees that use other forms of ICT are also likely to use e-mail for both work and personal reasons. Finally, increases in both self-reported productivity and distress are more common among ICT users than nonusers.

ICT Use, Work Extension, and Work Time

Is ICT-based work extension a factor shaping employee perceptions of increases in distress and productivity? If so, is this also connected to increases in work time? Logistic regression results in Tables 3 and 4 suggest a link between both forms of work extension and both outcomes. In model 1 in Table 3, we show the baseline distress model that controls for individual and job characteristics on the likelihood that employees report increases in distress. Two job-level characteristics, average weekly work hours and high levels of job satisfaction, predict the likelihood that

Table 3. Logistic Regression Results Documenting the Influence of ICT-Based Work Extension and Changes in Overall Work Time on the Likelihood of High Self-Reported Employee Distress ($N = 806$).

Independent Variables	Model 1		Model 2		Model 3		Model 4	
	Odds ratio	SE	Odds ratio	SE	Odds ratio	SE	Odds ratio	SE
Age (years)	1.009	0.008	1.015	0.008[+]	1.009	0.008	1.014	0.008[+]
% Female	1.331	0.202	1.455	0.206[+]	1.317	0.207	1.440	0.210[+]
% White	0.983	0.235	1.005	0.236	1.012	0.244	1.024	0.244
Education[a]								
% No HS degree	1.612	0.458	1.758	0.499	2.033	0.454	2.067	0.489
% HS degree	0.622	0.267[+]	0.668	0.281	0.754	0.275	0.750	0.287
% Some college	1.013	0.241	1.049	0.247	1.047	0.242	1.051	0.244
Relationship status[b]								
% Married	0.762	0.206	0.812	0.208	0.817	0.210	0.857	0.214
% Cohabiting	0.599	0.436	0.707	0.445	0.755	0.431	0.859	0.441
Income[c]								
% Less than $30K	0.632	0.317	0.762	0.326	0.671	0.318	0.779	0.331
% $30–49K	0.720	0.269	0.855	0.279	0.754	0.269	0.852	0.279
% $50–74K	0.606	0.277[+]	0.725	0.286	0.608	0.286[+]	0.702	0.298
Organization type[d]								
% Large corporation	1.455	0.369	1.663	0.374	1.461	0.361	1.701	0.375
% Medium-sized business	0.904	0.408	0.962	0.419	0.916	0.412	0.991	0.428
% Small business	1.105	0.365	1.133	0.375	1.029	0.361	1.068	0.378
% Federal/State/Local government	1.901	0.424	2.062	0.423[+]	2.046	0.435	2.294	0.445[+]
% Education	1.635	0.428	1.851	0.427	1.713	0.431	2.014	0.438
Job type[e]								
% Professional	0.926	0.335	0.893	0.328	0.898	0.348	0.890	0.345
% Manager/Exec/Bus. owner	1.003	0.383	0.794	0.403	0.930	0.396	0.771	0.415
% Clerical/Office/Sales	1.136	0.348	1.016	0.351	1.067	0.361	0.987	0.363
% Service	0.503	0.403[+]	0.472	0.405[+]	0.479	0.418[+]	0.438	0.418[+]
% Skilled trades	0.482	0.397[+]	0.480	0.405[+]	0.525	0.400	0.517	0.406
% Semi-skilled trades	0.533	0.460	0.576	0.467	0.555	0.463	0.576	0.471
% Self-employed	1.066	0.307	0.906	0.316	1.132	0.308	0.961	0.318
Average weekly work hours	1.023	0.009*	1.021	0.008*	1.021	0.009*	1.019	0.009*
% Satisfied with job	0.328	0.329***	0.340	0.317***	0.310	0.324***	0.323	0.315*
Level of job autonomy (1 = low to 5 = high)	1.013	0.081	0.998	0.081	1.065	0.083	1.050	0.083

Table 3. (*Continued*)

Independent Variables	Model 1		Model 2		Model 3		Model 4	
	Odds ratio	SE	Odds ratio	SE	Odds ratio	SE	Odds ratio	SE
Potential for job advancement (1 = low to 5 = high)	1.036	0.068	1.021	0.068	1.041	0.069	1.028	0.069
Job complexity (4 = low to 20 = high)	1.034	0.031	1.021	0.032	1.018	0.031	1.004	0.032
Frequency works at home (1 = never to 6 = everyday)	1.063	0.054	0.962	0.062	1.042	0.056	0.971	0.064
ICT-based work extension								
E-mail work extension (6 = none to 24 = a lot)			1.039	0.022+			1.013	0.023
Phone work extension (6 = none to 24 = a lot)			1.078	0.024**			1.087	0.024*
ICT use and changes in work time[f]								
Increases in overall work time					3.613	0.262***	3.398	0.267*
Decreases in overall work time					1.293	0.380	1.061	0.406
Constant	0.260	0.862	0.075	0.904**	0.216	0.859+	0.078	0.906*

Source: 2008 Pew Networked Workers data with imputed income.
[a]Comparison is college/advanced degree.
[b]Comparison is single.
[c]Comparison is $75K +.
[d]Comparison is nonprofit/other.
[e]Comparison is other.
[f]Comparison is no change in overall work time.
+$p < .10$; *$p < 0.05$; **$p < 0.01$; ***$p < .001$.

employees report a distress increase. For each additional hour of work per week, respondents are 2% more likely to report a distress increase, while high levels of job satisfaction are associated with a 67% decrease in the likelihood of experiencing greater stress at work. In model 2 in Table 3, we add information about levels of e-mail and phone work extension. Both have odds ratios greater than 1, although only the odds ratio for phone extension is statistically significant at conventional levels. For each unit increase in phone extension, employees are about 8% more likely to report

Table 4. Logistic Regression Results Documenting the Influence of ICT-Based Work Extension and Changes in Overall Work Time on the Likelihood of High Self-Reported Employee Productivity ($N = 806$).

Independent Variables	Model 1		Model 2		Model 3		Model 4	
	Odds ratio	SE	Odds ratio	SE	Odds ratio	SE	Odds ratio	SE
Age (years)	0.989	0.008	0.996	0.008	0.989	0.008	0.996	0.008
% Female	1.389	0.222	1.571	0.239+	1.369	0.223	1.554	0.237+
% White	0.994	0.258	1.029	0.273	1.005	0.262	1.039	0.276
Education[a]								
% No HS degree	0.383	0.458**	0.512	0.487	0.439	0.460+	0.554	0.488
% HS degree	0.417	0.275**	0.560	0.286*	0.489	0.286*	0.612	0.296+
% Some college	0.638	0.262+	0.788	0.278	0.654	0.266	0.796	0.275
Relationship status[b]								
% Married	1.242	0.208	1.445	0.213+	1.310	0.213	1.458	0.214+
% Cohabiting	0.888	0.426	1.094	0.441	1.007	0.416	1.164	0.434
Income[c]								
% Less than $30K	1.076	0.337	1.382	0.355	1.144	0.341	1.398	0.355
% $30–49K	1.411	0.312	1.843	0.327	1.490	0.316	1.842	0.327+
% $50–74K	1.297	0.316	1.656	0.345+	1.300	0.322	1.624	0.343
Organization type[d]								
% Large corporation	1.623	0.381	1.747	0.382	1.671	0.382	1.745	0.387
% Medium-sized business	1.276	0.408	1.364	0.400	1.320	0.404	1.370	0.403
% Small business	1.109	0.396	1.168	0.382	1.062	0.393	1.112	0.384
% Federal/State/Local government	0.979	0.446	0.985	0.471	0.986	0.452	0.976	0.476
% Education	0.473	0.461	0.430	0.450+	0.446	0.470+	0.416	0.460+
Job type[e]								
% Professional	1.492	0.399	1.346	0.434	1.433	0.399	1.347	0.431
% Manager/Exec/Bus. owner	1.646	0.429	1.193	0.459	1.418	0.430	1.113	0.463
% Clerical/Office/Sales	1.403	0.387	1.099	0.415	1.292	0.390	1.049	0.414
% Service	0.855	0.398	0.798	0.406	0.824	0.395	0.772	0.406
% Skilled trades	0.783	0.409	0.776	0.413	0.787	0.408	0.773	0.414
% Semi-skilled trades	0.411	0.446+	0.436	0.443+	0.407	0.445*	0.424	0.443+
% Self-employed	0.950	0.331	0.810	0.346	0.958	0.330	0.821	0.342
Average weekly work hours	1.015	0.009+	1.016	0.009	1.015	0.009+	1.015	0.009
% Satisfied with job	1.247	0.325	1.271	0.312	1.279	0.325	1.275	0.311
Level of job autonomy (1 = low to 5 = high)	0.994	0.079	0.959	0.083	1.021	0.081	0.977	0.084

Table 4. (Continued)

Independent Variables	Model 1		Model 2		Model 3		Model 4	
	Odds ratio	SE	Odds ratio	SE	Odds ratio	SE	Odds ratio	SE
Potential for job advancement (1 = low to 5 = high)	1.016	0.072	1.007	0.075	1.003	0.074	1.005	0.075
Job complexity (4 = low to 20 = high)	1.064	0.031*	1.055	0.034	1.056	0.032+	1.049	0.033
Frequency works at home (1 = never to 6 = everyday)	1.212	0.064**	1.043	0.070	1.181	0.064*	1.041	0.070
ICT-based work extension								
E-mail work extension (6 = none to 24 = a lot)			1.173	0.032***			2.035	0.421***
Phone work extension (6 = none to 24 = a lot)			1.014	0.026			1.667	0.681
ICT use and changes in work time[f]								
Increases in overall work time					3.008	0.384**	1.156	0.032+
Decreases in overall work time					2.979	0.658+	1.015	0.026
Constant	0.377	0.892	0.061	1.012**	0.316	0.891	0.064	1.001**

Source: 2008 Pew Networked Workers data with imputed income.
[a]Comparison is college/advanced degree.
[b]Comparison is single.
[c]Comparison is $75K +.
[d]Comparison is nonprofit/other.
[e]Comparison is other.
[f]Comparison is no change in overall work time.
+$p < .10$; *$p < 0.05$; **$p < 0.01$; ***$p < .001$.

increases in work-related distress. Thus, deciding (or being asked) to take or make work-related calls before or after work, on the weekend or when you are running errands, when you are sick, or on vacation – all markers of work extension – is positively associated with increases in employee distress.

A key question raised in recent literature concerns the role that ICT plays in increasing work hours and how this may shape employee distress. These data allow us to examine connections among ICT-based work time changes, work extension practices, and the likelihood that employees report increased distress or productivity. Model 3 in Table 3 examines the influence of employee reports that their ICT use has increased, decreased, or produced no change in overall work time on the likelihood of reporting a distress increase. Compared to employees who report no change in work time with respect to ICT use, employees who report that their ICT use has increased their overall work time are 261% more likely to also report an increase in distress. In model 4 in Table 3, we add information about e-mail and phone work extension to assess whether accounting for ICT-facilitated work extension will reduce the significance of the relationship between overall work time increases and distress. While there is a small decrease in the odds ratio after adding this information, the coefficient for ICT-based increases in overall work time remains a highly significant factor that is associated with greater distress in employees. As a whole, models 3 and 4 in Table 3 indicate that ICT-based work extension practices, particularly phone use, and increases in overall work time due to ICT use both independently influence the likelihood that employees report increases in distress. While we wondered if linkages between work extension practices facilitated through technology and distress could be explained by increases in work time, there is not clear evidence that longer work hours are the mechanism linking work extension and increased employee distress.

Model 1 in Table 4 documents the baseline productivity model that controls for individual and job characteristics in shaping the likelihood that employees report increases in self-rated job performance. In the baseline model, there are three central factors that shape these assessments including education level, level of job complexity, and the frequency of working from home. In terms of education, when compared with the college or better educated, all other educational groups are less likely to report productivity increases. Higher job complexity is also associated with a higher likelihood of reporting improvements in job performance. For each unit increase in job complexity, employees are about 6% more likely to report improvement. Similarly for each unit increase in the frequency of working from home, employees are 21% more likely to report improved performance. Model 2 in Table 4 illustrates what happens when we add information about both e-mail and phone work extension to model 1. First, e-mail-based work extension is highly significant. For each unit increase in e-mail-based work extension, employees are 17% more likely to report improvements in work productivity. Second, the odds ratios for both job complexity, and, especially, frequency of telecommuting, are reduced to nonsignificance. This suggests that the role that greater telecommuting plays in shaping productivity gains might be explained via use of e-mail in the ways captured by the extension variable (e.g., using e-mail after hours, on vacation, etc.). The telecommuting variable and the e-mail work extension variable are moderately correlated ($r = 0.48$), which no doubt indicates some overlap among the work behaviors captured by these measures conceptually. However, they are not so highly correlated that worries about multicollinearity come into play.

In general, models 3 and 4 in Table 4 suggest that ICT-based changes in work time are linked to productivity gains, largely via e-mail-based (rather than phone-based) work extension. For example, in model 3 in Table 4, we assess the role of changes in overall work time on the likelihood that employees report increased productivity. While both coefficients are positive, only the coefficient for increases in work time is significant at conventional levels. Model 3 indicates that, compared to employees who perceive no change in work time, employees who perceive an increase in their overall work time are 200% more likely to report increases in productivity. When we add information about ICT-based work extension (model 4 in Table 4), the coefficient for increased overall work time is no longer significant at conventional levels while the coefficient for e-mail-based work extension remains highly significant. One interpretation of this pattern is that e-mail-based work extension explains the link between increases in work time and better self-rated productivity.

Network Expansion and Type of ICT Use

How important is expanded network connectivity for today's employees, and how might work and personal communications mediated through different technology shape employee outcomes? The patterns summarized in Table 5 illustrate the role that expanded communication networks play in shaping both increased distress and productivity among employees. The first model documents that, when compared with employees who report that their ICT use has not increased the size of their networks, those employees that report that their networks have expanded "a lot" are also those with a greater likelihood (181%) of reporting increases in work stress. However, larger communication networks are also linked to productivity gains. The productivity model (2) shows that, compared to employees experiencing no increase in their networks, those employees whose ICT use has produced networks that have expanded "some" or "a lot" are much more likely (370% and 723%, respectively) to also report better

Table 5. Logistic Regression Results Documenting the Influence of Network Connectivity and Type of Work-Related ICT Use on Employee Self-Reported Distress and Productivity ($N = 806$).

Independent Variables	Increased Connectivity				Type of Work ICT Use			
	Model 1 (distress)		Model 2 (productivity)		Model 3 (distress)		Model 4 (productivity)	
	Odds ratio	SE	Odds ratio	SE	Odds ratio	SE	Odds ratio	SE
Age (years)	1.012	0.008	0.996	0.009	1.014	0.009	0.995	0.008
% Female	1.293	0.201	1.308	0.249	1.294	0.205	1.545	0.243[+]
% White	1.002	0.235	1.043	0.285	1.044	0.243	1.106	0.294
Education[a]								
% No HS degree	1.653	0.468	0.411	0.530[+]	2.195	0.485	0.627	0.470
% HS degree	0.672	0.270	0.480	0.297*	0.779	0.277	0.690	0.301
% Some college	0.976	0.240	0.550	0.291*	1.094	0.245	0.833	0.289
Relationship status[b]								
% Married	0.764	0.207	1.339	0.229	0.721	0.215	1.364	0.223
% Cohabiting	0.631	0.438	1.151	0.434	0.580	0.435	0.903	0.485
Income[c]								
% Less than $30K	0.776	0.321	1.770	0.379	0.783	0.326	1.742	0.383
% $30–49K	0.830	0.272	2.212	0.349*	0.769	0.271	1.894	0.337[+]
% $50–74K	0.651	0.282	1.535	0.358	0.599	0.279[+]	1.459	0.350
Organization type[d]								
% Large corporation	1.349	0.372	1.616	0.402	1.309	0.385	1.726	0.389
% Medium-sized business	0.880	0.412	1.401	0.425	0.775	0.424	1.410	0.415
% Small business	1.010	0.371	0.927	0.404	1.026	0.381	1.119	0.388
% Federal/State/ Local government	1.632	0.420	0.693	0.474	1.742	0.431	1.033	0.486
% Education	1.606	0.433	0.437	0.466[+]	1.677	0.439	0.437	0.419[+]
Job type[e]								
% Professional	0.999	0.333	1.510	0.450	0.958	0.338	1.752	0.454
% Manager/Exec/ Bus. owner	1.054	0.399	1.584	0.492	0.982	0.390	1.320	0.459
% Clerical/Office/ Sales	1.088	0.350	1.155	0.452	1.141	0.352	1.219	0.419
% Service	0.530	0.403	0.864	0.454	0.670	0.419	1.292	0.417
% Skilled trades	0.595	0.400	1.057	0.502	0.553	0.410	1.070	0.432
% Semi-skilled trades	0.656	0.463	0.500	0.516	0.743	0.473	0.663	0.463
% Self-employed	1.121	0.318	1.025	0.329	1.212	0.308	1.074	0.344
Average weekly work hours	1.022	0.009*	1.015	0.010	1.022	0.009*	1.011	0.008

Table 5. (*Continued*)

Independent Variables	Increased Connectivity				Type of Work ICT Use			
	Model 1 (distress)		Model 2 (productivity)		Model 3 (distress)		Model 4 (productivity)	
	Odds ratio	SE	Odds ratio	SE	Odds ratio	SE	Odds ratio	SE
% Satisfied with job	0.336	0.332**	1.258	0.343	0.302	0.342***	1.157	0.324
Level of job autonomy (1 = low to 5 = high)	1.028	0.083	1.015	0.086	1.016	0.083	1.034	0.085
Potential for job advancement (1 = low to 5 = high)	1.016	0.068	0.942	0.079	1.042	0.070	0.994	0.080
Job complexity (4 = low to 20 = high)	1.031	0.032	1.066	0.034+	1.037	0.032	1.051	0.033
Frequency works at home (1 = never to 6 = everyday)	1.039	0.055	1.179	0.063*	1.034	0.057	1.160	0.063*
ICT use and size of communication network[f]								
Expanded only a little	1.849	0.368+	1.130	0.319				
Expanded some	1.468	0.347	4.706	0.303***				
Expanded a lot	2.813	0.315**	8.232	0.302***				
Type of ICT used at work[g]								
E-mail for work colleagues					2.102	0.239**	3.874	0.248***
E-mail for family/friends					1.278	0.202	1.298	0.256
IM for work colleagues					1.656	0.265+	2.160	0.424+
IM for family/friends					0.495	0.310*	1.383	0.428
Texts to work colleagues					1.245	0.285	0.712	0.348
Texts to family/friends					1.134	0.247	1.419	0.273
SNS for work colleagues					0.358	0.512*	1.743	0.745
SNS for family/friends					1.712	0.399	1.028	0.580
Constant	0.113	0.885*	0.070	1.030*	0.102	0.907*	0.066	1.032**

Source: 2008 Pew Networked Workers data with imputed income.
[a]Comparison is college/advanced degree.
[b]Comparison is single.
[c]Comparison is $75K +.
[d]Comparison is nonprofit/other.
[e]Comparison is other.
[f]Comparison is "not at all."
[g]Comparison is "no use at work" across ICT categories.
+$p < .10$; *$p < 0.05$; **$p < 0.01$; ***$p < .001$.

productivity. Overall, models 1 and 2 in Table 5 provide support for our expectation that ICT-facilitated communications networks are linked to both distress and productivity increases.

The next set of models in Table 5 documents connections among different forms of ICT use at work and increased distress and productivity. When we account for the many different technologically mediated forms of communication that are measured in these data (e-mail, IM, texts, SNS) as well as both work and personal use while working, we see that only e-mail to communicate with work colleagues is connected to increased distress. Employees that use e-mail for work are 110% more likely to also report increased distress. However, it is interesting to note that using SNS to communicate with work colleagues is associated with a 64% *reduction* in the likelihood of reporting an increase in work stress. We also see that personal use of IM at work is linked to a 50% reduction in the likelihood of reporting a distress increase. Turning to the role that different types of ICT use play in shaping productivity gains, work-related e-mail use is the only form of ICT communication that appears associated with better self-reported work performance. Employees that use e-mail at work are 287% more likely to also report improved work performance. There is no evidence that personal forms of ICT use at work promote productivity improvements, contrary to our expectations and some previous research.

DISCUSSION AND CONCLUSION

Concerns about the ways in which an entrenched ICT infrastructure is reshaping work, and life outside of work, are prevalent. Indeed, companies like Volkswagen and Altos have publicly restricted or shunned e-mail use because of worries about the stressful blurring of work/life boundaries (Volkswagen, see No Author, 2011) and reductions in employee productivity (Altos, see Thompson, 2011). However, systematic research examining claims that using a variety of ICTs at work (including e-mail) is stressful for employees and bad for productivity have not been rigorously assessed drawing on more contemporary representative samples of workers. We add to knowledge about the role of work-related ICT use by examining how specific ICT-based work practices might influence both self-reported employee distress and productivity. Overall, we believe our findings point to five key implications of technological innovation for research and practice.

First, while our data show that, for most respondents, ICT use was not associated with increased distress, about a third of employees *do* report that ICT use is a factor shaping a more stressful work experience. Many more employees (69%) report that ICT use is enhancing productivity. Technology is influencing these employee experiences through different pathways, including via work-extension practices, influences on work time, the expansion of communication networks, as well as through a range of technologically based communication systems employees use to communicate with work colleagues, family, and friends while working.

Second, our data provide more detail on what work extension practices look like and illustrate that these technologically facilitated practices, while stressful for some, are also connected to perceptions of increased productivity. These data make clear that both e-mail and phones are being used by some employees to check in on work outside traditional work hours or work spaces, while they are sick, and while on vacation, consistent with the popular notion that ICT use is implicated in blurred work/personal boundaries. We also find that similar ICT practices do not produce uniform effects. Phone-based work extension is associated with self-reported increased distress among employees. In contrast, e-mail-based work extension is linked to self-reported improvements in work performance.

Why might this be? We can think of several possible explanations. First, it may be that more urgent requests with tighter deadlines occur via phone, rather than e-mail communication. It may also be that e-mail offers greater control over dealing with workplace requests and interactions relative to taking a call in real-time because of the asynchronous nature of this communication medium. It might just be harder to ignore a ringing phone than to refrain from checking one's e-mail at an inconvenient time. Further, the delay in e-mail response time may give employees greater control over their response and reactions in ways that are beneficial to them. Thus, technology differences may stem from differences in employee control over the technology (e-mail offers more?) or differences in urgency or context of communications (phones are used to convey more urgent, potentially stressful work-related communications?).

We should also emphasize that the age of the data may play a role in shaping the differences we identify between e-mail and phone-based work extension and employee outcomes. In 2008, when these data were collected, smart phones were new enough that Pew did not even track their adoption. We assume that few workers owned smart phones at the time of this survey. This is important because it is smart phones with Internet capabilities that facilitate mobile access to e-mail in some of the places identified in the work extension variable. Further, a smart phone will alert users via a vibration or tone when they receive an e-mail (making it harder to ignore and more similar to the "ringing" telephone effect we mention above). Given the prevalence of smart phones in the population now (58% of American adults owned a smart phone in 2014; see www.pewinternet.org), more recent data might not identify differences in distress or productivity that depend on work extension practices supported via e-mail or phone unless differences in employee control or variation in message urgency are important. Indeed, distinguishing e-mail and phones in a contemporary survey might not even make sense to many workers since both are accessible through a smartphone.

Connections among ICT-facilitated work extension and increased employee distress have clear implications for the work/life interface. Evidence of ICT-facilitated work extension suggests that some employees may be working outside traditional times and places, and that switch can be stressful for employees, perhaps because of increases in work/life conflict. In general, our findings extend and build on earlier work that point to the importance of ICT use, contact with work outside of normal times and spaces, and connections both to higher levels of work/family conflict and greater distress (Chesley, 2005; Voydanoff, 2005). Other research (Glavin et al., 2011) finds that frequent ICT-facilitated contact outside of work is associated with greater levels of guilt and distress among female employees, suggesting that greater opportunities for role blurring may be fueling conflicts between work and personal life in ways that enhance feelings of guilt in employed women. Our findings indicate that ICT-facilitated work extension may be creating more opportunities for the types of role blurring that previous research demonstrates can contribute to greater work/family conflict. However, the data also show that work extension is connected to self-reported work performance improvements. The same general mechanism that is leading work to be experienced as more stressful is also associated with employee reports that they are more productive. This is a reminder that technology practices are multifaceted and will not necessarily support uniformly positive or negative outcomes for the people that use them. However, identifying whether and how technology can be engaged to enhance the work/family interface is understudied outside of a focus on telecommuting and future research should engage this area more rigorously.

A third implication of this study concerns connections among technology use, longer work hours, and increases in employee distress and productivity. These results suggest that a small segment (15%) of the working population attributes increases in work time to ICT use (80% report no changes in work time). Among employees who report that their ICT use is connected to increases in their work time, there are connections to both increased distress *and* improved productivity. Further, this is the one instance where the likelihood of employee distress is higher than the likelihood of productivity improvements. In addition, in the case of enhanced productivity, the mechanism supporting these improvements appears to be the use of work-extension practices. In other words, longer hours are promoted via work extension in ways that enhance employee productivity.

We think links between technology use and changes in work hours and distress and productivity outcomes is important and requires greater future investigation. There is some previous evidence that engagement in technologically entrenched work systems can alter expectations about employee availability in ways that might increase overall workload. Given links between long hours and employee burnout, the fact that technology use is linked to perceptions of greater work time and distress for some employees is indicative of a potential technological downside for both employers and employees, although we assume links to enhanced productivity are welcome.

A fourth implication of this study concerns the role of expanded communication networks in work settings and links to employee outcomes. One of the much-touted benefits of the "network society" is expanded communication networks, which have generally been found to be beneficial for users (Rainie & Wellman, 2012). Overall, our results mirror past work that draws on the expansion of personal communication networks and links these to largely positive outcomes for employees. However, in the work context, our data point to the potential for threshold effects. For example, we find that employees who report that their work-related communications networks have expanded "some" are also more likely to report unequivocally enhanced productivity, with no distress increases. However, among employees who report that their communications networks have expanded "a lot," while there are still clear connections to productivity improvements, we also start to see links to increased distress. What this suggests is that there may be limits to how big we want employee communication networks to get. Some expansion of these networks is clearly positive from the perspective of potentially enhancing productivity. However, at some point, rapidly expanding networks may simply become unwieldy and difficult to manage for employees, adding to distress. Further investigation of the size and depth of work-related communication networks and links to employee experiences is an important are for future research.

The final important implication of this study is rooted in how different forms of technologically mediated communication at work shape employee experiences. The Pew data show that e-mail communication is one of the most prevalent forms of work-based ICT-mediated communication. Use of IM, texts, or SNS is much less prevalent at the time these data were collected. However, among ICT users, it is clear that ICT use at work engages employees both with their work colleagues and keeps at least some connected to family and friends while at work. Previous research suggests that ICT use to engage with family and friends can reduce levels of employee distress (Chesley, 2014). This is demonstrated here, as well, in that IMing to communicate with friends and family while working is associated with reductions in distress even as e-mail use to engage with work colleagues is linked to distress increases. It is also interesting that using social networking tools to communicate with work colleagues is associated with less distress. It may be that tools that are designed to enhance feelings of community and connection may help foster more supportive ties with coworkers. Of course, it may also be that more supportive coworkers are more interested in communicating with one another on these platforms to begin with. Finally, consistent with other patterns in this data and previous research (e.g., Mano & Mesch, 2010) e-mail use to communicate with work colleagues is clearly linked to productivity improvements. While some previous research has suggested that connectivity with family and friends while at work has the potential to enhance productivity via mechanisms like greater information and social support (Chesley et al., 2013), there is little support for the idea that personal forms of connectivity enhance productivity here. Even so, these patterns drive home that networked workers have networked personal lives. Employers that recognize this, and leverage it in the workplace, may be able to provide their employees with access to friends and family that can actually enhance work outcomes.

Our findings should be interpreted with several limitations in mind. First, the cross-sectional research design used in the Pew data collection establishes association but is not able to determine causality. While our analysis assumes that employing specific ICT-based work practices influences subsequent levels of employee productivity or distress, it may be that more productive or distressed employees are more likely to use ICT at work. However, in support of our arguments, we would note that the widespread use of ICT in workplaces likely dictates that the majority of workers *have* to use some type of ICT in order to complete work tasks — thus ICT use is probably no longer a choice, but a job requirement in many contemporary employment settings. Second, there is variation in the findings across the dependent variables (not every ICT-based work practice is related to productivity or distress), which suggests that nuances in work-related ICT use do influence employee outcomes, even among ICT users.

A second limitation is the age of the data we analyze. Technological innovations are rapid and significant changes in applications, and how they are used, can occur over just a few years. While the Pew data are old, they provide one of the only relatively recent sources of data on work-related ICT use drawn from a nationally representative sample of U.S. workers. Since much previous research in this area comes from small qualitative or organizational samples of employees drawn from specific industries or workplaces, or draws from national studies with very limited (and, by now, out of date) measures of ICT use (e.g., NSCW), we argue that it is critical to augment this previous research with findings from a broader, more representative sample of the workforce in order to gain a clear understanding of the role that ICT use is playing in shaping contemporary work. However, findings related to use of IM, texts, or social networking applications in these data, in particular, may not reflect current use by employees, as these applications were less entrenched in social behavior in 2008 than they are today.

A third limitation involves missing data. As is typical in survey research, we are missing responses on some variables. The most egregious missing data involved income information; however, analyses incorporating imputed income data using multiple imputation methods compared with analyses without imputed income data (not shown) suggest that our results are robust.

A fourth potential limitation of this study is the low survey response rate (24%). A common concern when response rates are low is that generalizability of the sample to the population is in doubt. However, the most recent research indicates that low response rates alone are not a solid indicator of data quality (Groves, 2006). A more worrisome source of bias is social processes that influence both participation in a survey and the outcome being measured. In this study, it is possible that individuals with high distress levels would be less likely to participate in the survey. However, if such a selection process were in place, it suggests that our results for distress are conservative and perhaps understate the size and scope of an ICT use–distress relationship.

Measurement limitations of key concepts should also be kept in mind when interpreting our results. All of our measures are based on employee self-reports. Thus, assessments of increases in work time, distress, or productivity are based on employee perceptions. These measures are a limitation of our data and we hope that future research can build on our findings using different measurement techniques. These data also lack sufficient measures distinguishing the family context of employees. In particular, variables that adequately capture caregiving responsibilities, like the numbers or ages of children, are likely important. We know, for example, that many parents of preteen and teenage children use cell phones and texting to monitor children when they are apart (Blair & Fletcher, 2011; Christensen, 2009; Rainie & Wellman, 2012). Thus, the presence of children of different ages could very well shape some forms of personal ICT use at work. Further, caregiving demands more generally are known factors that can affect ratings of both distress and productivity. Incorporating information about employee's family life, particularly with respect to caregiving responsibilities, is critical to improving our understanding about how ICT-based practices shape employees' work experiences.

Overall, this study points to technological innovation as an important factor influencing work extension and social network processes and connects this to changes in employee distress and productivity. The focus on productivity improvements is especially important given the emphasis that previous sociological research has placed on linking ICT use to problematic employee outcomes. Our findings illustrate that ICT use clearly has the potential to influence work processes that are reshaping the work/life interface in ways that are both problematic and helpful. The challenge for future research is to identify ICT-based work practices that can enhance the benefits of ICT use while reducing the costs, perhaps through a more consistent research focus on understanding the context of use within particular organizational settings.

REFERENCES

Acock, A. C. (2012). *A gentle introduction to STATA* (Rev. 3rd ed.). College Station, TX: Stata Press.

Ashforth, B. E., Kreiner, G. E., & Fugate, M. (2000). All in a day's work: Boundaries and micro role transitions. *Academy of Management Review*, 25(3), 472–491.

Baily, M. N. (2004). Recent productivity growth: The role of information technology and other innovations. In *FRBSF review* (pp. 35–41). San Francisco, CA: Federal Reserve Bank of San Francisco.

Barley, S. R., Meyerson, D. E., & Grodal, S. (2011). Email as a source and symbol of stress. *Organization Science*, 22(4), 887–906.

Bellavia, G. M., & Frone, M. R. (2005). Work-family conflict. In J. Barling, E. K. Kelloway, & M. R. Frone (Eds.), *Handbook of work stress* (pp. 113–148). Thousand Oaks, CA: Sage.

Blair, B. L., & Fletcher, A. C. (2011). The only 13-year-old on planet earth without a cell phone: Meanings of cell phones in early adolescents' everyday lives. *Journal of Adolescent Research*, *26*(2), 155–177.

Boswell, W. R., & Olson-Buchanan, J. B. (2007). The use of communication technologies after hours: The role of work attitudes and work-life conflict. *Journal of Management*, *33*(4), 592–610.

Brynjolfsson, E., & Hitt, L. M. (2000). Beyond computation: Information technology, organizational transformation and business performance. *The Journal of Economic Perspectives*, *14*(4), 23–48.

Brynjolfsson, E., & Hitt, L. M. (2003). Computing productivity: Firm-level evidence. *The Review of Economics and Statistics*, *85*(4), 793–808.

Castells, M. (2000). *The rise of the network society*. Malden, MA: Blackwell Publishers Inc.

Chesley, N. (2005). Blurring boundaries? Linking technology use, spillover, individual distress, and family satisfaction. *Journal of Marriage and Family*, *67*(December), 1237–1248.

Chesley, N. (2010). Technology use and employee assessments of productivity, workload, and pace of life. *Information, Communication & Society*, *13*(4), 485–514.

Chesley, N. (2014). Information and communication technology use, work intensification and employee strain and distress. *Work, Employment, and Society*, *28*, 581–610. doi:10.11 77/0950017013500112

Chesley, N., & Johnson, B. (2010). Information and communication technology, work, and family. In S. Sweet & J. Casey (Eds.), *Work and family encyclopedia*. Chestnut Hill, MA: Sloan Work and Family Research Network.

Chesley, N., Siibak, A., & Wajcman, J. (2013). Information and communication technology use and work-life integration. In D. A. Major & R. Burke (Eds.), *Handbook of work-life integration of professionals: Challenges and opportunities* (pp. 245–268). Northampton, MA: Edward Elgar.

Christensen, T. H. (2009). 'Connected presence' in distributed family life. *New Media & Society*, *11*, 433–451.

Clark, S. C. (2000). Work/family border theory: A new theory of work/family balance. *Human Relations*, *53*, 747–770.

Desjardins Financial Security. (2006). *Health is cool! 2006 survey on Canadian attitudes towards physical and mental health at work and play*. Retrieved from http://www.desjardinslifein surance.com/en/life-events/Documents/Health%20survey%202006%20Health%20is% 20cool.pdf

Desrochers, S., & Sargent, L. (2003). Boundary/border theory and work-family integration. In E. E. Kossek & M. Pitt-Catsouphes (Eds.), *Work and family encyclopedia*. Chestnut Hill, MA: Sloan Work and Family Research Network.

Duxbury, L., Towers, I., Higgins, C., & Thomas, A. (2006). From 9 to 5 to 24 and 7: How technology redefined the work day. In W. Law (Ed.), *Information resources management: Global challenges* (pp. 305–332). Hershey, PA: Idea Group Publishing.

Ellison, N. B., Steinfield, C., & Lampe, C. (2007). The benefits of Facebook "friends": Social capital and college students use of online social network sites. *Journal of Computer-Mediated Communication*, *12*(4), 1143–1168.

Fenner, G., & Renn, R. (2010). Technology assisted supplemental work and work-family conflict: The role of instrumentality beliefs, organizational expectations and time management. *Human Relations*, *63*(1), 63–82.

Glavin, P., Schieman, S., & Reid, S. (2011). Boundary-spanning work demands and their consequences for guilt and psychological distress. *Journal of Health and Social Behavior*, *52*, 43–57.

Gonzalez, V. M., & Mark, G. (2004). Constant, constant multi-tasking craziness: Managing multiple working spheres. Paper presented at the proceedings of the SIGCHI conference on human factors in computing systems (CHI '04), Vienna, Austria (pp. 113–120).

Groves, R. M. (2006). Nonresponse rates and nonresponse bias in household surveys. *Public Opinion Quarterly*, *70*(5), 646–675.

Hackett, E. J., Amsterdamska, O., Lynch, M. E., & Wajcman, J. (2008). *The handbook of science and technology studies*. Cambridge, MA: MIT Press.

Hampton, K. N., Sessions, L. F., Her, E. J., & Rainie, L. (2009). *Social isolation and new technology*. Washington, DC: Pew Internet and American Life Project. Retrieved from www.pewinternet.org

MacKenzie, D., & Wajcman, J. (Eds.). (1999). *The social shaping of technology*. Philadelphia, PA: Open University Press.

Madden, M., & Jones, S. (2008). *Networked workers internet and American life project*. Pew Research Center. Retrieved from http://www.pewinternet.org/

Mano, R. S., & Mesch, G. S. (2010). E-mail characteristics, work performance and distress. *Computers in Human Behavior*, *26*, 61–69.

Mark, G., Gudith, D., & Klocke, U. (2008). The cost of interrupted work: More speed and stress. Paper presented at the proceedings of the twenty-sixth annual SIGCHI conference on human factors in computing systems (CHI '08), Florence, Italy (pp. 107–110).

Nippert-Eng, C. E. (1996). *Home and work: Negotiating boundaries through everyday life*. Chicago, IL: University of Chicago Press.

No Author. (2011). Volkswagen turns off Blackberry email after work hours. *BBC News*, December 23. Retrieved from http://www.bbc.co.uk/news/technology-16314901

Perlow, L. (2012). *Sleeping with your smartphone: How to break the 24/7 habit and change the way you work*. Boston, MA: Harvard Business Review Press.

Rainie, L., & Wellman, B. (2012). *Networked: The new social operating system*. Cambridge, MA: MIT Press.

Rienties, B., Tempelaar, D., Pinckaers, M., Giesbers, B., & Lichel, L. (2010). The diverging effects of social network sites on receiving job information for students and professionals. *International Journal of Sociotechnology and Knowledge Development*, *4*, 39–53.

Rose, E. (2013). Access denied: Employee control of personal communications at work. *Work, Employment, and Society*, *27*(August), 694–710. doi:610.1177/0950017012460329

Schafer, J. L., & Graham, J. W. (2002). Missing data: Our view of the state of the art. *Psychological Methods*, *7*(2), 147–177.

Schieman, S., & Glavin, P. (2008). Trouble at the border? Gender, flexibility at work, and the work-home interface. *Social Problems*, *55*(4), 590–611.

StataCorp LP. (2013). *STATA multiple-imputation reference manual: Release 13*. College Station, TX: StataCorp, LP.

Stiroh, K., & Botsch, M. (2007). Information technology and productivity growth in the 2000s. *German Economic Review*, *8*(2), 255–280.

Thompson, D. (2011). The case for banning email at work. *The Atlantic*, December 1. Retrieved from http://www.theatlantic.com/business/archive/2011/12/the-case-for-banning-email-at-work/249252/#

Towers, I., Duxbury, L., Higgins, C., & Thomas, J. (2006). Time thieves and space invaders: Technology, work and the organization. *Journal of Organizational Change Management, 19*(5), 593–618.

Voydanoff, P. (2005). Consequences of boundary-spanning demands and resources for work-to-family conflict and perceived stress. *Journal of Occupational Health Psychology, 10*(4), 491–503.

Wajcman, J. (2006). New connections: Social studies of science and technology and studies of work. *Work, Employment, and Society, 20*(4), 773–786.

Wajcman, J., & Rose, E. (2011). Constant connectivity: Rethinking interruptions at work. *Organization Studies, 32*(7), 941–961.

Zickuhr, K., & Smith, A. (2012). *Digital differences*. Washington, DC: Pew Research Center's Internet and American Life Project. Retrieved from www.pewinternet.org

WHAT WOULD JESUS HAUL?: HOME, WORK, AND THE POLITICS OF MASCULINITY AMONG CHRISTIAN LONG-HAUL TRUCK DRIVERS

Rebecca L. Upton

ABSTRACT

Purpose — *This chapter explores how long-distance truckers in the contemporary United States navigate work and family obligations. It examines how Christianity and constructions of masculinity are significant in the lives of these long-haul drivers and how truckers work to construct narratives of their lives as "good, moral" individuals in contrast to competing cultural narratives which suggest images of romantic, rule-free, renegade lives on the open road.*

Methodology/approach — *This study is based upon ethnographic fieldwork, interviews, observations of long-haul truckers, and participation in a trucking school for eight months in 2005–2006 and an additional four months in 2007–2008. Using feminist grounded theory, I highlight how*

Christian trucking provides avenues through which balance is struck between work and family and between masculinity and other identities.

Findings — *Christian truckers draw upon older ideas about responsible, breadwinning fatherhood in their discourse about being good "fathers" while on the road. This discourse is in some conflict with the lived experiences of Christian truckers who simultaneously find themselves confronted by cultural narratives and expectations of what it means to be a good "worker" or a good "trucker."*

As these men navigate both work and social locations, gender expectations are challenged and strategies to ameliorate the work/family balance are essential.

Originality/value of chapter — *The chapter contributes to discourse on gender studies as well as to the reshaping of ideology and practices of work and family in contemporary American culture.*

Keywords: Long-haul trucking; work; family; religion; masculinity; United States

> The contemporary symbol of tradition and heroism ... the great American folk hero and romantic way of life. We believe he is the American truck driver. His trademark is an 18 wheeler and his way of life is tough, hard-driven, yet curiously romantic ... He has a distinctive set of values and knows right from wrong. He is a down-to-earth guy who's willing to give up creature comforts for the open road. He's married or single, has strong inclinations to family, but also yearns for his personal freedom. He lives a tough life, peppered with certain amounts of danger. He is confident, tough, and masculine. (Tobacco advertisement in *Overdrive* magazine, May 1981, p. 60)

> My wife describes me as regular family man, a guy who commutes to work, for work and then comes home to a family ... its more than that though ... I'd say, and I'm sorta embarrassed to say it like this, but its like being a contemporary cowboy ... or a cop ... we're out that keeping the streets safe and carrying more than the load, we're carrying a message. (Gary Carlson, 39, married father of two, self-identified Christian long haul trucker)

INTRODUCTION

Truck drivers embody many of the symbols of working families and the American dream. As renaissance-men-on-the-road and in seemingly Kerouac-fashion, they offer an image of unbounded freedom, exploration, and frontier renegade individualism. They are, as the advertisers for the tobacco company, Brown and Williamson so purposefully and deftly describe above, both heroic and down-to-earth. They demonstrate the complex and often competing constructions and expectations of modern day masculinity.

Truckers also embody ideas of patriotism and providership and literally find themselves at the intersections of cultural meanings and obligations of work and family while on the road. Described by some as "sailors on a concrete sea" and yet by others as "hazards of the highway," long-haul truck drivers are seemingly caught between competing narratives of responsible and renegade identity in popular culture (Hamilton, 2008; Lewis, 1999; Oullet, 1994; Stern, 1975). For Christian truck drivers in particular, these potentially pejorative stereotypes are in contrast with the more positive narratives and images that they choose to draw upon; truckers as good workers, good providers, good fathers, and good men. Christian truckers draw heavily upon the metaphor of Jesus as a messenger, as a lone savior who followed a path of his own and encountered numerous and morally challenging obstacles along the way. So too do they draw upon narratives and symbols of overcoming such obstacles in order to fulfill broader cultural obligations of fatherhood and providership. Christian truckers, in particular, embody and combine the older ideas about responsible and breadwinning fathers with over-simplified constructions of masculinity. At the same time however, they navigate far more contemporary contexts where workplaces and spaces have profound effects on work/family life and many of these men end up embodying entirely new forms of fatherhood and masculinity.

REVIEW OF THE LITERATURE

As Aune (2010) suggests, the study of fathering practices within contemporary evangelical Christianity is a relatively new field but one that has emerged and focused almost exclusively upon the lives of "mainstream" men in the United States. The scholarly discourse on fathering and Christianity has focused attention on particular communities and religious movements; attention to those who are positioned at the periphery of some of these discussions, such as truckers, have been left out almost entirely. Aune writes that too much of the literature of Christian fathers is subsumed in discussions of work and family rather than placing it squarely in the focus of fatherhood and evangelical Christians themselves (cf. Bartowski, 2004; Gallagher, 2003). Much of the literature on the Promise Keepers (another well-known Christian group) in the United States emphasizes the role of men as fathers, and suggests that among Christian fathers there is a demonstrated flexibility in terms of how to perform fatherhood (Bartowski, 2004). Little consensus exists however on how gender and family are *actually* negotiated by Christian fathers, particularly those who are considered marginal, such as the subpopulation of Christian truckers, and this research seeks to fill that gap. Others have observed the elasticity of concepts such as "dad" or "working father," both among more mainstream religious groups (Aune, 2010) and in the work and family literature more broadly. As Williams (2010) argues too, concepts of class and gender must enter into the discussion of what it means to be "working-class" in terms of income versus ideology (see also Alvarez & Collier, 1994; Belman & Monaco, 2001; Bolton, 1979). In this chapter I draw heavily upon the observations by Aune (2010), Bartowski (2004), Heath (2000), and Sumerau (2012) who also conducted qualitative studies of religiously identified fathers in the United States to suggest that among Christian truckers, where evangelical ideology is paramount and the discourse of the male head of household and "traditional" families is ubiquitous, the *elasticity* of the concepts of father, worker, and Christian is necessary in order to identify as a good Christian father and worker. This is particularly true because of the broader cultural discourse in the United States about truckers in general. Like Bartowski, who describes the Promise Keepers movement as engaged in "a relationship of 'distinctive engagement' with secular culture" (cited in Aune, 2010, p. 169), I see that Christian truckers also embrace many elements of contemporary culture while simultaneously espousing ideals that contrast with more "mainstream" values. I find that many Christian truckers rely heavily upon contemporary information technology and services and yet may simultaneously be engaged in more evangelical discourse and practices while on the road.

In order to address the flexibility of these concepts as well as the connections to work and family, I also build on the work of Civettini and Glass (2008), Heath (2000), and Wolkomir (2006) who suggest that male-based gender movements have had significant influence on family and work relations and obligations. These studies suggest that tensions embedded in Christian discourse lead many Christian truckers to constantly negotiate particularly gendered identities. They find themselves caught between conservative notions of masculinity and fatherhood in addition to more contemporary constructions of fatherhood as more nurturing. Heath suggests that early iterations of Christian male religious groups sought specifically to alter norms of masculinity and challenged men to rethink their roles in the family – "reestablishing" themselves as leaders in the family (2000, p. 423; see also Donovan, 1998). But among Christian truckers, the navigation of gender roles casts a wide net – as Connell (1987) suggests there is no single form of masculinity, but rather there may be multiple and even marginalized masculinities that emerge in concert with other social variables such as race or class. Similar then to the "distinctive engagement" argument that Aune (2010), Bartowski (2004), and others (cf. Coughlin, 2005) suggest then, in this work, it is clear that Christian truckers are navigating several paths along which both masculinity and Christianity are configured.

In the negotiation of fatherhood and provider, Christian truckers engage with variables of identity along class and race lines as well. Here, however, I am interested in how the truckers themselves come to view their navigation, their practices of fatherhood as both genuine and contradictory. While conservative Protestantism may have had a "domesticating" role (Wilcox, 2004) on men in evangelical groups, among Christian truckers, the very idea of domestic space and obligation has become challenged and must constantly be renegotiated. This chapter explores how the discourse of truckers themselves become evidence that they are both good fathers and good Christians and that these categories, while at times, seemingly in opposition to one another given a contemporary socio-political contexts, remain paramount in the language and stories that are told on the road.

While studies of masculinity suggest that the very idea of masculinity is constantly subject to debate and contest (Connell & Messerschmidt, 2005; Ducat, 2004; Heath, 2000; Kimmel, 1996), this chapter contributes to that discussion by providing more ethnographic evidence as to how those contests over identity are won, lost, or drawn. In this chapter, several of the cultural means and strategies which these truckers experience and utilize are explained and the importance of the struggle over contested identities as truckers, Christians, and men in the United States are highlighted in narrative. At times, "on the road Dads" are faced with very similar challenges and work/family obligations as those who are more or less "stay at home Dads" (I use that term as truckers often did, referring to non-truckers writ large as "stay at homes" even if they "went to work" in an office). The lens of Christian rhetoric and its salience to the crafting of masculine identity for on the road truckers offers a unique perspective and voices to some of the discussions of masculinity in contemporary American culture. These men embody (as do their trucks) a sense of what they describe as a "lost" responsibility on the part of men. They see themselves as would-be sinners, saints, saviors, and sailors on tarmac seas.

The Christian Concrete Cowboy

In the United States, the evangelical population accounts for approximately 20–40% of the population (Wuthnow, 2007). There are approximately 3.5 million truck drivers in the United States. Of those, about one in nine are independent owner operators and about 10% self-identify specifically as Christian truck drivers (Bureau of Labor Statistics, 2014). There are approximately 500,000 different trucking companies in operation in the contemporary United States and within the top 25 highest earning companies, at least 3 are recognized as specifically Christian trucking companies. One of the largest resources for Christian truck drivers of all kinds (whether independent owner operator or employed by a large company) is the Association of Christian Truckers (ACT) who, along with Truckers 4 Christ and the Christian Truckers Network, represent the leading organizations for Christian truck drivers.

Christian trucking organizations and their vehicles are often readily identifiable by certain signs and symbols while out on the road and in the public domain. Images such as scrolls, "Jesus fish" and large crosses adorn both bobtails (cabs) and the trailer load. Many online and truck-stop ministries provide literature and material for dissemination to both truckers and those they encounter. Tracts, or short treatises, usually in pamphlet form are often part of the markers of Christian trucker identity. "Tract men" are those who, along with marked vehicles, regularly identify as part of Christian trucking organizations and disseminate the pamphlets, other literature and are charged with carrying a message to other drivers and men. For many who were part of ACT, the public performance of a certain kind of masculinity, visibly as well as verbally identifying as a Christian trucker, was the subject of both public discourse on trucking and those engaged with the individual negotiation of such identities.

Organizations such as ACT operate, often literally, as vehicles and institutions through which the renegade, individual, and cowboy-esque stereotype of the long haulers gets mediated and recast as conforming to Christian and particularly "good" fatherhood – even while these men are on the road and literally away at work and not in the home. Through the narratives of Christian truckers as well as the positions espoused on the ACT and other websites, it is clear that these men seek to be "super-men" as they cast themselves rhetorically and in practice as men who "can do it all" and akin to biblical figures, are repeatedly tested on the road to redemption and success.

METHOD

This study examined the social construction of gender and the negotiation of work and family among Christian long-haul truck drivers. The study took place over eight months in 2005 and 2006 and four additional months in 2007 and 2008, during which time I rode with over 23 study participants and observed a Certified Driver License (CDL) school. In addition to the immersion in the CDL training school, I rode with nine different explicitly self-identified "hard-core" Christian truckers over several routes, one was a married couple with whom I rode several round trips from Indianapolis to the West Coast. Typically long-haul runs lasted anywhere from a few days "on the road" (through several Midwest states) to a weeklong round-trip (from Indiana to California).

Participant Observation

The primary method of data collection was overt participant observation at the CDL school and on the road with truck drivers based in the Midwest. The CDL school was not specifically or overtly religious in affiliation and so provided me with a general immersion in trucking culture to compare with the experiences and discourse of the specifically Christian truckers I observed. I attended three weeks of classes at the CDL school, often described as "just like boot camp for truckers," approximately 60 hours of classroom time and an additional 60 hours spent with novice drivers practicing skills, navigating hazards, and preparing for exams.

While on the road, participant observation was conducted at 10 different Christian truck stops and at over 40 "prayer meetings" at truck-stop chapels. I was able to record and transcribe 20 different sermons delivered at these chapels and these transcribed sermons were key in the analysis of the more institutional message espoused by Christian truckers and mobile ministries in general. These prayer meetings were held at truck-stop chapels (including several old trailers set on blocks at one end of a lot that are mobile chapels ready to be taken on the road) where worship, singing, and a commitment to Interstate Missionizing (praying and proselytizing) were iterated and described as "truck stop fellowship." I attended two truck "beauty pageants" during the fieldwork period (each pageant lasted for several days much like a conference or convention). I too analyzed the published literature, *tracts* (or fliers and pamphlets distributed by Christian trucking ministries), and audiotaped sermons as well as information available publicly on various Christian trucking organizations and that serve to promote a public idea of responsible, masculine, and Christian identity and to recruit new members "into the fold."

Interviews

In addition, I conducted structured interviews with 23 members of a CDL cohort, all 9 drivers that I rode with and 10 family members of those drivers who identified as Christian truckers. These interviews lasted anywhere between one and three hours in length. Participants for the project were found through a snowball sampling process.

The CDL cohort included 25 drivers and had a demographic distribution fairly representative of the US picture overall. The drivers I drove along with all had children and all but two were married at the time of the study. The majority of those with whom I rode were based in the Midwest states of Indiana and Michigan and identified as white; they were between the ages of 27 and 34. All of the drivers described themselves as middle class, even though some recognized that they might not be classified as middle class by others. For example, Ken described himself as "a regular middle class guy, we have a good family life, a nice home ... but no, I don't expect that other people think of us when we're out there on the road as middle class, as just like them, they think we're lower [class]." Ken and others reflect an ideology where despite having a middle-class income, he and others are viewed as working-class in terms of how they understand work and family, where work is viewed as something done to support the household.

Wages for long-haul truck drivers in the United States currently ranges from $40,000 to $100,000 per year (Bureau of Labor Statistics, 2014) for salaried long haulers (driving for a local company); independent owner operators can earn less or considerably more but are generally not salaried as company employed long haulers are. Some of the individuals involved in the study described themselves as career truckers and others were trucking as part of a long-term financial and life plan. Ken recalled how "I never thought I'd go into this for life, I was aiming to work a while on the road, save up for a franchise and then settle down more permanently back in

Columbus – I never imagined that this would be my home away from home all these years." This tension, between home and work and work as home is not a new one, but is certainly a key part of the narratives of truckers in general.

Analysis

My research used a feminist grounded theoretical approach (Charmaz, 2008; Glaser & Strauss, 1967; Wuest, 1995), in which theory emerged during the process of immersion in and examination of the research site. Open-ended field interviews, participant observation, Christian trucking websites, sermons, tracts, observations, and field notes data were coded thematically first by hand and then via MAXQDA software analysis. The coded data revealed that the primary discourse present among Christian long-haul truckers centered on particular themes (providership, marriage, masculinity and work, women and sex) of which the narratives that surrounded fatherhood were the most significant.

Examining fatherhood among Christian truckers requires a closer examination of narratives of fatherhood as well as the practice of fathering (cf. Dermott, 2007; Townsend, 1999). It also requires consideration of the context in which these narratives and practices arise, so the following section examines the public trucking discourse, interviews with Christian truck drivers and participant observation, and interviews with long-haul drivers and their companions.

MASCULINITY AND FATHERHOOD ON THE TRUCKING FRONTIER

Public Trucking Narratives

Trucking industry discourse on masculinity consistently highlights an almost hypermasculine and overtly masculine and male authoritarian presence on the road. The overarching theme in public discussions of masculinity and fatherhood at the CDL school was a concern with the "image" of truckers out on the road. Specifically as one instructor put it on one day early in the training session, "you represent the company, yourselves and men everywhere who put their lives on the line to do their duty." Much like military discourse, the notion of hypermasculine, individualized identity, and bravery are concepts emphasized in the public discourse of and by long-haul truckers. As Gill (1997) describes, "military service is one of the most important prerequisites for the development of successful subaltern manhood, because it signifies rights to power and citizenship and supposedly instills the courage that a man needs to confront life's daily challenges" (p. 527). In the CDL school several posters papered the walls of class and break rooms that included messages such as, "semis are the *real* monster trucks," "watch for four wheelers (passenger cars), they do not always watch for you," and "we too serve and protect" and "we are clean, courteous and caring." These messages conveyed a sense of power and space on the road as well as the obligation to care for others.

Gendered identity is key in the public discourse about long-haul trucking. As Heath (2000) and Wolkomir's recent (2012) work suggest, discourse about masculinity in groups such as the Promise Keepers or among competitive card players, relies heavily on the negation of women's roles in such arenas. With truckers, narratives and public discourse about the trucking industry mirror these observations. Very few women engage in long-haul trucking as employment and even fewer can be found in Christian trucker circles. There are purportedly level playing fields: trucking can be done by any driver once certified and women are often ironically considered "better" hires since they are assumed to be less likely to engage in dangerous behaviors while on the road and on the job. Yet women's contributions and work in particularly gendered fields are consistently downplayed, undervalued, and constructed as weaker (cf. Wolkomir, 2012).

For many truckers, there is a constant tension between being courteous, clean, and caring on the road and the renegade, hypermasculine, male. Even some who want no part of truck-stop religion say having the chapels has helped improve the truck driver's image. "The truck industry needs all the help they can get," said Jim Malone, 29, a driver interviewed in the *New York Times*, "when people think of us, they think of us as just fat and never taking showers and doing drugs. Ninety-nine percent of us have families just like regular people" (Belluck, 1998). As Ray Glazier, a 44-year-old trucker I spoke with at the CDL school in Florida described when I asked specifically about how Christian truckers, in particular, thought of themselves as "men,"

> I don't think you're going to find a big difference – I mean we're all raised here, you grow up knowing what you are supposed to do and be if you are a man – that's the whole thing, I think when you are educated or just grow up with your buddies, this is the stuff that you are taught. I think for the Christian guys that's the tricky part, when

do you decide that being a man is more important that being a Christian man, I'm not really sure that is an actual decision, I think all men here [in the US] are taught how to be men and we know what "masculine" is.

Similarly, Jeffrey Morales a trucker in his late fifties who had been involved with trucking for several decades observed that the differences between Christian and non-Christian truckers were really quite minimal and that the overarching and public narratives about masculinity and gender identity writ large in the United States had potentially far more relevance when it came to think about the construction of masculinity on the road. He said,

> It doesn't actually matter what your sexuality is either. I wouldn't say that men talk about that the way they used to, I can remember guys [laughs] who were constantly getting some from the lot lizards, but these days I guess that is less attractive to everyone, just a safety thing, like it came along with the safety regulations on the road, you had to practice safer sex. Anyway, I think that no matter what your beliefs about sex, so this goes for the Christian truckers and some of my buddies, it doesn't matter, you still understand what it takes to be a man in American culture, I think you could ask a fifth grader and they could tell you.

In a more recent *New York Times* article in fact, the significance of a traditional view of hypermasculinity is reiterated and, Kimmel's (1996) "hegemonic masculinity" is integral to the growing numbers of Christian men's groups (cf. Worthen, 2009).

Christian Trucker Narratives

But truckers are not just "like everyone else," and nor do they all profess similar ideology. For Christian truckers, the narrative and construction of masculinity becomes a much more carefully crafted one. Randall Balmer draws parallels between trucker missionaries and the circuit riders bringing horseback gospel to the pioneers and to the railroad preachers proselytizing train travelers. As Balmer states, "it's the hallmark of the evangelical movement, speaking the idiom of the people, going to the people wherever they are ... there's also a cachet of going to the worst places, going to the tenement areas, sending missions to the brothels. Truck stops can be pretty bleak, pretty godless places, and if you can shine a light there, you've really accomplished something" (cited in Belluck, 1998).

For many truckers, such as Gary Carlson, the married father of two young children quoted at the start of this chapter, the struggle to be both an available father figure and to fulfill his aspirations and obligations as part of a Christian-based trucking company has meant that he has had to craft a precarious balance between being a good father, husband, and worker while on the road. The road brings him in contact with the "hazards of sin and temptation" as he puts it, in addition to the work itself taking him away from his family.

Gary laughingly introduced himself at our first meeting at a well-known Christian truck stop on a major highway, "I'm the kind of guy they want as a poster image for truckers — I am a good guy, I'm not pushy and I'm not smarmy, I'm just setting a good example ... at least I hope so," he continued, "I'm the kind of guy you want to see out there, clean in body and mind [laughs]." Gary dresses the part too — with clean jeans and a freshly washed and ironed shirt, I met him first on one of his stops to shower and rest for the mandatory period. Seated in a small booth that was part of the mobile ministry trailer and rest stop, Gary first told me that he was first and foremost a Christian trucker, someone who tried to, in his words, "carry the message and practice what Jesus preached — he was a traveling guy too you know." He then described himself as a regular working family man, although as he put it, "without the stuffy suit and tie, not some guy in a monkey suit or uniform that you can't get to know, I'm open, I'm just your average guy, I could be your neighbor" and as a guy who "joined Calvary Trucking (a pseudonym) because I wanted everyone to know that I wasn't afraid to be a real guy and a real Christian at the same time."

What it means to be a "real" Christian and a "real man" were recurring themes throughout my travels with Christian truck drivers. The role of religious identity is integral to their lives and within the trucking industry writ large. In the past several years, the rise of Christian-based trucking companies has escalated. In the 1970s, ministries on the road grew and the trucker "chaplain" Jim Keyes mobilized many of the highway Christian truck stops. These stops and the groups themselves (similar as Aune, 2010 and others suggest about the Promise Keeper movement) have grown considerably in the 1990s and 2000s. Groups such as ACT emphasize that "[the] goal is to empower the truckers to be the next generation of Ministers" and, according to their website, Christian trucking corporations offer economic as well as spiritual opportunities for many in the long-haul industry. For many, driving with such a company affords an opportunity to craft a culturally powerful, stable, and public narrative while simultaneously building a middle-class income and lifestyle. Christian trucking discourse is what Aune describes as "primarily traditional in the sense that it seeks to restore an older discourse of fathering as responsibility and discipline" (p. 177).

For male truckers, the rhetoric that appears salient and mirrors many of their beliefs is found in the ideologies of groups such as the Promise Keepers and other "family" oriented Christian groups. These groups emphasize the importance of masculinity as embodied not *just* in an image of the Marlboro Man, though they certainly do not negate such an image. Indeed, much of their literature is accompanied by photos of hypermasculine, white, well dressed, and presumably heterosexual men. But male Christian truckers' identity is explicitly grounded in ideas of providership and traditional "family values." Financial, emotional, and familial supports are all important factors in the configuration of male, Christian trucker identity.

Dale, a younger friend of Gary's, described what he saw as the important qualities or prerequisites for the job:

> its like you have to be the *whole* package – what you see, really is what you get – you see good, clean, American men who are out there on the roads, braving some tough times, some tough challenges but we keep above it and are doing this for our families – we are trying to be good representatives of a God driven life and that's what you get, nothing more, nothing less, but the whole deal.

Both Gary and Dale agreed, "not everyone can do it, not everyone gets it or is cut out for this life, but pretty soon you know who is providing and who is just not." Ultimately it became a kind of unstated and (ironically) overstated contest about proving masculinity though various means. Townsend (1999) has suggested the masculine ideal of achieving the "package deal" – being good workers, fathers, husbands, and providers. Here, these narratives grow out of an approved (within the greater context of trucking) right-wing conservatism, biblical stories about fatherhood, and religious rhetoric about the importance of reestablishing/maintaining men as key to nuclear families and family organization. *All* truckers grappled with work and family tensions and obligations. For Christian truckers however, those tensions and obligations are brought into greater relief given their unique employment, their absence for the most part from the actual home, and the religious ideology that often frames masculinity and manhood in very different ways.

Masculinity in Motion: Embodiment and the Christian Trucker

Through subtle, and not-so-subtle symbols (chrome "Jesus" fish ornaments), narratives (testimonials from converts and drivers on websites), and performances of man and truck (through truck shows), it becomes clear just how complicated and interwoven concepts of religious, economic, and masculine identity have become for on the road truckers as they attempt to fulfill those myriad roles. Belonging to a Christian trucking company, driving for a company, or even just stopping at a Christian truck stop, it is clear that certain symbols and images of the American family are in busy contest with other key ideas about the long-haul truck driver. From the now ubiquitous "Jesus fish" icons (located at eye level on trailers so that they are visible to cars and other passenger vehicles) to "no lot lizard" decals (symbolized by a line across an encircled salamander) that clearly communicate the antiprostitution message of Christian truckers, the trucks themselves come to embody the ethos and image of the long-haul Christian truck driver. Not only are the drivers hardworking (or at least perceived to be) and good, moral beings, so too are their trucks. Independent owner operated bobtails (the front part of the cabs) and trailers are often decorated with a variety of images and messages from Christian literature. If not on the truck, the t-shirts and other paraphernalia sold inside the truck stops proclaim biblical messages adopted by Christian drivers and companies. Without exception, all of the drivers who identified as Christian truckers had either a truck with an identifiable symbol on the cab or trailer (a cross or scroll in the company title for example) or adorned the cab interior (or themselves) with crosses, chrome Icthus (or "Jesus fish") icons, baseball caps, t-shirts, and placards with biblical sayings. One of the most common t-shirts (and one that was given to me by several of my respondents at the conclusion of this study) or placard images is of a truck's grille as seen from a rear view mirror with the words "I press toward the mark for the prize of the high calling of God in Christ Jesus" with "Philippians 3:14" emblazoned underneath.

Some cabs and trailers are so highly decorated that drivers describe them as "Christmas trees" due to how heavily lit up the trucks are and the size of the Christian painted messages. Dale acknowledged that at times the messages can be intimidating. He described a friend,

> one of my buddies had a "tree" – it was all lit up, a huge cross on the front of the grill, will come barreling up behind some small four wheeler, that would put the fear of god in you! But it really was amazing, he was showing his pride and joy right there on the body of his truck, he's a Trucking for Jesus guy [a particular subgroup and company who display their motto along the entire length of the trailer] so you know, those guys aren't shy about what they're saying.

At times however being seen as a part of the "good guy's team" became highly competitive and certainly required the careful construction and maintenance of a particular masculinity. Similar to discourse on men and masculinity as perceived through the consumption of particular goods or activities (cf. Messner & Montez de Oca, 2005) it was not unusual for drivers and owners to speak about the physicality of their trucks. The trucks' "bodies" were things that could carry a powerful message and in ways that they saw as connected to their own selves and beliefs. The construction and extension of masculinity and Christianity through material goods is not an entirely new idea certainly but it carries great weight in the embodiment of these identities for truckers (cf. Worthen, 2009). Trucks of all types for example are entered into beauty contests, using the notion of beauty to demonstrate strength and as Gary put it, "a clean cab, a beautiful truck, that's a sign of a good, strong, clean soul, that's the kind of guy you want hauling your goods, carrying your burden, a clean body, a clean mind."

Christian truckers are actively engaged in everyday construction of their lives, their work, and what they haul as part of their particular, unique, and yet simultaneously all-American "good guy" identity as hard workers and good family men, even if they are from varied backgrounds and upbringings. In part, these men are caught in the interesting and often awkward space between stereotypes and individual experience. Certainly not all Christian truckers (nor truckers in general) fall into this space or find themselves actively negotiating stereotypical identities about what it means to be a "man, Christian, truck driver" or even "father," but for those that I worked with and rode with, these tropes were everywhere.

Recasting, Defining, and Defending Christian Masculinity

Some trust in chariots, (trucks) and some in horses, (engines); But we will remember the name of the Lord our God. They have bowed down and fallen; But we have risen and stand upright. (Psalm 20:7,8 – Theme scripture and song for Steering Wheel Ministries; parenthesis in original)

Time is running out to reach our fellow drivers for Jesus Christ ... rescue our fellow drivers from Hell so, men, lets team together and get this job done ... (webpage "call to arms" from Steering Wheel Ministries, an affiliate of the Association of Christian Truckers)

Truckers in general experience the tensions between being at home and being at work, being good men and yet having a part of the trucker persona on the road – independent, carefree, and rebellious. These tensions, these dual identities can present some difficulties on the road, at home, and for male identity on a day-to-day basis. Gary Carlson points out some of these tensions and the irony of long-haul trucking in the context of work and family discourse when he said,

> The funny thing about being a trucker is that people think you are a total rebel, or dangerous or something like that. Nobody really wants to be on the road with us, everyone thinks we're dangerous and gonna cause some big accident, you always turn on the radio or tv in the morning to hear about how some semi just jack knifed and caused a bunch of trouble. The thing is though, we are the ultimate providers, we are providing everyone in the US with their *stuff*, whatever it is, *we* provide it. When we are trying to get the stuff to where it is supposed to be and get held up, believe me, we aren't any happier than the customer. And frankly, we are, for the most part, good, honest men. We are like the perfect men – totally rough and able to drive big rigs, and yet we are working our butts off to get everyone their food and comforts of home.

For Gary and others, providing becomes an idea that is greater than simply the idea that he is providing financially for his own family. There is a defense of the ideology of both what it means to be a "man" in the contemporary United States in addition to the very public performance of being a good "provider" and a good "Christian" at the same time. While many Christian companies will not haul specific goods that are considered secular and luxury or even anti-Christian values (alcohol, certain kinds of pharmaceuticals, products deemed pornographic, and in some cases even cigarettes) the notion that a driver is providing and sharing a bounty with broader society while carrying a message of Christian faith was ever present. As Gary continued,

> Sure there are things we will not haul as part of Calvary, but that's part of the point, and yet its not. You see, its important to tell people what you will and will not haul, some things just add to the spiritual weakness of man, but on the other hand, you are carrying more than the load, you are carrying other people's loads for them, if you get my drift, you are providing them with goods for their own families so that they can do other kinds of work, they can think about what kind of men we are that we do dangerous work but we are pretty unnoticed unless you are on the highway, even then, you never really see the guy driving, but you see the truck and you see that he's Christian, or you start to wonder who this guy is driving for Calvary and what that's all about.

In addition to carrying a particular kind of message, Christian long-haul truckers described how their work really helped to define them in an era where they felt that being a good Christian was under "attack." Gary's friend Dale observed that,

> It is hard to be a Christian guy these days, people see you sometimes as kinda weak, puny, like a real mouse or something, like no matter how big you are, you are still going to back out of a fight, being a trucker kinda helps that a bit, makes them think twice about just who you might be, it complicates the picture and they think that maybe you have something that they don't or maybe that they start thinking that they need.

Dale's observation is in line with much of the writing in contemporary popular Christian literature on the concept of masculinity. For example, Paul Coughlin writes that "the problem with the wimpy Jesus of the popular imagination is that a 'meek and mild Jesus' eventually is a bore. He doesn't inspire us" (in O'Brien, 2008, p. 2). Brandon O'Brien describes the vitriol and vision that certain pastors have claimed as a notion of Christian masculinity and describes a pastor Mark Driscoll, who says that

> real men avoid the church because it projects a Richard Simmons, hippie queer Christ, that is no one to live for and is no one to die for, Jesus was not a long haired effeminate looking dude, rather he had callused hands and big biceps, this is the sort of Christ men are drawn to ... the ultimate fighting Jesus. (*Ibid.*)

For some Christian truckers, this discourse is appealing – they can fulfill an idea (however stereotyped) of themselves as good truckers, good workers, good men, and good Christians without suffering greatly in any arena – their identity as all of those things is solid and secure. O'Brien continues his description when he describes pastor Driscoll imagining Jesus as the model of maleness when he argues that,

> latte sipping Cabriolet drivers do not represent biblical masculinity, because real men like Jesus, Paul and John the Baptist, are dudes: heterosexual, win-a-fight, punch-you-in-the-nose-dudes In other words, Jesus is not a limp-wristed dress wearing hippie. The men created therefore in this image are not sissified church boys, they are aggressive, assertive and nonverbal.

On several occasions I read O'Brien's article aloud to truckers stopped at mobile ministries along major highways and in places like the Road Angel Café (now the Midwest Christian Truckers Retreat) on I-70, a truck stop ostensibly for anyone, but dedicated to passing along a message of Christianity. In discussions at these truck stops, in person and on the CB radio with other drivers, what became clear was that perspectives such as Driscoll's were not uncommon and were increasingly welcome. A trucker who I only know by the "handle" of Ty's Pop on the radio described himself as heavily tattooed, long haired but "glad that people don't just see me as some kinda outlaw, I'm a good example for kids, boys especially, I am a tough looking guy but a guy who could lie down with the lambs, I show them how it's a complicated picture, to call somebody a trucker or a Christian, really, just one thing doesn't give you the whole perspective."

These perspectives are welcomed not just by those who identified as Christian or who worked for a Christian company. The appeal of Christian trucking and trucking companies has reached the general trucking populace and more and more non-Christians reported stopping at truck stops and actually preferring not just the amenities at Christian stops but the security they afford. For some it's a place where their image as a good man, a good father, and husband is secure, many stop because they know it's a "safe place with good showers and no hassles." For others, primarily those who seek a revived masculine identity as a Christian, it affords the opportunity to be seen as something more than what Dale described as "sissies." He noted, "Nobody calls a trucker a sissy, if you are a Christian trucker, it's like you are even better, an even *better* man, a *real*, respectable man."

Family, Fathers, and Religion on the Road

Central too, to the discourse of truckers writ large, and as was clear through the narratives of Christian truckers, the tension between work and home became a pivotal point of navigation in discussions of masculinity.

Inherent to the very concept of long-haul trucking is the idea that one virtually lives in one's workplace. Cabs of bobtails are outfitted extremely well with places to sleep, microwaves to heat food on the go, the latest in computer equipment and GPS units, and many other comforts of "home." Great pride is taken in the maintenance and upkeep of the cab as part of the Christian trucker identity and not simply a result of observer effect. I rarely met a driver who filled the cab with trash or any sort of litter – typically too, when at home, entire families and certainly wives and girlfriends got involved in the care and upkeep of the cab. Gary Carlson's wife Sue for example, would spend hours on a Saturday when he was home, vacuuming, cleaning, dusting, wiping, and detailing the inside of Gary's cab. As she described,

> its something I can do for him when he's home – most of the time I am cleaning the house, but that is not something that goes with him, if I clean the truck, if I clean where he is most of the time, it's a reminder of home, of what is waiting for him back here. Something he doesn't want to lose or let go of, but he can take a little bit with him. Its something I can do for him, with him in a way.

A source of pride too, a clean cab is understood as a symbol of the kind of care and family work that individuals and couples are invested in *together*, even as they are on the road and geographically distant from family – they are still doing the "home" work.

Many cab interiors were decorated too with actual images from home – family photos, homemade gifts from children, favorite pillows, and knitted blankets were not uncommon. Bobtail cabs are among the most highly technical and IT advanced places in which I have ever been. Akin to the cockpits of jet airliners, cabs are places of high tech and highly safety-conscious machinations. Yet I was never in a cab that was without a "personal touch," the things, trappings from the home, made their way to work. Even for single or unmarried drivers, décor was important and photos, letters, even stuffed animals accompanied drivers across US highways.

As Hochschild (1997) points out, workplaces can become home places and home places and spaces come to work (and in this case, go on the road) in important ways. For truckers this was particularly and unsurprisingly the case and as the data from this study suggest, many relied upon the construction of that work/home space as the stage against which their construction of masculinity, sexuality, political, and Christian selves were cast. It became extremely important and clearly evident that the "work" of being a good man, a good Christian was intricately tied to the kind of work that long-haul truckers were engaged in and with what they came to see as their obligation or mission while performing those kinds of jobs. Yet, the work lives of long-haul truck drivers affect their home lives in ways that appear far greater than an everyday, middle-class, nine-to-five job might. Specifically, being at work requires being on the road, and being away from home for extended periods of time. As noted above, truckers and their families take care to send the home on the road. Even more importantly, the crafting of their identities as good workers, fathers, and moral men became heightened as the challenges to those identities became greater in their home lives.

While the home might come on the road, the idea that they bring "work" home with them is not something that truckers could relate to. Many wives and girlfriends too, felt that work should stay at work, it created enough complications in their everyday lives to begin with, as Peggy, the 27-year-old mother of two put it,

> This is my second marriage. The first one didn't work out because we were both traveling so much – I was trying to have a full time career and my then husband was a resident so he always had these crazy hours. So it just didn't work out, we would see each other at these odd times of day, one coming, the other going, and that gave us nothing to build a real future on. When I married Jim I had already changed my career and priorities. I really wanted a family and now we have the girls who are just wonderful and everything has been great – except I suppose that sometimes I feel like I'm reliving the same kind of marriage pattern you know? In this case we see each other at the end of runs (Jim Delaney drives from Indianapolis to Sacramento and Boise and back each week) and that's it. It's almost the same as seeing each other at the end of the workday

shift or in those small moments, but now the shifts are more like weeks and I have all this additional stuff to do. When Jim gets home from "work" [she puts the word in air quotes] he just wants to relax, play with the kids, be the fun guy away from work and yet there is all this stuff to do around the house – mowing, yardwork, bills, it's frustrating. I mostly feel like support staff when he's around and the total head CEO of the home when he's not.

Peggy's case is not atypical. Many spouses who stay behind experience similar tensions in negotiating the times their partners are away and times their partners when the partners are in town. Jane Sutton and her husband Frank spoke openly about these tensions and Jane described how she "felt irritated even though [she was] glad he was home, because mostly he gets all the joy from the kids and I get all the crap [laughs] I know that's selfish because of all that he does, but sometimes I want to be the hero, to have the kids make a 'welcome home' banner for me." Frank acknowledged these differences and noted that "I know it doesn't seem like it, but I have days and nights where I'd give anything to be doing the normal, boring, house stuff for Jane, to be home, to take out the trash and to clean gutters ... but I remember what I'm doing all this for and why I work hard on the road, it is all for them." For many, the seemingly logical solution is to go on the road together, and this works if there aren't kids in school and to be looked after. Stu and Stella Nichols travel together once a week on a long haul and have done so for the past four years. They are on the road together, "working together" away from home for over 40 weeks during the year. As Stu says, "this way we get to be together and work together, when we are home, we can focus on being there." Stella concurs, admitting that while not perfect, it is nice to be able to "get to know each other all over again now that the kids are gone in school, with their own lives" although she continues,

> There are days where it felt like when I was trying to say I was "working from home" when the kids were little. I was working part time for a small company who let me shift some of my work to hours I could be at home with the kids ... it really didn't work out because when I was thinking about work I was at home and thinking about the kids, I just couldn't neatly separate the two – there was no necessary separation between home and work and there are times when this feels like that too, but I still think it's the best thing for us now.

Another example illustrates the tensions that occur with this career and the potential tensions between work and family. Carrie Newcomb describes some of their family and work concerns,

> We have a fifteen year old daughter and an eleven year old son ... about two years ago, my husband worked in home renovation, crazy hours, like 60 hours a week but really

good money. And then the economy for construction and housing started to tank. His working those long hours we didn't have much time for each other and then it became a real, tangible financial issue. In order to help our family and our finances we decided we needed to move back to Indiana and that my husband would do what his uncle had done and learn to become a truck driver. I also learned things while he was going through training. The worst challenge for me was just being alone. I had the kids and all and they were a handful, but I felt alone and I cried every night for the weeks he was away [at truck driving school]. Even now, when he is away after his home time, I cry. Here is where technology helps a lot, his aunt and uncle never had things like cell phones, we have them and use them all the time, he calls me at least once a day sometimes more. Sometimes our conversations are long and sometimes they last just long enough for him to tell me that he's okay, parked for the night and is going to bed.

But as Carrie describes, technology and the tangible need for a better financial situation did not always help when her husband's work(place) was clearly a site where the family came under siege, whether it was real or imagined. For example she said, "at first I worried about everything while he was on the road, he told me about lot lizards, that's the slang for hookers, but more than that, I started worrying about weather, traffic, crazy people out there." From bad weather to poor drivers to poor road conditions, the hazards on the road, at the workplace for truckers are real (Renner, 1998). Carrie and others find solace and comfort through technology (website support groups for truckers' wives for example) but what about the truckers themselves?

Ed Newcomb is 39 and enjoys his current work driving a truck on long-haul trips. He says,

> I go from Indianapolis to parts of Nebraska about every week or so, it's a long trip, but you get used to it, I like seeing new things, I never traveled when I was a kid, I mainly grew up in foster homes and such, and then early on, Carrie and me, we were so focused on the kids and I was working crazy hours with the renovation business, we just never really got out much. It's not like driving is a vacation, don't get me wrong, it's totally work and when I'm at work, I'm at *work*. I am doing this so we can feel more secure, maybe save up enough money so I can be at home more. But ... and I tell you this honestly, the work is exciting and worth it, it's good money, I bring home a big paycheck and everybody is happy. My wife maybe not as much because we don't see each other and I really like some of the challenges out there, but I don't tell her that, mainly I tell her how much money I am able to make.

Ed's story, similar to other long-haul truckers, emphasizes the ability to provide financially for his family, and as some truckers suggested, to eventually provide for his extended family who were "at home." It is not uncommon for example for truckers to talk about saving money, putting away their savings in order to someday "settle down" and even invest in business opportunities such as local franchises and restaurants. For truckers, the appeal of being on the long haul, being out, on the highways, and being seen as a bit of a romantic renegade is tempered by the obligations and tensions they experience at home. Specifically, for many, the idea of being a good provider, a good father, and a good worker are at odds with a renegade image so often associated with truck driving. Many seek to disprove that image and whether Christian or not, find the opportunities offered through Christian trucking (and more generally truck stops) ideal ways in which to balance competing obligations between working on the road as truckers and being seen as Gary Carlson put it, as "good, honest men."

CONCLUSION

But surely not all men and truckers seek such a seemingly traditional or hegemonic model of masculinity? As Connell and Messerschmidt (2005) emphasize in a review of the concept of hegemonic masculinity, the internal contradictions and obligations that men experience need careful attention. Specifically, they call for more careful attention to gender hierarchies and the deconstruction of a single approach to understanding masculinity. It is insufficient they suggest, to say that there are only dual sets of masculine (or feminine) identities and urge the recognition of more complicated and ever shifting sets of identities which men encounter and must negotiate in different social contexts. In many ways the idea of Christian trucking and being a trucker for Christ solves this set of dueling identities. Most useful I find, is that similar to the work of Heath (2000), Aune (2010), and Wolkomir (2006), the narratives and public performance of trucking identity, in negotiation with specifically Christian trucking identity, can often belie a more contemporary and egalitarian sense of masculinity for men where women and men are seen as equals and partners in their work and family obligations. Central to this discourse is the navigation of being "at home" versus being "at work" and the concurrent obligations of identifying as a Christian trucker.

Being (or at least utilizing facilities) a Christian trucker offers men in the long-haul trucking industry narratives of themselves as independent and free, good providers, and good men while simultaneously rejecting a notion of themselves as emasculated weaklings.

Gary suggested at one point that in fact,

> I have a lot more freedom that my brother for example. He is a nine-to-five job kind of guy, wears a tie, works hard, is there at night for his family each and every night, but he is like one of those hamsters, you know, running around the wheel and just doing the same thing each day. He's there, but is he really *there*? I would say that while not every run I do is an adventure, some of them are pretty boring and the road can go on forever, that's what the CB is for ... but when you climb up in the cab, there's something about being out there, being on the road and whatever lies ahead is unknown. My brother doesn't have that I don't think. He's always listening to what someone else is telling him to do, not really his own master or boss.

The irony in Gary's statement of course is that truckers are rarely if ever their own true bosses – with regulations about driving time, stop-overs and rests, even independent owner operators were subject to the desires and schedules of others. But throughout the research it was clear that an identity that encompassed the excitement of a renegade, typically all American cowboy image that was increasingly woven together with an idea of a good father and provider with a family at home who he was taking care of was paramount. It is interesting that in contemporary American society television shows such as "Ice Road Truckers" for example have come to highlight the dangerous and masculine jobs that long-haul truckers engage in. Contemporary media plays incessantly upon this narrative of the tough and hard-driven man. Contemporary Christian discourse too has entered into a debate over how to reconcile masculinity and religiosity. For long-haul truckers, the solution can be found it seems in the adoption of or advocacy for Christian trucking companies and amenities.

Christianity is not seen as counter culture in this realm, but a way to perhaps reclaim or even *begin* to claim an identity as the super-man, a contemporary renaissance man with good morals, with good work ethics, with good behavior and all the while, with a secure identity as a "dude" and as an "ultimate fighting Jesus" kind of guy. In some contrast to what Anderson-Facile (2007) found in her research on Christian bikers, this research suggests that Christian truckers operate in an arena where synthesis of their myriad work and family obligations and identities are facilitated. For Anderson-Facile (2007), bikers were seen as perennially caught between dueling identities. In this research I suggest that it is less about the fixed or polarized identities that are offered to Christian truckers, but more about acknowledging that masculine identities and obligations are much more dynamic, fluid, and less polarized and stratified. What is interesting too is that even for non-Christian truckers, that social and symbolic arena and discourse is appealing in the negotiation of masculine identity as evidenced in the observations at the CDL school and through interview data.

This chapter offers insight through the use of ethnographic methods into the social life of long-haul truckers, and specifically Christian truckers, in this particular and unique social context. While the scope of this study is limited given the relatively small sample size, the ethnographic data that emerged is valuable in other disciplinary discussions of work and family and the sociology of religion. Those interested in gender studies will find this work an invaluable springboard for future studies of the negotiation of masculinity across work and cultural contexts. Given increased focus on workplace safety and health policies too, this study provides interesting insights into how contemporary middle-class Americans actively navigate those policies and benefits. All truck drivers are on the road and represent a type of rule-free renegade freedom, but they are ever immersed in American middle-class work culture, one that has long neglected the important intersections of gender and class (Williams, 2010). They must perform at work and find themselves over-performing family (work) when at home on limited schedules. By studying Christian truckers, as well as their families and partners, we can see that not only are work and family obligations negotiated in a variety of ways on the road, so too are notions of masculinity managed in different ways that allow concepts of masculinity, providership, fatherhood, and the whole "package deal" more opportunity for reconciliation. Rather than assume that Christian or evangelical identity separates those truckers from those more mainstream, it appears, as Aune (2010) found too, that Christian truckers, while actively espousing more traditional or conservative forms of masculinity as others do, simultaneously navigate contemporary fatherhood and providership while on the "road" through the use of Christian narratives and imagery. Whatever the claims of Christian truckers, the similar narratives between more mainstream truckers and men engaged in work/family balance writ large are striking. These men live out and profess particular narratives while at the same time, use mainstream discourse on work, family, and fatherhood to both normalize and reify their roles on the road.

REFERENCES

Alvarez, R. R., & Collier, G. A. (1994). The long haul in Mexican trucking: Traversing the borderlands of the north and the south. *American Ethnologist, 21*(3), 606–627.

Anderson-Facile, D. (2007). *Dueling identities: The Christian biker*. Lanham, MD: Lexington Books.

Aune, K. (2010). Fatherhood in evangelical Christianity: Negotiating with mainstream culture. *Men and Masculinities, 13*(2), 168–189.

Bartowski, J. P. (2004). *The promise keepers: Servants, soldiers, and godly men.* New Brunswick, NJ: Rutgers University Press.

Belluck, P. (1998). Drivers find new service at truck-stops: Old-time religion. *New York Times online*, February 1. Retrieved from http://www.nytimes.com/1998/02/01/us/drivers-find-new-service-at-truck-stops-old-time-religion.html

Belman, D. L., & Monaco, K. A. (2001). The effects of deregulation, de-unionization, technology, and human capital on the work and work lives of truck drivers. *Industrial and Labor Relations Review, 54*(2A), Extra Issue: Industry Studies of Wage Inequality, 502–524.

Bolton, R. (1979). Machismo in motion: The ethos of Peruvian truckers. *Ethos, 7*(4), 312–342.

Bureau of Labor Statistics, U.S. Department of Labor. (2014). Heavy and tractor-trailer truck drivers. *Occupational outlook handbook, 2014–15 edition.* Retrieved from http://www.bls.gov/ooh/transportation-and-material-moving/heavy-and-tractor-trailer-truck-drivers.htm

Charmaz, K. (2008). Views from the margins: Voices, silences, and suffering. *Qualitative Research in Psychology, 5*(1), 7–18.

Civettini, N. H. W., & Glass, J. (2008). The impact of religious conservatism on men's work and family involvement. *Gender & Society, 22*(2), 172–193.

Connell, R. W. (1987). *Gender and power.* Stanford, CA: Stanford University Press.

Connell, R. W., & Messerschmidt, J. W. (2005). Hegemonic masculinity: Rethinking the concept. *Gender & Society, 19*, 829–859.

Coughlin, P. (2005). *No more Christian nice guy.* Bloomington, MN: Bethany House.

Dermott, E. (2007). Fatherhood. In G. Ritzer (Ed.), *The Blackwell encyclopedia of sociology* (Vol. 4, pp. 1647–1650). Malden, MA: Blackwell.

Donovan, B. (1998). Political consequences of private authority: Promise keepers and the transformation of hegemonic masculinity. *Theory and Society, 27*, 817–843.

Ducat, S. J. (2004). *The wimp factor: Gender gaps, holy wars and the politics of anxious masculinity.* Boston, MA: Beacon Press.

Gallagher, S. (2003). *Evangelical identity and gendered family life.* New Brunswick, NJ: Rutgers University Press.

Gill, L. (1997). Creating citizens, making men: The military and masculinity in Bolivia. *Cultural Anthropology, 12*(4), 527–550.

Glaser, B. G., & Strauss, A. L. (1967). *The discovery of grounded theory: Strategies for qualitative research.* New York, NY: Aldine de Gruyter.

Hamilton, S. (2008). *Trucking country.* Princeton, NJ: Princeton University Press.

Heath, M. (2000). Soft-boiled masculinity: Renegotiating gender and racial ideologies in the promise keepers movement. *Gender and Society, 17*(3), 423–444.

Hochschild, A. R. (1997). *The time bind: When work becomes home and home becomes work.* New York, NY: Metropolitan Books.

Kimmel, M. (1996). *Manhood in America.* New York, NY: Free Press.

Lewis, T. (1999). *Divided highways.* New York, NY: Penguin Books.

Messner, M., & Montez de Oca, J. (2005). The male consumer as loser: Beer and liquor ads in mega sports media events. *Signs, 30*, 1879–1909.

O'Brien, B. (2008). A Jesus for real men: What the new masculinity movement gets right and wrong. *Christianity Today.* April 18.

Oullet, L. J. (1994). *Pedal to the metal: The work lives of truckers*. Philadelphia, PA: Temple University Press.

Overdrive. (1981). The owner operator trucking magazine. *Overdrive*, May, p. 60.

Renner, D. A. (1998). Cross country truck drivers: A vulnerable population. *Nursing Outlook*, 46(4), 164–168.

Stern, J. (1975). *Trucker: A portrait of the last American cowboy*. New York, NY: McGraw-Hill.

Sumerau, J. E. (2012). That's what a man's supposed to do: Compensatory manhood acts in an LGBT Christian church. *Gender & Society*, 26(3), 461–487.

Townsend, N. (1999). *The package deal: Marriage, work and fatherhood in men's lives*. Philadelphia, PA: Temple University Press.

Wilcox, W. B. (2004). *Soft patriarchs, new men: How Christianity shapes fathers and husbands*. Chicago, IL: University of Chicago Press.

Williams, J. C. (2010). *Reshaping the work family debate: Why men and class matter*. Cambridge, MA: Harvard University Press.

Wolkomir, M. (2006). *Be not deceived: The sacred and sexual struggles of gay and ex-gay Christian men*. New Brunswick, NJ: Rutgers University Press.

Wolkomir, M. (2012). You fold like a little girl: (Hetero) gender framing and competitive strategies of men and women in no limit Texas hold em poker games. *Qualitative Sociology*, 35(4), 407–426.

Worthen, M. (2009). Who would Jesus smack down? *New York Times*, January 11, p. MM20. Retrieved from http://www.nytimes.com/2009/01/11/magazine/11punk-t.html?pagewanted=all&module=Search&mabReward=relbias%3Ar&_r=0

Wuest, J. (1995). Feminist grounded theory: An exploration of the congruency and tensions between two traditions in knowledge discovery. *Qualitative Health Research*, 5, 125–137.

Wuthnow, R. (2007). *After the baby boomers: How twenty and thirty somethings are shaping the future of American religion*. Princeton, NJ: Princeton University Press.

POLICING WORK AND FAMILY: HOW WORKERS COPE WITH CONTRADICTIONS AND DILEMMAS OF IMPLEMENTING WELFARE-TO-WORK

Tiffany Taylor

ABSTRACT

Purpose — *In the United States, welfare-to-work workers are under scrutiny from everyone and must defend the program if they want to defend themselves as good workers and good people. I build on past research that has examined how workers manage their emotions to cope with dilemmas in their jobs in a number of settings including hospitals, nursing homes, restaurants, and airplanes.*

Methodology — *In this chapter, I draw on data from an in-depth case study of a rural North Carolina (USA) welfare office using data primarily from observations and interviews with 19 welfare-to-work workers.*

Findings — *Within this highly constrained and contradictory work environment, workers recreate and redefine themselves as good workers and good people while simultaneously punishing program participants. To achieve this difficult task, workers manage their emotions through two key strategies, using institutionalized rhetoric and tough love paternalism, to justify their actions toward participants.*

Originality/value — *I add to the existing literature by examining how welfare-to-work workers cope with the emotional and moral dilemmas of their jobs.*

Keywords: Work; family; welfare; paternalism; tough love; emotions

> But I will defend [the program]. Because I believe in it and I enjoy my job. And this is a job when I get up in the morning, even though it is Monday, where I don't mind putting my foot on the floor and I know when I am coming here that I know what I have got to do. And I think that we are all committed to it. (Kim, Line Supervisor)

It is not easy working in a county welfare-to-work program. Workers implementing the program, including caseworkers and supervisors, are under scrutiny from everyone. These workers have to deal with supervisors constantly monitoring them, participants who seem ungrateful and/or disrespectful, and a public that complains that government spending on welfare is a waste of their tax money. In this situation, as the quote says, workers have to defend the program to friends, strangers, and the general public, if they want to defend themselves. Further, welfare-to-work programs represent a rich convergence of work and family. Not only are the workers required to implement programs that police program participants' work and family lives, the workers themselves demonstrate that work and family are indeed not separate spheres. In this chapter, I highlight the infusion of work and family as workers cope with the dilemmas of implementing welfare-to-work programs.

Researchers have examined how workers cope with dilemmas in their jobs in a number of settings. Smith and Kleinman's (1989) study illustrates how medical students learn to manage their emotions to suppress feelings of disgust or arousal when coming into contact with patients' bodies. Lerum (2004) explores how restaurant servers use humor to deal with the stressful, high paced, highly interactive job of waiting tables. Other research looks at the emotional demands of such occupations as paid caregivers in nursing homes where some homes provide structured settings encouraging emotional interaction, while other homes discourage interaction (Lopez,

2006). Yet more research compares men and women's emotional labor in service sector jobs finding that, in addition to women's occupations, men's occupations often require that men do emotional labor (Leidner, 1993; Steinberg & Figgart, 1999).

I build on this literature by examining how welfare-to-work workers coped with the emotional and moral dilemmas of their jobs, and how they resolved the contradictions and conflicting ideologies of welfare reform. Current US welfare-to-work programs require invasive and strict surveillance of client behavior and layers of bureaucracy. And yet, the program does little to help clients transition from welfare to jobs that offer living wages. Within this challenging context, county workers in rural North Carolina wanted to be seen as good people, people who make a positive difference in the lives of the participants; therefore, they had to redefine their work as helpful and meaningful toward participants while simultaneously punishing them (see Taylor, 2013, 2014 for other aspects of being a "good worker"). To achieve this difficult task, workers had to manage their own emotions, but their emotion management techniques did not go unchallenged. Workers constantly dealt with dilemmas of their work environment that challenged their ability to be helpful workers and manage their emotions.

I begin by describing the worker's structural and organizational context. I find that workers used two key emotion management strategies to help them navigate dilemmas in being good workers: institutionalized rhetoric to legitimate actions and tough love paternalism. While both strategies were used to police program participants' work and family lives, the latter strategy illustrated how workers integrated their ideas of appropriate work and family behavior to justify their treatment of participants. A significant departure from the dominant discourse idealizing women's work and family balance, workers strongly emphasized paid work as the path to a successful balance.

LITERATURE REVIEW

The shift from Aid to Families with Dependent Children (AFDC) to Temporary Assistance for Needy Families (TANF) was fueled by critiques of AFDC as a program that fostered dependence on the government and fed what had come to be known as the "culture of poverty." This term is often used differently from how Lewis (1966) or even Moynihan (1965) intended. Lewis and Moynihan viewed the culture of poverty as being a response to extreme structural constraints, such as adapting to new urban environments or living in economically depressed areas. Over time, the "culture of poverty" has come to be seen more as a racialized cultural inferiority and less in terms of a reaction to structural constraints (Feagin, 2000; Hays, 2003; Quadagno, 1994). Those embracing "culture of poverty" ideology now use the term as follows: individuals inflicted with the culture of poverty are not white people; they lack values; they are not motivated, even lazy; they are sexually promiscuous; they do not delay gratification; and do not take responsibility for their own actions. Finally, instead of supporting themselves, they feel the government should support them. In short, people inflicted with the culture of poverty do not follow the rules.

While rules vary from state to state, welfare scholars note that some aspects of welfare reform act as "carrots" and some act as "sticks" (Corcoran, Danziger, Kalil, & Seedfeldt, 2000; Lichter & Jayakody, 2002). Carrots can include diversion programs meant to give temporary assistance and keep economically troubled folks from ever going on welfare. This might include cash or housing assistance (Corcoran et al., 2000). The other side of reform is the sticks, which are negative policies meant to change welfare participants' behavior. These include sanctions for not following the rules, stringent work-activity requirements, family caps, and time limits (Corcoran et al., 2000; Handler & Hasenfeld, 2007; Lichter & Jayakody, 2002).

The maximum time an individual can receive federal funding is 60 months (five years); however, states have the ability to limit this to less time. For instance, in North Carolina where the data for this study was gathered, individuals can receive aid for 24 consecutive months and then enter a period where they cannot receive benefits for 36 months. A participant can have two years on, three years off until they reach the federal lifetime ceiling of 60 months. Sanctions, or punishments for not following rules, result in temporary or permanent termination of benefits and can be unexpected. Sanctions can occur for a variety of reasons including failure to fill out a form proving a child has been vaccinated, not participating in mandatory work activities, or a felony drug conviction. In my research, the state and county policies and worker implementation practices emphasize sanctioning participants. While workers distress over having to sanction they must enforce these rules that may have disastrous consequences for the participants' families. Workers, then, must find a way to justify their actions. To do this, workers engage in emotional labor.

According to Hochschild (1979, 1983), people can manage emotions either through expressing appropriate emotions or suppressing inappropriate ones. What is appropriate or not is situational and based on norms of emotion expression that she calls "feeling rules." Emotion management can come in the form of surface acting, where the individual alters their emotional display without changing their underlying feelings, or deep acting in which the individual changes their inner feelings in order to create a behavioral response. An example of surface acting is a cashier half-heartedly saying "have a nice day" in a robotic, scripted fashion. Surface acting can certainly also be more convincing even if the person acting is only changing their emotional display. Deep acting, on the other hand, might require a person to psyche themselves up or even convince themselves of some inner feelings in order to behave appropriately. Workers in Smithgrove County,[1] not only engaged in emotional labor, they adopted what I refer to as "tough love paternalism" that was consistent with their working-class parenting styles.

Working and lower-class parents must prepare their children for the world of rules (Bernstein & Henderson, 1969; Hochschild, 1979; Kohn, 1977; Kohn & Schooler, 1978, 1982; Komarovsky, 1967; Lareau, 2003). Unlike middle-class adults and children, lower and working-class adults more often face serious consequences for even the slightest challenge to the rules and to authority. Over time then, working and lower-class parenting, as Lareau (2003) and others before her have found (Bernstein & Henderson, 1969; Hochschild, 1979; Komarovsky, 1967), involves teaching children deference to the rules. Children need to know the real world has rules and even the slightest infraction could result in the loss of a job. When jobs, any jobs, are hard to come by and your family is already living near or in poverty, this is disastrous.

In some ways, workers see punitive aspects of welfare policy as something that can be effective, but they also recognize that sanctions can put the family at risk. Many of the workers I interviewed said they wanted to make a positive difference in the participant's life. This ideology of helping others conflicted with institutionalized ideologies of program time limits, sanctions, and the culture of poverty. These conflicting ideologies created a number of problems for workers, problems they had to solve in order to feel good about themselves and the work they did.

LOCATION

The location chosen, Smithgrove County was selected for theoretical reasons. Workers in this county faced a number of serious challenges in helping participants successfully move from welfare-to-work. At the time of the study, the county was rural, had deindustrialized, and had high rates of unemployment and poverty. It also had a high number of program participants reaching state time limits (24 months in North Carolina). Faced with these enormous challenges, I wanted to see how workers in this county implemented welfare policy.

Smithgrove County is in eastern North Carolina where the economy has centered on cotton agriculture and textile manufacturing in the second half of the 20th century. Several small cities grew from mill towns that textile manufacturers constructed when they sought cheap labor that was socially and geographically isolated (Wood, 1986). Wealthy southerners essentially invited these firms to exploit the desperately poor white farmers as mill laborers, while using already exploited African American tenant and sharecropping farmers to harvest their supply of cotton (Tomaskovic-Devey & Roscigno, 1996, 1997). This historical economic development set into motion decades of exploitation and poverty (Anderson, Schulman, & Wood, 2000; Wood, 1986). Smithgrove County's racial makeup was attractive to companies at the time and the county has remained diverse (U.S. Census Bureau, 2000).

During 2007, when I was in the field, Smithgrove County was among 200 US counties with the highest poverty and unemployment rate (Bureau of Labor Statistics, 2007). More than a quarter of Smithgrove County's population was living in poverty (more than double the NC average) and more than 9 percent were unemployed (which was much higher than the NC rate of 5.5 percent). These figures simply illustrate that residents faced tough conditions that showed little promise of improving. Work opportunities were not plentiful and most jobs that were currently filled offered very low wages. Smithgrove County and the eastern part of the state never diversified their industrial base. This lack of industrial diversity proved disastrous for the economy by 2000. When the textile and apparel industries moved further south (first to the US Deep South and then to Central America) for cheaper labor, many people in this region were left without jobs (Anderson et al., 2000). In 2007, The Bureau of Labor Statistics reported retail as the largest industry in the county and the jobs in this sector paid less than $20,000 a year.

In North Carolina, TANF funding is used to support the "Work First" program discussed in this chapter. Like many states, North Carolina instituted time limited assistance, only offering assistance for 24 consecutive months and recognizing the federal 60-month lifetime limit. Family caps were also instituted and forbid additional assistance if a program participant becomes pregnant while receiving cash assistance. Finally, North

Carolina instituted work requirements for cash assistance. Workers use sanctions to enforce rules under TANF and Work First. In North Carolina sanctions result in case closure and the loss of cash assistance for the entire family for 30 days. Once the sanction period ends, then families can reapply for assistance. Compared to other states "toughness," Soss, Schram, Vartanian, and O'Brien (2001) find North Carolina to have adopted weak parent-only sanctions (though they switched to stricter full-family sanctions in 2005), strict work requirements, a time limit shorter than the federal limit, and a family cap. Overall, North Carolina policies are in the top-third of states in terms of "toughness."

METHODS

Data collection for this case study occurred from June 2006 until June 2007. While case studies vary in the methods employed, several methods were used in this project given the numerous benefits to using multiple methods in research including that the various methods serve as a check and balance, improving the reliability and validity of the data and findings (Hammersley & Atkinson, 1985; Marshall & Rossman, 1998). First, I conducted a thorough review of the policies and procedures relevant to the area of study, including welfare history and policy documents in the United States, North Carolina, and Smithgrove County. These included training manuals from the job readiness class, performance reviews, program policy manuals, and a variety of paperwork used by workers and participants on a daily basis.

I observed, as a participant and nonparticipant observer in a number of settings. These observations included shadowing workers as if I were training, sitting in on interviews with welfare participants, and sitting in the cubicle area observing phone and face-to-face interaction between workers and welfare participants. I also went on home visits to participants' homes and attended the job readiness class, as well as "Success Staffing" meetings in which Department of Social Service (DSS) workers and their community partners (nonprofit and other government agencies who provide services) met with welfare participants who were in danger of hitting time limits.

I also conducted 19 interviews with welfare service providers including all 13 caseworkers working in the county Work First program, three line supervisors, and the program manager. I also interviewed two employees responsible for interacting primarily with organizations in the community and secondarily with participants. One of these employees was employed full time with the DSS and the other was a liaison who worked out of the county's Chamber of Commerce but half of her time and salary was dedicated to DSS (she was the only person interviewed employed part time with DSS). In addition to spending more than a day each week meeting participants at the Employment Security Commission (ESC), these community liaisons were responsible for promoting the "Work Experience" program.

My 19 respondents were all women. While I did not find variation in responses by race, the office was racially diverse. Ten workers were white and nine were African American. Three of the caseworkers had received cash assistance through the DSS before becoming workers. An additional caseworker had once received county-coordinated outplacement assistance when the local textile mill closed. Overall, they had a great deal of experience with DSS. All of the supervisors even worked with DSS prior to the implementation of 1996 welfare reform policies. At the time of the study, the program manager had been with the DSS for more than 20 years. She was also one of the few workers in this division holding a four-year degree.

All interviews were semi-structured using techniques meant to elicit rich stories (Weiss, 1994). Interviews lasted between 30 minutes to over 2 hours, averaging just over an hour. I recorded all interviews, which were transcribed immediately. Interviews covered a range of topics including questions about the division of labor, effectiveness, and legitimacy. While the quotations in the results section were responses to a variety of questions, questions concerning what types of cases the worker cares the most or least about were important in this research since they generated rich stories about workers interactions with participants.

The data were analyzed using a grounded theory approach (Charmaz, 2001, 2006; Glaser & Strauss, 1967). As I conducted interviews, I began open (or line-by-line) coding data to uncover the emergent patterns concerning discretion that were present within and across interviews. Consistent with Lofland and Lofland (1995), after initially open-coding the data (using Atlas.ti — a qualitative software program), I used analytic memos to explore themes that emerged in the interview data and the observation data. While the interviews are the focus of the analysis, I used focused coding and subsequent analytic memos to analyze themes — similarities and contradictions — in the interview and relevant observation data. I report these themes in the following sections. I mostly refer to all workers (caseworkers and supervisors) as "workers" as findings did not vary by occupation. Unfortunately,

I interacted little with participants, so what I have presented are the workers' accounts of participants and cannot validate those accounts.

BEING A GOOD WORKER TO WHOM? IDENTITY DILEMMAS AND CONFLICTING IDEOLOGIES

While workers never articulated exactly what it means to be a "good worker," they were faced with conflicting ideologies concerning how to be a "good worker" and a "helper." When I asked workers why they became welfare-to-work workers, everyone I interviewed (with only one exception) said they wanted to help people. This was an identity that was very important to them, but how did they achieve it? On one hand, workers wanted to be helpful to the participants, and they saw this as part of being a good worker. On the other hand, to be a good worker to their bosses, they had to punish participants through sanctions. These sanctions had negative real life consequences for participants. Since workers felt they had to follow the rules and sanction participants to keep their jobs, they developed ways to legitimate the necessity of sanctioning as a way to help people. In this way, sanctioning came to be viewed as a lesson, or a way to teach participants how the real world works.

In my interview with Amanda who worked for both the DSS and the Chamber of Commerce, she dreadfully described sending "the letter." "The letter" as many workers called it, is a notice to the participant that they should complete some action (a form, apply for a certain job, etc.) within 10 days or their benefits will be terminated. One of Amanda's responsibilities was to work a few days a week at the local ESC office. Participants came in to the ESC office where she talked to them about job openings posted at the ESC. However, participants rarely did come in to see Amanda, and there did not appear to be a formal mechanism through which interaction between Amanda and participants was fostered.

Amanda went through all open jobs listed at the ESC and then matched Work First participants to the jobs. The participant received a notice from Amanda, not their worker, to apply for the job. If, after several days, the participant did not apply to the job through the ESC, Amanda sent them "the 10-day letter" stating the participant must comply with the request (in this case, apply for the job) within 10 days or have their benefits terminated. Amanda commented that people often called her upset once they received the letter. She stated they did not know who she was and that it was a challenge, but she "... makes sure by the end of the conversation they know that it was their responsibility to follow the rules." As she said this, she was visibly affected by these conversations. Her eyes watered and her hand and voice shook. This is a substantial change in her prior polished, extremely cheerful demeanor.

The participants' confusion over not having had any prior interaction with Amanda certainly made these interactions more difficult. Amanda's motivations for working with the DSS and wanting to help others also matter. Amanda was a teacher for many years but left because she felt she could not make a difference given the many constraints in our education system. Additionally, she was working as a teacher in a county with few resources and, as she told me, all three high schools were sanctioned due to failure to meet "no child left behind" requirements. Without being explicit about how, many times during the interview she noted always wanting to help people and make a difference. She said she was always that way as a teacher and felt constrained. She felt she could make a difference in her new job. Her job now is to sanction welfare participants for failing to comply with the rules, actions that seem in opposition to her motivations for taking her job. In fact, I would argue the punitive policies of welfare reform mirror the punitive educational policies of "no child left behind."

While Amanda has these conversations over the phone, workers often had them face-to-face. Carol, a supervisor, often characterized workers as "tender" which meant that they cared about their participants and doing their jobs well, but that sanctioning was particularly difficult. She also noted the ways in which it is difficult, saying:

> I think they get frustrated when someone just does not want to do. But I think on the other hand, some of them, because of the face-to-face, it hurts their feelings when they have to either sanction or terminate someone's case.

This face-to-face interaction or telephone interaction was emotionally difficult for workers and participants in several ways. Workers had to explain a seemingly endless number of rules to participants who were frustrated in trying to keep up with everything. The rules did not always seem fair to the workers or the participants. Regardless, workers said that the rules are the rules and they must be followed. Additionally, workers had to punish the participants through direct interactions (vs. a letter) that were over the phone or even worse, in person. This added to the emotional toll of the job.

Despite workers' frustration with the rules and sanctioning, almost all commented on how useful they felt sanctions were. This focus on the effectiveness of sanctions at first seems counter-intuitive, but it was not surprising given the pressure on workers to sanction. Workers redefined the act of sanctioning as a way to help participants. To the workers, sanctioning became the most effective way to get participants to follow the rules. Supervisors encouraged the workers to approach the participants with a disciplinarian attitude. Sarah, a supervisor, echoed other supervisors when she said:

> We really enforce that, at least going to the level of sanctions. [Workers] need to do what they are supposed to do. They need to go back in and just get over that. [Participants] need to know they are required to do these activities in order to get their check and if they are not going to do it, then they will be sanctioned. And if they do not step up, then they go to just Medicaid and in a month or two later can be back on [cash assistance].

Carol, another supervisor, added that workers must sanction to keep their job. Carol spoke at some detail that they relayed this to the participants as well, saying she tells participants, "state policy requires [the worker] to do this action and she would not be doing her job if she did not take this action." Supervisors relay to the participants that the worker was just following the policy and the rules. This served several purposes: it enforced workers sanctioning participants; it showed participants that workers also had rules to follow (thereby normalizing rule following); and it was an attempt to depersonalize the act of sanctioning (in a "just doing my job" way).

According to workers, it was common for participants "to fail to do" or not follow the rules. Workers needed to be prepared for that and they needed to withhold checks, sometimes for several months, to punish participants for not following the rules. Given the intensely punitive nature of welfare reform and given the dilemmas, conflicting ideologies, and contradictions in their work, how did workers negotiate their good worker identity? This is the focus of the following section.

EMOTION MANAGEMENT AND THE DIRTY WORK OF WELFARE REFORM

Workers in Smithgrove County engaged in emotional labor (Hochschild, 1979, 1983), specifically they did deep acting. To do this deep acting required a lot of work, but given the serious challenges to workers feeling like helpers and good workers, it was work they had to do. Workers used two main strategies to redefine the situation in a way that helped them suppress negative feelings and feel positive emotions. In order to feel positively about their actions, workers used language (including labeling those who do and don't do which I discuss below) to neutralize their behavior. Second, workers redefined themselves using tough love paternalism to help them feel like good workers, but also like good people.

Institutionalized Rhetoric: Those Who "Do" and Those Who "Don't Do"

Participant success depended on a number of factors, including the cooperation of both workers and participants. However, the burden was clearly placed on the participants. As such, workers sorted participants and labeled them as those who wanted help and those who did not. In Smithgrove County, the workers said specifically that there are those who "do" and those who "don't do." By "do," they meant do what you are supposed to do and follow the rules. The threat of sanctions kept participants on the "do" path. According to workers, those who were sanctioned either learned from it or they never really wanted help to begin with, thereby blaming the victim. Workers then were able to define sanctions as helpful, and this definition allowed the workers to see themselves as good workers. The strategy of sorting participants allowed workers to cast their behavior as objective or neutral, and it absolved them from the negative consequences of their actions (Sykes & Matza, 1957). This neutralizing was necessary for them to recreate sanctions as helpful and to solve their identity dilemma around being both a good worker and a good person.

Language is a powerful tool individuals use to neutralize their behavior (Scott & Lyman, 1968; Scully & Marolla, 1984; Snow & Anderson, 1987). Further, language can also be used in ways that help individual's form positive self-evaluations through interaction (Schwalbe, 1983; Schwalbe & Mason-Schrock, 1996; Schwalbe et al., 2000). For workers, institutionalized rhetoric was very important to feel good about sorting participants into categories of deserving (those who do) and undeserving (those who don't do). The institutionalized rhetoric legitimated and justified the workers' actions. The institutionalized ideology and rhetoric also helped the worker form a strong commitment to their group of coworkers who shared the same concepts and language and had stakes in feeling good about their work. This group commitment served as a constant reinforcement and source of support that sanctioning participants and following the rules was necessary. All of the workers were in this together – they had to use the punitive rules in ways that supported the team: the county.

The workers had the responsibility to punish participants deemed to be irresponsible. Using the language of "mutual responsibility" and the complementary "refusing to participate" allowed the workers to neutralize their own accountability and to blame the consequences of rule breaking on the participants (Godwin, 2004 finds this same technique used by parents with "troubled teens"). For instance, as Angela, a worker explained:

> If they don't do what they are supposed to, then we have to take their check away until they participate. And we do have some that will do very well. Some are making very good. And I have a lot that do not want to do anything and do not believe their check will be cut off.

Using the language of the participant choosing to participate helped the workers to feel that any negative consequence of sanctioning was really the participant's choice. Also note that the worker began by referring to the participants as "they" and "some," but eventually did not even refer to the participants directly saying she had "a lot" that did not want to do anything. In a way, she had taken the humanity from the participants. In our entire interview and in conversations, she rarely referred to the participants as participants in an individual sense. Her language referred to participants as a group or quantity.

Not following the rules meant the participant was falling into the category of "not doing," so the workers needed to remind the participant of their responsibility to follow the rules. If the participant did not respond, then the worker would "help" the participant by threatening to sanction them through the "10-day letter" or by sanctioning them if the participant did not comply with the request in the letter. As one worker, Julie, said, "You know [be]cause some people, you just got to, you got to be firm with. They just don't understand it any other way, you know." The workers said they hoped this would teach the participant about the consequences of not following rules in the "real world." Kathy discussed the effectiveness of sanctions saying:

> Unfortunately, sanctions have been one of our most effective ... because if you fail to do, then you will not get a check. And most of the time that does work, which is unfortunate, but that is the way it is.

Workers defined this punishment with institutionalized and seemingly less emotionally driven terminology. For instance, after the above quote, I responded, "a little negative reinforcement to get people to ..." and Kathy interrupted and corrected my terminology saying, "yep, monitoring. Uh hum." Kathy clearly preferred to say "monitoring," a much more legitimate term for something a government official would do. Saying "negative reinforcement" obviously called attention to the punishment in the action and places some responsibility (perhaps in the form of judgment) on the worker. The workers preferred officially to "monitor" as if that allowed them to detach from the process they help to recreate. Workers did not want to be perceived as judging the participants. They wanted to maintain an ideal of objectivity. As Julie, a worker, said,

> ... you know I don't look at it like I am better than them or anything, you know. It's a fact that we are all people. I'm not here to judge. God will do that. Let him do that. I'm here to do my job and my job is to help people.

Despite this resistance to being perceived as judgmental, workers had to judge participants if they wanted to keep their jobs. To judge participants they adopted the language of those who do and don't do as sort of a watered down version of the deserving and non-deserving poor. In this legitimating language it was not about what the participant deserves, it was about the participant *choosing* to follow rules. Recall that workers said participants "refuse to participate." Therefore, monitoring was important based on many of the workers' orientations toward participants. They often referred to participants as "multigenerational" meaning their mothers and perhaps even grandmothers had been on welfare. For some DSS workers this meant they unfortunately "were not taught the things you and I were taught," according to Amanda, the person who works as a liaison between the business community (through the Chamber of Commerce) and Work First. For others, like Kathy, this meant participants needed "retraining and rethinking" because some participants were unmotivated. Regardless of whether the worker blatantly described participants as lazy or used more subtle ways to describe them as value-deficient, most workers echoed some version of a "culture of poverty" orientation toward participants fused with institutionalized rhetoric to help them justify their actions.

Tough Love Paternalism

A second technique comes from workers' view that sanctioning was a way to teach participants about how the "real world" operates. Helping participants had less to do with assisting participants in finding jobs than teaching them that the real world has rules and low-wage workers need to follow the rules if they want to keep their jobs. Workers enacted "tough love" paternalism that was influenced by and reinforced class inequality.

The workers needed to feel like their work helped participants. They wanted to be good workers, but also to be good people. To do this, given the working-class roots of the workers, they adopted a "tough love" style of parenting where the rules were the rules and they needed no explanation (Hochschild, 1979, 1983; Lareau, 2003). This tough love style was emotionally trying, and it required the workers to suppress some emotions while expressing others. Workers needed to be tough "for" the participants. While this did not fit with so-called traditional notions of white middle-class motherhood, it did fit the workers' notions of motherhood.

While I never asked workers about their family lives, over the course of my time in the field I overheard or had a number of conversations with workers about getting children dressed and clean and getting children and husbands fed. For instance, one worker, in the midst of juggling a number of tasks, stopped suddenly to make a phone call. She had remembered that it was Wednesday night, commonly a night Southern Baptists have church services, and she had to go to church. She had prepared dinner for her husband and stepchildren in advance, but needed to call her husband with instructions on how to heat the dinner up in the microwave. This act was simply taken in stride as a mother[2] and wife's duty, getting your family fed even if you are not at home to serve the meal. Like many working women, these women left a difficult and stressful job to go home to a second shift of making dinner, cleaning house, and childcare. Some workers even did this work for grandchildren as their children went off to work second shift paid jobs.

One of the implications of workers balancing work and family is that they expect participants to be able to do the same. They often take on a "if I can do it, they can do it" attitude. In fact, several workers told me this exactly. For instance, Julie a worker who is married with children told me:

> But it's hard to justify giving a benefit to a person who is 37 years old and had two jobs in their life and worked one hour at one place and a week at the other. You know, okay. So if she gets another job she'll probably quit anyway ... . Because I'm 30 years old and I been making it somehow. What happened that you haven't been working? What were you doing before?

This worker, who had earlier told me how important it was to not be judgmental, here expressed her frustration with participants not working. After all, she seemed to say, she had to work and she made it.

The workers in Smithgrove County often evoked aspects of motherhood consistent with working-class motherhood found in prior research (Hochschild, 1979, 1983; Lareau, 2003). Additionally, being a mother was also about many things normally associated with traditional masculinity, such as being a provider. For these working-class, rural women in Smithgrove County, being a mother meant you did it all. Being a mother meant you made sacrifices so that your children got the best you could give them. Workers made this clear to me, each other, and to participants on a number of occasions. On one such occasion, the instructor of the county job readiness class described to participants what it meant to be a mother and to make sacrifices. The job readiness instructor spoke to the class about her 16-year-old son and having to provide for him. She told a story of applying to a fast food restaurant to be a biscuit maker from 5 am until 2 pm. An employee at the fast food restaurant told her she had too much education to work there. She said she wanted to cry, and did cry once she left. But she said she responded in pride "thank you Miss, have a nice day." She said she needed a job and a paycheck and it did not matter what that job was. She would make biscuits and sweep the parking lot if that was what it took. She told the students she would be proud to have a paycheck at the end of every two weeks. Then she said,

> You gotta step up to the plate and take it like a woman. You gotta be mama and woman. It's not what you want. It's what you have to do to provide.

Her words are meaningful in many ways. First, she gave the mixed gendered notion of stepping up to the plate, a sports analogy, but taking it like a woman, not a man. This captures the convergence of gendered expectations of being a mother, but also a provider. Being a mama and a woman means you take any job you can take to provide. Further, the underlying notion was that women were to provide. This was echoed by workers who said on numerous occasions to me and to participants that women should not count on a man (something that every worker and supervisor told me in these words at least once) to provide for their family. Women needed to put themselves in a position to provide if they could even if it meant sacrifice, such as taking a job one might think is beneath them, or not doing what you want, but what you need to do in order to provide.

On the one hand, workers expected their participants to be competent as the primary caregiver and provider in their households, but they also took a very paternalistic approach with participants. Often workers seemed to treat participants as wayward children and "mothered" them. Mothers reproduce class inequality, but they have to prepare their children for the world, even if it is the low-wage work world. Workers insisted that some participants' mothers have not taught them appropriate values, suggesting they see "value teaching" as work done by mothers. For instance,

Angela described the situation as she tells me that Supplemental Security Income (SSI) is

> ... welfare for people who have never worked. And there are a few honest to God good reasons that people get that, but if you've got momma and grandma getting a SSI check of $600 a month, an 18 year old daughter has got a baby and she's only getting $100 to $236. She [the daughter/participant] has not had the backbone in the household, the ethics of getting out and working and earning your own money. So sometimes we're the first time they ever heard that. There is pride working. There is pride in earning your paycheck.

According to workers, mothers were supposed to teach their children this. There was pride in working and in earning your *own* money and therefore not being welfare dependent. Mothers should be tough because problems arise when children have "not had the backbone in the family." Finally, it was an ethic, a moral issue, to want to get out and work. Mothers must teach this morality, these ethics.

Some DSS workers even described this moral teaching as nurturance. Amanda went out of her way in talking to me to describe how "we" (she and I) had been "afforded" many things that participants did not get. She said that, for instance, we had been taught at home the importance of education. She said a lot of people had not had that same "nurturance in the home." Unlike many of the workers, Amanda came from a middle-class background. She saw herself as different from the participants and distanced herself from them through her comments to me. On the one hand, she attempted to be empathetic and noted that she and I have privilege, which we do. In this regard she made attempts to bond with me through recognizing our commonalities in race, gender, and class. On the other hand, her well-intended words reinforced the culture of poverty ideology that poor mothers are failures. Beyond this, she reinforced traditional white middle-class femininity by associating teaching values with mothering. Perhaps this is not surprising given her former job as a teacher.

Additionally, workers negotiated the potentially problematic act of infantilizing participants by focusing on what they perceive as the participants' dependence on them for help. Well into our interview, one worker began talking about a participant as if she were a baby learning to walk. The exchange follows:

> Worker: Sometimes you have to make them feel like, you know, "I'm not here to tell you what to do. I'm here to sit with you on the things I do to help you through. You know I'll hold your hand as long as you need me to hold your hand, but when I start letting go of your hand you need to try and take a few steps on your own, but I'll always be here you know in case you need to call back."

Interviewer: Ever feel kind of like a mother to participants?

Worker: Yes. You have some that call you every day, two or three times a day wanting you to, umm, tell them what to do.

It is likely she would say this openly to a participant because she did not see the harm in comparing an adult participant's entry into the labor force with a baby taking its first steps. Even more, she said that the participant was dependent on her for help, but that she had to eventually break that dependence. Implicit in her comment was that she does enjoy the participant's momentary dependence. In fact, workers are very much dependent on participants, though the interdependence was clearly unequal. Without participants, workers would not have their jobs. Further, they got a sense of gratification from the participants' dependence, a sense that they were helping them out. Later in the interview, this same worker described a success story in which a participant got a job and then the worker called the case "my baby."

After the worker's initial response using the baby walking metaphor, I asked her if she ever felt like a mother to the participants. Her response again shows the gratitude and rewards workers gain from participants' dependence. The worker said that participants call two or three times a day because they want workers to tell them what to do. Again, this makes the worker feel needed and it is a signifier to workers that this is a participant who wants to "do." However, at the very same time, the participant's display of dependence justifies the worker's paternalistic and infantilizing behavior toward the participant. In other words, to these workers, participants are incapable of making their own decisions or judgments. They needed workers to tell them what to do.

DISCUSSION: TOUGH LOVE, EMOTION WORK, AND BEING A GOOD WORKER

While this study builds on the general research on work and emotion management and specifically on the research on emotions in service work, some findings differed from prior research. For instance, Limoncelli (2002) in her study of Work First trainings in California found that job service trainers worked hard to strip participants of their identity as good mothers and to replace it with a "universal worker" identity. Job readiness trainers urged participants not to focus on the self-esteem they gained from being good mothers, even to the point of arguing to the mothers that children are a lot of trouble. Given this, they argued the participants should learn the value of a hard day's work (as if being a good mother was not a hard day's work). In my setting, workers and the job readiness instructor urge participants to do it all. They had to provide for their family and in many cases be the only provider, but they also had to be good mothers who nurtured their children and prepared them for a world of low-wage or working-class work.

In many ways, the attempt to balance work and family is similar to what Hays (1997; see also Blair-Loy, 2003; Williams, 2000 for similar arguments) describes as "intensive mothering," but with one strong distinction. Intensive mothering involves not just the stress of balancing work and family, but also retaining and reinforcing femininity through what Hays describes as the "cultural contradictions of motherhood." According to Hays, women are required to be competitive in the workplace while also doing the second shift of housework at home. Even further though, women must do the "third shift" (Hochschild, 1997) and provide emotional support for their family.

While this is likely common for most mothers, Lareau (2003) finds some distinctions between middle-class mothers and working and lower-class mothers. Middle-class parents use what she calls the "logic of concerted cultivation" where parents (mostly mothers) do emotion and nurturing work to cultivate their children's talents. An unintended consequence of this mothering work is that middle-class children learn a sense of entitlement and communication skills that they use to question authority and institutions. This contrasts sharply with working and lower-class mothering, which Lareau (2003) calls "an assumption of natural growth." In these families, children are not intensely nurtured or cultivated. Children instead live in a world of freedom in their play lives and learn about constraint and what they cannot have or afford. Children learn to distrust institutions and not to challenge authority, just like their parents. Lareau (2003) argues that through these parenting strategies, the unfortunate and unintended outcome is the "transmission of differential advantages." In this way, it seems the middle-class parenting style is more consistent with Hays's (1997) intensive mothering, while the working-class mothers parent differently. As I have shown, workers in my study did some aspects of intensive mothering. Like many mothers, they worried about their children and being a good mother. The workers suggested that working is a way in which they sacrifice for their children, which is consistent with intensive mothering. Finally, the workers argue that since they did it all, they expected participants to do the same.

However, cultivating hidden talents was not crucial or feasible, given the conditions and environment in which these mothers – workers and participants – parent (see Kohn, 1977; Kohn & Schooler, 1978, 1982 for a discussion of social class and the reciprocal effects of job conditions and personality). Workers and participants must prepare their children for the world of rules. Goffman (1979) argues that we learn much about how to treat others through the parent–child relationship. Parents are often the main authority figure enforcing behavior as we grow up. Therefore, we learn from our parents how to treat subordinate others. As adults, we behave in a paternalistic way and infantilize those who seem as if they cannot take care of themselves, no matter how true this perception is. In Smithgrove County, workers often treated adult participants like children and justified this treatment by evoking the working-class ideas of "tough love" paternalism. This helped the workers' negotiate their good worker identities by drawing on their existing class beliefs about appropriate motherhood, as well as drawing on a history of paternalistic practices in a mill town.

Mill towns in the southeast were created by textile manufacturers. In an effort to support workers, all the while controlling them, textile manufacturers built houses, schools, churches, and whole towns, really, to concentrate former rural farm laborers around the cotton mills (Hall et al., 2000; Pope, 1965). Support and protection were exchanged for deference and hard work. Many of the workers in Smithgrove County are accustomed to mill paternalism. In this way, this historical practice provided a readily acceptable cultural script for workers: they were not trying to control participants; they were trying to help them. When workers combine mill paternalism with their "tough love" working-class parenting practices, the environment is ripe for the reproduction of class inequality or as Lareau (2003) termed it, the transmission of differential advantages.

CONCLUSIONS: SANCTIONING EQUALS HELPING

Throughout this chapter I have mentioned several times that workers said sanctions were effective or helpful, but they failed to provide any evidence of these claims. Instead, they relied on institutionalized rhetoric that neutralized their actions and tough love paternalism that helped them create the reality that sanctions were helping participants. Workers did not keep statistics on sanctioning success. They did not even tell stories of when they sanctioned someone and that turned the person around. In fact, they gave no evidence whatsoever that sanctioning participants actually was effective or helpful in assisting the participants in any way, much less to help them reach self-sufficiency. But in this sense, it did not have to be logical or empirically proven. They just need to believe it. Workers needed to believe that punishing the participants works just like punishing a child.

In fact, workers did worry too much about the contradictory logic they used in saying some participants do and others don't do. In many ways, sorting in this way put blame on the participant. More importantly though, workers' sorted participants in a way that essentialized the participant's noncompliance. This made it seem as if it was inherent that some participants "naturally" will not follow the rules. However, for sanctions to work, then people needed to be able to change, meaning they cannot be inherently or essentially someone who will not do. The workers argued they were not responsible for participants' failures. The worker told participants the rules as her end of the mutual responsibility agreement. The participant needed to hold up her end and "participate." Workers did not invent the wheel. They just turned it like they are supposed to. They were doing their jobs and participants needed to do theirs. Sometimes they needed to be threatened with the consequences of not following the rules. Sometimes they needed to be punished to learn their lesson. This was how the real world worked for the workers, and it was this version of the real world they enforced on the participants. Workers had to believe in the system if they were to do their job, which was doing the dirty work of welfare reform.

Welfare-to-work program workers represented a unique opportunity to investigate worker identity and emotion work. Since these workers actively police the work and family lives of participants and negotiate their own work and family lives, this study adds an innovative lens to the convergence of work and family. This lens allows a greater understanding for the importance of emotion work, especially in jobs that require workers to engage in punitive actions. Further, the contradicting and conflicting ideology of welfare reform offers challenges for the workers, but it also provided them with the institutionalized rhetoric to cope with those challenges. Paternalistic welfare ideology combined with mill paternalism and workers' own "tough love" approaches to parenting allow the workers to neutralize punitive actions and redefine them as effective and helpful for participants.

While my study focuses on one type of service worker, some research (Maynard-Moody & Musheno, 2003) suggests that emotion management techniques found in this study – institutionalized rhetoric and tough love paternalism – might be present among other service workers including police officers, counselors, and teachers. With the new economy becoming ever so service focused, it is possible that the results of this study might apply even more broadly to other service jobs. Workers in Smithgrove County certainly managed their emotions in a way that reflected an interesting blending of work and family, however there is no reason to think these workers were very unique.

NOTES

1. All names, county and individuals, are pseudonyms.
2. Workers very rarely discussed fathers of their children or the participants' children.

REFERENCES

Anderson, C. D., Schulman, M., & Wood, P. J. (2000). Globalization and uncertainty: The restructuring of southern textiles. *Social Problems*, *48*(4), 478–498. doi:10.1525/sp.2001.48.4.478

Bernstein, B., & Henderson, D. (1969). Social class differences in the relevance of language to socialization. *Sociology*, *3*(1), 1–20. doi:10.1177/003803856900300101

Blair-Loy, M. (2003). *Competing devotions: Career and family among women executives.* Cambridge, MA: Harvard University Press.

Bureau of Labor Statistics. (2007). *Current population study.* Retrieved from http://www.bls.gov/cps/

Charmaz, K. (2001). Grounded theory. In R. M. Emerson (Ed.), *Contemporary field research: Perspectives and formulations reader* (pp. 335–352). Prospect Heights, IL: Waveland Press.

Charmaz, K. (2006). *Constructing grounded theory.* Thousand Oaks, CA: Sage.

Corcoran, M., Danziger, S. K., Kalil, A., & Seedfeldt, K. S. (2000). How welfare reform is affecting women's work. *Annual Review of Sociology*, *26*, 241–269. doi:10.1146/annurev.soc.26.1.241

Feagin, J. (2000). *Racist America: Roots, current realities, and future reparations.* New York, NY: Routledge.

Glaser, B. G., & Strauss, A. L. (1967). *The discovery of grounded theory: Strategies for qualitative research.* Chicago, IL: Aldine.

Godwin, S. E. (2004). Managing guilt: The personal responsibility rhetoric among parents of "troubled" teens. *The Sociological Quarterly*, *45*, 575–596. Retrieved from http://www.jstor.org/stable/4120864

Goffman, E. (1979). *Gender advertisements.* New York, NY: Harper & Row.

Hall, J. D., Leloudis, J., Korstad, R., Murphy, M., Jones, L., & Daly, C. B. (2000). *Like a family: The making of a southern cotton mill world.* Chapel Hill, NC: University of North Carolina Press.

Hammersley, M., & Atkinson, P. (1985). *Ethnography: Principles in practice* (2nd ed.). New York, NY: Routledge.

Handler, J., & Hasenfeld, Y. (2007). *Blame welfare, ignore poverty and inequality*. New York, NY: Cambridge University Press.

Hays, S. (1997). *The cultural contradictions of motherhood*. New Haven, CT: Yale University Press.

Hays, S. (2003). *Flat broke with children: Women in the age of welfare reform*. New York, NY: Oxford University Press.

Hochschild, A. R. (1979). Emotion work, feeling rules, and social structure. *American Journal of Sociology*, *85*(3), 551–575. Retrieved from http://www.jstor.org/stable/2778583

Hochschild, A. R. (1983). *Managed heart: Commercialization of human feeling*. Los Angeles, CA: University of California Press.

Hochschild, A. R. (1997). *The time bind: When work becomes home and home becomes work*. New York, NY: Metropolitan Books.

Kohn, M. L. (1977). *Class and conformity: A study in values* (2nd ed.). Chicago, IL: The University of Chicago Press.

Kohn, M. L., & Schooler, C. (1978). The reciprocal effects of the substantive complexity of work and intellectual flexibility: A longitudinal assessment. *American Journal of Sociology*, *84*(1), 24–52. Retrieved from http://www.jstor.org/stable/2777977

Kohn, M. L., & Schooler, C. (1982). Job conditions and personality: A longitudinal assessment of their reciprocal effects. *American Journal of Sociology*, *87*(6), 1257–1286. Retrieved from http://www.jstor.org/stable/2779361

Komarovsky, M. (1967). *Blue-collar marriage*. New York, NY: Vintage Books.

Lareau, A. (2003). *Unequal childhoods: Class, race, and family life*. Los Angeles, CA: University of California Press.

Leidner, R. (1993). *Fast food, fast talk: Service work and the routinization of everyday life*. Berkeley, CA: University of California Press.

Lerum, K. (2004). Sexuality, power, and camaraderie in service work. *Gender & Society*, *18*(6), 756–776. doi:10.1177/0891243204269398

Lewis, O. (1966). *La vida: A Puerto Rican family in the culture of poverty – San Juan and New York*. New York, NY: Random House.

Lichter, D. T., & Jayakody, R. (2002). Welfare reform: How do we measure success? *Annual Review of Sociology*, *28*, 117–141. doi:10.1146/annurev.soc.28.110601.140845

Limoncelli, S. A. (2002). "Some of us are excellent at babies": Paid work, mothering, and the construction of "need" in a welfare to work program. In F. F. Piven, J. Acker, M. Hallock, & S. Morgan (Eds.), *Work, welfare, and politics: Confronting poverty in the wake of welfare reform* (pp. 81–94). Eugene, OR: University of Oregon Press.

Lofland, J., & Lofland, L. H. (1995). *Analyzing social setting: A guide to qualitative observation and analysis*. Belmont, CA: Wadsworth.

Lopez, S. H. (2006). Emotional labor and organized emotional care. *Work and Occupations*, *33*(2), 133–160. doi:10.1177/0730888405284567

Marshall, C., & Rossman, G. B. (1998). *Designing qualitative research* (3rd ed.). Thousand Oaks, CA: Sage.

Maynard-Moody, S., & Musheno, M. (2003). *Cops, teachers, counselors: Stories from the front lines of public service*. Ann Arbor, MI: The University of Michigan Press.

Moynihan, D. (1965). *The Negro family: The case for national action*. Washington, DC: Office of Policy Planning and Research, United States Department of Labor. Retrieved from http://www.dol.gov/dol/aboutdol/history/webid-meynihan.htm

Pope, L. (1965). *Millhands and preachers: A study of Gastonia*. New Haven, CT: Yale University Press.

Quadagno, J. (1994). *The color of welfare: How racism undermined the war on poverty.* New York, NY: Oxford University Press.

Schwalbe, M. L. (1983). Language and the self: An expanded view from a symbolic interactionist perspective. *Symbolic Interaction, 6*(2), 291–306. doi:10.1525/si.1983.6.2.291

Schwalbe, M. L., Godwin, S., Holden, D., Schrock, D., Thompson, S., & Wolkomir, M. (2000). Generic processes in the reproduction in inequality: An interactionist analysis. *Social Forces, 79*(2), 419–452. doi:10.2307/2675505

Schwalbe, M. L., & Mason-Schrock, D. (1996). Identity work as group process. *Advances in Group Processes, 13,* 113–147.

Scott, M. B., & Lyman, S. (1968). Accounts. *American Sociological Review, 33*(1), 46–62. Retrieved from http://www.asanet.org/journals/asr/american_sociological_review.cfm

Scully, D., & Marolla, J. (1984). Convicted rapists' vocabulary of motive: Excuses and justifications. *Social Problems, 31*(5), 530–544. doi:10.1525/sp.1984.31.5.03a00050

Smith, A. C., & Kleinman, S. (1989). Managing emotions in medical school: Students' contacts with the living and the dead. *Social Psychology Quarterly, 52*(1), 56–69. Retrieved from http://www.jstor.org/stable/2786904

Snow, D. A., & Anderson, L. (1987). Identity work among the homeless: The verbal construction and avowal of personal identities. *American Journal of Sociology, 92*(6), 1336–1371. Retrieved from http://www.jstor.org/stable/2779840

Soss, J., Schram, S. F., Vartanian, T. P., & O'Brien, E. (2001). Setting the terms of relief: Explaining state policy choices in the devolution revolution. *American Journal of Political Science, 45*(2), 378–395. doi:10.2307/2669347

Steinberg, R. J., & Figgart, D. M. (1999). Emotional demands at work: A job content analysis. *Annals of the American Academy of Political and Social Science, 561,* 177–191. Retrieved from http://www.jstor.org/stable/1049289

Sykes, G. M., & Matza, D. (1957). Techniques of neutralization: A theory of delinquency. *American Sociological Review, 22,* 664–670. Retrieved from http://www.jstor.org/stable/2089195

Taylor, T. (2013). Paperwork first, not work first: How caseworkers use paperwork to feel effective. *Journal of Sociology and Social Welfare, 40*(1), 9–27. Retrieved from http://wmich.edu/socialwork/journal/

Taylor, T. (2014). No discretion required: How welfare-to-work rural North Carolina caseworkers respond to the rules of welfare reform. *Sociological Inquiry, 84*(3), 412–434. doi:10.1111/soin.12038

Tomaskovic-Devey, D., & Roscigno, V. J. (1996). Racial economic subordination and white gain in the US South. *American Sociological Review, 61*(4), 565–589. Retrieved from http://www.jstor.org/stable/2096394

Tomaskovic-Devey, D., & Roscigno, V. J. (1997). Uneven development and local inequality in the US South: The role of outside investment, landed elites, and racial dynamics. *Sociological Forum, 12*(4), 565–597. Retrieved from http://www.jstor.org/stable/684733

U.S. Census Bureau. (2000). *State and county quickfacts.* Retrieved from http://quickfacts.census.gov/qfd/index.html#

Weiss, R. S. (1994). *Learning from strangers: The art and method of qualitative interview studies.* New York, NY: The Free Press.

Williams, J. (2000). *Unbending gender: Why family and work conflict and what to do about it.* New York, NY: Oxford University Press.

Wood, P. J. (1986). *Capitalism: The political economy of North Carolina.* Durham, NC: Duke University Press.

WHEN WORK BECOMES FAMILY: THE CASE OF LOW-WAGE CAREGIVERS

Naomi Gerstel and Dan Clawson

ABSTRACT

Purpose — *This chapter revisits a debate about the relationship between work and family and the conditions under which workers believe their jobs in the new economy offer an escape from families.*

Methodology/approach — *In contrast to prior research, the chapter uses multiple methods, including a random sample survey, intensive interviews with 221 respondents, and 615 hours of observations at eight sites in the health care sector.*

Findings — *The chapter shows that low-wage women nursing assistants — more than those in other health care occupations — develop strong connections to coworkers and patients whom they come to talk about as "family." It finds that more than doctors, nurses, or EMTs, the CNAs seek an escape from home and a pull to people at work not only because they develop strong relations on the job and have more inclusive notions of family, but also because they face more difficulties at home. These difficulties at home are created in part by the unpredictable schedules and low wages offered by their jobs. These make home life more difficult, which paradoxically leads them to turn to their jobs.*

Research limitations/implications — *The analysis and findings show the ongoing power of unequal social relations — organized around class and gender and their intersection — in shaping the recursive relationship of jobs and families.*

Keywords: Work hours; class; gender; family; caregivers; family policy

People say the family is a haven in a heartless world. And it is the job which *is* the heartless world. This chapter reverses that understanding — showing the ways workers reject the view that their own families are havens or escapes from their jobs and instead use the metaphor of "family" to describe the positive social relations they find at the workplace.

Media pundits and political candidates often use the "family" as a metaphor to evoke widely shared images of connection and attachment. Many corporations use "the family" as metaphor to describe the workplace, as a way to appeal to workers, increase loyalty, and boost the bottom line (Gerstel, 2011). Because metaphor means "understanding one kind of thing or experience in terms of another" (Lakoff, 1992), the use of metaphor this way "not only helps make sense of activities but also structures them" (Kovecses, 2010, p. 68). It helps shape employees' expectations and relationships — both on the job and at home.

To explore this metaphorical usage of "family" and its consequences on the ground, the chapter focuses on one group of disadvantaged workers — certified nursing assistants (CNAs, almost exclusively female) — and briefly compares them to three other groups in the health care system — two advantaged, doctors (mostly male) and nurses (almost exclusively female), as well as another working class group, Emergency Medical Technicians (EMTs, also mostly male). We show that it is especially the low-wage women caregivers who talk of their relations at work, or at least some of those relations, as "family" and think of these relations as an escape from home.

This may seem something of a paradox. CNAs typically work under difficult conditions — with low wages, unpredictable hours, as well as little authority or control. Nationally, all nursing assistants working in nursing homes are at significant risk of injury: For example, in a typical year, 17.3 percent get back injuries, and another 15.6 percent get other strains or pulled muscles.[1] CNAs recognize, complain about, and sometimes protest these job conditions (Lopez, 2006; see Clawson & Gerstel, 2014, for a detailed discussion of their work conditions and complaints). As we will show, however, they also turn some of their job relations into "family" — seeking and finding connection with both coworkers and patients (or, as they are called in some nursing homes, residents). We argue that this seeming paradox can be explained at least in part by the recursive relationship between paid work and family: jobs that are difficult, unpredictable, and provide few material benefits produce stresses at home and these sometimes send workers back to the job as an escape from their homes.

The chapter examines two sets of factors that lead CNAs sometimes to choose work over staying home and to use the rhetoric of family to describe their jobs. First, these low-wage workers develop strong connections at work to both patients and coworkers, and they talk of these as "family" — referring to patients as either children or parents and coworkers as partners and siblings. Second, conditions at work increase problems at home which, in turn, sometimes lead them to turn to and value the family-like relations at work. We then briefly argue that this combination of factors does not apply, or applies with diminished force, to the other occupations we studied.

LITERATURE REVIEW

Perhaps the most common media and popular understanding of the family is as a haven, a bedrock of support in a tough world (Lasch, 1977). According to this argument if people could afford to do so, they would prefer to spend time at home — the place people look for warmth, freedom, and emotional support — rather than on the job, which is the site of strife, control, and exploitation.

In *The Time Bind*, Arlie Hochschild (1997) challenged that view, making the provocative argument that employees flee the pressures of home for the relief provided by their jobs. Hochschild reminded us that much stress and conflict, even exploitation, occurs at home while much support and personal reward occurs at the workplace. She argued that because employees look to paid work as an escape from family life, many do not take advantage of institutional policies that allow workers time off to be with their families. Based on intense observations at one corporation — a so-called "family friendly" one — Hochschild argued that such companies offer time off, but employees prefer to stay at work rather than go home.

Hochschild's book generated much controversy. Criticizing her for studying only one organization, a number of researchers used survey data of employees and found that only a small proportion said they preferred time at work to time at home (Clarkberg & Moen, 2001; Kiecolt, 2003; Maume & Bellas, 2001; Reynolds, 2005). Hochschild could reasonably respond that survey preferences likely reflect cultural expectations of what people believe they should say (Pager & Quillian, 2005); in practice people might choose to work longer hours, even while saying in a survey that they preferred shorter hours. Damaske, Smyth, and Zawadzki (2014) examined the level of the stress hormone cortisol in 122 workers and found lover levels of stress on the job than at home. In this chapter, we use multilevel data (including interviews and observations at a number of organizations) not only to argue that Hochschild was onto something important that many have rebutted but also to extend her argument by suggesting that it is often jobs that make families stressful which, in turn, leads the employees to turn back to relationships at work for a sense of connection.

Another set of research addresses this issue from a different angle, examining the relationship — or the "spillover" of moods or experiences — between home and job. Instead of insisting on their separation, numerous work-life scholars have pointed to positive and negative "spillover" with strains (Ferguson, 2012; Grzywacz, Almeida, & McDonald, 2002) or pleasures (Pedersen, Minnotte, & Mannon, 2009; Voydanoff, 2005) in one domain — whether the job or family — shaping the experience in the other. This line of research tends to assume that problems in one domain spill over to create problems or stress in another domain (negative work-to-home or home-to-work spillover) or that positive emotions in one domain spill over to create positive emotions or less stress in another domain (positive spillover in either direction) (Sandberg et al., 2013; for review, see Roehling, Moen, & Batt, 2003). We, too, argue negative experiences in one can create negative experiences in the other. But, we also examine and find that *negative* experiences in one domain can prompt *positive* emotions in another domain. That is, rather than only analyzing the transfer of the same mood from one domain to another (i.e., difficult work experiences make home life more difficult), we also analyze the ways in which people then seek greater engagement in a different setting (in this case the job) if experiences in the first setting (here the home) are unsettling or challenging.

We further specify these arguments by suggesting that workers think and talk of relations at work as family, a kind of spillover that is shaped by gender, race, and class – distinctions that Hochschild mostly ignores. First gender: On the one hand, some research suggests that mothers report they suffer more than fathers if they feel paid work does not allow them to have enough time with their husbands or children (Nomaguchi, Milkie, & Bianchi, 2005). On the other hand, Larson, Richards, and Perry-Jenkins (1994) compared the emotional states experienced by mothers and fathers during daily activities both at home and on the job by asking participants to report on these emotional states at random times on the pagers they carried. Mothers reported more positive states on the job (because they faced more burdens at home). Fathers reported more positive states in the home, "partly because they spent more of this time in personal and recreational activities and partly because they experienced more choice, even during family work" (p. 1034). Thus, we might expect that Hochshchild's argument and the spillover argument would apply to women more than men. And, as this chapter shows, it does.

Almost half of the CNAs we studied were Black or Latina; in none of the other occupations were they as much as 6 percent. For many middle class whites "the family" means primarily spouse and children. For Latina and Black women (especially those who are low wage), "family" is far more inclusive, likely to involve more contact, help, and reliance on siblings, grandparents, aunts, uncles, nieces, nephews, and cousins and even fictive kin (Gerstel, 2011; Sarkisian & Gerstel, 2012). Thus CNAs, many of whom are Black and Latina, might be particularly open to using the rhetoric of family for a wider range of relations.

What of class? We might expect that compared to less advantaged workers, those more advantaged would be more drawn to work as an escape, given the more favorable conditions they find there (Jacobs & Gerson, 2004). At the same time, we might expect the disadvantaged would face more difficult conditions not only on the job but at home which might, in turn, lead them to turn back to the workplace. Difficult job conditions, research shows, create conflicts at home (Kelly, Moen, & Tranby, 2011; Presser, 2003). Class and gender may interact: for example, low-wage women might be more likely to turn to the workplace as an escape from their homes. This accords with what Rubin (1976, pp. 159, 169) found in her study of the working class a generation ago: "For the [working class] men in such jobs, bitterness, alienation, resignation, and boredom are the defining features of the work experience. For them ... work is a requirement of life, hours to be gotten through until you can go home." In contrast, women's "attitudes toward their work are varied, but most find the work world a satisfying place – at least when compared to the world of the housewife. ... There is, perhaps, no greater testimony to the deadening and deadly quality of the tasks of the housewife than the fact that so many women find pleasure in working at jobs that by almost any definition would be called alienated labor." We ask whether the outcome Rubin describes still holds today – even as women are far less likely to be housewives.

DATA AND METHODS

Data for this chapter comes from research we conducted on the jobs and families of paid caregivers in the Northeast. In the larger study on which this chapter is based, we examined four occupations chosen to create a two by two, gender by class table: nursing assistants and nurses, EMTs, and physicians. Given limited space, we focus in this chapter on nursing assistants, with brief comparisons to the other occupations. (For more detailed discussion of methodology, see Clawson & Gerstel, 2014).

In our data and in national data, the large majority of CNAs (89 percent) are women, who are paid less (average income $21,000) than any of the other occupations we studied. The three other occupations include physicians (70 percent male, class advantaged, average income $155,640 for family physicians to $225,360 for surgeons), registered nurses (94 percent female, class advantaged, $67,720), and EMTs (73 percent male, class disadvantaged, $33,330) (U.S. Department of Labor, Bureau of Labor Statistics, 2010). According to our survey, while the majority of those in the three other occupations are married, fewer than half of CNAs are. The average age of interview respondents in all the occupations was quite close, with CNAs and nurses' median age at 38 years; physicians and EMTs at 42 years.

We studied these health care occupations for reasons both substantive and methodological. A crucial methodological advantage is that, at least in the Northeastern area where we conducted the research, employees in all of these occupations must register with the state, making it possible to draw a random sample. Health care is in some sense the prototypical industry of our time – a part of the growing service sector rather than the diminishing manufacturing sector. In 2010 health care accounted for 17.5 percent of total GDP.

The chapter uses three types of data. First, we mailed 800 surveys, to a random sample of 200 in each occupation; the overall response rate was 64.5 percent, more than 50 percent for every occupation. Second, we observed for 615 hours at eight sites, two for each of four different kinds of organizations: (1) two nursing homes, including a high end stand-alone nonprofit 200 bed facility and a less upscale 120 bed mid-range chain facility; most nursing assistants are employed in nursing homes; (2) two hospitals including an urban teaching hospital, employing over 5,000 people and a community hospital, employing about 1,000 people, both nonprofit. Within each hospital, we observed both an emergency floor and a medical floor. Hospitals do employ nursing assistants but they are outnumbered by nurses in these settings; (3) two doctors' offices, including a family practitioner and a specialist surgical practice, where doctors, nurses, as well some nursing assistants are employed; (4) two EMS centers, including a public fire station and a private for-profit company – the only site employing only one of our occupational groups (the EMTs). Field notes for each visit were recorded during and completed following each observation. We developed and used a coding scheme with a focus on paid work, family, and time and then coded field notes using NVivo8.

Third, we did intensive face-to-face interviews with 221 people, three-quarters with direct-care providers (distributed across the four occupations; about one-quarter of them survey respondents) and one-quarter with others who shape hours and schedules in these occupations (including administrators, schedulers, human resources personnel, and union reps). This produced a total of 53 interviews with CNAs (3 men and 50 women), 50 with doctors (11 of whom were women), 84 with nurses (12 of whom were men), and 30 with EMTs (nine of whom were women). Averaging well over an hour, interviews included questions about the number, timing, policies, preferences, and feelings concerning paid and unpaid work hours as well as the character and quality of their relationships in what we have come to call a "web of time" – including administrators and supervisors, patients and coworkers as well as partners, children and extended family members. We transcribed all interviews, developed a coding scheme covering relevant work and family themes (including the number of times they spoke of work as "family") and used NVivo8 to code them.

Note two data limitations. First, given the number of interviews, we do not focus on variations within each occupation, for example, nursing assistants working in hospitals versus nursing homes, although we note that nursing assistants in nursing homes were more likely to talk about attachment to residents (probably because patients stay considerably longer in nursing homes). Second, our ability to systematically analyze and compare the off-gender cases in each occupation (i.e., male nursing assistants) is hindered by data and space limitations.

ANALYSIS

Family as Metaphor and Work as Escape: Nursing Assistants and Patients

To explore the Hochschild argument, we asked: "Some people tell us that they use work as a way to get away from their families. Do you ever feel that way?" The response was overwhelming: Seventy-seven percent of the CNAs agreed. And this view of work as an escape also spontaneously came up often among CNAs – 40 percent of them brought it up in other parts of their interviews when we were not asking direct questions about it (compare this to 7 percent for male doctors, 19 percent for male EMTs, and 25 percent for female nurses – a difference to which the latter part of the chapter will return).

The CNAs use the metaphor of family to describe the residents they care for and invoke these relationships as an explanation for why they might want to escape their "real" family. Adriana, a Latina CNA, muses about the residents: "They're my babies – my people. I would do anything for them." Adriana then compares their relations to her "real" family: "You come there every day and you see them, some of them they get so happy when they see you, you be like, 'Okay, not even my momma gets so happy when she sees me [laughs].'" Sofia, another Latina assistant, only 25 years old, who is a single mother with a young child at home, seems wise for her age: "When they [residents] end up leavin', if they goin' back home, trust me, you're gonna miss them. You be like, 'Oh, ok, I miss this person,' you get like attach, I get attach."

For these women, the meaning of family they find with residents comes not only from giving much needed care but also from gaining appreciation, sometimes from those who come from very different walks of life. Tasha, a Latina single mother with two young children, said "We're not strangers, we're the people that take care of them." Not only did she say, "We're like their family," she continued by saying: "they're my family." What did she mean? She tells us she could talk to them: "you wanna know, I love to talk to them." She also told us that she admires and learns from them: "I learn so much from these elderly people, it's not even funny. I know what they used to do. I love to ask all that. So, that's something I always do." Although her job sometimes makes that hard and the nursing home seems not to value these social relations formed on their job, the CNAs do:

> Sometimes, you don't have the time. Nah, everybody, not going really by the books, sometimes, but yeah, I love to communicate with the residents and talk to them. Even

Jerry [a resident she cared for], I sit there and ask him how he was a lawyer. And you know, you learn a lot from them, from talking to them and asking about their lives.

This thinking even leads them to contrast their jobs favorably to those earning much higher wages. For example, Rodolfo, a Latino, one of the few male CNAs, first emphasizes: "This is not an easy job. I don't care what anybody tells you, we have a lot to do as aides. A lot. Dealin' with a lot of people. A lot of your time is sacrificed doin' this stuff, you know. And, uh, there's a lot of times even when people are passin' away, you're there talkin' to 'em right when they go." Then he went on to favorably contrast his job as a CNA to that of physicians because he felt like he and the patients are like "family." As he put it, "Doctors might be the ones who, like, go in there and fix everything, but, we're family to these people. We spend more time with 'em, we're family. We treat them like family." What did Rodolfo mean by "family"? What he means is that residents confide in him: "Like, I have people talk to me about things that they probably never told anybody else. But because they confide in me and things like that, just sit there and listen to 'em ... it's, it's an experience for both." And he added: "They argue with us, just like a family member does." Though in his early forties, he recounts how these cross-class relations socialize him, teaching him about a world to which he would not otherwise have access:

> I'm learning because I'm still young ... I'm still learning about, you know, everything they've gone through and I'm like wow, it's amazing. It's, like I said, we're their family. I remember them, like, a resident who talked to me about her whole life story. And, when she passed away, I knew who she was. I mean, she told me everything. How she was born, how she came from Italy. How she heard her father and mother had nothing, and owned a small piece of land which grew ... and now today, the land is actually, uh, Mountain Community College. You know? (laughs)

He concludes with an affectionate phrase often used in old-fashioned affairs of the heart: "She was just a sweetheart." The paradox is that some used these metaphorical families to contrast with their "real" families – with whom they have little relaxed time. Constantly using the colloquial phrase "you know" – which implies (and promotes) a shared understanding, he went on: "You know, I spend more time with these people than I do with my own children. You know, I'd be lucky to spend eight hours with my kids."

Although facing high death rates among those they care for, these CNAs do not develop, and don't think they should, the kind of "detached concern" that Lieff and Fox (1963) thought so important for doctors who see so much death and dying. We saw staff cry about residents. CNAs come in on their days off to check on residents.[2] Sometimes the CNAs will say "We're just ass-wipers, that's all we are" but on the other hand it is a job they can and do feel good about, taking care of human beings that matter to them. When asked "So why did you like it here?" a White married CNA responded: "I dunno. I like the people. I love the residents. I mean, the residents ... they're just ... they're like family. You know?" As others have noted, employers can pay them low wages not only because hands-on care work is generally devalued but also because personal relations with residents can substitute for financial compensation (Dodson & Zincavage, 2007; Folbre, 2012). One Black CNA sounded a common theme: "When I first became a CNA, they always told us don't get too attached to the residents. But I was talkin' to a nurse last night, and I'm like, how you not get attached to them? ... . I love these residents."

Coworkers as Family

Not only did the residents become at-work family, so did coworkers. Speaking of her coworkers, Linda — a White CAN — says: "Pretty much it's more like a family sort of thing, you know, we're all together." Explicitly contrasting "the family" she finds with coworkers to "the family" she finds at home, a Black CNA says: "what I think about my coworkers, more of a family, because we spend more hours with them than even our families."

Turning coworkers into family appears to be associated with particular structural conditions CNAs encounter on the job. Time of shift matters: Some tell us there is more companionship on the night shift when fewer managers, supervisors, or residents' "real" family members are around. Compared to the more hectic day shift, there is also more down time on the night shift which allows personal relations among coworkers to develop. While most patients were asleep, we observed CNAs sharing details about their personal lives. Some say particular floors, and not others, become like family: "With the girls on the Baker unit on 3 to 11, we all know pretty much everything about everyone in everyone's family. We seem more like we are a family." They usually use "family" to refer to coworkers at roughly the same level, not to supervisors or bosses (although bosses might use it to refer to subordinates). Organizational context further shapes these ties: the CNAs are more likely to form ties with coworkers when they work in nursing homes than when they work in hospitals, perhaps because the nursing homes provide a considerably larger pool of nursing assistants to draw from. Multiyear stays characteristic of residents of nursing homes (more than other health settings) give them time to build relationships. Nested within these characteristics, many particular alliances among coworkers seem simply based on personality and personal attraction. Whatever the structural and personal forces shaping them, these relations with coworkers are important substitutes or supplements for the relationships they find at home.

Escaping the Family
In addition to the attractions of patients and coworkers, CNAs talk about the other side — the stress they face *at home* that leads them to turn to their jobs. In part, that stress comes from the low wages they make which makes their home lives difficult. Many are single mothers (itself associated with low wages) and if they have partners, those partners are often either unemployed or also earn very low wages. Barbara, a nursing home scheduler, notes "I've had people in here when we have a heat wave — everybody shows up. ... Whether they don't have air conditioning at home ... ."

CNAs offer a number of explanations for why they see work as an escape from home. Some emphasize the comforts of paid work and, in doing so, contrast it to their homes. A married Black CNA who earned $25,000 a year uses the evocative image of a tasty dessert to contrast her job to her less appealing home. This nursing assistant, whom we interviewed in her apartment, spoke evocatively of her job as an "ice cream cone," reporting "I feel better when I'm at work. I feel, you know how some people, they drown theirself in the bottle because sometimes they'd be so miserable and unhappy? That's me. To me at work is ... it's like a big old ice cream cone." We asked "Because?" and her answer: "Sometimes I just don't want to be here" as she motioned around her dark apartment.

These CNAs also talk of their paid work relationships in terms of time: although their jobs sometimes make it difficult to spend predictable time with their "real" families, they spend a lot of time with coworkers and residents and that turns them into "family." Explicitly contrasting "the family" she finds with coworkers to "the family" she finds at home, a Black CNA says: "what I think about my coworkers, more of a family, because we spend more hours with them than even our families. Because by the time you know, that I work seven to three, by the time I go home, I'm tired, I want to rest. You don't even have much time for your family." Job hours can reduce involvement at home, in part because it creates exhaustion there, which in turn make people at work more attractive.

More often, CNAs talk of the emotional void or burdens they encounter at home – also in part a product of their difficulties on the job. They volunteer for that suddenly available extra shift (as so many do) not just because they need the money, but because relations at work offer relief from those at home – which ironically become difficult because of job conditions, whether low wages or unpredictable time over which they have little control. A number of those who speak in these terms are single mothers who emphasize the dreariness they face at home as an explanation for the pull of the job. One unmarried Puerto Rican mom with two children under 12 points to her small, crowded apartment, "I really, you see my apartment, it's very lonely here, it is very lonely" (which she does not feel about her job). Some single mothers highlight their appreciation for the distraction from the stresses of home that work can provide – as does this 21-year-old Latina CNA who earns less than $20,000 a year:

> Like any other person at the house, sometimes you need to get away and I feel like, you know, when I work, you're just busy on working so you don't focus on whatever's going at home or whatever problem you have, you don't focus on it, you're focusing at your job. That's the reason why I like to work because your mind is off of things that you're so worried about at home.

A Black single mother says she would cut back on her hours if she could, "if money wasn't an issue," so she could have more time with her children. The unpredictable shifts that their employers suddenly offer makes it difficult to raise her kids the way she would like. But after talking about the stresses of home, she quickly switches to focus on escaping home for the draw of her job: "I still would pick up [extra hours], because you need that adult environment, you know. Because when you're around your kids all the time, sometimes you do get a little stressed out. ... you just need that outlet to get out, or either – you know, even when you come to work and it's a little stressful at times, you're around other adults, so it passes by a little better." This single mother concludes, capturing what so many tell us even while expressing confusion about its legitimacy: "I don't know if it makes any sense ... Work as an escape."

A Black single mother is particularly emphatic about the stress of children as a cause of her draw to work. She cut short her sick leave because of that draw:

> Q: So for a fractured ankle and a broken toe you missed a week? Only a week?
>
> R: Yeah, I should have been out longer, but sometimes it's depressing when you're at home. You know when you're home you should be homely, and it's like it's not ... . It's like everybody's yelling at me, everybody's wanting things done; it's more peaceful if I

go into work. Do you ever feel that way sometimes? Because sometimes when I'm here [interview took place in her apartment] on my days off it's like everything is just caving in, and when I'm at work I feel that peace.

How did these low-wage single mothers take care of their families, especially their children, given their unpredictable hours and need to volunteer for extra shifts? They have to rely on a number of different types and combinations of child care – itself a stressful experience. They cannot afford the flexible support of nannies, stay-at-home partners, or often even the kind of day care centers we found among the more advantaged. A limited subset of CNAs – those who worked the day shift and had public vouchers – do rely on day care centers as the first option. Day care centers, however, were unavailable on the every-other-weekend schedule that most CNAs must work, and they are unavailable when a CNA unexpectedly picks up an evening or night shift. In some cases the children's father provided care, whether or not the mother and father were still together. More than any of the other occupational groups, however, the CNAs depended on extended kin. Three-quarters of the CNAs rely on their (non-spouse) relatives – their mothers, sisters, brothers, cousins, aunts – for an important fraction of their child care. These kin help make it possible to pick up more (and unpredictable) extra work shifts. These extended families often not only provide important support but also add extra work and tension in a system that depends on reciprocity (Gerstel & Clawson, 2014). At the same time, reliance on these kin indicates and depends on their inclusive notion of family – which they then apply to people at work.

When we began examining CNAs' talk of escaping their homes to go to their jobs, we hypothesized it was because so many were single mothers. Further analysis proved us wrong. The *married* CNAs also emphasized the pull of the job as an escape from the home. Shalamar, a Black CNA, mentions both her nagging husband and teenage son: "Sometimes my husband, he been nagging me. And my son will be giving me a lot of talking; I just want to get out. Sometimes, I enjoy going to work." Sally, a White CNA, also emphasizes her escape from her teenager and husband:

> Q: Sometimes people tell us that they use work as a way to get away from their families. Have you ever felt that way?
>
> R: Oh, sometimes I feel like that, especially with teenagers. Definitely. Sometimes it's nice just to go to work. Definitely.
>
> Q: Tell me more.
>
> R: Ohh, I think, too, when we go to work, we can just vent with our friends and it makes you feel better, and makes things easier to adjust to at home. Sometimes when

> I'm aggravated with my husband, I can't wait to get outta there! Cause I think if I stayed home, I'd be nitpicking more and arguing more, so it's better that I just leave for 8 hours.

Other married women emphasize escaping from their husbands. Melissa, a Black CNA whose two children are grown, holds two full time jobs and remarks: "Even though me and my husband don't see each other, so we can get along better that way [laughs]." Nancy, a White married CNA with grown children, first denies the pull of work, but changes her mind in the middle of a sentence:

> Q: Sometimes people have told us that they go to work as a way to get away from their families.
>
> R: Really?
>
> Q: Is that anything that, I mean sometimes ...
>
> R: No, no, I never. That's never crossed my mind [laughs] except for now, that my husband is, you know, his back operation and everything, and he's always sittin' in that kitchen saying, "Ohh, ohh." [laughs]

Like single mothers, the married mothers also talk of their teenagers as the reason for conflict at home. Ana is a young married Latina with one teenage child. She emphasizes the loneliness she feels at home and the companionship she finds with residents: "I am always home by myself, and my son. So, it is stressing, it gets depressing when you just doing nothing. So, I just wanna work." Again, we probe: "But it definitely feels sometimes like you'd rather be there than here [the apartment where the interview took place]?" And she continues with the same line of thought: "Yeah, but because it's like, sometimes you're stressed and if you stay in the house, it gets more stressing. So, but when you're working like the residents can make you laugh or, you know, you can make them laugh, you could have a better day over there than in your house."

Sometimes it is a young child from whom married CNAs seek relief. One 25-year-old married mom who worked the day shift reports why she cut short her leave:

> I had my son, and then I'm like, I cannot wait to go back to work, because with him I think sometimes I work more even being at home than here, with him, because he is – he's non-stop. He's into everything. He's so curious. SO, there's days when I'm just like, oh, I can't wait until I get to work. At least I'm not chasing someone around, you know, 24-7.

As others have argued, a life course approach helps us understand the particular tensions from which employees seek relief (Moen, 2003). Many

CNAs who talked of the draw of work were escaping the demands of parenting – both of young children and teenagers. But as we have seen, some also sought an escape from the demands of marriage – marriages which sometimes suffered because of job demands.

Who Escapes? Comparing CNAs to Doctors, EMTs, and Nurses

More than three-quarters of the CNAs (77 percent) talked about sometimes preferring work to home; only 25 percent of nurses, 19 percent of EMTs, and 7 percent of doctors did so. The factors we have identified – the pull of patients, the pull of coworkers, and the wish to escape home – help explain these differences.

The Pull of Patients
CNAs in nursing homes have long-term relations with residents, relations sometimes lasting years, in stretches of 8 hours, involving intimate personal care and repeated interactions. CNAs themselves noted that in hospitals they did not get to know the patients. One day in a hospital, a CNA commented: "I used to work in a nursing home as a CNA. I made less money. But at least there, you got to know the patients, what we call the residents. You had a personal relationship with them."

None of the other occupations come close to the CNA nursing home relations with patients. Hospital nurses care for patients for 8 or 12 hours at a stretch, but the care is less intimate or hands-on and the average hospital stay in the United States has decreased substantially and is now less than five days (Centers for Disease Control and Prevention, 2014). Primary care practitioners may have long-term relations with patients, but generally see them for relatively short visits, are an ever-smaller fraction of all doctors, and even they have come increasingly to spend less time with their patients. EMTs deal with someone in a crisis situation and the entire encounter is typically over within an hour.

To be sure, some doctors talked about the pulls to the job. But their explanations were very different from those of the CNAs. Using a "rhetoric of constraint," physicians often assert and assume that they have to stay long hours at work. This is seen as inevitable, or duty, not because of close (never mind family-like) relations with patients.

One EMT used a love metaphor to talk about the attraction of the work itself, but it was the work, not the patients, that exerted a pull. But work in his eyes was more like an illicit love affair than a family:

I've always said this: EMS is a jealous lover ... Like an old flame it's always in the back of my mind ... I'm married and I have a respectable life but I have this naughty girl on the side, and that's what EMS is like. It's like my dirty little secret. I'll take my girls to the park, I'll teach them how to ride their bikes, and in the back of my mind I'm thinking tomorrow night I go back to work, tomorrow night's my first night, I wonder what that's going to bring. It's always back there.

The Pull of Coworkers

Doctors, nurses, and EMTs found coworkers one of the attractions of work. One EMT explained: "If I were on a call and any one of my teammates got hurt or worse, I'd be devastated, because it's a family group." Another EMT uses the language of family to describe the shared holidays and domestic work: "It's like a second family. I actually look forward to going into work because you get real close with the people that you work with. Yesterday was a holiday, so we knew it would probably be slow and we didn't have any inspections, so we actually cooked a big like Thanksgiving dinner." EMTs, more than any other occupation, also note the downside of their work "family": "There can be some pretty good arguments amongst each other, because if I'm doing 40 hours [of overtime], you're not doing any, I feel like I'm taking more of the workload on, and you're not doing anything .... there's personality differences, big ones, inside the firehouses. It's not the big happy family that ... [is] portrayed on TV." Then he concludes: "It's just like any family, there's brothers and sisters fighting." Another develops this same theme: "We [firefighters] are like a big dysfunctional family. We're like brothers and sisters, we talk about each other, fights like a soap opera." These men seem to have a less romantic view of families than the CNAs.

The pull of coworkers was powerful for some nurses. One said: "The reason I've stayed in the same job for 18 years is ... We're family." This sort of statement was, however, much less common for nurses or EMTs than for CNAs and not a single physician talked this way.

Escaping Home

Members of the other three occupations all had significantly higher household incomes than CNAs; they also are more likely to have spouses who have higher incomes than CNA spouses. CNAs and their families are thus much more likely than those in other occupations to experience the stress that comes from being unable to pay bills or from kids not having the material possessions that other kids have. This may be one reason why members of the other occupations are less likely to talk about home circumstances pushing them to work more.

Doctors are least likely to bring up the draw of work over home. The average private practice doctor — the lowest paid of doctors — makes on average about eight times what an average nursing assistant earns. They often have spouses and nannies to pick up domestic responsibilities, even when they face unpredictable job hours. They buy more substantial houses, less tension, and healthier families. Only one doctor uses the term "family" to describe work. And this was a woman doctor who said that she and the staff regularly have lunch together, and "we look forward to that, we have fun. At this point I feel like some of these people are more like my family than my family."[3] Not a single male doctor used the rhetoric of family that way. One male doctor told us: "When people ask me what is your hobby, the answer is my family. My family is my hobby." Although his family "would like to have more of me around them," they had full lives with his reduced presence; his teenagers are, as he saw it, "self-sufficient" — a conception of teenagers it is hard to imagine coming from mothers. A home life that is structured to enable someone to view teenagers as self-sufficient, and family as a hobby, is a home life sheltered from stresses that push others to escape to work. Even if the long and unpredictable hours that doctors choose to stay on the job might suggest they are seeking an escape from home, they do not talk, and likely think, of their actions this way; instead they talk of these extra hours as serving patients' needs and meeting peer pressure. Doctors talk about peers encouraging one another to work long hours, celebrating those who do and befuddled by or stigmatizing those who don't. As one physician describes doctors, "the ones who work the most are looked up to ... You have to work harder; that gets respect. When you work more ... that's a big badge."

EMTs, like doctors, had little to say about families pushing them to want to spend more time at work; the reverse was more likely. Tom, for example, a full time EMT with a wife who also works full time, explained why he would not go in for overtime money: "If I haven't been home with my wife for a bit, and maybe I was gone all day and we just both got home and we just had dinner, and I'm going to open a nice bottle of wine ... . I would never go in [for an overtime call] if she just walked through the door and I haven't seen her all day, there's no way I'm going to get up and say, 'yeah, I'll be back in an hour and a half.'"

A significantly higher proportion of the female nurses than the male EMTS or doctors (but not as a high a proportion as the CNAs) say they go to work to escape the demands they face at home — they talk of facing dishes, floors to clean, demanding children, difficult husbands. One nurse, a married mother of two teenage kids who works in a nursing home, says:

"My home life has been no picnic, believe me ... my husband's a pain in the ass. My kids they ... give me trouble too." She went on to describe the nursing home residents, "as my second family." But she is one of only two currently married nurses who uses the rhetoric of family.

Though relatively few nurses use the family metaphor to describe their work, they nonetheless occasionally speak of their jobs as an escape. Rosanna – like many respondents in Hochschild's sample – explains that she does not take full advantage of family friendly policies because she is drawn back to work.

> I never took a four month leave of absence. Because I went nuts at home. I had to have more in my life than that. I made arrangements to take a four month leave of absence when I had my first child, and I went back in six weeks. ... And when my youngest one was born, I took two weeks off and I went back.

Part of the explanation for their feelings is that the majority of nurses do more domestic labor than their partners. One nurse whose husband is a self-employed consultant comments dramatically and sarcastically: "My husband's hands would disintegrate if they hit dish water!"

Although some nurses insist they want to escape to work and do so more often than those in either of the male occupations, this formulation only appears in about a quarter of the nurse interviews,[4] far less than in the CNAs' interviews. Moreover, these are not simply women responding to external constraints or to husbands who earn a living but refuse to do their share in the daily work of the home. Some nurses spoke of liking to cook family meals, garden, or wanting to see their elderly parents and especially to care for their children. As one explains: "Well, the big thing is that I like to be home with my kids."

These nurses, unlike the CNAs, often can and do take advantage of policies at work that allow them to take the time away from work to care for their families. As one administrator in a hospital complained about her nursing staff, "They are always FMLAing me." To be sure, some nurses talk about stresses at home. Some talk about attractions to work. This is not equivalent, however, to talking about using work as a way to escape family or seeing work as family. That they did far less than the CNAs.

CONCLUSION

Dichotomous thinking is misleading in many circumstances, and certainly when dealing with work and family. Presumably no one would defend a simple dichotomy of "work bad; family good" but in practice such views often shape the thinking of both ordinary people and academic analysts. Garson (1975, p. 219) wrote that "Real work is a human need, perhaps right after the need for food and the need for love. It feels good to work well." It should not surprise us that people seek a balance, that they value work. If work becomes too demanding, it can only be resisted by a powerful alternative force, and most often that force is family. But work can provide not only a sense of accomplishment and social connections; it can also provide a sense of escape from one's family. At the same time, this discussion of work and family shows the powerful ideological draw of the latter or at least the cultural rendition of it as the key institution to which people are (or should be) drawn. It shows the meaning and perhaps romanticization of what counts as family.

Even though much research has stressed the ways parenting is often stressful (e.g., see Simon, 2008), we show that it is not primarily children that lead workers to want to escape their homes. This is similar to the findings of Damaske and colleagues (2014): In their recent research that received a great deal of media attention, they found people − with and without children − were less stressed on the job than at home.

This is, nonetheless, in part a story of inequality, one that varies by gender, race, and class. More than men, women − CNAs and nurses − are likely to talk of their jobs as offering an escape. It is, however, most often the low-wage (frequently Black and Latina) CNAs who explicitly state that they look to their jobs for an escape from their often stressful families; they are also the ones who most often use "family" as a metaphor for their relations at work. This underscores two points.

First, difficult work conditions contribute to difficult home conditions which lead some employees to turn back to their jobs − a causal relationship only implicit in Hochschild's *Time Bind*. While she emphasizes that the problems at home contrast with the satisfactions on the job, we agree but also suggest a recursive relationship: unpredictable job hours and inadequate pay may create problems at home which, in turn, lead workers to turn back to their jobs to find satisfying relationships. This process indicates not only the particularly damaging effects of low-wage jobs but also the irony of these workers' sentiments and language. The rhetoric of family, paradoxically, is used to describe the domain (the worksite) that low-wage workers are attracted to − they say it is a place where they find connection, intimacy, and meaning − even while they want to escape from the very place, that is, families, that their rhetoric invokes. Family remains a pervasive and powerful cultural symbol, but one transferred to the workplace.

These workers are not inventing this language; they are drawing on a metaphor that is very much a part of corporate rhetoric. McDonalds talks of itself as "a family" where "happy time is family time" and its executive center is a "home office." The president and CEO of Walmart recently said: "At Walmart, we are family" (Duke, 2012). Larry Page, cofounder and chief executive of Google, remarked: "It's important that the company be a family, that people feel that they're part of the company, and that the company is like a family to them" (Page, 2012). The use of family as metaphor for relations on the job is intended to sustain attachment to those jobs. As Lakoff and Johnson (1980, p. 458) suggest, "The very systematicity that allows us to comprehend one aspect of a concept in terms of another .... will necessarily hide other aspects of that concept." Using "family" to describe the workplace may help accommodate workers to oppressive jobs and help conceal or at least assuage some problems on the job.

We are also proposing a second reason why CNAs are most likely to use this metaphor to describe their relations on the job: family means something different to the low-wage women workers than it does to the affluent. As we argue elsewhere (Gerstel & Clawson, 2014; Sarkisian & Gerstel, 2012), their view of family outside of the workplace is extended rather than nuclear which is to say broader and more inclusive. Extending it to the workplace may become less of a stretch. The coworkers are sometimes described as sweethearts, confidants, or adults with whom to discuss intimate matters. The residents are sometimes described as good parents or as lovable children. These CNAs also talk of knowledge and practical care — the indicators many work and family scholars have emphasized — when they speak of why people at their worksites are "family."

Such processes may be more likely to obtain in care work than in other low-wage occupations. Care work involves a set of relationships and tasks that involve intimacy and repeated interactions which may facilitate thinking of care recipients and coworkers as "family." Our analysis suggests that shared intimacy (high emotions, shared information, and practical care) is key to these care workers' family claims. The factors leading people to see coworkers as family do not necessarily coincide with care work, but relations with clients inherent in care work are absent in many other kinds of work. Rubin's earlier arguments, in concert with Hochschild's general frame, would seem to indicate that working class women generally — including those in different kinds of jobs — might use the family metaphor and think of the workplace as an escape. For example, Kim (2009) describes "the family" that formed among immigrant restaurant workers (see Nelson, 2014). Specifying the work and family conditions under which work becomes or is viewed as family would be a useful extension of this chapter's argument.

Not all health workers conceptualize jobs as family or emphasize that they want to escape their "real" families. Doing so depends not on only on the conditions of their jobs but on the conditions of their families — both of which are tied to gender and class. We find this view is more often espoused by women, probably because they carry more of the domestic responsibilities and may well have less power at home than do men. This may be because the two groups of men have it relatively easy at home and have less need to escape. So too men are probably less likely than women to use family as a metaphor for cultural reasons; some EMTs substituted the metaphors of an "illicit love affair" and, more often, a "team" — perhaps masculinized versions of connection; at the same time, when these men did use a family metaphor to talk of the valued relations at work, they were more likely to describe these connections as conflicted (as fighting siblings, for instance).

But the fact that men are less likely to say they use the job to escape their family may also have another cause: a gap between what they say (and maybe believe) and what they do. The men rarely say they want to escape their families — but in our study the men work 20 hours a week more than the women. One form of male privilege may be the ability to claim — to others and to themselves — that they love family and are devoted to it, and at the same time to choose work hours that reduce time with family. EMTs typically present their extra hours as needed to maintain the family's income; doctors most frequently present their extra hours as required to meet the needs of patients. As one physician said, "How can you justify being late for the kids' graduation ceremony to see somebody else's child in the emergency room?" But, this doctor went on to say, "that happens every day," as he is continually forced (at least as he sees it) by external circumstances, by his commitment to his patients and pressure from peers, to make work the priority over family. In this self-understanding (or self-presentation), the physician does not say he seeks to escape family. Instead he comes to believe there is no way to restructure the workplace, and every day a potentially life-and-death decision requires choosing work over family.

It comes as no surprise that class and gender matter to family life but what is particularly striking here, especially as a specification of Hochschild's argument, is their interaction. Although women are more likely to espouse this view, it is not all women who do so. This view of family as an escape, we found, is most often espoused by low-wage women workers whose material conditions at home are more likely to be difficult – as our observations and interviews make clear, the home surroundings that their jobs make possible are smaller, darker, and less compelling than those in the other occupations. This view of work as "family" or an escape is less often espoused by the more advantaged women: Nurses typically do not see their coworkers or patients as family. It may be because of work conditions – the shorter patient stays in hospitals where most nurses are employed means they have less intimate ties to those patients. It may be because of their greater resources that nurses not only have more satisfactory conditions at home but also have greater power to reshape organizations to meet these family demands which, in turn, eases life at home. Finally, it may be that nurses in our study were focused on "doing gender" (Deutsch, 2007) in ways that pull them to motherhood and home. The nurses could afford to "do gender" (in conventional ways) while the low-wage CNAs could not. (For an elaboration of this aspect of the argument, see Gerstel & Clawson, forthcoming.)

Perhaps what we analyze here at the micro level is parallel to what happens at the macro level: an ideological celebration of family coming in conflict with lived reality. At the macro level, people often react with anger at any challenge to the sanctity and priority of "the family" as it is imagined, but this is combined with a set of economic and political forces that impose penalties for motherhood. When academics study this, the implicit message is often that family and motherhood should be more valued. But we should also remember the costs of family. What we see here at the micro level is parallel: (some) people (sometimes) choose work over family, due both to the attractions of work and to the downside of their families' situation which are connected. People sometimes want to be away from the home – even when they have a broken ankle or young child. This is a useful reminder of a now largely forgotten, but once standard, feminist critique of families.

NOTES

1. Data from Table 45 of the Nursing Home Nursing Assistant national survey, to be found at http://www.cdc.gov/nchs/data/nnhsd/Estimates/nnas/Estimates_InjVac_Tables.pdf#45 and accessed on September 2, 2010.
2. A practice that Dodson and Zincavage (2007) also report.
3. We interviewed 11 women doctors and found divisions of the sort Blair-Loy (2003) found among women executives she studied: only 3 of the women physicians work full time and have stay-at-home spouses, 4 work full time and also have

primary responsibility for both child care and housework, and 4 work part time. This is consistent with national data showing 40 percent of women doctors now work part time (Sibert, 2011). See Clawson and Gerstel (2014) for further discussion of these women doctors.

4. Almost none of the male nurses bring this up and the one who did explicitly disagreed.

ACKNOWLEDGMENTS

We gratefully acknowledge research support provided by the National Science Foundation (grant # SES-0549817 and SES-0959712), the Sloan Foundation, the Russell Sage Foundation, the National Association of Emergency Medical Technicians (NAEMT), the Political Economy Research Institute (PERI), the University of Massachusetts Future of Work Project, and Conti Award. We are grateful to Mary Ann Clawson, Jill Crocker, Lisa Dodson, Lisa Harvey, Rosanna Hertz, Arlie Hochschild, James Jasper, Margaret Nelson, Maureen Perry-Jenkins, Rhacel Parrenas, Natalia Sarkisian, Donald Tomaskovic-Devey, and Robert Zussman for comments on earlier versions of this argument.

REFERENCES

Blair-Loy, M. (2003). *Competing devotions: Career and family among women executives*. Cambridge, MA: Harvard University Press.

Centers for Disease Control and Prevention. (2014). *Faststats: Hospital utilization (in non-federal short-stay hospitals)*. Retrieved from http://www.cdc.gov/nchs/fastats/hospital.htm

Clarkberg, M., & Moen, P. (2001). Understanding the time-squeeze: Married couples preferred and actual work-hour strategies. *American Behavioral Scientist, 44*(7), 1115–1136.

Clawson, D., & Gerstel, N. (2014). *Unequal time: Class, gender and family in employment schedules*. New York, NY: Russell Sage Foundation Press.

Damaske, S., Smyth, J., & Zawadzki, M. (2014). Has work replaced home as a haven? Re-examining Arlie Hochschild's time bind proposition with objective stress data. *Social Science & Medicine, 115*, 130–138.

Deutsch, F. (2007). Undoing gender. *Gender & Society, 21*(1), 106–127.

Dodson, L., & Zincavage, R. (2007). "It's like a family": Caring labor, exploitation, and race in nursing homes. *Gender & Society, 21*(6), 905–928.

Duke, M. (2012, June 1). *Walmart shareholder's meeting "Walmart's enduring values"*. Retrieved from http://news.walmart.com/executive-viewpoints/walmarts-enduring-values

Ferguson, M. (2012). You cannot leave it at the office: Spillover and crossover of coworker incivility. *Journal of Organizational Behavior, 33*(4), 571–588.

Folbre, N. (2012). *For love and money*. New York, NY: Russell Sage Foundation.
Garson, B. (1975). *All the livelong day: The meaning and demeaning of routine work*. Garden City, NY: Doubleday.
Gerstel, N. (2011). Rethinking families and community: The color, class, and centrality of extended kin ties. *Sociological Forum*, 26(1), 1−20.
Gerstel, N., & Clawson, D. (2014). Low wage care workers: Extended family as a strategy for survival. In M. Duffy, A. Armenia, & C. Stacey (Eds.), *Caring on the clock* (pp. 179−188). Brunswick, NJ: Rutgers University Press.
Gerstel, N., & Clawson, D. (forthcoming). Class advantage and the gender divide: Flexibility on the job and at home. *American Journal of Sociology*.
Gerstel, N., & Sarkisian, S. (2006). Marriage: The good, the bad, and the greedy. *Contexts*, 5(4), 16−22.
Grzywacz, J., Almeida, D., & McDonald, D. (2002). Work−family spillover and daily reports of work and family stress in the adult labor force. *Family Relations*, 52(1), 28−36.
Hochschild, A. (1997). *The time bind: When work becomes home and home becomes work*. New York, NY: Metropolitan.
Jacobs, J., & Gerson, K. (2004). *The time divide: Work, family and gender inequality*. Cambridge, MA: Harvard University Press.
Kelly, E., Moen, P., & Tranby, E. (2011). Changing workplaces to reduce work-family conflict: Schedule control in a white-collar organization. *American Sociological Review*, 76(2), 265−290.
Kiecolt, J. (2003). Satisfaction with work and family life: No evidence of a cultural reversal. *Journal of Marriage and Family*, 65(1), 23−35.
Kim, E. C. (2009). "Mama's family": Fictive kinship and undocumented immigrant restaurant workers. *Ethnography*, 105(4/5), 497−513.
Kovecses, Z. (2010). *Metaphor: A practical introduction*. New York, NY: Oxford University Press.
Lakoff, G. (1992). The contemporary theory of metaphor. In A. Ortony (Ed.), *Metaphor and thought* (2nd ed., pp. 202−251). Cambridge: Cambridge University Press.
Lakoff, G., & Johnson, L. (1980). *Metaphors we live by*. Chicago, IL: University of Chicago Press.
Larson, R. W., Richards, M. H., & Perry-Jenkins, M. (1994). Divergent worlds: The daily emotional experience of mothers and fathers in the domestic and public spheres. *Journal of Personality and Social Psychology*, 67(6), 1034−1048.
Lasch, C. (1977). *Haven in a heartless world*. New York, NY: Basic Books.
Lieff, H., & Fox, R. (1963). Training for detached concern in medical students. In H. Leiff (Ed.), *The psychological basis of medical practice* (pp. 12−35). New York, NY: Harper & Row.
Lopez, S. (2006). Culture change management in long-term care: A shop-floor view. *Politics and Society*, 34(1), 55−80.
Maume, D., & Bellas, M. (2001). The overworked American or the time bin? *American Behavioral Scientist*, 44(7), 1137−1156.
Moen, P. (2003). *It's about time*. Ithaca, NY: Cornell University Press.
Nelson, M. (2014). *The paradoxes of fictive kinship*. Unpublished.
Nomaguchi, K., Milkie, M., & Bianchi, S. (2005). Time strains and psychological well-being: Do dual-earner mothers and fathers differ? *Journal of Family Issues*, 26(6), 756−792.

Page, L. (2012). *Google should be like a family*. Interview with CNN Money. Retrieved from http://tech.fortune.cnn.com/2012/01/19/best-companies-google-larry-page/. Accessed on January 19.

Pager, D., & Quillian, L. (2005). Walking the talk? What employers say versus what they do. *American Sociological Review, 70*(3), 355–380.

Pedersen, K., Minnotte, G., & Mannon, S. (2009). Workplace policy and environment, family role quality and positive family to work spillover. *Journal of Family and Economic Issues, 30*(1), 80–89.

Presser, H. (2003). *Working in a 24/7 Economy*. New York, NY: Russell Sage Foundation.

Reynolds, J. (2005). In the face of conflict: Work-life conflict and desired work hour adjustments. *Journal of Marriage and Family, 67*(5), 1313–1331.

Roehling, P., Moen, P., & Batt, R. (2003). Spillover. In P. Moen (Ed.), *It's about time: Couples and careers* (pp. 101–121). Ithaca, NY: Cornell University Press.

Rubin, L. (1976). *Worlds of pain*. New York, NY: Basic Books.

Sandberg, J., Harper, J., Hill, J., Miller, R., Yorgason, J., & Day, R. (2013). What happens at home does not necessarily stay at home. *Journal of Marriage and Family, 75*(4), 808–821.

Sarkisian, N., & Gerstel, N. (2012). *Nuclear family values, extended family lives: The power of race, class, and gender*. New York, NY: Routledge Press.

Sibert, K. (2011). Don't quit this day job. *New York Times*, June 11, p. WK9.

Simon, R. (2008). The joys of parenthood, reconsidered. *Contexts, 7*(2), 40–45.

U.S. Department of Labor, Bureau of Labor Statistics. (2010). *National occupational employment and wage estimates*. Retrieved from http://www.bls.gov/oes/2010/may/oes_nat.htm

Voydanoff, P. (2005). Toward a conceptualization of perceived work-family fit and balance: A demands and resources approach. *Journal of Marriage and Family, 67*(4), 822–836.

IS WORK-FAMILY CONFLICT A MULTILEVEL STRESSOR LINKING JOB CONDITIONS TO MENTAL HEALTH? EVIDENCE FROM THE WORK, FAMILY AND HEALTH NETWORK

Phyllis Moen, Anne Kaduk, Ellen Ernst Kossek, Leslie Hammer, Orfeu M. Buxton, Emily O'Donnell, David Almeida, Kimberly Fox, Eric Tranby, J. Michael Oakes and Lynne Casper

ABSTRACT

Purpose — *Most research on the work conditions and family responsibilities associated with work-family conflict and other measures of mental health uses the individual employee as the unit of analysis. We argue that work conditions are both individual psychosocial assessments and objective characteristics of the proximal work environment, necessitating multilevel analyses of both individual- and team-level work conditions on mental health.*

Methodology/approach — *This study uses multilevel data on 748 high-tech professionals in 120 teams to investigate relationships between team- and individual-level job conditions, work-family conflict, and four mental health outcomes (job satisfaction, emotional exhaustion, perceived stress, and psychological distress).*

Findings — *We find that work-to-family conflict is socially patterned across teams, as are job satisfaction and emotional exhaustion. Team-level job conditions predict team-level outcomes, while individuals' perceptions of their job conditions are better predictors of individuals' work-to-family conflict and mental health. Work-to-family conflict operates as a partial mediator between job demands and mental health outcomes.*

Practical implications — *Our findings suggest that organizational leaders concerned about presenteeism, sickness absences, and productivity would do well to focus on changing job conditions in ways that reduce job demands and work-to-family conflict in order to promote employees' mental health.*

Originality/value of the chapter — *We show that both work-to-family conflict and job conditions can be fruitfully framed as team characteristics, shared appraisals held in common by team members. This challenges the framing of work-to-family conflict as a "private trouble" and provides support for work-to-family conflict as a structural mismatch grounded in the social and temporal organization of work.*

Keywords: Work-family conflict; multilevel; job conditions; stress; psychological distress; emotional exhaustion

Sociologists and social epidemiologists (cf., Berkman & Kawachi, 2000; House, 2002; Kawachi & Berkman, 2003; Krieger, 2011; Moen & Chesley, 2008; Oakes & Kaufman, 2006; Pearlin, Schieman, Fazio, & Meersman, 2005) have theorized social structures and contexts — more than individual attributes — as fundamental to individual stress, health, and well-being. Some have keyed in on specific social environments, such as social networks (Christakis & Fowler, 2007, 2008), schools (Aveyard, Markham, & Cheng,

2004), and residential neighborhoods (Sampson, Morenoff, & Gannon-Rowley, 2002). But most adults spend most of their waking hours *on the job*, meaning that the majority of nonfamily interactions are with coworkers, not neighbors or (nonwork) friends (Dahlin, Kelly, & Moen, 2008). Arguably the most potent forces affecting the stress or, conversely, the mental health, of workers lie within the understudied proximal social environments of paid work (Quick & Tetrick, 2011; Sennett, 1998). Moreover, members of work teams may have a shared sense of work-to-family conflict and well-being, both as a result of common conditions on the job and crossover in the assessments of coworkers within a team.

Even though it is commonly thought of as a characteristic of individuals, work-to-family conflict may be a stressor characterizing workgroups as well, socially patterned such that some teams experience greater levels of work-to-family conflict than others. Work-to-family conflict is typically viewed as a private trouble of individual workers, a stressor that can be reduced if they do a better job at "balancing" their multiple roles. But if work-to-family conflict differs across teams in identifiable ways, it suggests the primacy of job conditions in producing or reducing stressors affecting whole teams. Alternatively, if work-to-family conflict operates exclusively at the level of individual employees then more customized solutions may be called for. Some teams may also experience higher or lower collective levels of stress or well-being, again suggesting that team-level conditions or interventions may be key to enhancing the quality of life – and consequently the engagement and productivity – of employees.

We consider team members' collective perceptions of their job conditions and the ways employees perceive their job conditions as individuals. We investigate: (1) Are work-to-family conflict and mental health outcomes patterned at the team level, such that some teams experience greater work-to-family conflict and well-being than others? (2) Does work-to-family conflict operate as a mediator between job conditions and stress/mental health measures, at either the individual or team levels? (3) Are some groups more vulnerable to the negative mental health effects of work-to-family conflict than others?

This study makes three contributions to understanding work and family in the 21st century. First, we assess the primacy of the work environment in shaping of employees' work-to-family conflict and mental health. Like other key social contexts (neighborhoods, classrooms, networks), work environments shape life chances and life quality. This is important from a policy and practice perspective because interventions aimed at changing work environments may be more effective and reach a broader population than those aimed at changing individuals' coping behaviors (e.g., worksite stress reduction workshops, yoga).

Second, we focus on information technology (IT) employees in a high-tech organization, an increasingly central component of the twenty-first century economy. As part of a larger study by the Work, Family and Health Network (WFHN), we collected data on IT employees in a large U.S. firm that we call TOMO. We are particularly interested in these professional and technical workers because their jobs represent both the promise (in terms of new technologies) and the perils (in terms of global off-shoring and rising time pressures) of white-collar employment today.

Third, this study underscores the importance of multilevel analysis of work-to-family conflict and mental health. We analyze one positive measure of mental health − job satisfaction − and three negative measures − emotional exhaustion, perceived stress, and psychological distress − using multilevel data on IT workers ($N=748$ employees in 120 work teams). Perceived stress and psychological distress in particular have a long history as indicators of the stress process (Almeida & Wong, 2009; Pearlin, 2010; Pearlin et al., 2005).

BACKGROUND

Growing numbers of employees are reporting work-family conflict (Aumann, Galinsky, & Matos, 2011). Work hours, time pressures, supervisor and workplace support, and employees' control over their time (all measured at the individual level) have been shown to predict work-family conflict and mental health outcomes as experienced by individuals, as have job control and job demands (e.g., Hammer, Kossek, Yragui, Bodner, & Hanson, 2009; Kossek, Pichler, Bodner, & Hammer, 2011; Moen, Kelly, & Huang, 2008; Moen, Kelly, & Lam, 2013; Moen, Kelly, Tranby, & Huang, 2011). Moreover, work-family conflict has been associated with mood, anxiety, and substance disorders (Frone, 2000; Frone, Russell, & Barnes, 1996; Grzywacz & Bass, 2003), less healthy behaviors (Allen & Armstrong, 2006), high cholesterol, high body mass index, and poor physical stamina (Van Steenbergen & Ellemers, 2009), musculoskeletal disorders (Hammer, Cullen, Neal, Sinclair, & Shafiro, 2005; Hämmig, Knecht, Läubli, & Bauer, 2011), more self-reported chronic disease and obesity, all-cause sickness, and sickness absence (Sabbath, Melchior, Goldberg, Zins, & Berkman, 2012) as well as worse mental health and poorer self-rated health (Beutell,

2010). Because work-to-family conflict is a prime example of chronic role strain, "the felt difficulty in fulfilling role obligations" (Goode, 1960, p. 483) and is experienced as a chronic stressor, we theorize it may be a key mediator between job conditions and health – here mental health – outcomes.

Individual-Level Predictors

There are a number of studies of the effects of the work environment on work-to-family conflict and mental health outcomes; these typically rely on individuals' assessments of the psychosocial job conditions in which they work. Consider the large body of scholarship on the impacts of job control, defined by Karasek (1979, p. 290) as an employee's "potential control over his tasks and his conduct during the working day." Building on Karasek and Theorell (1990), scholars have found that individual-level perceptions of job control (i.e., control over how work is done) has both direct and buffering effects in reducing the risks of job demands and the impacts of stressors on health and well-being (see reviews by de Lange, Taris, Kompier, Houtman, & Bongers, 2003; Hausser, Mojzisch, Niesel, & Schulz-Hardt, 2010). Job control has been linked to exhaustion and depressive symptoms (e.g., Mausner-Dorsch & Eaton, 2000), psychological distress (Dalgard et al., 2009), physiological stress responses (e.g., Lundberg, 1996), blood pressure and mood (e.g., Rau & Triemer, 2004), and work-family conflict and strain (e.g., Thomas & Ganster, 1995).

Work-family researchers are increasingly focusing on *schedule control* as a distinct form of control at work, arguing that many employees are stressed because they do not feel in control of their *working time*. Individual assessments of schedule control appear to be related to, but distinct from, traditional measures of job control (Moen et al., 2008) and have been linked to lower work-family conflict and/or better reported health in cross-sectional (Moen et al., 2008; Thomas & Ganster, 1995), longitudinal (Grzywacz, Casey, & Jones, 2007), quasi-experimental studies (Kelly, Moen, & Tranby, 2011; Moen et al., 2013; Moen et al., 2011) and one randomized field trial (Kelly et al., 2014). However, some studies raise the issue of whether the greater autonomy and flexibility associated with job and schedule control might be detrimental for work-to-family conflict because it heightens the demands and pressures of work and blurs work-life boundaries (Blair-Loy, 2009; Glavin & Schieman, 2012; Kossek, Lautsch, & Eaton, 2006; Moen, Lam, Ammons, & Kelly, 2013; Roeters, Van der Lippe, & Kluwer, 2010; Schieman, Milkie, & Glavin, 2009). Greater flexibility in work schedules may also lead to greater family demands and pressures, culminating in higher levels of work-family conflict (Hammer, Neal, Newsom, Brockwood, & Colton, 2005).

Scholars have also integrated social support into occupational health models, considering both supportive organizational climates and support from managers. Employees who perceive their organization to be supportive of family responsibilities report less work-to-family conflict (e.g., Allen, 2001). Understanding of concrete ways that supervisors support employees' family and personal lives has been advanced recently with new measures of "family-supportive supervisor behaviors" (FSSB; see Hammer et al., 2009) and a meta-analysis of the contributions of family-supportive supervisor support as compared to more general measures of supervisor support (Kossek et al., 2011).

This body of evidence to date using the individual as the unit of analysis offers important insights as to the distribution of both psychosocial job conditions and mental health outcomes across individuals. But such studies often draw on surveys of random samples of employees in different types of jobs located in a wide range of organizational contexts and therefore cannot investigate team-level conditions as either predictors or outcomes. Taken together, the extant evidence underscores the significance of individual perceptions of job conditions for work-to-family conflict and mental health outcomes, but cannot promote understanding as to what types of work environments appear optimal, such as which team-level conditions predict teams' experience of work-to-family conflict and mental health outcomes or whether work-to-family conflict operates as an intervening mechanism between job conditions and mental health.

Team-Level Analyses

Multilevel analyses of work-to-family conflict and stress outcomes that analyze individuals within the social organization of their work teams are rare, although there are some path-breaking exceptions. Team characteristics, such as team decision-making and job rotation, were found to be associated with job anxiety (Cruz & Pil, 2011) while team-level cohesiveness and support moderated the relationship between team job demands and emotional exhaustion (Westman, Bakker, Roziner, & Sonnentag, 2011). Hammer, Saksvik, Nytrø, Torvatn, and Bayazit (2004) found that organizational norms governing work performance and social relations were significantly related to job stress. Some studies tie team-level perceptions of job demands and control to psychological health symptoms and sick days (Van Yperen & Snijders, 2000) and to self-reported health as well as other outcomes (Kossek et al., 2012). Furthermore, Bakker, van Emmerik, and Euwema (2006) find that team-level burnout and work engagement are related to individual burnout and work engagement after controlling for individuals' job demands and resources. These shared assessments also affect businesses; O'Neill et al. (2009) found that organizational work-family climate (time expectations, career consequences of using work-family benefits, and manager support for family) measured at both individual and worksite levels were associated with hotel employees' organizational commitment and turnover intentions.

Other studies consider work-to-family conflict explicitly. Bhave, Kramer, and Glomb (2010) used a sample of nonfaculty employees at a large Midwestern university in the United States to examine the effects of work-to-family conflict and support within work groups on individual employees' work-to-family conflict. Their results suggest that work group level work-to-family conflict influences individual work-to-family conflict over and above the shared work environment. Similarly, van Emmerik and Peeters (2009) used multilevel analyses on data from a sample of employees in a Dutch municipality, finding that team-level work-to-family conflict was associated with individual-level work-to-family conflict, net of team and individual job demands.

Taken together, these innovative studies point to the value of multilevel theory and analysis (Bliese & Jex, 2002; Klein & Kozlowski, 2000). But none made the "groupness" of job conditions, work-to-family conflict, and mental health measures a central focus as we do here, or investigated the

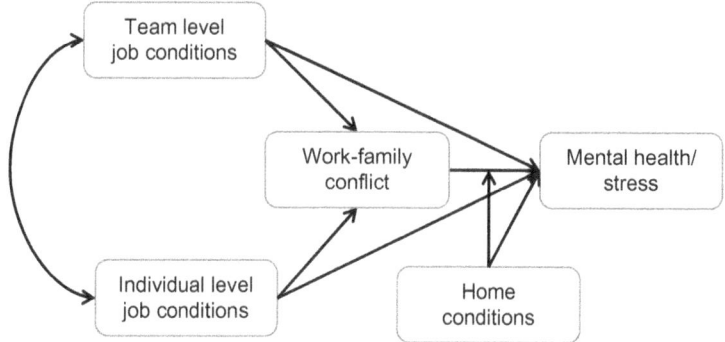

Fig. 1. Multilevel Pathways to Employees' Mental Health/Stress Outcomes.

potential mediating effects of work-to-family conflict on a range of stress/ mental health measures. Neither did they examine whether some employees are more vulnerable to the effects of work-to-family conflict than others. We build on and extend these studies by examining both team-level and individual-level job conditions, work-to-family conflict, and mental health outcomes, hypothesizing the relationships shown in Fig. 1.

RESEARCH QUESTIONS

Our first research question is: *Are work-to-family conflict and mental health outcomes patterned at the team level, such that some teams experience greater work-to-family conflict and stress than others?* Following Bhave et al. (2010) and van Emmerik and Peeters (2009) we argue that work-to-family conflict and at least some mental health outcomes vary systematically across teams, as do job conditions. We anticipate that perceived stress and psychological distress may vary more across employees than teams, in light of individual-level differences in personal characteristics and unmeasured individual differences (such as each employees' unique past experiences and current goals and expectations). Thus the strongest argument is for teams to share work-to-family conflict, job satisfaction, and emotional exhaustion (a component of burnout), since team members share the same team structure, the same supervisor, and the same work, as well as working with one another.

Our second research question is: *Does work-to-family conflict (at either the individual or team levels) operate as a mediator between job conditions and mental health measures?* Related to this question, we also address: *What job conditions predict team-level work-to-family conflict and mental health outcomes?* We anticipate that team and individual appraisals of high job demands will be associated with higher work-to-family conflict and poorer mental health, while higher team and individual appraisals of job control, schedule control, and FSSB will be linked to lower work-to-family conflict and better mental health (Baltes, Briggs, Huff, Wright, & Neuman, 1999; Hammer et al., 2009; Kossek et al., 2011; Thomas & Ganster, 1995), as will a supportive organizational work-family climate (Kossek, Colquitt, & Noe, 2001). Additionally, we consider team-level job insecurity as a source of stress that may affect mental health (Burgard, Brand, & House, 2009; Ferrie et al., 2001; Lam et al., 2015). Teams reporting greater job insecurity may be working less effectively together as a team. For example, anxiety about losing one's job may push employees to act more competitively with each other or provide less support to coworkers. Generally, we expect that individuals' own perceptions of working conditions are most proximal and will matter most for individual outcomes but team-level job conditions may also be important predictors of teams' and individuals' work-to-family conflict.

Our third research question is: *Are some subgroups more vulnerable to the deleterious mental health effects of work-to-family conflict?* We theorize gender, parental status, and caregiving responsibilities as key markers of vulnerability, proposing that work-to-family conflict effects may be especially pronounced for those with heavy home demands, with those sandwiched between caring for children and caring for infirm relatives especially at risk.

METHOD

Research Design

As part of a larger study by the WFHN, we collected and analyzed data on teams of IT employees in a large U.S. firm that we call TOMO. The WFHN study seeks to promote understanding of the impact of working conditions on work, family life, and health outcomes (see Bray et al., 2013; King et al., 2012). This chapter uses data from a survey of TOMO employees nested in teams that range in size from 4 to 28. TOMO was selected based on its size, the ability to logistically support data collection, and its openness to an intervention introduced after these data were collected. Because of the centralized organizational structure of the firm, recruitment to the study involved agreements with top leadership over all work units in this division, but individuals chose whether to participate in the survey.

Participants and Procedure

Managers and nonsupervisory employees were eligible to participate in the study if they were located in the two principal metropolitan locations of TOMO and were classified as employees rather than independent contractors. Of 1,182 nonsupervisory employees and 221 managers (who received a separate, substantially similar survey) eligible for the computer-assisted personal interview (CAPI), 1,044 completed it for a 78% response rate. Because we are interested in group-level characteristics, our analytic sample includes only teams with four or more CAPI respondents (including managers); these restrictions limited our sample size to 782 employees. We also restricted our sample to respondents who did not have missing values for any of the covariates.[1] These restrictions resulted in an analytic sample of 748 employees in 120 teams.

We first investigated the distribution and "groupness" of job conditions, work-to-family conflict, and mental health outcomes. Second, we assessed whether team-level job conditions were associated with work-to-family conflict and the mental health of teams. We hypothesized that teams with more demanding or less supportive working conditions would have stronger team-level patterns of work-to-family conflict and some mental health outcomes (such as job satisfaction and emotional exhaustion) compared to teams reporting less stressful environments. We then fit multilevel models of individual employees' work-to-family conflict and mental health outcomes. Finally, we estimated whether work-to-family conflict at the individual or team level operates as a mediator between job conditions and mental health outcomes using the method outlined by Baron and Kenny (1986).

Work-to-Family Conflict

Work-to-family conflict is measured using a scale developed and validated by Netemeyer, Boles, and McMurrian (1996) with individual items measured on a five-point scale, ranging from 1 (*Strongly Disagree*) to 5 (*Strongly Agree*). Examples of questions in the work-to-family conflict scale include "The demands of your work interfere with your family or personal time" and "Due to your work-related duties, you have to make changes to your plans for family or personal activities." We consider work-to-family conflict at the team and individual level as both outcomes and mediators. For team-level models, we use the team mean to operationalize work-to-family conflict as an outcome. For multilevel models, however, we use the percent individuals on the team with high (≥ 4) work-to-family conflict to operationalize work-to-family conflict at the team level in order to mitigate potential identification problems that would occur by including both the team mean and individual work-to-family conflict in our models (see Bakker et al., 2006).

Mental Health Outcomes

Job satisfaction is assessed using an established scale by Cammann, Fichman, Jenkins, and Klesh (1983). The three items allow responses ranging from *Strongly Disagree* to *Strongly Agree* on a five-point scale. A sample item is: "In general, you like working at your job."

Emotional exhaustion is assessed using that component of the Maslach Burnout Inventory. We use three items with frequency responses ranging from *Every Day* to *Never* on a seven-point scale. A sample item is: "You feel emotionally drained from your work."

Perceived stress is assessed using a well-known scale by Cohen, Kamarck, and Mermelstein (1983) shown to predict many mental and physical health outcomes. We use four items with frequency responses ranging from *Very Often* to *Never* on a five-point scale. This scale is additive, and theoretical values range from 4 to 20. A sample item is: "During the past 30 days, how often have you felt confident about your ability to handle your personal problems?" (reverse coded). Perceived stress is only included on the employee survey.

Psychological distress is a widely used scale for mental health screening (the K6) which has been clinically validated (Kessler et al., 2003). It is a six-item additive scale, with a possible range from 6 to 30 and responses from 1 (*None of the time*) to 5 (*All of the time*). Two questions in the scale are: "During the past 30 days, how much of the time did you feel so sad nothing could cheer you up?" and "During the past 30 days, how much of the time did you feel nervous?"

Independent Variables

Collective appraisals of job conditions are obtained by aggregating reports by team members. Bliese and Jex (2002) note that "the group-level measure, by virtue of being a shared perception, can be considered more of an objective rating of the environment than can the individual-level assessment" (pp. 271–272). These collective appraisals of job demands, control, and support are operationalized as the percent individuals on the team with high values (usually ≥4) on the job condition. This approach mitigates potential identification problems that would occur by including both the team mean and individual job condition variables in our models (Bakker et al., 2006). Both team-level and individual-level psychosocial job conditions were derived from established scales or measures (see Appendix). We include organizational work-family climate (which assesses expectations of sacrificing family and personal life for the sake of work), FSSB, schedule control, job demands, job control, hours worked (in a typical week in this job), and job insecurity. Models also include gender, parental status, marital status, race/ethnicity, whether the respondent has children age 18 or under living at home, whether the respondent cares for an adult relative for three or more hours per week over the past six months, and a birth cohort variable constructed using respondent's age.

Statistical Analysis

We first computed intraclass correlation coefficients (ICCs) and other descriptive statistics, assessing whether within-team correlations are higher than between-team correlations. We then fit models predicting work-to-family conflict, job satisfaction, and emotional exhaustion at the team level (due to their high ICCs). We next fit multilevel models that include both team- and individual-level characteristics theorized to predict individual employees' work-to-family conflict, using both team-level and individual perceptions of job conditions as well as employees' sociodemographics, testing also for any effects of team-level work-to-family conflict on individuals' perceptions of work-to-family conflict. We then tested whether work-to-family conflict mediates the relationship between job conditions and mental health outcomes. In addition to these main models, we also examined moderating effects by fitting models that included interactions between work-to-family conflict and various subgroups. In simplest notation, the multilevel models are of the format:

$$Y_{ij} = \alpha + \beta_1 X_{1ij} + \beta_2 X_{2j} + \zeta_j + \epsilon_{ij}$$

Y_{ij} is the outcome for an individual i in work team j, α is the intercept, X_{1ij} is the vector of individual conditions and characteristics for an individual i in team j. X_{2j} is the vector of work team conditions for team j. ζ_j is a random intercept and remains constant for all members of the team but potentially varies across teams. ϵ_{ij} is the individual error component that varies between individuals.

RESULTS

Means and standard deviations or percentages of dependent and independent variables are shown in Table 1. A total of 38% of respondents in the analytic sample were women, 46% had children age 18 or under, 23% were providing care for an adult relative, and 9.2% of employees were "sandwiched" between caring for children and an infirm adult. There are, not surprisingly, strong

Table 1. Collective and Individual Assessments of Work-Family Conflict, Mental Health/Stress Outcomes, and Job Conditions.

	Team-Level		ICC	Individual-Level	
	Mean	Standard deviation		Mean	Standard deviation
Work-family conflict					
Work-to-family conflict scale (1–5)	3.11	0.51	0.18	3.10	0.94
Percentage of team with high work-family conflict (≥4)	0.23	0.20			
Mental health/stress outcomes					
Job satisfaction scale (1–5)	3.99	0.43	0.17	3.98	0.78
Emotional exhaustion scale (1–7)	4.29	0.77	0.13	4.26	1.53
Perceived stress scale (4–20)			0.06	8.53	2.61
Psychological distress scale (6–30)			0.01	10.83	3.18
	Percentage of team "high"				
Team and individual job conditions					
Organizational work-family climate scale (1–5, 5 = best)	0.13	0.15	0.15	2.75	0.88
FSSB scale (1–5)	0.54	0.25	0.19	3.82	0.79
Schedule control scale (1–5)	0.32	0.22	0.14	3.56	0.69
Job demands scale (psychological job demands | 1–5)	0.39	0.25	0.14	3.61	0.71
Job control scale (decision authority | 1–5)	0.62	0.23	0.09	3.85	0.69
Hours worked per week	0.33	0.24	0.14	46.01	5.88
Job insecurity (1–4)	0.32	0.25	0.10	2.25	0.73
Manager (vs. employee) respondent				0.14	0.34
Team structure controls					
Core IT versus other business functions	0.36	0.48			
Team size (roster, including 1 manager per team)	11.02	5.48			
No manager CAPI respondent on Team	0.13	0.33			
Surveyed after merger announcement				0.43	0.50
Individual sociodemographics					
Birth cohort					
Gen X, ages 30–45, born 1965–1980			0.10	0.49	0.50
Trailing Edge Boomers, ages 46–54, born 1956–1964			0.02	0.33	0.47
Leading Edge Boomers, ages 55–64, born 1946–1955			0.04	0.18	0.38
Children age ≤18 at home			0.04	0.47	0.50
Female			0.13	0.38	0.49
Married/partnered			0.01	0.81	0.40

Table 1. (*Continued*)

	Team-Level		ICC	Individual-Level	
	Mean	Standard deviation		Mean	Standard deviation
Caregiver for adult relative			0.00	0.23	0.42
Race/ethnicity					
White, non-Hispanic			0.14	0.68	0.47
Asian or Pacific islander			0.25	0.22	0.42
Other race/ethnicity (nonwhite, non-Asian)			0.02	0.10	0.30

Note: $N = 748$ individuals in 120 teams. In the "Team and Individual Job Conditions" section, "team-level" is the team mean of the individual-level responses within each team unless otherwise indicated.

correlations between individual-level and team-level assessments of job conditions, ranging between .38 and .45 (table available from authors).

Question #1: Do Team Members Collectively Experience Work-to-Family Conflict and Mental Health?

Does work-to-family conflict operate only through the lens of individuals, or do team members share this stressor? ICCs, which gauge the proportion of variance in a variable that is between groups as compared to the total variance in that variable, can theoretically range from 0 to 1 (Raudenbush & Bryk, 2002). A high ICC means that there is a patterned "groupness" to that measure, and that team members share some commonality regarding it. Generally ICCs above .10 are considered high for psychosocial measures.

Work-to-family conflict has a statistically significant ($p < .001$) and high ICC of .18, indicating that almost one-fifth of the total variance of work-to-family conflict is attributable to team membership. This demonstrates that work-to-family conflict varies systematically across teams as well as across individuals. The ICCs for job satisfaction (.17) and emotional exhaustion (.13), also high and statistically significant ($p < .001$), indicate that these mental health outcomes similarly vary across teams. These outcomes both explicitly address the job context. By contrast, the ICCs for perceived stress and psychological distress are much lower and the group-level component is not statistically significant, possibly because individual differences in terms of family status and other nonwork factors might better predict whether individual employees experience perceived stress or psychological distress.

A number of job conditions also have high ICCs; specifically, organizational work-family climate, FSSB, schedule control, job demands, and work hours are all .14 or above. These high ICCs show that much of the variability in job conditions is attributable to differences across teams. This supports our theoretical emphasis on job conditions, work-to-family conflict, and some mental health measures as constituting not only employees' individual assessments but also the collective experiences of team members.

Question #2: Does Work-to-Family Conflict Operate as a Mediator between Job Conditions and Mental Health Outcomes?

To address this question at the team level, we first fit team-level (ecological) models with team measures of both outcomes and independent variables. Five team-level job conditions are associated with teams' degree of work-to-family conflict (see Table 2, Model 1). Team-level assessments of high job demands and long (≥ 50 per week) work hours are both positively associated with higher mean work-to-family conflict, while team-level assessments of a supportive organizational climate, a supervisor supportive of family concerns, and schedule control are all negatively related to teams' work-to-family conflict. This model highlights both the collective experience by teams of work-to-family conflict, and the fact that teams with intensive work – putting in long hours with high job demands – report high work-to-family conflict, while teams with supportive organizational climates, supportive supervisors, and control over their schedules have lower collective appraisals of work-family conflict. Thinking about work-family conflict as varying across teams underscores that (1) teams differ in the nature of their working conditions and (2) some job conditions are associated with higher or lower team-level work-to-family conflict. This suggests that team-level job conditions *can be changed* in ways that might reduce the collective experience of work-to-family conflict.

Turning to mental health outcomes, recall that both job satisfaction and emotional exhaustion vary across teams. We find teams with greater job resources (supportive organizational climates, family supportive supervisors, greater job control) tend to experience greater job satisfaction, while teams with high job demands tend to experience lower job satisfaction (Table 2, Model 2). Teams with greater job resources (family supportive supervisors, schedule control) also are more apt to report lower collective

Table 2. Team-Level Predictors of Team-Level Work-Family Conflict, Job Satisfaction, and Emotional Exhaustion.

	(1) Team Mean Work-to-Family Conflict		(2) Team Mean Job Satisfaction		(3) Team Mean Job Satisfaction		(4) Team Mean Emotional Exhaustion		(5) Team Mean Emotional Exhaustion	
	Coefficient	Standard error	Coefficient	Standard error	Coefficient	Standard error	Coefficient	Standard error	Coefficient	Standard error
Team job conditions (proportions of individuals in each team with "high" values on job conditions)										
Percentage of team perceiving supportive org. work-family climate (≥4)	−1.084***	(0.248)	0.601*	(0.243)	0.480+	(0.263)	−0.403	(0.359)	0.221	(0.359)
Percentage of team perceiving family supportive supervisor (≥4)	−0.329*	(0.148)	0.340*	(0.145)	0.303*	(0.148)	−0.691**	(0.214)	−0.502*	(0.202)
Percentage of team with high schedule control (≥4)	−0.434*	(0.169)	0.179	(0.166)	0.131	(0.170)	−0.733**	(0.245)	−0.483*	(0.232)
Percentage of team with high job demands (≥4)	0.551***	(0.153)	−0.373*	(0.151)	−0.311+	(0.159)	1.497***	(0.222)	1.180***	(0.217)

	(1)	(2)	(3)	(4)	(5)
Percentage of team with high job control (≥4)	0.043 (0.166)	0.506** (0.163)	0.511** (0.163)	0.027 (0.241)	0.003 (0.223)
Percentage of team working 50 or more hours/week	0.560*** (0.155)	0.020 (0.153)	0.083 (0.161)	0.329 (0.225)	0.007 (0.220)
Percentage of team with high job insecurity (3 or 4)	0.126 (0.148)	−0.230 (0.145)	−0.216 (0.146)	0.609** (0.215)	0.537** (0.199)
Team mean work-to-family conflict			−0.112 (0.094)		0.575*** (0.129)
Constant	3.049*** (0.184)	3.540*** (0.181)	3.881*** (0.339)	4.084*** (0.267)	2.331*** (0.463)
Observations	120	120	120	120	120
R-squared	0.587	0.424	0.432	0.613	0.674

Note: Standard errors in parentheses. The above table shows results from OLS models. Models also control for team business function, team size, presence of manager CAPI respondent in each team, and timing of a merger announcement.
+ $p<0.10$, * $p<0.05$, ** $p<0.01$, *** $p<0.001$.

emotional exhaustion, while teams with greater job demands and job insecurity are more likely to experience higher emotional exhaustion. We observe no statistically significant relationship between team-level work-to-family conflict and team members' collective job satisfaction (Table 2, Model 3), suggesting that *team-level* work-to-family conflict does not mediate the relationship between job conditions and team means of job satisfaction. However, there is evidence that work-to-family conflict at the team level does serve as a partial mediator between job conditions and a team's collective sense of emotional exhaustion (comparing Model 5 with Model 4 in Table 2).

We then examine whether team-level job conditions predict individual outcomes (see Table 3). Model 1 in Table 3 shows team-level supportive climate is significantly associated with lower work-to-family conflict, while employees in teams with greater job control (often associated with greater responsibilities) report higher work-to-family conflict. Note that these findings are net of individual workers' own sense of the organizational climate, job control, and other job conditions.

Some team-level job conditions also predict individual mental health outcomes, net of individuals' own perceptions of their job conditions. Specifically, employees in teams with a supportive organizational climate or with lower job demands report greater job satisfaction, even net of their own individual assessments of these and other job conditions (Table 4, Model 1). And employees in teams with greater job demands or greater job insecurity experience greater emotional exhaustion, again net of individual job conditions (Table 4, Model 3). All of these coefficients attenuate slightly once work-to-family conflict (measured at both the team and individual levels) are included (Table 4, Models 2 and 4), but only one meets the Baron and Kenny (1986) criteria for mediation. The relationship between team-level supportive climate and individual-level job satisfaction is mediated by individual employees' sense of work-to-family conflict.

Turning to individual-level effects, relationships between employees' perceptions of their job conditions and their mental health outcomes are, as hypothesized, mediated by their sense of work-to-family conflict. For example, the relationship between individual perceptions of the organizational climate, schedule control, and job control, on the one hand, and all the mental health outcomes, on the other, is mediated by individuals' work-to-family conflict. These job conditions affect mental health in part through the mechanism of work-to-family conflict. The models in Table 4 also show that work-to-family conflict mediates the relationship between

Table 3. Team- and Individual-Level Predictors of Individual Employees' Work–Family Conflict.

	(1) Individual Work-Family Conflict		(2) Individual Work-Family Conflict	
	Coefficient	Standard error	Coefficient	Standard error
Team job conditions (proportions of individuals in each team with "high" values on job conditions)				
Percentage of team perceiving supportive org. work-family climate (≥4)	−0.439*	(0.202)	−0.222	(0.194)
Percentage of team perceiving family supportive supervisor (≥4)	−0.047	(0.127)	0.074	(0.123)
Percentage of team with high schedule control (≥4)	−0.069	(0.138)	0.082	(0.133)
Percentage of team with high job demands (≥4)	−0.016	(0.127)	−0.105	(0.121)
Percentage of team with high job control (≥4)	0.281*	(0.138)	0.221+	(0.131)
Percentage of team working 50 or more hours/week	0.077	(0.130)	−0.126	(0.128)
Percentage of team with high job insecurity (3 or 4)	0.203	(0.128)	0.045	(0.125)
Percentage of team with high work-family conflict (≥4)			0.906***	(0.155)
Individual job conditions				
Organizational work-family climate scale (1–5, 5 = best)	−0.280***	(0.032)	−0.264***	(0.032)
FSSB scale (1–5)	−0.154***	(0.036)	−0.145***	(0.035)
Schedule control scale (1–5)	−0.152***	(0.042)	−0.156***	(0.041)
Job demands scale (psychological job demands ǀ 1–5)	0.418***	(0.039)	0.401***	(0.038)
Job control scale (decision authority ǀ 1–5)	−0.085*	(0.040)	−0.080*	(0.040)
Hours worked per week	0.042***	(0.005)	0.041***	(0.005)
Job insecurity (1–4)	0.027	(0.036)	0.036	(0.035)
Manager (vs. employee) respondent	−0.026	(0.071)	−0.016	(0.070)
Individual sociodemographics				
Birth cohort (Gen X omitted)				
Trailing Edge Boomers, ages 46–54, born 1956–1964	−0.035	(0.056)	−0.034	(0.055)
Leading Edge Boomers, ages 55–64, born 1946–1955	0.077	(0.074)	0.073	(0.072)

Table 3. (*Continued*)

	(1) Individual Work-Family Conflict		(2) Individual Work-Family Conflict	
	Coefficient	Standard error	Coefficient	Standard error
Children age ≤18 at home	0.124*	(0.053)	0.101+	(0.053)
Female	0.030	(0.050)	0.027	(0.049)
Married/partnered	0.059	(0.062)	0.054	(0.060)
Caregiver for adult relative	−0.004	(0.055)	−0.014	(0.054)
Race/ethnicity (white omitted)				
Asian or Pacific islander	0.026	(0.066)	0.004	(0.064)
Other race/ethnicity (nonwhite, non-Asian)	−0.131+	(0.078)	−0.116	(0.077)
Constant	2.932***	(0.153)	2.783***	(0.147)
Model fit information and random effects				
Observations	748		748	
Number of groups	120		120	
Team variance	0.006		0.000	
Individual variance	0.376		0.365	
ICC	0.015		0.000	
Proportion of team-level variance explained	0.964		1.000	
Proportion of individual level variance explained	0.477		0.492	
Proportion of total variance explained	0.563		0.582	
BIC	1,600		1,573	

Note: Standard errors in parentheses. Models also control for team business function, team size, presence of manager CAPI respondent in each team, and timing of a merger announcement.
$+ p < 0.10$, $* p < 0.05$, $** p < 0.01$, $*** p < 0.001$.

long work hours and both emotional exhaustion and psychological distress. Additionally, we find that employees who report that their supervisor is supportive of family concerns (higher FSSB) are more likely to have higher job satisfaction, while employees with higher job insecurity are more likely to report greater psychological distress.

These findings add evidence that both individuals' own assessments *and* the collective assessments by team members of job conditions are important

Table 4. Team- and Individual-Level Predictors of Individual Employees' Mental Health/Stress Outcomes.

	(1)		(2)		(3)		(4)	
	Job Satisfaction				Emotional Exhaustion			
	Coefficient	Standard error	Coefficient	Standard error	Coefficient	Standard error	Coefficient	Standard error
Team job conditions (percentages of individuals in each team with "high" values on job conditions)								
Percentage of team perceiving supportive org. work-family climate (≥4)	0.503*	(0.226)	0.405+	(0.228)	0.219	(0.370)	0.551	(0.350)
Percentage of team perceiving family supportive supervisor (≥4)	−0.064	(0.141)	−0.096	(0.142)	−0.321	(0.233)	−0.260	(0.221)
Percentage of team with high schedule control (≥4)	−0.076	(0.154)	−0.119	(0.157)	−0.256	(0.253)	−0.183	(0.240)
Percentage of team with high job demands (≥4)	−0.295*	(0.143)	−0.276+	(0.143)	0.476*	(0.233)	0.472*	(0.219)
Percentage of team with high job control (≥4)	0.193	(0.155)	0.237	(0.154)	0.234	(0.253)	0.032	(0.237)
Percentage of team working 50 or more hours/week	0.093	(0.145)	0.150	(0.151)	−0.044	(0.238)	−0.133	(0.231)
Percentage of team with high job insecurity (3 or 4)	−0.210	(0.141)	−0.155	(0.144)	0.472*	(0.235)	0.304	(0.224)
Individual job conditions								
Organizational work-family climate scale (1–5, 5 = best)	0.096**	(0.033)	0.062+	(0.034)	−0.293***	(0.061)	−0.097	(0.060)
FSSB scale (1–5)	0.188***	(0.037)	0.169***	(0.037)	−0.089	(0.068)	0.017	(0.064)
Schedule control scale (1–5)	0.081+	(0.043)	0.065	(0.043)	−0.259**	(0.079)	−0.155*	(0.074)
Job demands scale (psychological job demands | 1–5)	0.001	(0.040)	0.050	(0.042)	0.638***	(0.074)	0.348***	(0.074)
Job control scale (decision authority | 1–5)	0.330***	(0.041)	0.320***	(0.041)	−0.283***	(0.077)	−0.225**	(0.071)

Table 4. (Continued)

	Job Satisfaction				Emotional Exhaustion			
	(1)		(2)		(3)		(4)	
	Coefficient	Standard error	Coefficient	Standard error	Coefficient	Standard error	Coefficient	Standard error
Hours worked per week	−0.004	(0.005)	0.001	(0.005)	0.030***	(0.009)	0.001	(0.009)
Job insecurity (1–4)	−0.010	(0.036)	−0.008	(0.036)	0.036	(0.068)	0.019	(0.064)
Manager (vs. employee) respondent	−0.102	(0.072)	−0.107	(0.071)	0.164	(0.135)	0.184	(0.125)
Work-family conflict mediators								
Percentage of team with high work-family conflict (≥4)			−0.201	(0.185)			0.155	(0.285)
Individual work-family conflict scale (1–5)			−0.111**	(0.038)			0.685***	(0.066)
Individual sociodemographics								
Birth cohort (Gen X omitted)								
Trailing Edge Boomers, ages 46–54, born 1956–1964	0.082	(0.057)	0.077	(0.057)	0.001	(0.106)	0.023	(0.099)
Leading Edge Boomers, ages 55–64, born 1946–1955	0.195**	(0.075)	0.204**	(0.075)	−0.005	(0.140)	−0.062	(0.130)
Children age ≤18 at home	−0.059	(0.055)	−0.042	(0.055)	0.167+	(0.101)	0.076	(0.095)
Female	0.056	(0.052)	0.060	(0.051)	0.009	(0.095)	−0.010	(0.088)
Married/partnered	0.076	(0.063)	0.083	(0.063)	−0.142	(0.117)	−0.183+	(0.109)
Caregiver for adult relative	0.020	(0.056)	0.021	(0.056)	−0.152	(0.105)	−0.153	(0.097)
Race/ethnicity (white omitted)								
Asian or Pacific islander	0.180**	(0.068)	0.188**	(0.067)	−0.626***	(0.124)	−0.649***	(0.115)
Other race/ethnicity (nonwhite, non-Asian)	0.206*	(0.080)	0.188*	(0.080)	−0.273+	(0.148)	−0.182	(0.138)
Constant	3.971***	(0.172)	3.984***	(0.173)	4.070***	(0.280)	4.156***	(0.266)

	(5)		(6)		(7)		(8)	
	Perceived Stress				Psychological Distress			
	Coefficient	Standard error	Coefficient	Standard error	Coefficient	Standard error	Coefficient	Standard error
Model fit information and random effects								
Observations	748		748		748		748	
Number of groups	120		120		120		120	
Team variance	0.023		0.023		0.000		0.000	
Individual variance	0.382		0.377		1.367		1.184	
ICC	0.058		0.057		0.000		0.000	
Proportion of team-level variance explained	0.781		0.786		1.000		1.000	
Proportion of individual level variance explained	0.247		0.256		0.325		0.416	
Proportion of total variance explained	0.340		0.349		0.413		0.491	
BIC	1,640		1,642		2,555		2,461	
Team job conditions (percentages of individuals in each team with "high" values on job conditions)								
Percentage of team perceiving supportive org. work-family climate (≥4)	−1.512+	(0.783)	−1.289	(0.788)	−0.967	(0.885)	−0.512	(0.886)
Percentage of team perceiving family supportive supervisor (≥4)	0.705	(0.499)	0.570	(0.503)	0.365	(0.559)	0.480	(0.559)
Percentage of team with high schedule control (≥4)	−0.115	(0.539)	−0.069	(0.540)	−0.281	(0.607)	−0.147	(0.608)
Percentage of team with high job demands (≥4)	−0.567	(0.490)	−0.534	(0.486)	−0.529	(0.558)	−0.563	(0.553)
Percentage of team with high job control (≥4)	−0.125	(0.534)	−0.286	(0.529)	0.258	(0.607)	0.004	(0.600)
Percentage of team working 50 or more hours/week	0.068	(0.498)	0.071	(0.511)	−0.207	(0.570)	−0.378	(0.583)

Table 4. (Continued)

	(5)		(6)		(7)		(8)	
	Perceived Stress				Psychological Distress			
	Coefficient	Standard error	Coefficient	Standard error	Coefficient	Standard error	Coefficient	Standard error
Percentage of team with high job insecurity (3 or 4)	0.630	(0.496)	0.575	(0.499)	0.770	(0.563)	0.522	(0.568)
Individual job conditions								
Organizational work-family climate scale (1–5, 5 = best)	−0.424**	(0.130)	−0.228+	(0.135)	−0.377*	(0.147)	−0.143	(0.152)
FSSB scale (1–5)	−0.212	(0.140)	−0.102	(0.140)	−0.117	(0.163)	0.008	(0.162)
Schedule control scale (1–5)	−0.399*	(0.164)	−0.289+	(0.164)	−0.335+	(0.190)	−0.215	(0.188)
Job demands scale (psychological job demands | 1–5)	0.639***	(0.157)	0.394*	(0.164)	0.711***	(0.177)	0.369*	(0.187)
Job control scale (decision authority | 1–5)	−0.529***	(0.159)	−0.488**	(0.157)	−0.712***	(0.183)	−0.643***	(0.181)
Hours worked per week	0.002	(0.019)	−0.025	(0.019)	0.048*	(0.021)	0.014	(0.022)
Job insecurity (1–4)	0.198	(0.143)	0.179	(0.141)	0.474**	(0.163)	0.457**	(0.161)
Manager (vs. employee) respondent	0.000	(0.000)	0.000	(0.000)	−0.506	(0.322)	−0.479	(0.317)
Work-to-family conflict mediators								
Percentage of team with high work-family conflict (≥4)			−0.354	(0.639)			0.476	(0.721)
Individual work-to-family conflict scale (1–5)			0.652***	(0.148)			0.796***	(0.167)
Individual sociodemographics								
Birth cohort (Gen X omitted)								
Trailing Edge Boomers, ages 46–54, born 1956–1964	−0.249	(0.223)	−0.217	(0.220)	−0.588*	(0.255)	−0.561*	(0.251)

Leading Edge Boomers, ages 55–64, born 1946–1955	−0.266	(0.286)	−0.330	(0.283)	−0.798*	(0.334)	−0.867**	(0.329)
Children age ≤18 at home	0.465*	(0.212)	0.409+	(0.210)	0.046	(0.243)	−0.068	(0.240)
Female	0.415*	(0.197)	0.401*	(0.194)	0.553*	(0.227)	0.531*	(0.224)
Married/partnered	−0.171	(0.239)	−0.200	(0.235)	−0.775**	(0.280)	−0.825**	(0.275)
Caregiver for adult relative	0.409+	(0.218)	0.414+	(0.215)	0.485+	(0.251)	0.480+	(0.247)
Race/ethnicity (white omitted)								
Asian or Pacific islander	−0.129	(0.257)	−0.127	(0.254)	0.473	(0.296)	0.438	(0.292)
Other race/ethnicity (nonwhite, non-Asian)	−0.951**	(0.307)	−0.868**	(0.303)	−0.721*	(0.355)	−0.611+	(0.350)
Constant	8.578***	(0.596)	8.781***	(0.601)	10.616***	(0.671)	10.666***	(0.673)
Model fit information and random effects								
Observations	646		646		748		748	
Number of groups	120		120		120		120	
Team variance	0.000		0.000		0.000		0.000	
Individual variance	5.169		5.017		7.837		7.577	
ICC	0.000		0.000		0.000		0.000	
Proportion of team-level variance explained	1.000		1.000		1.000		1.000	
Proportion of individual level variance explained	0.206		0.230		0.211		0.238	
Proportion of total variance explained	0.243		0.266		0.221		0.247	
BIC	3,082		3,076		3,861		3,849	

Note: Standard errors in parentheses. Models also control for team business function, team size, presence of manager CAPI respondent in each team, and timing of a merger announcement.
+ $p<0.10$, * $p<0.05$, ** $p<0.01$, *** $p<0.001$.

in understanding work-to-family conflict, job satisfaction, and emotional exhaustion. By contrast, it is their own perceptions of job conditions that appear most directly predictive of employees' perceived stress and psychological distress. We have also shown that work-to-family conflict operates as a mediator between some job conditions and mental health outcomes. However, the direct effects of job conditions on mental health remain, even after controlling for the indirect effects through work-to-family conflict.

Question #3: Are Some Subgroups More Vulnerable to the Deleterious Mental Health Effects of Work-to-Family Conflict?

It may be the case that work-to-family conflict (measured at either level) is more linked to the mental health and stress of some employees than others. To investigate this, we fit models like the even-numbered models in Table 4 with additional interaction terms between work-to-family conflict (at both levels) and employees' birth cohort, gender, combined gender and parental status, and adult caregiving status. We found only two statistically significant interactions. Fig. 2 shows that individuals in teams with higher work-to-family conflict — where more than half the team experiences high work-to-family conflict — who themselves care for an adult relative but do not have children at home tend to experience greater psychological distress than their peers who care for adult relatives and also have children. This points to caregiving for adult relatives as a private trouble that may not be as recognized as an "acceptable" time demand within teams. Perhaps adult caregivers who do not have children are focusing their full attention on caregiving for aging parents or other relatives, leading to greater psychological distress for themselves. It could be that "sandwiched" employees see that their coworkers are also experiencing high conflict from work to family and this puts their own difficulties in perspective. Fig. 3 shows that for a given level of individual work-to-family conflict above 3 (out of 5), members of Generation X (born 1965–1980) with higher levels of work-to-family conflict tend to experience greater psychological distress than members of either the leading edge (born 1946–1955) or the trailing edge (born 1956–1964) of the large Boomer age-cohort. This could reflect that Gen X'ers are in the middle of raising their families as well as building their careers, making them more vulnerable to work-to-family conflict as a chronic stressor in their lives.

Mental Health 203

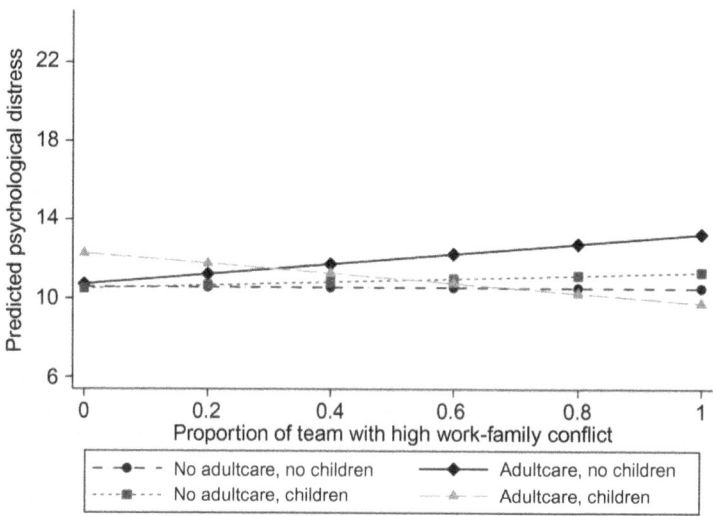

Fig. 2. Individuals Caring Only for Infirm Adults in Teams with High Work-Family Conflict Experience More Psychological Distress.

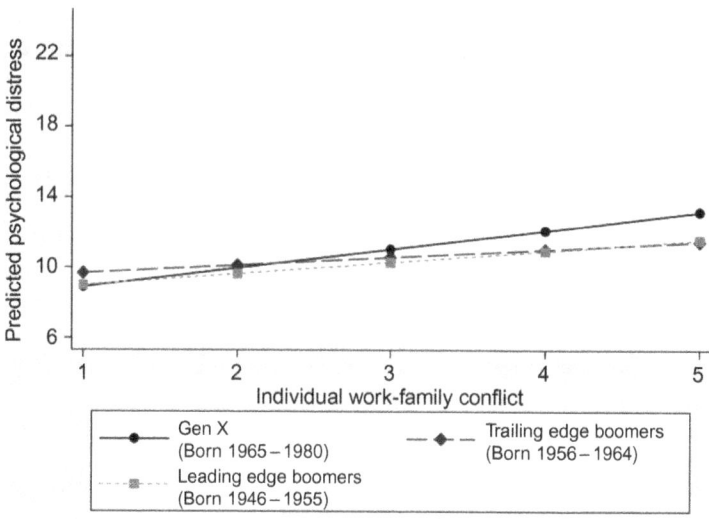

Fig. 3. Gen X'ers with High Work-Family Conflict Report Higher Psychological Distress than Boomers.

DISCUSSION AND CONCLUSIONS

Teams as a Focus of Theorizing and Analysis

Using individuals as the exclusive unit of analysis (as is the case in most mental health research) perpetuates conceptualization of individual rather than contextual forces shaping well-being. Thinking about and estimating the effects of team characteristics on both team-level and individual-level work-to-family conflict and mental health provides a structural framing of the demands and resources on the job that shape the mental health and life quality of employees. Our multilevel findings extend the conclusions from a meta-analysis of over 60 studies (Byron, 2005) conducted at the individual level that work conditions (in our study, a supportive climate, family-supportive supervisors, job control, schedule flexibility, and job demands) are more important predictors of work-to-family conflict than are family variables, while sociodemographic characteristics such as gender and parental status may be more relevant to mental health outcomes.

We have shown that both work-to-family conflict and job conditions, traditionally measured at the individual level, can be fruitfully framed as *team* characteristics, shared appraisals held in common by team members. Thinking about teams as varying in their degree of work-to-family conflict, job satisfaction, and emotional exhaustion suggests that the circumstances under which they work matter for their collective as well as individual well-being. Consider the case of work-to-family conflict, often framed as a private trouble of individual employees, a problem of "balance" rather than a structural mismatch grounded in the social and temporal organization of work (Moen & Roehling, 2005). The fact that we show work-to-family conflict is patterned at the team level challenges this "private troubles" framing. Rather, our findings suggest that work-to-family conflict varies across different team environments. Similarly, job satisfaction and emotional exhaustion are socially distributed across teams.

We have also shown that work-to-family conflict, particularly as measured at the individual level, is a key mechanism linking job conditions to individual employees' mental health outcomes. However, job conditions continue to affect well-being, over and above the indirect effects through work-to-family conflict. Executives and managers interested in employee engagement and productivity would do well to attend the conditions of work that reduce both individual- and team-level work-to-family conflict and promote their employees' mental health.

Note that we find that work-to-family conflict seems to have similar effects for women and men alike, suggesting that job conditions associated with work-to-family conflict may have broad impacts across the workforce. We do find that employees with elder care responsibilities in teams with high work-to-family conflict report higher psychological distress, but this may reflect the hidden nature of elder care as a chronic stressor. The fact that members of the Gen X age-cohort are more apt than Boomers to report higher psychological distress under conditions of high work-to-family conflict suggests that age, cohort, and life stage should be better theorized, rather than simply "controlled for," to promote understanding of mental health.

Implications for Future Research

Our findings suggest important future research directions. First, work-family and mental health research could be advanced if teams — shared environments with identifiable characteristics — were to be theorized and investigated in the same ways classrooms, neighborhoods, and networks have been. Second, little is known about the mechanisms shaping team-level conditions. Studies should consider the mechanism of crossover, often used to suggest that working conditions of one individual "crosses over" to affect the experience of others (Almeida & Wong, 2009). There is also the possibility that team members working under similar (adverse or supportive) conditions will experience these conditions in similar ways. Thus the same excessive job demands or rigid supervisor may elicit work-to-family conflict in most members of that team. Both mechanisms — crossover and similar job conditions — may be operating simultaneously. These suggest rich possibilities for understanding the specific ways that shared social context affects work-to-family conflict and mental health.

Third, we found team conditions to be more strongly associated with work-to-family conflict, job satisfaction, and emotional exhaustion than with perceived stress or psychological distress in this IT workforce, but additional research is needed in different organizational sectors and more varied outcomes. Clearly, multilevel modeling that locates employees within the multiple social contexts of their lives can be a fruitful research direction (cf., Bliese & Jex, 2002; Hammer et al., 2004). In all of this work, we would advocate for continued attention to the various ways that caregiving and home demands affect these relationships.

Implications for Policy and Practice

Krieger (2011, p. 31) points out, "to the extent there is spatiotemporal and/or social variation ... it suggests modifiable causes are at play, whose mechanisms could presumably be altered by informed action." Team-level patterns are just such "spatiotemporal and social variations." Identifying team-level factors related to employee well-being is the first step in identifying ways of promoting healthy work environments. This is potentially a key policy issue for employers as well as governments, especially in light of the fact that work-to-family conflict and stress have increased over time, for men as well as women (Bond, Thompson, & Prottas, 2002; Casper, Eby, Bordeaux, Lockwood, & Lambert, 2007; Eby, Casper, Lockwood, Bordeaux, & Brinley, 2005; Sorensen et al., 2011).

The real test of organizational- or team-level effects is in fact whether *changes in them* cause changes in health, stress, and well-being outcomes. Experimental or quasi-experimental designs introducing change in team environments are necessary for understanding causal paths, given issues of selection and interdependence. However, analysis of team-level conditions has important research and policy implications, moving the focus to ways of *changing the social environments of work* rather than differences across individuals (cf., Hammer, Kossek, Anger, Bodner, & Zimmerman, 2011; Kelly et al., 2011; Kelly et al., 2014; Moen et al., 2011). Intervention studies investigating the impacts of changes in the social environment of work are ultimately necessary to fully understand these social processes, opening up new horizons in the study of work, family, and health.

NOTE

1. For respondents who answered at least 75% of the questions in a scale, we averaged their response to the remaining questions and used that as their scale score, rather than treating the overall response for that respondent as missing.

ACKNOWLEDGMENTS

This research was conducted as part of the Work, Family and Health Network (www.WorkFamilyHealthNetwork.org), which is funded by a cooperative agreement through the National Institutes of Health and the Centers for Disease Control and Prevention: Eunice Kennedy Shriver National Institute of Child Health and Human Development (Grant # U01HD051217, U01HD051218, U01HD051256, U01HD051276), National Institute on Aging (Grant # U01AG027669), Office of Behavioral and Social Sciences Research, and National Institute for Occupational Safety and Health (Grant # U01OH008788, U01HD059773). Grants from the National Heart, Lung, and Blood Institute (Grant #R01HL107240), William T. Grant Foundation, Alfred P. Sloan Foundation, and the Administration for Children and Families have provided additional funding. The contents of this publication are solely the responsibility of the authors and do not necessarily represent the official views of these institutes and offices. Special acknowledgment goes to Extramural Staff Science Collaborator, Rosalind Berkowitz King, Ph.D., and Lynne Casper, Ph.D., for design of the original Workplace, Family, Health and Well-Being Network Initiative. The authors gratefully acknowledge support from the University of Minnesota's Building Interdisciplinary Research Careers in Women's Health (BIRCWH) Program (5K12HD055887) and the Minnesota Population Center (5R24HD041023), both funded through grants from the Eunice Kennedy Shriver National Institute for Child Health and Human Development (NICHD). We wish to express our gratitude to the worksites, employers, and employees who participated in this research and made this publication possible.

REFERENCES

Allen, T. D. (2001). Family-supportive work environments: The role of organizational perceptions. *Journal of Vocational Behavior, 58,* 414–435.

Allen, T. D., & Armstrong, J. (2006). Further examination of the link between work-family conflict and physical health: The role of health-related behaviors. *American Behavioral Scientist, 49*(9), 1204–1221.

Almeida, D. M., & Wong, J. D. (2009). Life transitions and daily stress processes. In G. H. Elder, Jr. & J. Z. Giele (Eds.), *The craft of life course research* (pp. 41–162). New York, NY: Guilford Press.

Aumann, K., Galinsky, E., & Matos, K. (2011). *The new male mystique.* New York, NY: Families and Work Institute.

Aveyard, P., Markham, W. A., & Cheng, K. K. (2004). A methodological and substantive review of the evidence that schools cause pupils to smoke. *Social Science and Medicine, 58,* 2253–2265.

Bakker, A. B., van Emmerik, H., & Euwema, M. C. (2006). Crossover of burnout and engagement in work teams. *Work and Occupations, 33*(4), 464–489.

Baltes, B., Briggs, T., Huff, J., Wright, J., & Neuman, G. (1999). Flexible and compressed workweek schedules: A meta-analysis of their effects on work-related criteria. *Journal of Applied Psychology, 84*, 496–513.

Baron, R. M., & Kenny, D. A. (1986). The moderator-mediator variable distinction in social psychological research: Conceptual, strategic, and statistical considerations. *Journal of Personality and Social Psychology, 51*(6), 1173–1182.

Berkman, L. F., & Kawachi, I. (2000). *Social epidemiology.* New York, NY: Oxford University Press.

Beutell, N. J. (2010). Health, supervisor support, and workplace culture in relation to work-family synergy. *Psychological Reports, 107*, 3–14.

Bhave, D., Kramer, A., & Glomb, T. (2010). Work–family conflict in work groups: Social information processing, support, and demographic dissimilarity. *Journal of Applied Psychology, 95*, 145–158.

Blair-Loy, M. (2009). Work without end?: Scheduling flexibility and work-to-family conflict among stockbrokers. *Work and Occupations, 36*, 279–317.

Bliese, P. D., & Jex, S. (2002). Incorporating a multilevel perspective into occupational stress research: Theoretical, methodological, and practical implications. *Journal of Occupational Health Psychology, 7*, 265–276.

Bond, J. T., Thompson, C., & Prottas, D. (2002). *Highlights of the national study of the changing workforce 2002.* New York, NY: Families and Work Institute.

Bray, J., Kelly, E., Hammer, L., Almeida, D., Dearing, J., King, R., Buxton, O. (2013). *An integrative, multilevel, and transdisciplinary research approach to challenges of work, family, and health.* Research Triangle Park, NC: RTI Press. RTI Press Publication No. MR-0024-1303. Retrieved from http://www.rti.org/rtipress

Burgard, S. A., Brand, J. E., & House, J. S. (2009). Perceived job insecurity and worker health in the United States. *Social Science and Medicine, 29*, 777–785.

Byron, K. (2005). A meta-analytic review of work-family conflict and its antecedents. *Journal of Vocational Behavior, 67*, 169–198.

Cammann, C., Fichman, M., Jenkins, G. D., & Klesh, J. (1983). Michigan organizational assessment questionnaire. In S. E. Seashore, E. E. Lawler, P. H. Mirvis, & C. Cammann (Eds.), *Assessing organizational change: A guide to methods, measures, and practices* (pp. 71–138). New York, NY: Wiley-Interscience.

Casper, W. J., Eby, L. T., Bordeaux, C., Lockwood, A., & Lambert, D. (2007). A review of research methods in IO/OB work-family research. *Journal of Applied Psychology, 92*(1), 28–43.

Christakis, N. A., & Fowler, J. H. (2007). The spread of obesity in a large social network over 32 years. *The New England Journal of Medicine, 357*, 370–379.

Christakis, N. A., & Fowler, J. H. (2008). The collective dynamics of smoking in a large social network. *The New England Journal of Medicine, 358*, 2249–2258.

Cohen, S., Kamarck, T., & Mermelstein, R. (1983). A global measure of perceived stress. *Journal of Health and Social Behavior, 24*, 386–396.

Cruz, K. S., & Pil, F. K. (2011). Team design and stress: A multilevel analysis. *Human Relations, 64*(10), 1265–1289.

Dahlin, E. C., Kelly, E., & Moen, P. (2008). Is work the new neighborhood? Social ties in the workplace, family, and neighborhood. *The Sociological Quarterly, 49*, 719–736.

Dalgard, O. S., Sørensen, T., Sandanger, I., Nygård, J. F., Svensson, E., & Reas, D. L. (2009). Job demands, job control, and mental health in an 11-year follow-up study: Normal and reversed relationships. *Work & Stress, 23*(3), 284–296.

de Lange, A. H., Taris, T. W., Kompier, M. A., Houtman, I. L., & Bongers, P. M. (2003). The very best of the millennium: Longitudinal research and the demand-control-support model. *Journal of Occupational Health Psychology, 8*, 282–305.

Eby, L. T., Casper, W. J., Lockwood, A., Bordeaux, C., & Brinley, A. (2005). Work and family research in IO/OB: Content analysis and review of the literature (1980–2002). *Journal of Vocational Behavior, 66*, 124–197.

Ferrie, J. E., Shipley, M. J., Marmot, M. G., Martikainen, P., Stansfeld, S. A., & Davey Smith, G. (2001). Job insecurity in white-collar workers: Toward an explanation of associations with health. *Journal of Occupational Health Psychology, 6*, 26–42.

Frone, M. R. (2000). Work-family conflict and employee psychiatric disorders: The national comorbidity survey. *Journal of Applied Psychology, 85*, 888–895.

Frone, M. R., Russell, M., & Barnes, G. M. (1996). Work-family conflict, gender, and health-related outcomes: A study of employed parents in two community samples. *Journal of Occupational Health Psychology, 1*, 57–69.

Glavin, P., & Schieman, S. (2012). Work–family role blurring and work–family conflict: The moderating influence of job resources and job demands. *Work and Occupations, 39*(1), 71–98.

Goode, W. J. (1960). A theory of role strain. *American Sociological Review, 25*, 483–496.

Grzywacz, J. G., & Bass, B. L. (2003). Work, family, and mental health: Testing different models of work-family fit. *Journal of Marriage and Family, 65*(1), 248–261.

Grzywacz, J. G., Casey, P. R., & Jones, F. A. (2007). The effects of workplace flexibility on health behaviors: A cross-sectional and longitudinal analysis. *Journal of Occupational and Environmental Medicine, 49*, 1302–1309.

Hammer, L. B., Cullen, J. C., Neal, M. B., Sinclair, R. R., & Shafiro, M. (2005). The longitudinal effects of work-family conflict and positive spillover on depressive symptoms among dual-earner couples. *Journal of Occupational Health Psychology, 10*, 138–154.

Hammer, L. B., Ernst Kossek, E., Bodner, T., & Crain, T. (2013). Measurement development and validation of the Family Supportive Supervisor Behavior Short-Form (FSSB-SF). *Journal of Occupational Health Psychology, 18*(3), 285–296. doi:10.1037/a0032612

Hammer, L. B., Kossek, E. E., Anger, W. K., Bodner, T., & Zimmerman, K. (2011). Clarifying work-family intervention processes: The roles of work-family conflict and family supportive supervisor behaviors. *Journal of Applied Psychology, 96*, 134–150.

Hammer, L. B., Kossek, E. E., Yragui, N. L., Bodner, T. E., & Hanson, G. C. (2009). Development and validation of a multidimensional measure of Family Supportive Supervisor Behaviors (FSSB). *Journal of Management, 35*, 837–856.

Hammer, L. B., Neal, M. B., Newsom, J., Brockwood, K. J., & Colton, C. (2005). A longitudinal study of the effects of dual-earner couples' utilization of family-friendly workplace supports on work and family outcomes. *Journal of Applied Psychology, 90*, 799–810.

Hammer, T. H., Saksvik, P. Ø., Nytrø, K., Torvatn, H., & Bayazit, M. (2004). Expanding the psychosocial work environment: Workplace norms and work-family conflict as correlates of stress and health. *Journal of Occupational Health Psychology, 9*, 83–97.

Hämmig, O., Knecht, M., Läubli, T., & Bauer, G. F. (2011). Work-life conflict and musculoskeletal disorders: A cross-sectional study of an unexplored association. *BMC Musculoskeletal Disorders, 12*, 1–12.

Hausser, J., Mojzisch, A., Niesel, M., & Schulz-Hardt, S. (2010). Ten years on: A review of recent research on the job demands-control (support) model and psychological well-being. *Work and Stress, 24*, 1–35.

House, J. S. (2002). Understanding social factors and inequalities in health: 20th century progress and 21st century prospects. *Journal of Health and Social Behavior*, 43, 125–142.
Karasek, R., Brisson, C., Kawakami, N., Houtman, I., Bongers, P., & Amick, B. (1998). The Job Content Questionnaire (JCQ): An instrument for internationally comparative assessments of psychosocial job characteristics. *Journal of Occupational Health Psychology*, 3, 322–355.
Karasek, R. A. (1979). Job demands, job decision latitude, and mental strain: Implications for job redesign. *Administration Science Quarterly*, 24, 285–307.
Karasek, R. A., & Theorell, T. (1990). *Healthy work: Stress, productivity and the reconstruction of working life*. New York, NY: Basic Books.
Kawachi, I., & Berkman, L. F. (2003). *Neighborhoods and health*. New York, NY: Oxford University Press.
Kelly, E. L., Moen, P., & Tranby, E. (2011). Changing workplaces to reduce work-family conflict: Schedule control in a white-collar organization. *American Sociological Review*, 76, 1–26.
Kelly, E. L., Moen, P., Oakes, J. M., Fan, W., Okechukwu, C., Davis, K. D., ... Casper, L. M. (2014). Changing work and work-family conflict evidence from the work, family, and health network. *American Sociological Review*, 79(3), 485–516. doi:10.1177/0003122414531435
Kessler, R. C., Barker, P. R., Colpe, L. J., Epstein, J. F., Gfroerer, J. C., Hiripi, E., ... Zaslavsky, A. M. (2003). Screening for serious mental illness in the general population. *Archives of General Psychiatry*, 60, 184–189.
King, R. B., Karuntzos, G., Casper, L. M., Moen, P., Davis, K., Berkman, L., ... Kossek, E. (2012). Work-family balance issues and work-leave policies. In R. J. Gatchel & I. Z. Schultz (Eds.), *Handbook of occupational health and wellness* (pp. 323–340). New York, NY: Springer.
Klein, K. J., & Kozlowski, S. W. J. (2000). From micro to meso: Critical steps in conceptualizing and conducting multilevel research. *Organizational Research Methods*, 3, 211–236.
Kossek, E., Hammer, L., Bodner, T., Petty, R., Michel, N., & Yragui, N. (2012). A multi-level model of antecedents of work-family support and linkages to health and work outcomes. Paper presented at National Academy of Management meeting, Boston, MA.
Kossek, E., Lautsch, B. A., & Eaton, S. (2006). Telecommuting, control and boundary management: Correlates of policy use and practice, job control, and work-family effectiveness. *Journal of Vocational Behavior*, 68, 347–367.
Kossek, E., Pichler, S., Bodner, T., & Hammer, L. B. (2011). Workplace social support and work-family conflict: A meta-analysis clarifying the influence of general and work-family specific supervisor and organizational support. *Personnel Psychology*, 64, 289–313.
Kossek, E. E., Colquitt, J. A., & Noe, R. A. (2001). Caregiving decisions, well-being, and performance: The effects of place and provider as a function of dependent type and work-family climates. *Academy of Management Journal*, 44, 29–44.
Krieger, N. (2011). *Epidemiology and the people's health: Theory and context*. New York, NY: Oxford University Press.
Lam, J., Fox, K., Fan, W., Moen, P., Kelly, E. L., Hammer, L., & Kossek, E. (2015, forthcoming). Manager characteristics and employee job insecurity around a merger announcement: The role of status and crossover. *The Sociological Quarterly*.

Lundberg, U. (1996). Influence of paid and unpaid work on psychophysiological stress responses of men and women. *Journal of Occupational Health Psychology, 1*(2), 117–130.

Maslach, C., & Jackson, S. (1986). *Maslach burnout inventory manual* (2nd ed.). Palo Alto, CA: Consulting Psychologists Press.

Mausner-Dorsch, H., & Eaton, W. W. (2000). Psychosocial work environment and depression: Epidemiologic assessment of the demand-control model. *American Journal of Public Health, 90*(11), 1765.

Moen, P., & Chesley, N. (2008). Toxic job ecologies, time convoys, and work-family conflict: Can families (re)gain control and life-course "fit"? In K. Korabik, D. S. Lero, & D. L. Whitehead (Eds.), *Handbook of work–family integration: Research, theory, and best practices* (pp. 95–122). New York, NY: Elsevier.

Moen, P., Kelly, E. L., & Huang, Q. (2008). Work, family, and life-course fit: Does control over work time matter? *Journal of Vocational Behavior, 73,* 414–425.

Moen, P., Kelly, E. L., & Lam, J. (2013). Healthy work revisited: Do changes in time strain predict well-being? *Journal of Occupational Health Psychology, 18*(2), 157–172.

Moen, P., Kelly, E. L., Tranby, E., & Huang, Q. (2011). Changing work, changing health: Can real work-time flexibility promote health behaviors and well-being? *Journal of Health and Social Behavior, 52*(4), 404–429.

Moen, P., Lam, J., Ammons, S., & Kelly, E. L. (2013). Time work by overworked professionals: Strategies in response to the stress of higher status. *Work and Occupations, 40*(2), 79–114.

Moen, P., & Roehling, P. (2005). *The career mystique: Cracks in the American dream.* Boulder, CO: Rowman & Littlefield.

Netemeyer, R. G., Boles, J. S., & McMurrian, R. (1996). Development and validation of work–family conflict and family-work conflict scales. *Journal of Applied Psychology, 81,* 400–410.

Oakes, J. M., & Kaufman, J. S. (2006). *Methods in social epidemiology.* San Francisco, CA: Jossey-Bass.

O'Neill, J. W., Harrison, M. H., Cleveland, J., Almeida, D., Stawski, R., & Crouter, A. C. (2009). Work-family climate, organizational commitment, and turnover: Multilevel contagion effects of leaders. *Journal of Vocational Behavior, 74,* 18–29.

Pearlin, L. I. (2010). The life course and the stress process: Some conceptual comparisons. *The Journals of Gerontology Series B: Psychological Sciences and Social Sciences, 65B*(2), 207–215.

Pearlin, L. I., Schieman, S., Fazio, E. M., & Meersman, S. C. (2005). Stress, health, and the life course: Some conceptual perspectives. *Journal of Health and Social Behavior, 46*(2), 205–219.

Quick, J. C., & Tetrick, L. E. (2011). *Handbook of occupational health psychology* (2nd ed.). Washington, DC: American Psychological Association.

Rau, R., & Triemer, A. (2004). Overtime in relation to blood pressure and mood during work, leisure, and night time. *Social Indicators Research, 67*(1–2), 51–73.

Raudenbush, S. W., & Bryk, A. S. (2002). *Hierarchical linear models* (2nd ed.). Thousand Oaks, CA: Sage.

Roeters, A., Van der Lippe, T., & Kluwer, E. S. (2010). Work characteristics and parent–child relationship quality: The mediating role of temporal involvement. *Journal of Marriage and Family, 72,* 1317–1328.

Sabbath, E. L., Melchior, M., Goldberg, M., Zins, M., & Berkman, L. F. (2012). Work and family demands: predictors of all-cause sickness absence in the GAZEL cohort. *The European Journal of Public Health, 22*(1), 101–106. doi:10.1093/eurpub/ckr041

Sampson, R. J., Morenoff, J. D., & Gannon-Rowley, T. (2002). Assessing neighborhood effects: Social processes and new directions in research. *Annual Review Sociology, 28*, 443–478.

Schieman, S., Milkie, M. A., & Glavin, P. (2009). When work interferes with life: Work-nonwork interference and the influence of work-related demands and resources. *American Sociological Review, 74*, 966–988.

Sennett, R. (1998). *The corrosion of character: The personal consequences of work in the new capitalism*. New York, NY: W. W. Norton & Co.

Sorensen, G., Stoddard, A., Stoffel, S., Buxton, O. M., Sembajwe, G., Hashimoto, D., ... Hopcia, K. (2011). The role of the work context in multiple wellness outcomes for hospital patient care workers. *Journal of Occupational Environmental Medicine, 53*, 899–910.

Thomas, L. T., & Ganster, D. C. (1995). Impact of family-supportive work variables on work-family conflict and strain: A control perspective. *Journal of Applied Psychology, 80*, 6–15.

van Emmerik, I. J. H., & Peeters, M. C. W. (2009). Crossover specificity of team-level work-family conflict to individual-level work-family conflict. *Journal of Managerial Psychology, 24*(3), 254–268.

Van Steenbergen, E. F., & Ellemers, N. (2009). Is managing the work-family interface worthwhile?: Benefits for employee health and performance. *Journal of Organizational Behavior, 30*, 617–642.

Van Yperen, N. W., & Snijders, T. A. B. (2000). A multilevel analysis of the demands-control model: Is stress at work determined by factors at the group level or the individual level? *Journal of Occupational Health Psychology, 5*, 182–190.

Westman, M., Bakker, A. B., Roziner, I., & Sonnentag, S. (2011). Crossover of job demands and emotional exhaustion within teams: A longitudinal multilevel study. *Anxiety, Stress, and Coping, 24*(5), 561–577.

APPENDIX

Table A1. Description of Scales/Questions.

Scale	Source	Variable Description	Cronbach's Alpha	Range
Work-to-family conflict	Netemeyer (1996)	The demands of your work interfere with your family or personal time. The amount of time your job takes up makes it difficult to fulfill your family or personal responsibilities. Things you want to do at home do not get done because of the demands your job puts on you. Your job produces strain that makes it difficult to fulfill your family or personal duties. Due to your work-related duties, you have to make changes to your plans for family or personal activities. *Response Choices (reversed): 1 = Strongly Disagree, 2 = Disagree, 3 = Neither, 4 = Agree, 5 = Strongly Agree*	0.91	1–5
Job satisfaction	Cammann et al. (1983)	In general, you like working at your job. In general, you are satisfied with your job. You are generally satisfied with the kind of work you do in this job. *Response Choices (reversed): 1 = Strongly Disagree, 2 = Disagree, 3 = Neither, 4 = Agree, 5 = Strongly Agree*	0.86	1–5
Burnout (emotional exhaustion)	Maslach and Jackson (1986)	You feel emotionally drained from your work. How often do you feel this way? You feel burned out by your work. How often do you feel this way? You feel used up at the end of the workday. How often do you feel this way?	0.89	1–7

Table A1. (*Continued*)

Scale	Source	Variable Description	Cronbach's Alpha	Range
		Response Choices (reversed): *1 = Never, 2 = A few times a year or less, 3 = Once a month or less, 4 = A few times a month, 5 = Once a week, 6 = A few times a week, 7 = Every day*		
Perceived stress	Cohen et al. (1983)	During the past 30 days, how often have you felt that you were unable to control the important things in your life? During the past 30 days, how often have you felt confident about your ability to handle your personal problems? During the past 30 days, how often have you felt that things were going your way? During the past 30 days, how often have you felt difficulties were piling up so high that you could not overcome them? *Response Choices (not reversed):* *1 = Very often, 2 = Fairly often, 3 = Sometimes, 4 = Almost never, 5 = Never*	0.76	4–20
Psychological distress	Kessler et al. (2003)	During the past 30 days, how much of the time did you feel so sad nothing could cheer you up? During the past 30 days, how much of the time did you feel nervous? During the past 30 days, how much of the time did you feel restless or fidgety? During the past 30 days, how much of the time did you feel hopeless? During the past 30 days, how much of the time did you feel that everything was an effort?	0.77	6–30

Table A1. (*Continued*)

Scale	Source	Variable Description	Cronbach's Alpha	Range
		During the past 30 days, how much of the time did you feel worthless? *Response Choices (reversed): 1 = None of the time, 2 = A little of the time, 3 = Some of the time, 4 = Most of the time, 5 = All of the time*		
Organizational work-family climate scale	Kossek et al. (2001)	In your workplace, employees are generally expected to take time away from their family or personal lives to get their work done. In your workplace, employees are expected to put their families or personal lives second to their jobs. In your workplace, employees are expected to make work their top priority. *Response Choices (not reversed): 1 = Strongly Agree, 2 = Agree, 3 = Neither, 4 = Disagree, 5 = Strongly Disagree*	0.79	1–5
FSSB	Hammer et al. (2009); Hammer et al. (2013)	Your supervisor makes you feel comfortable talking to him/her about my conflicts between work and nonwork. Your supervisor works effectively with employees to creatively solve conflicts between work and nonwork. Your supervisor demonstrates effective behaviors in how to juggle work and nonwork issues. Your supervisor organizes the work in your department or unit to jointly benefit employees and the company. *Response Choices (reversed): 1 = Strongly Disagree, 2 = Disagree, 3 = Neither, 4 = Agree, 5 = Strongly Agree*	0.88	1–5

Table A1. (*Continued*)

Scale	Source	Variable Description	Cronbach's Alpha	Range
Schedule control	Modified from Thomas and Ganster (1995)	How much choice do you have over when you take vacations or days off? How much choice do you have over when you can take off a few hours? How much choice do you have over when you begin and end each workday? How much choice do you have over the total number of hours you work each week? How much choice do you have over doing some of your work at home or at another location, instead of [insert company name/ location]? How much choice do you have over the number of personal phone calls you make or receive while you work? How much choice do you have over the amount or times you take work home with you? How much choice do you have over shifting to a part-time schedule (or full-time if currently part-time) while remaining in your current position if you wanted to do so? *Response Choices (reversed): 1 = Very Little, 2 = Little, 3 = A moderate amount, 4 = Much, 5 = Very Much*	0.79	1–5
Psychological job demands scale	Karasek et al. (1998)	You do not have enough time to get your job done. Your job requires very fast work. Your job requires very hard work. *Response Choices (reversed): 1 = Strongly Disagree, 2 = Disagree, 3 = Neither, 4 = Agree, 5 = Strongly Agree*	0.58	1–5

Table A1. (*Continued*)

Scale	Source	Variable Description	Cronbach's Alpha	Range
Job insecurity	Used in General Social Survey	Thinking about the next 12 months, how likely do you think it is that you will lose your job or be laid off? *Response Categories (reversed): 1 = Not at all likely, 2 = Not too likely, 3 = Fairly Likely, 4 = Very Likely*		1–4

THE RELATIONSHIP OF WORK UNIT PRESSURE TO SATISFACTION WITH WORK–FAMILY BALANCE: A NEW TWIST ON NEGATIVE SPILLOVER?

Jacquelyn Boone James, Marcie Pitt-Catsouphes, Tay K. McNamara, David L. Snow and Patricia L. Johnson

ABSTRACT

Purpose — *We explore: (1) the effects of work unit pressure on employees' satisfaction with work–family balance (S-WFB); (2) the effects of individual-level job and family pressures on S-WFB; and (3) the extent to which schedule control moderates the negative influences of work unit pressure and other demands on employee S-WFB — among employees in a large healthcare system.*

Methodology — *The data come from employee responses to the baseline survey (n = 3,950) administered in September 2012, and from administrative* unit-level data (445 units) showing the extent to which units were "on-budget" (within 5 percent), "over-budget," or "under-budget."

Findings – *Practices associated with cost containment in a healthcare system of 10,000 employees in the United States appear to have a negative impact on employee S-WFB. Working in a unit that is "under-budget" is negatively associated with individual S-WFB. Employees with high job demands, longer hours, responsibilities for children and/or adults, also reported lower S-WFB than employees without these characteristics.*

Research limitations/implications – *Research is limited by lack of measures specific to healthcare workers, the use of baseline data only, and sample size for some of the analyses.*

Social implications – *Schedule control makes a difference even under high work pressure. The lack of interactions among variables that typically moderate relationships between work pressures and S-WFB suggests the need for more support for healthcare workers under the strain of cost containment.*

Originality/value of the chapter – *We include an objective indicator of unit-level job pressures on individual employees, thus identifying specific ways that work stress affects S-WFB.*

Keywords: Job demands; family demands; schedule control; satisfaction with work–family balance

INTRODUCTION

It has long been acknowledged that the work–family interface is complex and multifaceted (Barnett, 1996; Dilworth, 2004; James, Barnett, & Brennan, 1998; MacDermid & Harvey, 2006; Westman, 2001). Experiences at work and at home have been associated with both positive and negative spillover from work to home, and home to work (Barnett, 1996; Bronfenbrenner, 1986; Chesley, 2005; Dilworth, 2004; Frone, 2003; Kossek, Colquitt, & Noe, 2010) and thus with satisfaction with work–family balance (S-WFB) (Valcour, 2007). Grzywacz and Marks (2000) have drawn from ecological theory to suggest that contextual factors, both work and family demands and expectations, and other aspects of job satisfaction can affect these outcomes. Variables such as work pressure and/or negative interactions at work have been seen to affect negative work to home spillover (e.g., Frone, Russell, & Cooper, 1992; Frone, Yardley, & Markel, 1997; Greenhaus & Parasuraman, 1987). The findings of previous investigations that have focused on context have elevated the academic discourse about the work−family interface; however, it is important to note that these studies have focused on subjective measures of pressure on individual employees. Importantly, we were unable to find published articles about studies that focused on the impact of work unit pressures, measured by objective indicators, which could contribute to S-WFB experienced by individual employees.

The purpose of this chapter is threefold, to explore: (1) the effects of work unit pressure (in this case, unit performance in meeting financial metrics) on employees' S-WFB; (2) the effects of individual-level job and family pressures on employees' S-WFB; and (3) the extent to which schedule control moderates the negative influences of work unit pressure and other job and family demands on employee S-WFB − among employees working in a large healthcare system.

EMPIRICAL AND THEORETICAL BACKGROUND

Researchers and practitioners have expended considerable effort to better understand the extent to which individuals are satisfied with their abilities to be successful in both their work and family domains. Resource and demand theory (Bakker & Demerouti, 2007) has been used to examine the extent to which the demands in one domain deplete resources of time and/or energy for meeting obligations in another creating conflict or strain (Voydanoff, 2005). Thus, more demands and fewer resources lead to decreased S-WFB (Bakker, ten Brummelhuis, Prins, & van der Heijden, 2011; Barham, Gottlieb, & Kelloway, 1998; Besen, Matz-Costa, James, & Pitt-Catsouphes, 2012; Glavin & Schieman, 2012).

WORK−FAMILY BALANCE

The concept of WFB has been seen as a measure of employees' perceptions of their capability of meeting their own standards for obligations at home and at work (Higgins, Duxbury, & Johnson, 2000). There has been some confusion in the scholarly literature about the differences between WFB and other terms (Allen, Johnson, Kiburz, & Shockley, 2013; Guest, 2002; Valcour, 2007). As noted by Carlson, Grzywacz, and Zivnuska (2009), most work−family researchers have operationalized WFB as the absence of work−family conflict (Grzywacz, Almeida, & McDonald, 2002; Moen, Fan, & Kelly, 2013). Voydanoff (2005) and others have used person− environment fit theory to argue that the more adequate measure of successful negotiation of the work−family interface is one that assesses the extent to which there is a good fit between one's preferences for time, energy, and effort spent in one domain versus the other (Pitt-Catsouphes & Matz-Costa, 2008). Valcour (2007) suggests that it is particularly important to determine the extent to which employees are satisfied with the degree of balance they have. Valcour's measure incorporates not only individuals' assessments of WFB, but also has an affective component, that is, how they feel about it.

There also is extensive literature about the social context of work (Blair-Loy & Wharton, 2002; Duffy, Ganster, Shaw, Johnson, & Pagon, 2006; James, McKechnie, & Swanberg, 2011; Wayne, Shore, & Liden, 1997). Indeed, most workplaces are structured into units or teams; they are not just a collection of individuals. As pointed out by Bakker, Westman, and van Emmerik (2009), such shared environments may create contagion effects such that difficulties experienced by one member of a team or unit can transmit to others (see also Westman, 2001). Yet, most previous investigations of the ways in which work demands affect family life have used individual reports of work pressures; unit-level demands are seldom assessed for the ways in which they might affect individual S-WFB. This study makes a contribution to the literature about work−family interface by examining the relationships between work pressures exerted on a work unit (measured as the unit's performance with regard to meeting financial metrics) and the levels of S-WFB reported by employees working in that unit, while also assessing the contributions of individual-level work and family stressors.

Efforts to unravel work−family conundrums are especially important in the healthcare sector where the workforce is predominantly female and older, and where the concern about work−family conflict is higher than in other industry sectors (Sweet, Pitt-Catsouphes, Besen, Hovhannisyan, & Pasha, 2010). In the context of longer lives and longer careers (James, Pitt-Catsouphes, Coplon, & Cohen, 2013) the necessity of caregiving for spouses or aging parents is on the rise among workers, some of whom are caring for both children and parents (Gastfriend, James, & McNamara, 2012).

Importantly, Sweet et al. (2010) found that healthcare workers are more likely to report difficulty in concentrating on work because of family, find it more difficult to fulfill family responsibility because of work, and more likely to come home from work too tired to do household chores than are employees in other job sectors.

It has been said that the healthcare sector is "in some sense the prototypical industry of our time, just as automobiles were the prototypical industry of the 1930s" (Gerstel, Clawson, & Huyser, 2007, p. 370). Healthcare accounts for approximately 18 percent of the total U.S. GDP (World Bank, 2011) and operates in an environment of intensive effort to stem rising costs. Thus, according to Gerstel et al. (2007), there are concomitant demands for longer hours and alternative schedules. While some healthcare systems have embraced new ways of working, including the provision of flexible work arrangements as one solution for optimizing schedule control and enhancing S-WFB, many have not (Sweet et al., 2010). Importantly, some employers in this sector report many barriers to doing so (e.g., Bailyn, Collins, & Song, 2007; Harton, Marshburn, Kuykendall, Poston, & Mears, 2012).

DEMANDS/PRESSURES AT WORK

The job demands/control theory (JDC) and related job demands/resources theory propose that, in general, higher work demands in the context of inadequate resources to meet those demands lead to stress, strain, and other negative outcomes for individual workers (Bakker & Demerouti, 2007; Bakker et al., 2011; Karasek, 1979; Schaufeli, Bakker, & Van Rhenen, 2009). As defined by Voydanoff, "Demands are structural or psychological claims associated with role requirements, expectations, and norms to which individuals must respond or adapt by exerting physical or mental effort" (2005, p. 823).

Individuals, however, work within organizations, which are under pressures of their own emanating from such sources as the state, through regulatory and governmental agencies, the professions, public and private interest groups, and consumers (Goodstein, 2013). Organizational work units are themselves under pressures to comply with metrics set by the organization. Individual employees then have pressures associated with their own responsibilities on the job. As noted above, research on the work−family interface has primarily focused on this latter type of "job pressure." Thus, there is a need to focus greater attention on examining the effects of pressures exerted on teams or units within organizations.

Work Unit Pressure

Work units share experiences, norms, and expectations. They are often evaluated as a group; for example, unit performance might be gauged against organizational expectations for unit productivity and related costs. Such expectations can create a type of pressure on the unit. Some pressures can be measured as the sum of individual team members' collective assessment of their experiences such as perceptions of their supervisor's expectations and the unit's efficacy (Bakker et al., 2009). In this chapter, we examine pressure on work units as indicated by the unit's success in meeting budgetary metrics. The managers of work units within the healthcare system under investigation here are required to accurately anticipate census levels, staffing needs, and other administrative costs for their units to develop a proposed budget. Once this budget is approved, they are then evaluated on their ability to manage this budget effectively. A key metric used to determine this is the extent to which they are over- or under-budget on a monthly basis. To be either over- or under-budget by more than 5 percent is considered a sign of poor management and, as such, brings scrutiny from organizational leaders.

According to key informants for the organization, a manager who is either over- or under-budget has to be prepared to explain how he or she missed the target, especially if this pattern continues for more than a month or so. This metric is also used as an indicator of competency in annual performance appraisals and will impact overall scores and eligibility for merit increases. It is clearly established within the organization that the manager's role is to ensure the effective, efficient, and sustainable use of human and financial resources. If budgets cannot be brought into compliance, managers can be dismissed. In these ways, each unit, and thereby the employees working in that unit, is under considerable pressure to comply with these targets. The expectation to "get in line in terms of budget metrics" is a demand felt by everyone. Those managers who are consistently over-budget by more than 5 percent each month can be seen as ineffective in their management of the unit and are under pressure to reduce expenditures for staffing and other resources. Having a budget that is consistently over-budget, except when justified as due to unanticipated increases in patient volumes and related costs, is seen as a serious issue. On the other hand, work unit pressures may be greater in those units that are under-budget by more than 5 percent, since they are expending less on staffing and other resources to complete their defined tasks than has been determined as necessary for optimal unit performance. This can occur for a variety of reasons including high turnover and churn (resulting in positions not being filled at specific times and salary expenses being lower as a result).

In this chapter, we explore the relationship between this type of organizational pressure on the work unit and S-WFB. We expect that being either over- or under-budget will be negatively associated with S-WFB, with the possibility that this effect will be strongest for employees in work units that are under-budget. On the basis of the job demands-control model, we expect that employees in units that move from under-budget to on-budget will show corresponding increases in S-WFB (since resources are being added), while those in units that move from over-budget to on-budget will show decreases in S-WFB (since resources are being reduced).

Individual-Level Work Hours

Work hours represent another type of job demand experienced by individual employees (Valcour, Ollier-Malaterre, Matz-Costa, Pitt-Catsouphes, & Brown, 2011). Numerous investigations have found that perceptions of excessive work hours/more hours than "the ideal" are associated with increased work–family conflict and/or diminished S-WFB (Frone, Russell, & Cooper, 1997; Grandey, Cordeiro, & Michael, 2007; Major, Klein, & Ehrhart, 2002; Valcour, 2007; Voydanoff, 2005; Wallace, 1997, 1999). In addition, there are indications that long work hours (or work hours that go beyond the number of "ideal" work hours) are associated with decreased perceptions of organizational support (Forret & de Janasz, 2005). Thus, here we consider work hours to be another indicator of job pressure.

Job Demands

Karasek's (1979) JDC model would suggest that high job demands (e.g., perceptions of the need for working fast, working hard, dealing with disruptions) would be negatively associated with S-WFB and would in fact increase the negative association between other sources of work pressure and S-WFB. Karasek in fact specified that job demands included "psychological stressors involved in accomplishing the work load, stressors related to unexpected tasks and stressors of job-related personal conflict" (1979, p. 291). In the current economic climate of the healthcare sector, job demands may have increased as organizations have struggled to stem rising costs (Gerstel et al., 2007).

DEMANDS/PRESSURES AT HOME

It is widely assumed that caregiving responsibilities represent demands from the family (see, e.g., Abendroth, van der Lippe, & Maas, 2012; Barnett, Marshall, & Singer, 1992; Williams, 2000). Among working families today, the ensuing time constraints for both men and women have been assumed to spawn much of the research on the ways that responsibilities at work affect satisfaction with life at home (Dilworth, 2004). Research suggests that both the presence and the number of children add to parental demands and therefore lower S-WFB (summarized by Dilworth, 2004). Especially in the healthcare sector, which is predominated by older women (Sweet et al., 2010), caregiving responsibilities for adults are also likely to negatively affect S-WFB.

MODERATOR VARIABLE – SCHEDULE CONTROL

Schedule Control

Previous theory and research emphasize that the extent to which employees feel that they have control over the way their time is spent during the day is related to S-WFB and conflict (Glavin & Schieman, 2012; Thomas & Ganster, 1995). Schedule control may be thought of as some level of autonomy with regard to "starting and finishing times, breaks, days off, vacations and the number of work hours" (Geurts, Beckers, Taris, Kompier, & Smulders, 2009). The ability to have some say in the schedule that is created and the ability to make decisions are said to be important indicators of job control (Bakker & Demerouti, 2007). Perceived schedule control may reduce the impact of both work and family pressures (Casey & Grzywacz, 2008; Day, Sibley, Scott, Tallon, Ackroyd-Stolarz, 2009; Geurts et al., 2009), and serve to moderate the negative relationships between work and family demands and S-WFB.

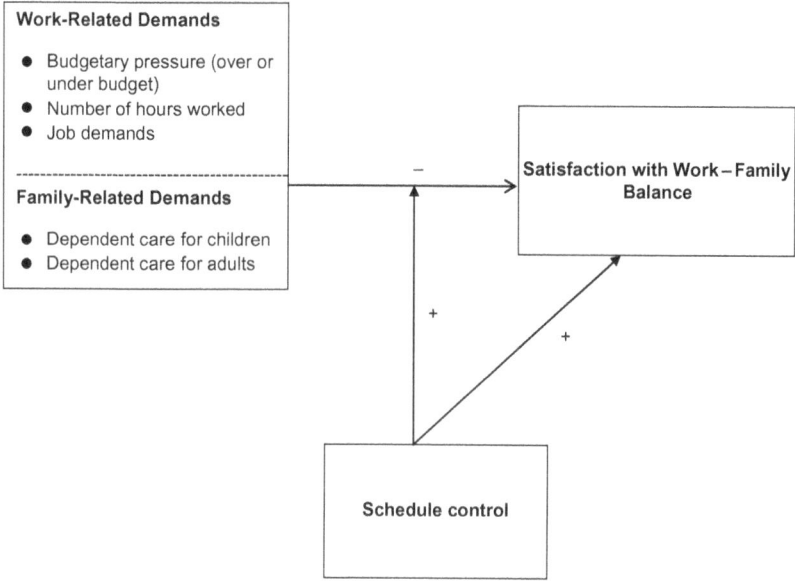

Fig. 1. Conceptual Model.

Fig. 1 shows the expected relationships among the key study variables. The JDC model would suggest that both work-related and family-related demands are negatively associated with S-WFB, while schedule control is positively associated with S-WFB. Further, we expect that schedule control will serve to "buffer" the negative effects of the work and family demands.

INDIVIDUAL FACTORS

Other individual factors such as gender, age, health status, level of education, and organizational site are also important contextual factors which may affect S-WFB. In addition, satisfaction with job security and benefits is especially important in the new economy (Sweet, Moen, & Meiksins, 2007). Therefore, we add several dimensions of job satisfaction (including constructive relationships, job security, culture of respect, and benefits with monetary value) that also may influence S-WFB. The effects of these variables are controlled for in each of the analyses.

DATA AND METHODS

Sample

This study is part of an ongoing initiative by the Sloan Center on Aging & Work at Boston College to examine the impact of a workplace flexibility initiative on employee and business outcomes. The study took place at a large regional healthcare organization in the United States (ModernMedical, a pseudonym) from September 2012 to January 2014. Employees at ModernMedical are similar to healthcare workers in general with respect to age, gender, and educational attainment (Sweet et al., 2010).

Most of the data for this chapter come from employee responses to the baseline survey, which took place in September 2012, and from administrative unit-level data provided by the organization. The baseline questionnaire covers important topics related to work- and family-level pressures as well as other known predictors of S-WFB, including schedule control, and demographic and economic factors.

All employees and managers who were employed at ModernMedical in August 2012 ($N=8,916$) were invited to participate in the baseline survey, The Boston College Study of the [ModernMedical] Health System; 3,950 employees and managers completed it (response rate = 44.3 percent). We omitted managers from the analyses presented here ($N=405$). We also excluded 332 observations because of highly problematic responses related to the operating expenses figures. For 12 work units, this was manifested in the form of a negative or zero actual expenses figure for the current year. For 12 work units, it was manifested as a negative or zero target operating expenses figure. For 45 work units, target or actual expenses were not available. For an additional two work units, the internal database indicated that they exceeded their target operating expenses by 1,000 percent or more in the past month. Feedback from human resource representatives at the site confirmed that these were not errors, but represented work units with atypical situations (e.g., grant funded rather than funded through the organization's main operating budget).

Of the remaining 3,213 observations, we omitted 388 because they were missing 75 percent or more of the items used in these analyses. We used chained equations to impute data for the remaining cases (Royston, 2004). Our final analysis did not include 36 cases from the final imputed data because those cases were missing data on all dependent variables, resulting in an analysis sample of 2,789 respondents. This represented 71 percent of the original sample of employees and 31 percent of the targeted population.

Within the remaining cases, the median item nonresponse was 6.4 percent, with a range of 5.9–12.0 percent. The items with nonresponse greater than 10 percent were consistently those in the demographic sections (age, gender, and health) and the job satisfaction variables. Due to the imputation method, this may have led to slightly larger (i.e., more conservative) standard errors for these variables. After excluding individuals with insufficient data, there were 2,789 observations in 445 units, ranging from 1 to 60 observations per unit (average of 6.3).

Measures

Dependent Variable – Employee-Level Satisfaction with Work–Family Balance
We measured S-WFB using the mean of five items from Valcour's (2007) scale. Items asked respondents to rate how satisfied they were with (1) "the way you divide your time between work and personal or family life," "The way you divide your attention between work and home," "How well your work life and your personal or family life fit together," "Your ability to balance the needs of your job with those of your personal or family life," and "the opportunity you have to perform your job well and yet be able to perform home-related duties adequately." Each item ranged from 1 ("very dissatisfied") to 6 ("very satisfied"). Higher values indicated higher S-WFB.

Work-Related Demands
We included three variables measuring work-related demands: budgetary pressure, work hours, and job demands.

Budgetary Pressure. Budgetary pressure was defined in terms of the deviation of the work unit's actual operating expenses from target operating expenses, expressed as a percentage. Our measures of actual and target total operating expenses at the work unit-level are the sum of wages and salaries and other operating expenses from ModernMedical's internal financial compliance database. The percent deviation from target is defined as the dollar difference between actual and target total operating expenses for the month of September 2012, as a percentage of the target. With the input and assistance of site contacts, we identified a "5 percent" threshold at which a work unit would need to provide explanations of their deviation from their target budgets. For the purposes of this study, spending 5 percent or more below their target budget in the most recent month constituted being "under-budget." Spending 5 percent or more above their target budget in the most recent month constituted being "over-budget."

Number of Hours Worked. We used responses to the question, "In a typical week, how many hours do you work?" We treated this variable as categorical to account for nonlinearity in effect.

Job Demands. Job demands (alpha = 0.83) was the mean of six Likert-type items based on Karasek's job content questionnaires, each ranging from 1 ("strongly disagree") to 6 ("strongly agree"). The items were: (1) "I do not have enough time to get my job done"; (2) "My job requires very fast work"; (3) "My job requires very hard work"; (4) "My job requires excessive work"; (5) "My job involves conflicting demands"; and (6) "I have many interruptions and disturbances in my job." The first five of these items were based on the five psychological demands items from Karasek's original Job Content Questionnaire (Karasek, Brison, Kawakami, Houtman, & Bongers, 1998), while the sixth item relates to the items regarding the "hecticness" of work added (Karasek, 1985).

Family-Related Demands
We included two measures of family demands: dependent care for children and dependent care for adults. The question for dependent care for children is as follows: "Do you have any children under the age of 19?" For adult care, the questions are: "Do you provide care for or support to a family member age 65 or older who needs assistance?" and "In the previous questions, we have asked about care that you provide to children under the age of 19 and care you provide to those 65 and older. Do you provide regular care to anyone else?" Each of these variables was coded 0 ("no dependent care responsibilities") or 1 ("dependent care responsibilities"). We replicated all models including interactions between the two dependent care variables, but results for interaction terms were not statistically significant.

Moderator Variable – Schedule Control
Following Thomas and Ganster (1995) we measured schedule control (Cronbach's alpha = 0.78) using a seven-item scale with values that range from 1 ("no control") to 4 ("a lot of control"). Items asked respondents to rate the amount of control they had over: (1) "when you take vacations or days off," (2) "when you can take a few hours off," (3) "when you begin and end each workday," (4) "the amount of times you work unanticipated

overtime," (5) "the amount of times you devote time beyond regularly scheduled hours," (6) "shifting to a part-time schedule if you wanted to do so," and (7) "the total number of hours your work each week." One item was omitted (i.e., whether the employee could work at home) from this scale because it was highly correlated with the type of work done.

Control Variables
Control variables included: age in years, gender, health, education, number of hours worked per week, job satisfaction, and work location.

Age. We calculated age based on year of birth and the year at time of interview. In preliminary models, we treated age as categorical, continuous with a quadratic term, or continuous with additional dummy variables (e.g., whether age 50) to test for nonlinearity of effect. Due to nonsignificance of these models, we opted for the simpler continuous version.

Gender. Gender was a dichotomous variable coded 0 if male and 1 if female.

Education. We treated education as interval, but the item itself was based on highest degree of educational attainment, coded: (1) "less than high school," (2) "high school diploma or GED," (3) "some college," (4) "2-year college degree," (5) "bachelor's degree," (6) "some graduate training or graduate school," and (7) "graduate degree." In preliminary models, we treated this variable as categorical. Due to the small number of cases in some categories (i.e., four categories comprised less than 10 percent of the sample each), we replicated all models treating education as interval. The main findings of this study were similar in size, direction, and level of significance for both versions of education.

Health. Health was a continuous measure, based on two survey questions: "How would you rate your physical health these days?" and "How would you rate your mental health these days?" A score of zero corresponds to "worst possible health" and a score of 10 corresponds to "perfect health." The sum of the two items, which could range from 0 to 20, is used as the measure of health due to the high correlation between the two measures (alpha = 0.75). Multivariate models were replicated using physical health only and mental health only to ensure that the major conclusions of the chapter were similar.

Satisfaction with Job Conditions. Employees' rated their satisfaction with nine aspects of their employment using a scale that ranges from 1 ("very dissatisfied") to 6 ("very satisfied") (Cronbach's alpha = 0.90). They were asked, "We would like to know your assessment of the following resources/policies available to employees, so how satisfied are you with the following ..." The nine options are: (1) "your job security," (2) "your compensation," (3) "benefits that have monetary value," (4) "opportunities for learning and development," (5) "health and wellness resources," (6) "opportunities to engage in meaningful work," (7) "clear and effective information in respect to employment security," (8) "clear and effective promotion of respect, inclusion, and diversity," and (9) "clear and effective promotion of constructive relationships." Not applicable was also an option but was coded as missing for the purpose of scale creation. It is possible that coding "not applicable" responses in this way influenced the relatively high item nonresponse of these variables.

Work Location. Employees were grouped according to where they worked within the healthcare organization in one of four sites. We dummy coded this variable in multivariate models.

Analytic Strategy

Both our descriptive and multivariate results used 25 imputed datasets. For the descriptives, we computed F-tests for differences between S-WFB means. For multivariates, we used ordinary least squares regression for each of 25 imputed datasets, then combined the results using the methods described in Rubin (1987). This method results in point estimates that are typically more accurate than using listwise deletion, combined with standard errors that are slightly increased to account for variation between imputations. We centered all interval-level predictors. Product–term interactions were included.

RESULTS

Table 1 provides descriptive and bivariate statistics – 27.3 percent of employees were in departments that were under-budget, 50.2 percent were over-budget, and 22.5 percent were on-budget. Further analysis of the operating costs data indicated that those budgets considered under-budget spent 12 percent less than their goal, on average (median), while those over-budget spent 21 percent more than their goal, on average (median).

The percentages in each category provide some insight into the work and family demands of employees in this organization. A substantial number indicated working more than 40 hours/week (40.5 percent). Most considered their job demands at work to be relatively high (60.3 percent) and a substantial number had a dependent child (45.8 percent) or a dependent adult (13.8 percent). In general, a large percentage of employees believed their schedule control was high (61.2 percent). Consistent with healthcare organizations throughout the nation, a large percentage of the workers were ages 50 or older (35.6 percent) and female (83.7 percent). They considered themselves in good health in general (high = 92 percent). Slightly less than half had a bachelor's degree or more (44.3 percent), and they were typically satisfied with other aspects of their jobs (91.5 percent).

Due to the nature of the imputed data, we provide F-tests from OLS regressions in which S-WFB was the outcome variable and each variable (individually) was a dummy-coded categorical predictor. For dichotomous variables, such as female, this is equivalent to a t-test. All variables, even if we consider them interval in the multivariate models, are categorical in this table.

The mean S-WFB score was 22.6. Given the item wording and response categories of the variables making up this measure, we can understand this score as falling between somewhat and moderately satisfied. Most of the predictors were significantly associated with S-WFB in the directions we would expect. For instance, employees working 50 or more hours per week had substantially lower S-WFB (a mean of 19.1, compared to about 23.3 for employees working 40 hours per week, $F = 34.84$, $p < .01$). Similarly, employees with high demands, in the form of job demands ($F = 199.71$, $p < .01$), a dependent child ($F = 38.36$, $p < .01$), or a dependent adult ($F = 3.39$, $p < .10$), had significantly lower S-WFB. Workers with high schedule control had significantly greater S-WFB ($F = 392.73$, $p < .01$). Older employees ($F = 13.23$, $p < .01$), employees in better health ($F = 169.99$, $p < .01$), and less highly educated employees ($F = 16.68$, $p < .01$) also had higher S-WFB. Employees who were satisfied with other aspects of their jobs were also more likely to be satisfied with WFB ($b = 193.64$, $p < .01$). Perhaps as interesting as the differences discussed above, the bivariate statistics indicate that budgetary pressure ($F = 0.56$, $p > .10$), gender (female, $F = 1.10$, $p > .10$), and site ($F = 1.91$, $p > .10$) were not significantly associated with S-WFB.

Table 1. Descriptive Statistics.

	Percent	Satisfaction with Work–Family Balance (S-WFB)	
		Mean	F-test
Total sample	100.00	22.62	
Budgetary pressure			0.56
Under-budget (by 5 percent or more)	27.29	22.43	
On-budget (within 5 percent)	22.55	22.73	
Over-budget (by 5 percent or more)	50.16	22.68	
Number of hours worked			34.84***
<40 hours	35.23	22.84	
40 hours	45.43	23.33	
41–49 hours	12.53	21.39	
50+ hours	6.82	19.10	
Job demands (potential range: 6–36)			199.71***
Low ($\leq$21)	39.73	24.51	
High (22+)	60.27	21.38	
Dependent care for children			38.36***
No	54.22	23.26	
Yes	45.78	21.87	
Dependent care for adult			3.39*
No	86.23	22.71	
Yes	13.77	22.10	
Schedule control (potential range: 7–28)			392.73***
Low ($\leq$17)	38.81	20.00	
High (18+)	61.19	24.29	
Age in years			13.23***
<30 years	14.58	21.87	
30–39 years	25.69	22.07	
40–49 years	24.11	22.25	
50+ years	35.63	23.59	
Gender			1.10
Male	16.26	22.90	
Female	83.74	22.57	
Health status (potential range: 0–20)			169.99***
Low ($\leq$10)	8.05	17.73	
High (11+)	91.95	23.05	
Education			16.68***
Low (less than a bachelor's degree)	55.70	23.03	
High (bachelor's degree or more)	44.30	22.11	
Satisfaction with job conditions (potential range: 9–54)			193.64***
Low ($\leq$31)	8.50	17.55	
High (32+)	91.50	23.09	

Table 1. (*Continued*)

	Percent	Satisfaction with Work–Family Balance (S-WFB)	
		Mean	*F*-test
Site			1.91
Site 1	64.00	22.62	
Site 2	20.54	22.97	
Site 3	12.15	22.35	
Site 4	3.30	21.54	

Source: Authors' calculations based on the Boston College Study of the ModernMedical Health System, baseline survey.
Note: $N = 2,789$.
$*p < .10$; $***p < .01$.

Table 2 shows an OLS regression analysis predicting S-WFB. Work-related demands were associated with lower S-WFB, as were family-related demands. These included budgetary pressure (being under-budget, $b = -0.91$, $p < .01$), number of hours worked ($b = -0.09$, $p < .01$, job demands ($b = -0.11$, $p < .01$), dependent care for children ($b = -1.83$, $p < .01$), and dependent care for adults ($b = -0.78$, $p < .01$). Schedule control was associated with higher S-WFB ($b = 0.26$, $p < .01$). Thus, employees whose units were operating at least 5 percent under-budget (which likely reflects that staffing is leaner than allowed) are significantly less likely to be satisfied with their WFB. Employees with greater demands in the form of hours, job demands, and child and adult caregiving responsibilities also report significantly lower satisfaction with WFB.

Interaction terms provide insight into the ways in which schedule control moderated both work-related and family-related demands. All interval-level predictors were centered at zero, so that the coefficients for main effects can be interpreted as the effects when the moderator variable is at zero. Schedule control moderated the association between budgetary pressure and S-WFB (schedule control × under-budget, $b = 0.15$, $p < .05$), such that the negative association was attenuated when schedule control was high. The same was true of dependent care for children. Dependent care for children was negatively associated with S-WFB, but the association was smaller at higher levels of schedule control. We replicated these models testing for the potential moderating roles of schedule control for job demands and dependent care for adults, but omitted these terms from the final model due to nonsignificance. The effects of being over-budget, both for main

Table 2. OLS Regression Predicting Satisfaction with Work–Family Balance (S-WFB).

	b	SE	β	t
Work-related demands				
Budgetary pressure (Ref = On-budget)				
Under-budget	−0.91	0.34	−0.07	−2.67***
Over-budget	−0.45	0.30	−0.04	−1.50
Number of hours worked	−0.09	0.01	−0.13	−8.72***
Job demands	−0.11	0.01	−0.13	−7.88***
Family-related demands				
Dependent care for children (Ref = None)	−1.83	0.38	−0.15	−4.77***
Dependent care for adults (Ref = None)	−0.78	0.26	−0.05	−2.95***
Schedule control	0.26	0.05	0.21	4.83***
Controls				
Age in years	0.02	0.01	0.03	1.95*
Gender (Female = 1)	−1.07	0.25	−0.07	−4.24***
Health	0.39	0.03	0.20	12.69***
Education	−0.31	0.07	−0.07	−4.63***
Satisfaction with job conditions	0.18	0.01	0.25	14.62***
Site (Ref = Site 1)				
Site 2	0.25	0.23	0.02	1.08
Site 3	−0.22	0.28	−0.01	−0.81
Site 4	−1.05	0.50	−0.03	−2.08**
Interaction terms				
Schedule control × Under-budget	0.15	0.07	0.06	2.07**
Schedule control × Over-budget	0.07	0.06	0.04	1.03
Dependent care for children × Under-budget	1.47	0.51	0.08	2.88***
Dependent care for children × Over-budget	1.10	0.45	0.08	2.42**
Schedule control × Dependent care for children	0.17	0.08	0.09	2.06**
Schedule control × Dependent care for children × Under-budget	−0.27	0.11	−0.08	−2.46**
Schedule control × Dependent care for children × Over-budget	−0.12	0.10	−0.04	−1.23
Constant	24.51	0.34		71.41***
R^2		0.39		
Adjusted R^2		0.38		

Source: Authors' calculations based on the Boston College Study of the ModernMedical Health System, baseline survey.
Note: $N = 2,789$. $F (25, 2756.1) = 68.26$***. Twenty-five imputed datasets are used, with an average relative variance increase of 0.0193. All interval-level predictors are centered at their means.
*$p < .10$; **$p < .05$; ***$p < .01$.

effects and interactions, were in the same direction as those for under-budget although were not statistically significant.

The two-way interactions between schedule control and budgetary demands were significant, for under-budget ($b = 1.47$, $p < .01$) as was the three-way interaction between schedule control, under-budget, and dependent care for children ($b = -0.27$, $p < .05$). Fig. 2 graphically illustrates these

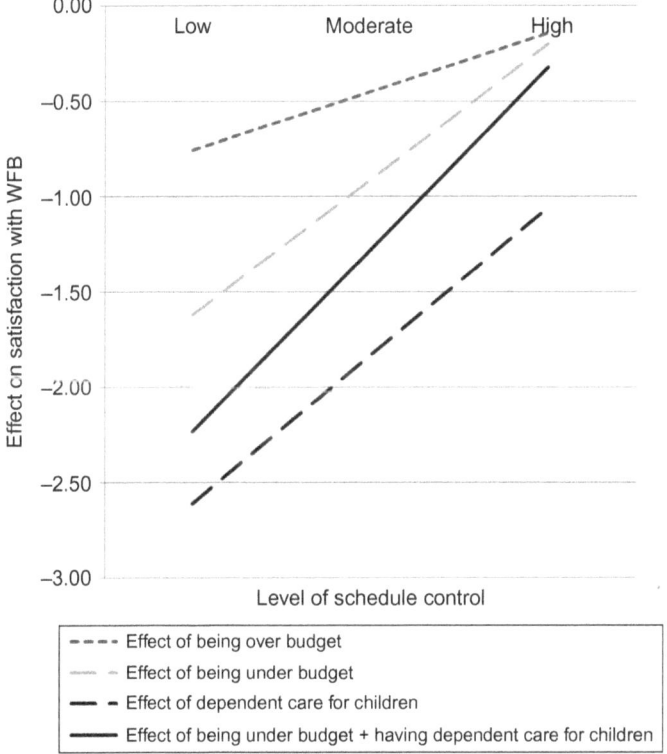

Fig. 2. Effects of Budgetary Demands and Dependent Child Care on Satisfaction with Work−Family Balance. *Source*: Authors' calculations based on the Boston College Study of the ModernMedical Health System, baseline survey. *Note*: Twenty-five imputed datasets are used, with an average relative variance increase of 0.0193. Coefficients reported in this figure are based on main effects and interaction terms from the OLS regression shown in Table 2. For "effect of being under-budget" and "effect of being over-budget," the reference group is being "on-budget." For "effect of dependent care for children," the reference group is "respondents without dependent children."

relationships, with zero representing the effect for those who are on-budget and do not have dependent care responsibilities for children. Four groups of effects are shown: the effect of being over-budget (with no dependent care for children), the effect of being under-budget (with no dependent care for children), the effect of dependent care for children (with on-budget), and the combined effect, taking into account all relevant interaction terms, of being under-budget and having dependent care for children (i.e., a "worst case" scenario). Each of these four combinations are shown for those with low (one standard deviation below the mean), moderate (at the mean), and high (one standard deviation above the mean) schedule control.

The results indicate that low schedule control exacerbates the gap between those with high demands and those with low demands (i.e., the "zero" baseline of on-budget and no dependent care for children). High schedule control narrows the gap almost to zero for three groups (being over-budget, being under-budget, and being under-budget plus having dependent care for children). The effect of dependent care for children, for employees whose work units are on-budget, is a notable exception. The negative association between dependent care for children and schedule control is smaller for those with high schedule control than for those with low schedule control. However, even at high schedule control, the negative association remains substantial.

Results for control variables indicated that older workers ($b = 0.02$, $p < .10$), men (female, $b = -1.07$, $p < .01$), employees in good health ($b = 0.39$, $p < .01$), less educated employees ($b = -0.31$, $p < .01$), employees working fewer hours ($b = -0.09$, $p < .01$), and employees who were more satisfied with their jobs in general ($b = -0.09$, $p < .01$) tended to have higher S-WFB. We also noted some site effects (site 4, $b = -1.05$, $p < .05$).

DISCUSSION

In this chapter we provide evidence that current practices associated with keeping costs under control in a large healthcare system of over 10,000 employees in the United States have a negative impact on employee satisfaction with their ability to manage both their work and family responsibilities. Employees in units that are under-budget report significantly lower S-WFB scores than do employees in units where budget targets are being met. When the work unit is over-budget the relationship is also negative, although not significantly so. Similarly, employees who work more than 40 hours per week, perceive high job demands, or have dependent care responsibilities also report lower S-WFB than do those who do not.

While the concept of "spillover" is typically focused on domain to domain impact at the individual level (for the same person) (Grzywacz et al., 2002), to date, there is no term in the literature for spillover experienced by the same person first as a member of the work unit and then at the individual level. It would seem, however, that some aspects of the relationships between work unit pressures and S-WFB are similar to spillover. Thus, we see these results as supporting our contention that the pressure on an organizational unit to comply with specified budget targets, especially when failing to meet them, may interfere negatively with unit members' family responsibilities and thus represent a new twist on spillover.

This is not a trivial concern as S-WFB (or lack of it) has been identified as a central issue for both employees and organizations (Valcour, 2007), especially in the healthcare sector where work−family conflict is particularly high relative to other job sectors (Sweet et al., 2010). In fact, declining work−life balance scores among employees at ModernMedical (as determined by their internal surveys) were an important factor in the organization's decision to participate in the study (Cahill et al., 2013). According to Gerstel et al. (2007), as healthcare employers have shifted from a "logic of care" to a "logic of cost," there is also evidence that there has been a loss of employee commitment (p. 374). While employers themselves are under similar pressures from many sources, and have good reasons for their focus on costs, findings suggest that they look for ways to balance this concern with similar concern for employees and their needs to manage competing responsibilities outside of work.

Thus, we examined longitudinal data for insight into what happens to employees whose work units are under-budget, but later meet budget targets. In auxiliary analyses (not shown due to low sample size), we compared the results from the survey reported in this chapter to data collected on the same employees one year later. We found that S-WFB increased slightly if a work unit was on-budget approximately one year later ($N=177$). We might speculate that, if the unit was operating under-budget but then had "extra" resources for bringing the expenditures up to the budgeted level, that is, they had more resources than before. In line with Karasek's (1979) Job Demands and Control model, the availability of such resources should reduce stress. On the other hand, employee S-WFB seemed to decrease slightly if work units that were over-budget at baseline succeeded in meeting budget targets ($N = 515$). We might speculate that if units were operating over-budget, their leaders were expending a certain level of resources to get the work done. If unit leaders had to bring the budget into line to comply with budget targets, then employees in the unit had to do the same work with fewer resources. In turn, these circumstances would introduce stress at the work unit-level.

Competing responsibilities of home and work are of course at the heart of the study of work and family and their intersection. In keeping with other research (e.g., Abendroth et al., 2012; Barnett, 1996; Greenhaus & Beutell, 1985; Van Daalen, Willemsen, & Sanders, 2006), we found that employees with either children under the age of 19 or adults in need of their care reported lower S-WFB than employees without those responsibilities. As the healthcare sector is notoriously older and female (Sweet et al., 2010), the significance of both child and adult care responsibilities in relation to S-WFB is worthy of note.

The results of this study indicate that work-related and family-related demands have negative associations with S-WFB. This is consistent with existing literature, but unlike almost all previous research using the job demands-control model, we had access to data on the potential association between budgetary pressures (at the work unit-level) and S-WFB (at the individual level). We found that being in a work unit that was under-budget was associated with lower S-WFB, as were job demands, number of hours worked, dependent care for children, and dependent care for adults.

We also found that schedule control was positively associated with S-WFB. In addition, higher levels of schedule control buffered the negative effects attributable to budgetary demands (under-budget) and dependent care for children, but the interactions with the other demand measures (number of hours worked, dependent care for adults, and job satisfaction) were not statistically significant.

Finally, good management practices also affect S-WFB. Indeed we found evidence of a direct effect of satisfaction with job conditions on S-WFB, suggesting that attention to a full array of successful "people practices" might enhance S-WFB. Compared to employers in other industry sectors, employers in the healthcare sector have expressed more concern about their ability to provide competitive pay and benefits than employees in other job sectors (Sweet et al., 2010). Similarly, Sweet et al. report that healthcare sector employers provide fewer flexible work options than other employers (see also Thomas & Ganster, 1995). Despite evidence of the direction effect of satisfaction with job conditions with S-WFB, we did not find a moderating effect of satisfaction with job conditions on the relationship between work pressure and S-WFB. It is possible that the pressure to comply with budget targets overrides most of the potential mitigating influences of job conditions.

In sum, we believe this chapter contributes to the literature in several ways. First, we study a large multisite regional healthcare system in the midst of healthcare reform (Gapenski & Pink, 2011). Second, we include in our model a measure of an organizational metric representing pressure on the work unit rather than one derived from the subjective experience of the individual, or even the sum of a team's assessment, thus putting a new spin on "spillover." The link between an objective measure of productivity or compliance with budget guidelines, that is, demands placed on the work unit as a whole and employee-level S-WFB thus represents a relatively new trail to travel with respect to organizational pressures on employees and how these pressures uniquely influence the interface between work and family. As Lambert (1999) has pointed out long ago, cost control strategies appear to trickle down and affect employees and their work−family concerns. And finally, the fact that schedule control did not moderate relationships between certain work pressures and S-WFB suggests that we need to continue to search for innovative ways to deal with healthcare system employees under the strain of cost controls. This is largely consistent with previous literature using the job demands-control model. While the main effects of demands and control are substantial and well-supported, the buffering effects of control (and of support, in the job demands-control-support model) often receive only mixed support. Our results suggest that schedule control does provide a buffer against the negative pressure of some demands (e.g., budgetary demands, dependent care for children). However, for other demands (e.g., job demands, number of hours worked) social support from supervisors and coworkers may offer a more effective buffer than schedule control. Further, it is possible that the negative effects of some demands are not easily mitigated and require directly reducing the demand itself.

Our study is not without limitations. First, because our results referred to healthcare workers, some of the standard measures we included were not fine-tuned for this population. For instance, one of the items included in the schedule control measure referred to whether the employee could work at home, but certain occupations (e.g., nurses) may not be able to work at home. While additional analyses suggest that the schedule control measure is nearly identical with and without this item (a correlation of 0.98), this remains a concern. Second, our results are derived from baseline data that are part of a longitudinal study, and only limited data are available on how the change in budgetary conditions over time might affect S-WFB. Our analysis of operating expense data from this organization indicates that work units that are under-budget tend to remain under-budget, those that are on-budget tend to remain on-budget, and those that are over-budget tend to remain over-budget. However, many work units fluctuate between two or three budgetary categories, raising questions about whether fluctuations in budgetary pressures are more important than the level of pressures. Third, due to sample size we could not fully assess the potentially nonlinear effects of our predictors without making the models unstable. We replicated all models using quadratic terms (and interactions with quadratic terms). Although results were similar, they suggest that job demands and job satisfaction may have slightly nonlinear effects in larger samples. Similarly, the highly significant results for both child and adult care suggest that workers with both types of care responsibilities might be under substantially more pressure. When we replicated our models including a "sandwich generation" dummy variable (i.e., both child and adult care), the results were not statistically significant. This may have been due to the relatively small number of workers in our sample with both types of responsibilities (less than 5 percent of the sample). Fourth, due to limitations in the time and resources that the healthcare organization could devote to the study, some measures were not ideal. For instance, we did not have a dispositional measure. This could be problematic in light of measures such as job satisfaction, for which employee responses might reflect disposition as much as the objective quality of the job. We replicated our analysis omitting job satisfaction, and found that the results were similar. Finally, while our measure of "work unit pressure" represents a novel approach to understanding the issues in question, further research is needed to more fully explain the relationship of unit-level influences on individual-level outcomes such as S-WFB. On the other hand, if our initial findings are supported and built upon by additional research, we suggest that innovative approaches to handling cost-containment measures might be found.

ACKNOWLEDGMENTS

We are grateful to the Alfred P. Sloan Foundation for supporting this work through a grant to the Sloan Center on Aging & Work at Boston College (#2011-6-23): Assessing the Business Impact of Time & Place Management Policies — What's Age Got to Do with It? We are grateful to the leaders of "ModernMedical" for their willingness to support research within their organization, and to the many hourly and exempt workers who graciously shared their time and experiences with us. We offer special thanks to the senior vice-president of human resources at ModernMedical, who, along with her colleagues on the Oversight Committee, has worked with us over the past year to make our efforts mutually beneficial to the organization and to our research agenda.

REFERENCES

Abendroth, A., van der Lippe, T., & Maas, I. (2012). Social support and the working hours of employed mothers in Europe: The relevance of the state, the workplace, and the family. *Social Science Research*, *41*(3), 581−597. doi:10.1016/j.ssresearch.2011.12.008

Allen, T. D., Johnson, R. C., Kiburz, K. M., & Shockley, K. M. (2013). Work−family conflict and flexible work arrangements: Deconstructing flexibility. *Personnel Psychology*, *66*(2), 345−376. doi:10.1111/peps.12012

Bailyn, L., Collins, R., & Song, Y. (2007). Self-scheduling for hospital nurses: An attempt and its difficulties. *Journal of Nursing Management*, *15*(1), 72−77. doi:10.1111/j.1365-2934.2006.00633.x

Bakker, A. B., & Demerouti, E. (2007). The job demands-resources model: State of the art. *Journal of Managerial Psychology*, *22*(3), 309−328. doi:10.1108/02683940710733115

Bakker, A. B., ten Brummelhuis, L. L., Prins, J. T., & van der Heijden, F. M. M. A. (2011). Applying the job demands−resources model to the work−home interface: A study among medical residents and their partners. *Journal of Vocational Behavior*, *79*(1), 170−180. doi:10.1016/j.jvb.2010.12.004

Bakker, A. B., Westman, M., & van Emmerik, I. H. (2009). Advancements in crossover theory. *Journal of Managerial Psychology*, *24*(5), 206−219. doi:10.1108/02683940910939304

Barham, L. J., Gottlieb, B. H., & Kelloway, E. K. (1998). Variables affecting managers' willingness to grant alternative work arrangements. *The Journal of Social Psychology*, *138*(3), 291−302. doi:10.1080/00224549809600382

Barnett, R. C. (1996). *Toward a review of the work−family literature: Work in progress.* Wellesley, MA: Center for Research on Women.

Barnett, R. C., Marshall, N. L., & Singer, J. D. (1992). Job experiences over time, multiple roles, and women's mental health: A longitudinal study. *Journal of Personality and Social Psychology*, *62*(4), 634−644. doi:10.1037/0022-3514.62.4.634

Besen, E., Matz-Costa, C., James, J. B., & Pitt-Catsouphes, M. (2012). Factors buffering against the effects of job demands: How does age matter? *Journal of Applied Gerontology*. doi:10.1177/0733464812460430

Blair-Loy, M., & Wharton, A. S. (2002). Employees' use of work−family policies and the workplace social context. *Social Forces*, *80*(3), 813−845. doi:10.1353/sof.2002.0002

Bronfenbrenner, U. (1986). Ecology of the family as a context for human development: Research perspectives. *Developmental Psychology*, *22*(6), 723−742. doi:10.1037/0012-1649.22.6.723

Cahill, K., James, J., Pitt-Catsouphes, M., DeAngelis, K. L., Lawler, S., Hartman, D., & Snow, D. L. (2013, January 22). *The Boston College Study of the [ModernMedical] Health System: Highlights from the pilot TPM initiative baseline survey*. Chestnut Hill, MA: The Sloan Center on Aging & Work at Boston College.

Carlson, D., Grzywacz, J. G., & Zivnuska, S. (2009). Is work–family balance more than conflict and enrichment? *Human Relations*, 62(10), 1459–1486. doi:10.1177/0018726709336500

Casey, P. R., & Grzywacz, J. G. (2008). Employee health and well-being: The role of flexibility and work–family balance. *Psychologist-Manager Journal. Special Issue: Work-Life Effectiveness: Implications for Organizations*, 11(1), 31–47. doi:10.1080/10887150 801963885

Chesley, N. (2005). Blurring boundaries? Linking technology use, spillover, individual distress, and family satisfaction. *Journal of Marriage and Family*, 67(5), 1237–1248.

Day, A. L., Sibley, A., Scott, N., Tallon, J. M., & Ackroyd-Stolarz, S. (2009). Workplace risks and stressors as predictors of burnout: The moderating impact of job control and team efficacy. *Canadian Journal of Administrative Sciences*, 26(1), 7–22. doi:10.1002/CJAS.91

Dilworth, J. E. L. (2004). Predictors of negative spillover from family to work. *Journal of Family Issues*, 25(2), 241–261.

Duffy, M. K., Ganster, D. C., Shaw, J. D., Johnson, J. L., & Pagon, M. (2006). The social context of undermining behavior at work. *Organizational Behavior and Human Decision Processes*, 101(1), 105–126.

Forret, M., & de Janasz, S. (2005). Perceptions of an organization's culture for work and family: Do mentors make a difference? *Career Development International*, 10(6–7), 478–492. doi:10.1108/13620430510620566

Frone, M. R. (2003). Work–family balance. In J. C. Quick & L. E. Tetrick (Eds.), *Handbook of occupational health psychology* (pp. 143–162). Washington, DC: American Psychological Association. doi:10.1037/10474-007

Frone, M. R., Russell, M., & Cooper, M. L. (1992). Antecedents and outcomes of work–family conflict: Testing a model of the work–family interface. *Journal of Applied Psychology*, 77(1), 65–78.

Frone, M. R., Russell, M., & Cooper, M. L. (1997). Relation of work–family conflict to health outcomes: A four-year longitudinal study of employed parents. *Journal of Occupational and Organizational Psychology*, 70(4), 325–335.

Frone, M. R., Yardley, J. K., & Markel, K. S. (1997). Developing and testing an integrative model of the work–family interface. *Journal of Vocational Behavior*, 50(2), 145–167.

Gapenski, L. C., & Pink, G. H. (2011). *Understanding healthcare financial management* (6th ed.). Chicago, IL: Health Administration Press.

Gastfriend, J., James, J. B., & McNamara, T. K. (2012, April). Workability, flexibility, and caregiving: Findings from the generations of talent study. Presented as part of a panel, Innovations in the Workplace for Caregivers. American Society on Aging Conference, Washington, DC.

Gerstel, N., Clawson, D., & Huyser, D. (2007). Explaining job hours of physicians, nurses, EMTs, and nursing assistants: Gender, class, jobs, and families. *Research in the Sociology of Work*, 17, 369–399.

Geurts, S. A. E., Beckers, D. G. J., Taris, T. W., Kompier, M. A. J., & Smulders, P. G. W. (2009). Worktime demands and work–family interference: Does worktime control buffer the adverse effects of high demands? *Journal of Business Ethics, 84*(Suppl. 2), 229–241. doi:10.1007/s10551-008-9699-y

Glavin, P., & Schieman, S. (2012). Work–family role blurring and work–family conflict: The moderating influence of job resources and job demands. *Work and Occupations, 39*(1), 71–98. doi:10.1177/0730888411406295

Goodstein, J. D. (2013). Institutional pressures and strategic responsiveness: Employer involvement in work–family issues. *The Academy of Management Journal, 37*(2), 350–382.

Grandey, A. A., Cordeiro, B. L., & Michael, J. H. (2007). Work–family supportiveness organizational perceptions: Important for the well-being of male blue-collar hourly workers? *Journal of Vocational Behavior, 71*(3), 460–478. doi:10.1016/j.jvb.2007.08.001

Greenhaus, J. H., & Beutell, N. J. (1985). Sources of conflict between work and family roles. *Academy of Management Review, 10*, 76–88.

Greenhaus, J. H., & Parasuraman, S. (1987). A work-nonwork interactive perspective of stress and its consequences. *Journal of Organizational Behavior Management, 8*(2), 37–60. doi:10.1300/J075v08n02_04

Grzywacz, J. G., Almeida, D. M., & McDonald, D. (2002). Work–family spillover and daily reports of work and family stress in the adult labor force. *Family Relations, 51*(1), 28–36. Retrieved from http://www.jstor.org/stable/3700296

Grzywacz, J. G., & Marks, N. F. (2000). Reconceptualizing the work–family interface: An ecological perspective on the correlates of positive and negative spillover between work and family. *Journal of Occupational Health Psychology, 5*(1), 111–126. doi:10.1037/1076-8998.5.1.111

Guest, D. E. (2002). Perspectives on the study of work-life balance. *Social Science Information, 41*(2), 255–279.

Harton, B. B., Marshburn, D., Kuykendall, J., Poston, C., & Mears, D. A. (2012). Self-scheduling: Help or hindrance? *Nursing Management, 43*(1), 10–12. doi:10.1097/01.NUMA.0000409929.92460.cd

Higgins, C., Duxbury, L., & Johnson, K. L. (2000). Part-time work for women: Does it really help balance work and family? *Human Resource Management, 39*(1), 17–32.

James, J. B., Barnett, R., & Brennan, R. (1998). The psychological effects of work experiences and disagreements about gender-role beliefs in dual earner couples: A longitudinal study. *Women's Health: Research on Gender, Behavior, and Policy, 4*(4), 341–368.

James, J. B., McKechnie, S., & Swanberg, J. E. (2011). Predicting employee engagement in an age-diverse retail workforce. *Journal of Organizational Behavior, 32*(2), 173–196. doi:10.1002/job.681

James, J. B., Pitt-Catsouphes, M., Coplon, J., & Cohen, B. (2013). Optimizing the long future of aging: Beyond involvement to engagement. In R. J. Burke, C. L. Cooper, & J. Field (Eds.), *Sage handbook of aging, work and society* (pp. 477–492). London: Sage. doi:10.4135/9781446269916

Karasek, R. A. (1979). Job demands, job decision latitude, and mental strain: Implications for job redesign. *Administrative Science Quarterly, 24*(2), 285–308.

Karasek, R. A. (1985). *Job content questionnaire and user's guide*. Lowell, MA: University of Massachusetts Lowell, Department of Work Environment.

Karasek, R. A., Brison, C., Kawakami, N., Houtman, I., & Bongers, P. (1998). The Job Content Questionnaire (JCQ): An instrument for internally comparative assessments of psychosocial job characteristics. *Journal of Occupational Health Psychology, 3*(4), 322–355.

Kossek, E. E., Colquitt, J. A., & Noe, R. A. (2010). In C. Gatrell, G. L. Cooper, & E. E. Kossek (Eds.), *Caregiving decisions, well-being, and performance: The effects of place and provider as a function of dependent type and work–family climates*. Northampton, MA: Elgar: International Library of Critical Writings on Business and Management.

Lambert, S. J. (1999). Lower-wage workers and the new realities of work and family. *Annals of the American Academy of Political and Social Science, 562*, 174–190.

MacDermid, S. M., & Harvey, A. (2006). The work–family conflict construct: Methodological implications. In *The work and family handbook: Multi-disciplinary perspectives, methods, and approaches* (pp. 567–586). Mahwah, NJ: Lawrence Erlbaum Associates.

Major, V. S., Klein, K. J., & Ehrhart, M. G. (2002). Work time, work interference with family, and psychological distress. *Journal of Applied Psychology, 87*(3), 427–436. doi:10.1037/0021-9010.87.3.427

Moen, P., Fan, W., & Kelly, E. L. (2013). Team-level flexibility, work–home spillover, and health behavior. *Social Science & Medicine, 84*, 69–79. doi:10.1016/j.socscimed.2013.02.011

Pitt-Catsouphes, M., & Matz-Costa, C. (2008). The multi-generational workforce: Workplace flexibility and engagement. *Community, Work & Family, 11*(2), 215–229.

Royston, P. (2004). Multiple imputation of missing values. *Stata Journal, 4*, 227–241.

Rubin, D. B. (1987). *Multiple imputation for nonresponse in surveys*. New York, NY: Wiley.

Schaufeli, W. B., Bakker, A. B., & Van Rhenen, W. (2009). How changes in job demands and resources predict burnout, work engagement, and sickness absenteeism. *Journal of Organizational Behavior, 30*(7), 893–917. doi:10.1002/job.595

Sweet, S., Moen, P., & Meiksins, P. (2007). Dual earners in double jeopardy: Preparing for job loss in the new risk economy. In B. A. Rubin (Ed.), *Workplace temporalities* (Vol. 17, pp. 437–464). Research in the Sociology of Work. London: Emerald Group Publishing Limited.

Sweet, S., Pitt-Catsouphes, M., Besen, E., Hovhannisyan, S., & Pasha, F. (2010). Talent pressures and the aging workforce: Responsive action steps for the health care and social assistance sector. Industry Sector Report No. 2.1.0. Sloan Center on Aging & Work at Boston College, Chestnut Hill, MA. Retrieved from http://www.bc.edu/research/agingandwork/meta-elements/pdf/publications/TMISR02_HealthCare.pdf

Thomas, L. T., & Ganster, D. C. (1995). Impact of family-supportive work variables on work–family conflict and strain: A control perspective. *Journal of Applied Psychology, 80*(1), 6–15. doi:10.1037/0021-9010.80.1.6

Valcour, M. (2007). Work-based resources as moderators of the relationship between work hours and satisfaction with work–family balance. *Journal of Applied Psychology, 92*(6), 1512–1523.

Valcour, M., Ollier-Malaterre, A., Matz-Costa, C., Pitt-Catsouphes, M., & Brown, M. (2011). Influences on employee perceptions of organizational work-life support: Signals and resources. *Journal of Vocational Behavior, 79*(2), 588–595. doi:10.1016/j.jvb.2011.02.002

Van Daalen, G., Willemsen, T. M., & Sanders, K. (2006). Reducing work–family conflict through different sources of social support. *Journal of Vocational Behavior, 69*(3), 462–476.

Voydanoff, P. (2005). Toward a conceptualization of perceived work–family fit and balance: A demands and resources approach. *Journal of Marriage and Family*, *67*(4), 822–836.

Wallace, J. E. (1997). It's about time: A study of hours worked and work spillover among law firm lawyers. *Journal of Vocational Behavior*, *50*(2), 227–248. doi:10.1006/jvbe.1996.1573

Wallace, J. E. (1999). Work-to-nonwork conflict among married male and female lawyers. *Journal of Organizational Behavior*, *20*(6), 797–816.

Wayne, S. J., Shore, L. M., & Liden, R. C. (1997). Perceived organizational support and leader-member exchange: A social exchange perspective. *The Academy of Management Journal*, *40*(1), 82–111. doi:10.2307/257021

Westman, M. (2001). Stress and strain crossover. *Human Relations*, *54*, 717–751. doi:10.1177/0018726701546002

Williams, J. (2000). *Unbending gender: Why family and work conflict and what to do about it*. New York, NY: Oxford University Press.

World Bank. (2011). *Population aging: Is Latin America ready?* Washington, DC: The World Bank. Retrieved from http://go.worldbank.org/Z7MBL2H0M0

GIVING CARE AND PERCEIVING DISCRIMINATION: THE SOCIAL AND ORGANIZATIONAL CONTEXT OF FAMILY RESPONSIBILITIES DISCRIMINATION

Lindsey Trimble O'Connor, Julie A. Kmec and Elizabeth C. Harris

ABSTRACT

Purpose — *Discrimination against workers because of their family responsibilities can violate federal law, yet scholars know little about the context surrounding perceived family responsibilities discrimination (FRD). This chapter investigates both the types of caregiving responsibilities that put workers at risk of FRD and the organizational contexts that give rise to perceived FRD.*

Methodology/approach — *We identify features of FRD which make detecting it particularly difficult and theorize the mechanisms by which caregiving responsibilities and organizational contexts lead to perceived*

FRD. We draw on data from the 2008 National Study of the Changing Workforce for our empirical analysis.

Findings — *Caregivers who provide both child and eldercare are more likely to perceive FRD than caregivers who provide one type of care, as are people who experience high levels of family-to-work interference and who spend more daily time on childcare. Certain family-friendly and meritocratic organizational contexts are associated with lower perceived FRD.*

Research limitations/implications — *We measure perceptions, not actual discrimination on the basis of family care responsibilities. Our research cannot pinpoint the factors which intensify or lessen actual discrimination, just perceptions of it.*

Originality/value — *By pinpointing the characteristics of organizations in which perceived FRD occurs, this chapter shows how organizations can create workplaces in which perceived FRD is less likely.*

Keywords: Family responsibilities discrimination; caregiving; work and family

Researchers have documented the presence of a bias against family caregivers at work — particularly mothers and fathers who have significant caregiving responsibilities or who signal a need for flexible work arrangements (Williams, 2000; Williams, Blair-Loy, & Berdahl, 2013). Although no federal law explicitly prohibits family responsibilities discrimination (FRD), the U.S. Equal Employment Opportunity Commission (EEOC) determined that decision-making on the basis of a worker's family caregiving status can violate federally protected workplace rights (EEOC, 2007). FRD, especially against mothers, has received attention on major television networks, radio, and blogs (Still, 2006; Williams & Bornstein, 2008) and although we are unaware of research investigating peoples' knowledge of their workplace rights as caregivers, FRD claims have grown dramatically in recent years while employment discrimination cases decided by federal district courts have fallen (Calvert, 2010, p. 7), suggesting growth in workers' knowledge of caregiving rights.

Despite growth in FRD claims, researchers know little about the process by which working caregivers come to recognize FRD, much less decide to challenge their employers with a formal complaint. To date, research tends to focus on the coverage of FRD law (Williams & Bornstein, 2008), the types of caregivers who file FRD claims (Still, 2006), or on the ways caregiving triggers stereotypes that workers are uncommitted to work (Correll, Benard, & Paik, 2007). Only recently have researchers examined who perceives FRD. For example, Adams, Heywood, and Miller (2012) found that women with high levels of work−family conflict perceive more FRD than women with low conflict and that women with family caregiving responsibilities who are employed in supportive environments and with supportive supervisors and coworkers experience little FRD.

We ask: what family caregiving responsibilities and organizational contexts are associated with perceived FRD? In asking this question, our study makes three distinct contributions to this emerging body of research. First, we distinguish FRD from other types of employment discrimination, paying attention to the unique features of FRD that may make it particularly difficult for working caregivers to recognize when it occurs. Second, our study is among the first to identify the caregiving responsibilities most associated with FRD. Third, building on Adams et al. (2012), we identify the organizational contexts in which working caregivers perceive FRD. In particular, we explore how family-supportive and meritocratic work cultures − the latter of which signals fair employment practices − impact FRD.

We assess workers' *perceptions* of FRD, not *actual* discrimination against caregivers or formally filed charges of FRD and so we cannot draw conclusions about what factors increase or decrease actual FRD, only what influences perceptions of it. Studying workers' perceptions of FRD and the contexts that shape them is important because acknowledgment of being discriminated against is necessary before workers can take action against discrimination. Perceived discrimination also affects workers' well-being, engagement, and productivity; workers who perceive workplace discrimination − whether or not they are actually victimized − have poorer physical and psychological health than workers who do not (Goldman, Gutek, Stein, & Lewis, 2006; Pavalko, Mossakowski, & Hamilton, 2003), and report feeling powerless, dissatisfied, and uncommitted to work (Ensher, Grant-Vallone, & Donaldson, 2001). Finally, identifying the organizational contexts that give rise to or lessen perceived FRD provides employers and policy-makers a starting point for reducing it.

Analyses of 2008 National Study of the Changing Workforce (NSCW) data reveal that people who provide both child and eldercare are more likely to perceive FRD than people who provide a single type of care. Caregivers with high levels of family-to-work interference perceive more

FRD than caregivers with low levels and childcare providers who spend more daily time on caregiving perceive more FRD than those who spend less. Organizational context influences perceived FRD; working caregivers are unlikely to perceive FRD when they feel they can advance their careers despite taking time off to provide care, when it is easy to take time off to provide care, when they feel their supervisors support their family lives, and when they believe their managers are honest and ethical.

FAMILY RESPONSIBILITIES DISCRIMINATION

Family responsibilities discrimination (FRD) occurs when an employer makes employment decisions about a worker on the basis of his or her assumed or real caregiving responsibilities (Center for WorkLife Law, 2012). Unlike other forms of employment discrimination, no single federal law prohibits FRD. For example, FRD might amount to unlawful disparate treatment under Title VII of the Civil Rights Act of 1964 if an employer acts on stereotypes that men should not engage in family caregiving because they are poorly suited for it, or that women are uncommitted to paid work when they do (EEOC, 2007; Kelly, 2005). An employer who subjects caregivers to harassment based on stereotypes of mothers may also be legally liable for creating a hostile work environment based on sex (EEOC, 2007). Employment decisions based on a woman's pregnancy status (or plans to become pregnant) may violate the federal Pregnancy Discrimination Act while discrimination against individuals who request or take family leave may violate the federal Family and Medical Leave Act (Center for WorkLife Law, 2012).

PERCEIVING WORKPLACE DISCRIMINATION

Despite these legal protections for caregivers, perceiving FRD when it occurs may be challenging. Of course, it can be difficult for workers to recognize *any* form of workplace discrimination. To begin, victims of workplace discrimination are frequently unaware they are being mistreated because discrimination is subtle (Hirsh & Cha, 2008; Stainback & Tomaskovic-Devey, 2012). Even when workers acknowledge discrimination, some fail to admit to its presence in their lives because of the psychological and financial costs of doing so (Kaiser & Major, 2006). Perceiving discrimination also requires workers' knowledge of antidiscrimination laws and that they identify their personal experiences as violations of law (Hirsh & Kmec, 2009). In fact, workers' response to discrimination depends on their perceptions of their employment rights almost as much as the treatment itself (Burstein & Monaghan, 1986). In short, workers must "name" and "blame" an act as discrimination (Felstiner, Abel, & Sarat, 1980, p. 631). Although FRD may be difficult to perceive, below we discuss why some working caregivers perceive it more than others.

VARIATION IN PERCEPTIONS OF FRD

Caregiving Responsibilities

We expect that one's responsibilities as a caregiver affect perceived FRD. First, the type of caregiving one engages in — childcare or eldercare — should affect perceived FRD. Childcare carries with it the intimation of choice. In the United States, demographic shifts in childbearing patterns make parenthood appear to be a chosen social status rather than an inevitable part of the life course. For example, compared to 30 years ago, two times as many women today have not had a child by the end of their reproductive years (Bianchi, 2012). Trends like this one have resulted in parenthood being seen as a chosen social status whose timing parents control rather than an expected part of the life course (Kricheli-Katz, 2012).

The perception of parenthood as a choice may have important implications for perceived FRD (see Kricheli-Katz, 2012). When a personal situation is viewed as a choice, others tend to interpret the situation as being of the individual's own making and under his or her control (Savani, Stephens, & Markus, 2011). What is more, when someone allegedly chooses a social status and experiences negative outcomes as a result of that alleged choice, others blame the person for his or her negative experiences (Weiner, Perry, & Magnusson, 1988). These attitudes exist alongside the perception that the management of family and workplace demands is a personal rather than societal or employer responsibility (Gornick & Meyers, 2005). To the extent that individuals view parenthood as a chosen, controlled responsibility, parents who experience mistreatment at work because of their childcare responsibilities may view mistreatment as an appropriate response to that choice, an attitude that may lead to a failure on parents' part to perceive FRD.

In contrast, eldercare obligations are often not chosen but responsibilities that workers must accept in response to a family member's deteriorating health. Eldercare is becoming an increasingly inevitable part of the life course as the overall population ages and smaller family size limit the number of children available to care for elderly relatives (Bianchi, 2012). What is more, while many childcare providers typically have nine months to prepare for caregiving, eldercare is frequently the response to an unanticipated and often devastating event (i.e., a stroke or dementia diagnosis) (Smith, 2004). The unforeseen nature of eldercare may lead eldercare providers to reevaluate the widely held idea that caregiving is a personal problem with a personal solution (see Levitsky, 2008), prompting them to think that mistreatment because of their care responsibilities is unfair. In short, eldercare providers may be less likely than parents to accept the idea that differential treatment at work is a tolerable trade-off for caregiving.

Caregivers who engage in simultaneous care for elderly relatives and children — those in the so-called "sandwich" generation — may perceive more FRD than caregivers who provide just one type of care because they are more likely to be overburdened with extensive responsibilities (Riley & Bowen, 2005). Extensive caregiving responsibilities can lead to greater FRD because they are disruptive to work, limiting an employed caregiver's ability to be an "ideal worker," one who devotes full time, uninterrupted hours to paid work with few — preferably no — caregiving disruptions (Blair-Loy, 2003; Williams, 2000). Employers expect their employees to be ideal workers, labeling those who are unable or unwilling to live up to this ideal as uncommitted to their work, and penalizing them with fewer rewards (Blair-Loy, 2003; Williams, 2000). As such, those with extensive demands (i.e., care for children *and* elderly relatives) may be targeted for FRD more than caregivers with less extensive demands (i.e., care for children *or* elderly relatives).

Workers typically internalize ideal work characteristics, believing single-minded commitment to work is a sign of their moral worth, dedication, and productivity (Blair-Loy, 2003). As a result of workers "buy-in" to the ideal worker norm, they may have difficulty "naming" mistreatment as discrimination believing instead their employer has a right to demand, and they have a duty to provide, a singular dedication to work (see Pugh, 2015) and that their employer has a right to mistreat workers who violate norms (Kmec, O'Connor, & Schieman, 2014). Workers with extensive caregiving responsibilities, however, may reevaluate the validity of those demands. For example, in a study of long-term care providers, Levitsky (2008) found that caregivers who were unable to manage their care responsibilities viewed their situation as unfair and in need of remedying and subsequently felt that families should not bear the brunt of caregiving. To the extent that caregivers with extensive demands feel they are unable to meet their responsibilities, they may be less likely to buy-in to ideal worker norms and more likely to attribute mistreatment to FRD on the part of their employer than their own inadequacies.

In sum, we expect parents to perceive little FRD because parenting is seen as a chosen social status and mistreatment stemming from this choice is interpreted as "deserved." Because eldercare may feel like less of a choice than parenting and eldercare responsibilities may prompt a reevaluation of employers' support for caregivers, we anticipate that eldercare providers will perceive more FRD than childcare providers. We suspect that caregivers with both child and eldercare responsibilities will perceive the most FRD; extensive caregiving demands put them at high risk of actual FRD and the nature of their caregiving responsibilities may make them particularly likely to recognize mistreatment as FRD. In addition to testing whether dual elder and childcare responsibilities result in perceived FRD, we investigate additional measures of the extent of working caregivers' responsibilities, including family-to-work interference, daily time spent on caregiving, and the number and age of care recipients.

Organizational Context

The organizational context of the workplace — specifically, employers' support for caregivers and the extent to which employers are meritocratic — may shape workers' perceptions of FRD. We define an organization as having a "family-supportive" context when it allows employees schedule control to facilitate the combination of work and family responsibilities as well as having a supportive culture — one in which employees feel their family responsibilities will not diminish advancement opportunities and their family lives are supported by supervisors and coworkers. An organization with a "meritocratic" context is one in which employers' decision-making processes (about all aspects of employment, not just work–life support) are transparent (Castilla & Benard, 2010). Below we discuss two divergent ways these contexts might affect perceptions of FRD.

Although counterintuitive, family-supportive and meritocratic contexts may *increase* perceptions of FRD. First, a family-supportive context may signal to workers that difficulties in balancing family caregiving with work are not problems that workers must personally resolve, but rather responsibilities that partly fall to the employer. In this case, this organizational context may shift workers' expectations, prompting them to believe that employers share some responsibility for helping balance family and work demands. When working caregivers do not believe they shoulder the entire responsibility of combining work and family, they may have an easier time recognizing FRD when it occurs. Caregivers employed in family-supportive and meritocratic contexts may also be more conscious of their rights than working caregivers in unsupportive or non-meritocratic contexts and better able to identify troubling actions as FRD (see Hirsh & Kmec, 2009). Finally, a meritocratic work culture may foster FRD, much like it has been linked to gender and race workplace inequality (Castilla, 2008; Castilla & Benard, 2010) because employers in meritocratic work cultures may come to believe they are objective and fair when in reality they act on stereotypes. For these reasons, working caregivers may perceive greater FRD in family-supportive or meritocratic work contexts than unsupportive or non-meritocratic ones.

Alternatively, a family-supportive and meritocratic context may reduce perceived FRD because actual FRD might occur less frequently in these contexts. Family-supportive and meritocratic contexts may lead working caregivers to feel free to discuss and support one another around family issues (Perlow, 2012), and so caregiving responsibilities may trigger less FRD from supervisors and coworkers.

Workers in family-supportive and meritocratic contexts may not believe their employer could engage in discriminatory behavior because they appear supportive of caregivers and have transparent operating policies that should minimize FRD. In such settings, working caregivers who face negative treatment may attribute FRD to factors outside of discrimination (e.g., their own shortcomings). The "one-way honor system" characteristic of today's workplace in which some workers expect little in return from their employers and invalidate negative reactions in response to employer mistreatment (Pugh, 2015) may amplify the perception that employers "do no wrong." Along these same lines, workers may be unlikely to perceive FRD in family-supportive and meritocratic settings because these settings signal employer commitment to workers, prompting workers to want to respond with the same kind of commitment (Beauregard & Henry, 2009). Social exchange perspective suggests that workers will want to reciprocate "good will" to their employers when they feel like their employers are putting in "extra" effort (Kossek & Friede, 2006). In fact, workers in family-supportive contexts feel more committed and productive than workers employed at organizations that are not family-supportive (Eaton, 2003). When employed caregivers feel positive about their employer, they may respond in kind and be unlikely to name mistreatment as FRD. Overall, organizational context can operate to either increase or decrease perceived FRD.

DATA AND METHODS

We use the 2008 NSCW, a nationally representative sample of 3,502 non-institutionalized U.S. workers, 18 years or older, who were employed in the civilian labor force at the time of data collection (Families and Work Institute (FWI), 2008). The NSCW questionnaire was administered by the FWI via telephone using random digit dialing and achieved a 54.6 percent response rate (FWI, 2011a). The 2008 NSCW is ideal for studying the social and organizational context of family responsibility discrimination; it is the only data set to our knowledge that contains measures of perceived FRD, family responsibilities that put workers at risk of experiencing FRD, and job and organization characteristics.

We restrict the original NSCW sample in several ways. First, we limited our sample to 2,769 wage and salary workers who worked for someone else. Self-employed workers ($n = 733$), have control in creating their workplace culture and so the factors that affect perceived FRD are likely to differ for them compared to workers employed by someone else. The NSCW questionnaire asked *all* respondents about perceptions of FRD so we restricted the sample to include: (1) parents or guardians of children under the age 18 who lived with the respondent for at least half of the year, or (2) those who reported providing care for an elderly relative or in-law in the five years leading up to the survey. We excluded 10 respondents with missing values on our outcome, leaving us with a sample of 1,897 working caregivers.

Dependent Variable

We created our outcome of interest, perceived FRD, using the survey item, "do you feel in any way discriminated against on your job because of your family caregiving responsibilities, such as the care of children, elderly parents, or other family members?" Respondents answered "yes" or "no" so we coded this variable "1" if a respondent felt discriminated against on the basis of their caregiver responsibilities and "0" if they did not.

Focal Independent Variables

Caregiver Responsibilities

We include a series of dichotomous variables measuring whether a respondent provided childcare, eldercare, or both types of care. Childcare provider (omitted) is coded "1" if a respondent was the parent or guardian of at least one child under the age of 18 who lived with the respondent for at least half of the year and "0" if the respondent was not. Eldercare provider is coded "1" if a respondent provided care to a relative or in-law 65 years old or older in the five years preceding the survey and "0" if a respondent did not. Child and eldercare provider is coded "1" if a respondent had simultaneous child and eldercare responsibilities and "0" if they provided only one type of care.

We account for the extent to which a respondent perceived that family life interfered with work (family-to-work interference) with an index of the following five items: How often ... (1) "... have you not been in as good a mood as you would like to be at work because of your personal or family life?" (2) "... has your personal life kept you from concentrating on your job" (3) "... have you not had enough time for your job because of your family or personal life?" (4) "... [in the past three months] has your family or personal life drained you of the energy you needed to do your job?" (5) "... has your family or personal life kept you from doing as good a job at work as you could?" Responses range from 1 to 5 with higher values indicating higher levels of interference ($\alpha = 0.87$).

Among childcare providers, we account for the daily minutes a respondent spent on childcare with a continuous measure, minutes on childcare.[1] We denote the presence of young children in the household with a dichotomous variable, child under six, coded "1" if respondents had a child under the age of six living with them for at least half of the year and "0" if they did not.[2] We include a measure of the number of children under the age of 18 who lived with the respondent for at least half of the year, a measure that ranges from 1 to 4+. Among those with eldercare responsibilities, we measure the number of elderly relatives a respondent cared for with a dichotomous variable, provided care to multiple elders, coded "1" if a respondent provided care to more than one elderly relative and "0" if they provided care to just one.

Family-Supportive Context

We measure the extent to which a respondent perceived his or her workplace to be supportive of family with three sets of variables. The first is the number of schedule control options a respondent perceived to be available at work, created by summing the following four dichotomous variables (each coded "1" if a respondent believed s/he was allowed to change their schedule in that way and "0" if not): (1) "Are you allowed to work part of your regular paid hours at home?" (2) "Are employees in your organization allowed to work a compressed workweek for part or all of the year?" (3) "Can you choose your own starting and quitting times within some range of hours?" (4) "Are you able to temporarily change your starting and quitting times on short notice when special needs arise if you check with your supervisor or manager?" The measure ranges from 0 to 4.

Second, we consider whether respondents perceived negative career consequences for taking time off or modifying their schedules to meet caregiving responsibilities. We created a variable called time off does not prevent advancement from a respondent's level of agreement with the single item: "At the place where you work, employees who ask for time off for personal or family reasons or try to arrange different schedules or hours to meet their personal or family needs are less likely to get ahead in their jobs or careers" with responses coded 1 (strongly agree) to 4 (strongly disagree).

We include a measure of a respondent's perception of the difficulty of taking time off for personal or family reasons, a measure we call easy to take time off, from the item: "How hard is it for you to take time off during your work day to take care of personal or family matters – very hard, somewhat hard, not too hard, or not at all hard?" Responses range from 1 to 4 and were coded so that higher values indicate that the respondent perceives less difficulty in taking time off.

Finally, we include two measures of interpersonal support at work. The first, supervisor support for family, is a 5-item index of supervisors' sensitivity to work–life issues, including: (1) "My supervisor or manager is fair and doesn't show favoritism in responding to employees' personal or family needs." (2) "My supervisor or manager is responsive to my needs when I have family or personal business to take care of – for example, medical appointments, meeting with child's teacher, etc." (3) "My supervisor or manager is understanding when I talk about personal or family issues that affect my work." (4) "I feel comfortable bringing up personal or family issues with my supervisor or manager." (5) "My supervisor or manager really cares about the effects that work demands have on my personal and family life" ($\alpha = 0.87$). Values for the index range from 0 to 4, where higher values indicate more family-related support from supervisors.[3] The second is a coworker support index of the items: (1) "How much do you agree or disagree with the following statement: I feel I am really a part of the group of people I work with." (2) "I have the support from coworkers that I need to do a good job." (3) "I have support from coworkers that helps me to manage my work and personal or family life" ($\alpha = 0.76$). Responses range from 0 to 4, with higher values indicating that a respondent perceived higher levels of coworker support.[4]

Meritocratic Context

Four questionnaire items indicate the extent to which respondents perceived their workplaces to be meritocratic. Two measures tap into a respondent's perception that workplace decisions were made fairly, a key aspect of a meritocratic workplace: (1) a dichotomous variable, performance-based work rewards, coded "1" if a respondent believed his or her pay, bonuses, and promotions were directly related to his or her performance and "0" if not, and (2) an ordinal-level variable, honest and ethical managers, created from the item: "Managers in my organization behave honestly and ethically when dealing with employees and clients or customers," coded from 1 to 4 with higher values indicating greater agreement with the statement.

We account for establishment size because larger work establishments tend to have formalized personnel practices and equal employment offices which "signal" fairness in personnel decision-making (Bisom-Rapp, 1999; Edelman, 1992; Hirsh & Kornrich, 2008). Establishment size is a four-category ordinal-level variable coded: 1 = less than 50 coworkers at respondents' work location, 2 = 50−249 coworkers, 3 = 250−999 coworkers, and 4 = 1,000 + coworkers.

Finally, because public sector employers are held to different standards than private sector employers (Wilson, Roscigno, & Huffman, 2013) in ways that may affect workers' knowledge of their rights surrounding caregiving, we include a measure of public sector coded "1" if a respondent's work establishment was in the public sector and "0" if in the private or nonprofit sector.

Control Variables

We include controls for a respondent's sex (a dichotomous variable coded "1" for women and "0" for men) and race (a dichotomous variable coded "1" if black, Hispanic, or another non-white race and "0" if white). Women are more likely to be responsible for family caregiving − and hence be the target of FRD − than men (Bianchi, 2012). Furthermore, racial minorities are the most frequent targets of race-based discrimination and so they may be more aware of any type of discrimination than whites.

We include a continuous measure of respondent age as it may be connected to ability to name unfair treatment as FRD. Older workers are more often the targets of discrimination at work than are younger workers (Bendick, Jackson, & Romero, 1997), which may make older workers more attuned to all types of discrimination, including FRD. On the other hand, younger workers increasingly express dissatisfaction with the work–life balance of previous generations and may demand more flexibility from their employers (FWI, 2011b). These views could lead younger workers to question their employers' actions surrounding caregiving as fair or legal. A worker's tenure with their employer might affect perceptions of FRD as the length of time with an employer increases one's opportunity to be exposed to FRD. Job tenure is a continuous measure of the number of years a respondent worked for his or her current employer.

Because knowledge of workplace rights might increase with education, we control for a respondent's education level with a four-category ordinal-level variable coded: 1 = has an H.S. diploma, GED, or less, 2 = has some postsecondary education, 3 = has a 4-year college degree, and 4 = a postgraduate degree. Because marriage might expose workers to different family caregiving responsibilities, models include a dichotomous measure of marital status coded "1" if a respondent was married for the first time, remarried, or living with someone as a couple and "0" if single, divorced, widowed, or separated and not living with someone as a couple. We control for the presence of others (i.e., relatives, friends, etc.) who lived in the respondents' household. These people might require care from the respondent or might help offset some of the respondents' caregiving responsibilities, influencing respondents' risk of experiencing FRD. Others in the household is coded "1" if a respondent reported having at least one other person living in their household and "0" if not.

Following Adams et al. (2012), we control for job satisfaction and employee engagement. Job satisfaction is an index created by averaging responses to two items: (1) "All in all, how satisfied are you with your job – very satisfied, somewhat satisfied, not too satisfied, or not satisfied at all?" and (2) "I am satisfied with my opportunities for advancement – strongly agree, somewhat agree, somewhat disagree, and strongly disagree" ($\alpha = 0.63$). Responses range from 1 to 4 and higher values indicate greater satisfaction. We created an ordinal measure of *employee* engagement using responses to the following four items: (1) "When I'm at work, time passes very quickly." (2) "I really look forward to going into work most days."

(3) "How much effort do you put into your job beyond what is required — a lot, some, only a little, or none?" and (4) "How often do you think about good things related to your job when you're busy doing something else — very often, often, sometimes, rarely, or never?" ($\alpha = 0.59$). We averaged the responses to these four items and then divided the average scores into three categories: 1 = low (<1.5), 2 = moderate (1.5–2.5), and 3 = high levels of engagement (2.6–4).

Manager/professional is a dichotomous variable coded "1" if a respondent worked in a managerial or professional occupation at the time of the survey and "0" if not. We control for whether a respondent was a union member or part of a collective bargaining agreement (coded "1" if so and "0" if not) because union membership might increase workers' knowledge of their rights as caregivers. Finally, we control for respondents' work status because part-time workers are more frequent targets of FRD than full-time workers (Epstein, Seron, Oglensky, & Saute, 1999). Part-time schedule is coded "1" if a respondent thought their employer considered their job to be part-time and "0" if full time.

Analytic Strategy

We estimate logistic regression models because our outcome of interest is dichotomous. We begin by regressing perceived FRD on the caregiving responsibilities measures and the controls to examine which caregiving responsibilities are associated with perceived FRD. Next, we estimate separate models for child and eldercare providers to examine whether child- and eldercare-specific responsibilities affect perceived FRD. Finally, we test the relationship between organizational contexts and perceived FRD.[5] We use multiple imputation to handle missing data (Allison, 2001).[6]

RESULTS

Few respondents — just 8 percent — perceived FRD (see Table 1).

In our sample of caregivers, approximately 37 percent engaged in childcare, 41 percent provided eldercare, while 22 percent provided both. On average, childcare providers spent 180 minutes per day on childcare-related activities and had 1.82 children under the age of 18. Nearly 38 percent had

Table 1. Descriptive Statistics ($n = 1,897$).

	Mean	Standard Error	Minimum	Maximum
Perceived FRD	0.08	–	0	1
Focal independent variables				
Caregiving responsibilities				
Childcare provider	0.37	–	0	1
Eldercare provider	0.41	–	0	1
Both child and eldercare provider	0.22	–	0	1
Family-to-work interference	2.17	0.02	1	5
Minutes per day spent on childcare ($n = 1,122$)	180.49	4.85	0	1,440
Child under the age of 6 ($n = 1,122$)	0.38	–	0	1
Number of children under 18 ($n = 1,122$)	1.82	0.03	1	4
Provided care to multiple elders ($n = 1,198$)	0.41	–	0	1
Family-supportive context				
Number of schedule control options	1.48	0.03	0	4
Time off does not prevent advancement	2.86	0.02	1	4
Easy to take time off for family	2.84	0.02	1	4
Supervisor support for family	2.98	0.03	0	4
Coworker support	3.42	0.02	0	4
Meritocratic context				
Performance-based work rewards	0.51	–	0	1
Honest and ethical managers	3.23	0.02	1	4
Establishment size	2.09	0.03	1	4
Public sector	0.26	–	0	1
Control variables				
Female	0.55	–	0	1
Minority	0.18	–	0	1
Age	44.91	0.26	18	99
Job tenure	9.14	0.20	1	50
Education	2.42	0.02	1	4
Married/living with a partner	0.71	–	0	1
Others in household	0.23	–	0	1
Job satisfaction	3.22	0.02	1	4
Engagement	2.30	0.01	1	3
Managerial/professional occupation	0.46	–	0	1
Member of a union	0.19	–	0	1
Part-time job	0.15	–	0	1

Source: 2008 National Study of the Changing Workforce.
Descriptive statistics are adjusted to account for NSCW's sampling design, a stratified by region, unclustered random probability sample.

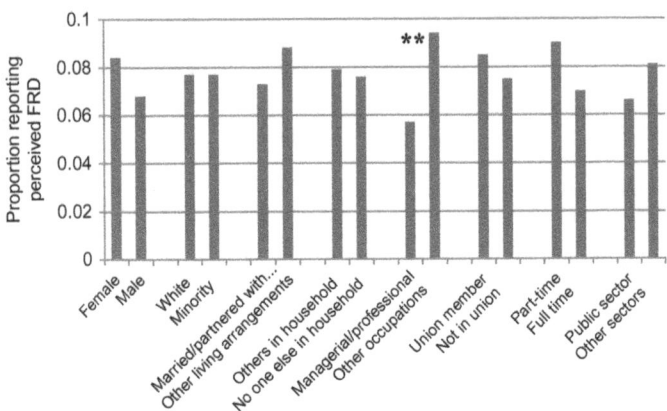

Fig. 1. Perceived FRD by Select Demographic Characteristics ($n = 1,897$). *Source*: 2008 National Study of the Changing Workforce. *Notes*: Analyses are adjusted to account for NSCW's sampling design, a stratified by region, unclustered random probability sample. **$p < .01$ (two-tailed tests).

children under the age of 6 in their household. Finally, 41 percent of eldercare providers cared for more than one elderly person at the same time.

Fig. 1 shows perceived FRD by select demographic characteristics. Means comparison tests show that perceived FRD does not vary by respondents' sex, race, marital status, residence with others, union membership, work status, or sector.

Those respondents employed in managerial or professional occupations, however, perceive significantly lower levels of FRD than respondents employed in other occupations.

Table 2 includes results from logistic regression models predicting perceived FRD. In Model 1, we regress our measure of perceived FRD on the caregiving responsibilities measures and control variables.

Eldercare providers are just as likely to perceive FRD as childcare providers. The odds of perceiving FRD among caregivers who provide child and eldercare simultaneously are 2.14 times the odds of childcare providers. The coefficients for provided eldercare and provided both types of care were significantly different at the $p < .001$ level (test not shown), suggesting that caregivers who provide both types of care perceive more FRD than caregivers who provide just eldercare. Family-to-work interference also increases perceived FRD; a one-unit increase in reported family-to-work interference yields a 72 percent increase in the net odds of perceived FRD.

Table 2. Logistic Regression Estimates of Caregiving Responsibilities on Perceived FRD Among Child and Eldercare Providers.

	Model 1: All Care Providers		Model 2: Childcare Providers		Model 3: Eldercare Providers	
	β	$\exp^\beta$	β	$\exp^\beta$	β	$\exp^\beta$
Focal independent variables						
Caregiving responsibilities						
Eldercare provider	−0.17	0.84	−		−	
	(0.26)					
Both child and eldercare provider	0.76***	2.14	0.80***	2.23	0.98***	2.65
(*omitted: childcare provider*)	(0.23)		(0.24)		(0.25)	
Family-to-work interference	0.54***	1.72	0.54***	1.72	0.51***	1.66
	(0.13)		(0.15)		(0.16)	
Daily minutes on childcare	−		0.001*	1.001	−	
			(0.0005)			
Child under the age of 6	−		0.23	1.22	−	
			(0.32)			
Number of children under 18	−		−0.01	0.99	−	
			(0.14)			
Provided care to multiple elders	−		−		0.57	1.77
					(0.30)	
Control variables						
Female	0.35	1.42	0.31	1.36	0.29	1.34
	(0.20)		(0.26)		(0.25)	
Minority	−0.23	0.80	−0.38	0.68	0.18	1.20
	(0.26)		(0.31)		(0.31)	
Age	−0.02	0.98	−0.02	0.97	−0.01	0.99
	(0.01)		(0.02)		(0.01)	
Job tenure	0.02	1.02	0.01	1.01	0.03*	1.03
	(0.01)		(0.02)		(0.01)	
Education	0.01	1.01	0.00	1.00	−0.08	0.93
	(0.11)		(0.14)		(0.14)	
Married/living with a partner	−0.10	0.91	−0.08	0.92	−0.06	0.94
	(0.22)		(0.30)		(0.26)	
Others in the household	0.03	1.03	0.00	1.00	−0.01	0.99
	(0.26)		(0.37)		(0.28)	
Job satisfaction	−1.25***	0.29	−1.23***	0.29	−1.15***	0.32
	(0.14)		(0.18)		(0.16)	
Engagement	−0.25	0.78	−0.27	0.76	−0.23	0.79
	(0.17)		(0.22)		(0.21)	
Managerial/professional occupation	−0.38	0.68	−0.29	0.75	−0.44	0.65
	(0.25)		(0.30)		(0.31)	
Member of a union	0.22	1.24	0.33	1.39	0.26	1.29

Table 2. (Continued)

	Model 1: All Care Providers		Model 2: Childcare Providers		Model 3: Eldercare Providers	
	β	$\exp^\beta$	β	$\exp^\beta$	β	$\exp^\beta$
	(0.23)		(0.28)		(0.28)	
Part-time job	0.03	1.03	0.21	1.23	0.07	1.07
	(0.26)		(0.32)		(0.32)	
Constant	0.92		0.86		−0.16	
N	1,897		1,122		1,198	

Source: 2008 National Study of the Changing Workforce.
Standard errors in parentheses. Analyses are adjusted to account for NSCW's sampling design, a stratified by region, unclustered random probability sample. *$p < .05$; ***$p < .001$ (two-tailed tests).

Although working a managerial or professional job was associated with reduced FRD in our bivariate analysis, the effect weakened after accounting for caregiving responsibilities and controls. Among the control variables in this model, only job satisfaction is significant and negatively related to FRD ($\exp^\beta = 0.29$, $p < .001$).

Model 2 (Table 2) displays results from the model testing the relationship between the additional childcare-specific measures of caregiving responsibilities and perceived FRD among childcare providers only. Childcare providers who also provide eldercare are more likely to perceive FRD than people who only provide childcare ($\exp^\beta = 2.23$, $p < .001$) and higher levels of family-to-work interference among childcare providers is associated with greater perceived FRD ($\exp^\beta = 1.72$, $p < .001$). Daily time spent on childcare affects perceived FRD. For each additional minute a respondent spends on childcare, the net odds he or she perceives FRD increases by 0.01 percent ($p < .05$).[7] Neither the presence of young children nor number of children in the respondent's household are statistically significant.

Model 3 (Table 2) presents the findings from the analysis of eldercare providers. Eldercare providers who are also engaged in childcare or who have high levels of family-to-work interference perceive FRD. We find no evidence that eldercare providers who care for multiple elderly persons report greater perceived FRD than those who care for just one. One control measure stands out for its significance; among eldercare providers, job tenure is positively associated with greater perceived FRD ($\exp^\beta = 1.03$, $p < .05$).

Table 3. Logistic Regression Estimates of Organizational Context Variables on Perceived FRD among Child and Eldercare Providers.

	Model 1	
	β	$\exp^\beta$
Focal independent variables		
Caregiving responsibilities		
Eldercare provider	−0.26	0.77
	(0.28)	
Both child & eldercare provider (*omitted: childcare provider*)	0.69**	2.00
	(0.25)	
Family-to-work interference	0.43***	1.53
	(0.13)	
Family-supportive context at work		
Number of schedule control options	0.16	1.17
	(0.09)	
Time off does not prevent advancement	−0.54***	0.58
	(0.10)	
Easy to take time off for family	−0.51***	0.60
	(0.11)	
Supervisor support for family	−0.20*	0.82
	(0.08)	
Coworker support	0.03	1.03
	(0.16)	
Meritocratic context at work		
Performance-based work rewards	−0.03	0.97
	(0.23)	
Honest and ethical managers	−0.26*	0.77
	(0.12)	
Establishment size	0.14	1.15
	(0.10)	
Public sector	0.18	1.20
	(0.29)	
Constant	3.10***	
N	1,897	

Source: 2008 National Study of the Changing Workforce.
Standard errors in parentheses. Analyses are adjusted to account for NSCW's sampling design, a stratified by region, unclustered random probability sample. Model includes controls for sex, race, age, job tenure, education, marital status, presence of others in the household, job satisfaction, engagement, managerial or professional occupation, union status, and part-time status. *$p < .05$; **$p < .01$; ***$p < .001$ (two-tailed tests).

Table 3 displays results from a model that tests the effects of family-supportive and meritocratic workplace contexts on perceived FRD for the full sample of caregivers (both child *and* eldercare providers).

Three measures of a family-supportive context emerge as important predictors of perceived FRD. First, caregivers who feel that taking time off to care for family responsibilities is unrelated to their workplace advancement are less likely to perceive FRD than respondents who feel otherwise. Specifically, a one-unit increase in respondents' belief that time off does not prevent advancement yields a 42 percent decrease in the net odds of perceived FRD. Second, caregivers who find it easy to take time off during the day for caregiving or personal responsibilities perceive less FRD than caregivers who do not find it easy to take time off; a one-unit increase in respondents' perceptions of ease of taking time off yields a 40 percent decrease in the net odds of perceived FRD. Finally, caregivers who feel supported in their personal lives by their supervisors are less likely to perceive FRD than caregivers who do not ($\exp^{\beta} = 0.82$, $p < .05$). Furthermore, respondents' perceptions that their managers are honest and ethical in interacting with employees and clients/customers, one indicator of a meritocratic context, is associated with lower perceived FRD. A one-unit increase in respondent belief that their managers are honest and ethical yields a 23 percent decrease in the net odds of perceived FRD ($p < .05$). None of the remaining measures of family-supportive or meritocratic context are significantly related to perceived FRD.

DISCUSSION AND CONCLUSIONS

This chapter considers the social and organizational factors associated with perceived mistreatment at work because of one's role as a caregiver. Specifically, we investigate the caregiving responsibilities and organizational contexts associated with perceived FRD. Eight percent of working caregivers in our sample perceived FRD. While we are unaware of any research which examines actual FRD rates in the workplace, the extensive body of research on the stigma and penalties working caregivers face (Correll et al., 2007; Williams et al., 2013) lead us to believe that perceived FRD is underreported in our sample. We suspect this is the result of the pervasive idea that caregiving − and parenting in particular − is a personal choice (Kricheli-Katz, 2012) and widely accepted ideal worker norms (Blair-Loy, 2003; Williams, 2000). It is also possible that the low rate of FRD stems from the relative novelty of the recognition of workers' caregiving rights in 2008 (the year our data were collected). Nonetheless, our analyses show that perceived FRD is associated with particular caregiving responsibilities and organizational contexts.

Who Perceives FRD?

We began by investigating the types of caregiving responsibilities that are associated with perceived FRD. To our surprise, we found no evidence that childcare providers perceive less FRD than eldercare providers, despite having thought that childbearing trends make parenting appear to be a personal choice to be handled solely by parents (Kricheli-Katz, 2012). An alternative explanation, and one that supports our finding, is that eldercare, like childcare, is viewed as a choice under one's control because of a growing tendency for people to contract out personal tasks, like care of elderly relatives, to third-party servicers (Hochschild, 2012). While eldercare is now an inevitable part of the life course (Bianchi, 2012), its outsourcing may be increasingly socially accepted and even expected. In fact, the most common type of voluntary support that employers offer eldercare providers is information and referrals to eldercare services (Smith, 2004). This type of support may inadvertently send the message that employers expect workers to outsource their eldercare. In light of these alternative care services, eldercare providers who are unwilling (or unable) to outsource eldercare may come to view eldercare provision as their "choice," accept mistreatment as an appropriate trade-off for that choice, and fail to recognize FRD when it occurs.

Consistent with our expectations, we found that caregivers who provide both child and eldercare perceive more FRD than caregivers who provide just one type of care, as do people with high levels of family-to-work interference. In fact, providers of both child and eldercare perceive more FRD than providers of one type even after accounting for family-to-work interference. Our finding rules out the possibility that extensive interference prompts dual child and eldercare providers to identify FRD and "blame" their employers for it if it occurs and hints that they might be more frequent targets of FRD than caregivers who provide one type of care. Data limitations prohibit us from further teasing out the exact mechanisms linking dual child and eldercare with perceived FRD. Future studies that pair data on actual FRD or biased attitudes toward caregivers (e.g., through audit studies) with data on perceived discrimination in the same workplace offer one way to disentangle these mechanisms.

Our finding that caregivers who provide both child and eldercare perceive more FRD than caregivers who provide one type of care implies that employers and policy-makers can expect to see growth in perceived FRD as more workers anticipate taking on eldercare responsibilities (Aumann, Galinsky, Sakai, Brown, & Bond, 2008). Given the connection between perceived discrimination and measures of worker well-being, job satisfaction, and engagement (Ensher et al., 2001; Goldman et al., 2006; Pavalko et al., 2003), to attract and retain productive workers employers will likely have an increasing economic incentive to create work environments in which caregivers with both child and eldercare responsibilities feel supported.

Analyses also revealed how the extent of child- and eldercare-specific responsibilities affect perceived FRD. Among childcare providers, each additional minute a childcare provider spends on childcare a day increases the odds he or she perceives FRD. Neither the presence of young children nor caring for multiple children or elders affected perceived FRD, perhaps because the presence of young or multiple children or elders does not adequately capture the extent of providers' responsibilities that put them at risk of perceiving FRD. For example, care for children with chronic illnesses or disabilities results in more stress and work−family conflict for caregivers than care for children without these conditions (Stewart, 2013). These sorts of caregiving responsibilities may better capture the behaviors that put caregivers at risk of being targeted for FRD or that foster the attitudes which prompt them to recognize FRD when it occurs. Future research on FRD should consider the specific needs of care recipients (e.g., their health, the type of care required, etc.), not simply their presence, age, or quantity.

The Role of Organizational Context

Some aspects of a family-supportive and meritocratic context increase perceived FRD more than others. First, employed caregivers perceive less FRD when they believe they can get ahead at work − even if they take time off or rearrange their work schedules for personal or family reasons − than when they believe taking time off will slow their advancement. Like Adams et al. (2012), we find that the perception that it is easy to take time off during work hours and having supervisor support for family life lowers perceived FRD. It appears that workplaces that foster a sense of support, rather than censure, for workers' family responsibilities yield lower perceived FRD. We proposed several explanations as to how these contexts could lead to less perceived FRD; actual FRD might occur less frequently, working caregivers feel free to discuss and support one another around family issues, or workers who face FRD may attribute it to factors outside of discrimination because they believe their employer has transparent operating policies that minimize FRD. Without data on actual FRD or more detailed measures of workplace culture and interactions, we can only conclude that workplace context is salient for perceived FRD. Future research should explore the mechanisms by which these aspects of a family-supportive context lead to less perceived FRD, as well as examine whether family-supportive characteristics lead to reduced FRD or just reduced perceptions of it.

Surprisingly, the number of schedule control options a respondent perceives to be available is unrelated to perceived FRD. These findings suggest that that while workers may benefit from greater schedule control (Kelly, Moen, & Tranby, 2011), they are just as likely as caregivers who do not have access to schedule control to feel their family responsibilities mark them as targets for mistreatment. Of course, our measure taps perceptions of available options, not actual options, and workers rarely feel schedule control options are available to use when the broader workplace culture is unsupportive of them (Epstein et al., 1999). Schedule control availability appears then to matter less for FRD than a generally supportive work culture. We also found that coworker support did not influence perceived FRD. Perceived support from one's coworkers may only matter for perceived FRD – or matter differently – in an organization whose culture or context already provides broader support for the combination of paid work and family.

One attribute of a meritocratic context is linked to perceived FRD: a belief that one's manager is honest and ethical in dealing with employees, clients, and customers is associated with lowered perceived FRD. Honest and ethical managers may engage in fewer discriminatory behaviors than dishonest and unethical managers resulting in less actual *and* perceived FRD, however meritocratic work cultures do not guarantee employment decisions are free of sex and race biases (Castilla & Benard, 2010). We suspect that the power of a meritocratic culture for reducing FRD lies in its ability to convince working caregivers that their managers are incapable of discrimination, a suspicion we hope is the topic of future investigation.

No additional meritocratic workplace attributes (e.g., the presence of performance-based awards, workplace size, or sector) influenced perceived FRD. It may be that our measures of meritocratic work context are limited. For example, a respondent might reply with his or her immediate supervisor in mind – the supervisor who has the greatest opportunity to engage in FRD – when answering questions about managerial honesty and ethics, but sector dynamics signal characteristics about the broader organization and perceived FRD may tie more closely to one's immediate and most frequently experienced work setting. In short, sector may be too distant to influence perceived FRD. Our categorical workplace size measure cannot capture distinctions between workplaces with 250 or 500 employees, distinctions that might affect operating policies that influence employer ability to engage in FRD. Future research should identify additional workplace features, including monetary benefits for family care, that might lead working caregivers to perceive their employers as fair and meritocratic regarding workers' caregiving rights.

Data Limitations

We would be remiss if we did not discuss the limitations of our analyses. As with any research that uses survey data to examine perceived discrimination, we cannot determine whether a respondent was actually a victim of FRD. On some level, this distinction is irrelevant; perceptions – whether accurate or not – are real to workers and result in negative outcomes (see Ensher et al., 2001; Goldman et al., 2006). Still, future research could do more to differentiate between actual FRD, perceived FRD, and the formal filing of FRD claims by workers.

We draw on data collected in 2008, one year after the EEOC published its guidance stating family caregiving discrimination can be an illegal form of discrimination (EEOC, 2007). Since it takes time for policy change or guidance to take hold at work, we likely understate perceived FRD. Recent data might yield higher levels of perceived FRD given that increased perceptions may yield increased publicity of FRD, publicity found to subsequently result in more FRD claims (Still, 2006).

Despite these limitations, our research has implications for researchers, organizational change agents, and policy-makers. For researchers studying FRD, our findings underscore the importance of paying attention to the diversity of caregivers' responsibilities, as well as to the context of their workplaces, to better understand their work experiences. Organizational change agents should also recognize that caregivers have divergent experiences and so policies that are designed with one type of caregiving in mind (i.e., childcare) may not support or benefit all caregivers. Because workplace characteristics shape perceptions of FRD, our results show how employers can influence the experiences of their caregiving employees; they can, at minimum, ensure their employees understand their rights as caregivers and, more specifically, support those who want to alter when, where, and how they will do their work and ensure that attending to their family responsibilities will not slow their career progression. Much like the EEOC did with its 2007 guidance regarding caregiving at work, policy-makers can mount a campaign whose primary goal is to inform workers of their caregiving rights. We suspect this is a particularly important step in eradicating FRD given the cultural pressures workers face to blame themselves for negative treatment, rather than their employers. The growing share of workers with caregiving responsibilities paired with the pervasive biases against caregivers in the labor market (Correll et al., 2007; Williams, 2000), suggests that perceived FRD promises to be an ongoing problem. We stand to gain from future research that continues to identify the contours of perceived FRD.

NOTES

1. Two respondents reported spending over 24 hours a day on childcare. We coded these respondents as missing for minutes on childcare. Findings do not change in substantive ways when we exclude these respondents from analyses.
2. We explored alternative ways of accounting for the presence of young children, including a continuous measure of the age of a respondent's youngest child, and a dichotomous measure of the presence of children under three. Results were similar across models.
3. We coded 283 respondents without an immediate supervisor as "0" on the supervisor support for family measure.
4. We use the NSCW's pre-created index of coworker support. We coded 11 respondents who reported that they usually worked alone as "0" on this index because they were not asked questions about coworker support. We considered creating an organizational culture index combing all of the variables we used to create time off does not prevent advancement, easy to take time off, supervisor support for family, and coworker support; however we decided to test the separate effects of these four variables since each measures a unique aspect of organizational culture.
5. Following Lee and Forthofer (2006), we adjust our analyses to account for the NSCW's complex sampling design, a stratified by region, unclustered random probability sample. We do not weight descriptive or multivariate analyses.
6. Using conventional p-values, the pattern of findings for our focal independent variables are substantively similar whether we use listwise deletion or multiple imputation.
7. Another way of interpreting this finding is that for each additional hour a childcare provider spends on childcare a day, the odds he or she perceives FRD increase by 6 percent.

REFERENCES

Adams, S. J., Heywood, J. S., & Miller, L. A. (2012). Caregivers, firm policies and gender discrimination claims. *Review of Economics of the Household, 12*, 359–377.

Allison, P. (2001). *Missing data.* Thousand Oaks, CA: Sage.

Aumann, K., Galinsky, E., Sakai, K., Brown, M., & Bond, J. T. (2008). *The elder care study: Everyday realities and wishes for change.* New York, NY: Families and Work Institute. Retrieved from http://familiesandwork.org/site/research/reports/elder_care.pdf

Beauregard, T. A., & Henry, L. C. (2009). Making the link between work-life balance practices and organizational performance. *Human Resource Management Review, 19*, 9–22.

Bendick, M., Jackson, C. W., & Romero, J. H. (1997). Employer discrimination against older workers: An experimental study of hiring practices. *Journal of Aging and Social Policy, 8*, 35–46.

Bianchi, S. M. (2012). *Family change and time allocation in American families.* New York, NY: Alfred P. Sloan Foundation. Retrieved from http://workfamily.sas.upenn.edu/wfrn-repo/object/1tu90df23ih550x4

Bisom-Rapp, S. (1999). Bulletproofing the workplace: Symbol and substance in employment discrimination law practice. *Florida State University Law Review, 26*, 959–1049.

Blair-Loy, M. (2003). *Competing devotions: Career and family among women executives.* Cambridge, MA: Harvard University Press.

Burstein, P., & Monaghan, K. (1986). Equal employment opportunity and the mobilization of law. *Law & Society Review, 20*, 356–388.

Calvert, C. T. (2010). *Family responsibilities discrimination: Litigation update 2010.* San Francisco, CA: The Center for WorkLife Law. Retrieved from http://www.worklifelaw.org/pubs/FRDupdate.pdf

Castilla, E. (2008). Gender, race, and meritocracy in organizational careers. *American Journal of Sociology, 113*, 1479–1526.

Castilla, E., & Benard, S. (2010). The paradox of meritocracy in organizations. *Administrative Science Quarterly, 55*, 543–576.

Center for WorkLife Law. (2012). *Family responsibilities discrimination.* San Francisco, CA: Author. Retrieved from http://worklifelaw.org/frd/faqs/. Accessed on August 4, 2014.

Correll, S. J., Benard, S., & Paik, I. (2007). Getting a job: Is there a motherhood penalty? *American Journal of Sociology, 5*, 1297–1339.

Eaton, S. C. (2003). If you can use them: Flexibility policies, organizational commitment, and perceived performance. *Industrial Relations: A Journal of Economy and Society, 2*, 145–167.

Edelman, L. (1992). Legal ambiguity and symbolic structures: Organizational mediation of law. *American Journal of Sociology, 97*, 1531–1576.

Ensher, E. A., Grant-Vallone, E. J., & Donaldson, S. I. (2001). Effects of perceived discrimination on job satisfaction, organizational commitment, organizational citizenship behavior, and grievances. *Human Resource Development Quarterly, 12*, 53–72.

Epstein, C. F., Seron, C., Oglensky, B., & Saute, R. (1999). *The part-time paradox: Time norms, professional lives, family, and gender.* New York, NY: Routledge.

Equal Employment Opportunity Commission. (2007). *Enforcement guidance: Unlawful disparate treatment of workers with caregiving responsibilities.* Washington, DC: Author. Retrieved from http://www.eeoc.gov/policy/docs/caregiving.html

Families and Work Institute. (2008). *2008 national study of the changing workforce*. New York, NY: Author.
Families and Work Institute. (2011a). *National study of the changing workforce: Guide to public-use files*. New York, NY: Author.
Families and Work Institute. (2011b). *Generation & gender in the workplace*. New York, NY: Author. Retrieved from http://familiesandwork.org/site/research/reports/genandgender.pdf
Felstiner, W. L., Abel, R. L., & Sarat, A. (1980). Emergence and transformation of disputes: Naming, blaming, claiming. *Law & Society Review, 15*, 631–654.
Goldman, B. M., Gutek, B. A., Stein, J. H., & Lewis, K. (2006). Employment discrimination in organizations: Antecedents and consequences. *Journal of Management, 32*, 786–830.
Gornick, J. C., & Meyers, M. K. (2005). *Families that work: Policies for reconciling parenthood and employment*. New York, NY: Russell Sage Foundation Publications.
Hirsh, E., & Cha, Y. (2008). Understanding employment discrimination: A multilevel approach. *Sociology Compass, 2*, 1989–2007.
Hirsh, E., & Kmec, J. A. (2009). Human resource structures: Reducing discrimination or raising rights awareness? *Industrial Relations, 48*, 512–532.
Hirsh, E., & Kornrich, S. (2008). The context of discrimination: Workplace conditions, institutional environments, and sex and race discrimination charges. *American Journal of Sociology, 113*, 1394–1432.
Hochschild, A. R. (2012). *The outsourced self: Intimate life in market times*. New York, NY: Metropolitan Books.
Kaiser, C. R., & Major, B. F. (2006). A social psychological perspective on perceiving and reporting discrimination. *Law & Social Inquiry, 31*, 801–830.
Kelly, E. L. (2005). Discrimination against caregivers? Gendered family responsibilities, employer practices, and work rewards. In L. B. Nielsen & R. Nelson (Eds.), *Handbook of employment discrimination research: Rights and realities* (pp. 353–374). Dordrecht, Netherlands: Springer.
Kelly, E. L., Moen, P., & Tranby, E. (2011). Changing workplaces to reduce work-family conflict schedule control in a white-collar organization. *American Sociological Review, 76*, 265–290.
Kmec, J. A., O'Connor, L. T., & Schieman, S. (2014). Not ideal: The association between working anything but full time and perceived unfair treatment. *Work and Occupations, 41*, 63–85.
Kossek, E. E., & Friede, A. (2006). The business case: Managerial perspectives on work and the family. In M. Pitt-Catsouphes, E. E. Kossek, & S. A. Sweet (Eds.), *The work–family handbook: Multi-disciplinary perspectives, methods, and approaches* (pp. 611–628). Mahwah, NJ: Lawrence Erlbaum Associates Press.
Kricheli-Katz, T. (2012). Choice, discrimination, and the motherhood penalty. *Law & Society Review, 46*, 557–586.
Lee, E. S., & Forthofer, R. N. (2006). *Analyzing complex survey data*. Thousand Oaks, CA: Sage.
Levitsky, S. R. (2008). What rights? The construction of political claims to American health care entitlements. *Law & Society Review, 42*, 551–590.
Pavalko, E. K., Mossakowski, K. N., & Hamilton, V. J. (2003). Does perceived discrimination affect health? Longitudinal relationships between work discrimination and women's physical and emotional health. *Journal of Health and Social Behavior, 44*, 18–33.

Perlow, L. (2012). *Sleeping with your smartphone: How to break the 24/7 habit and change the way you work*. Boston, MA: Harvard Business Review Press.

Pugh, A. J. (2015). *The tumbleweed society: Working and caring in an age of insecurity*. New York, NY: Oxford University Press.

Riley, L. D., & Bowen, C. (2005). The sandwich generation: Challenges and coping strategies of multigenerational families. *The Family Journal, 13*, 52–58.

Savani, K., Stephens, N., & Markus, H. R. (2011). The unanticipated interpersonal and societal consequences of choice: Victim-blaming and reduced support for the public good. *Psychological Science, 22*, 795–802.

Smith, P. (2004). Elder care, work, and gender: The work-family issue of the 21st century. *Berkeley Journal of Employment and Labor Law, 25*, 351–399.

Stainback, K., & Tomaskovic-Devey, D. (2012). *Documenting desegregation: Racial and gender segregation in private-sector employment since the Civil Rights Act*. New York, NY: Russell Sage Foundation Publications.

Stewart, L. (2013). Family care responsibilities and employment: Exploring the impact of type of family care on work-family and family-work conflict. *Journal of Family Issues, 34*, 113–138.

Still, M. C. (2006). *Litigating the maternal wall: U.S. lawsuits charging discrimination against workers with family responsibilities*. San Francisco, CA: The Center for WorkLife Law. Retrieved from http://www.worklifelaw.org/pubs/FRDreport.pdf

Weiner, B. E., Perry, R. P., & Magnusson, J. (1988). An attributional analysis of reactions to stigma. *Journal of Personality and Social Psychology, 55*, 738–748.

Williams, J. (2000). *Unbending gender: Why family and work conflict and what to do about it*. New York, NY: Oxford University Press.

Williams, J. C., Blair-Loy, M., & Berdahl, J. (2013). Cultural schemas, social class, and the flexibility stigma. *Journal of Social Issues, 69*, 209–234.

Williams, J. C., & Bornstein, S. (2008). The evolution of "FReD": Family responsibilities, discrimination, and developments in the law of stereotyping and implicit bias. *Hastings Law Journal, 50*, 1311–1358.

Wilson, G., Roscigno, V., & Huffman, M. L. (2013). Public sector transformation, racial inequality, and downward occupational mobility. *Social Forces, 91*, 975–1006.

POLICY OR EMPOWERMENT? POLICY ENVIRONMENTS, POLITICAL EMPOWERMENT, AND WORK−FAMILY CONFLICT

Leah Ruppanner

ABSTRACT

Purpose − To investigate the association between country-level differences in childcare enrollment, the presence of affirmative action policy, and female parliamentary representation and individual-level conflict between work and family.

Methodology/approach − This study applies data from the 2002 International Social Survey Program (n = 14,000 +) for respondents in 29 countries and pairs them with macro-level measures of childcare enrollment, the presence of affirmative action policy, and female parliamentary representation. I estimate the model using hierarchical linear modeling (HLM 7) and also assess cross-level interactions by gender and parental status.

Findings − The models show that female parliamentary representation has a robust negative association with individual-level reports of *work−family and family−work conflict. These associations do not vary by gender or parental status. Also, mothers report less family−work conflict in countries with more expansive childcare enrollment, indicating that this welfare policy benefits the intended group.*

Research limitations/implications − *This research implies that greater female parliamentary representation has widespread benefits to all citizens', rather than just women's or mothers', work−family and family−work conflict. Additional longitudinal research would benefit this area of study.*

Practical implications − *This research suggests that increasing female parliamentary representation at the country-level may promote work−life balance at the individual-level. It also indicates that public childcare enrollment benefits women through lower family−work conflict which may encourage continuous maternal labor force participation and reduce economic gender inequality.*

Originality/value − *This chapter builds on an emerging area of work−family research applying multilevel modeling to draw empirical links between individual work−family experiences and macro-level structural variation.*

Keywords: Work−family conflict; childcare enrolment; female parliamentary representation; affirmative action; maternal labor force participation; economic gender equality

Today, many individuals simultaneously balance work and home demands. Boundaries between work and family are often porous contributing to inter-role conflict, deteriorated health, depression, and stress (Allen, Herst, Bruck, & Sutton, 2000; Glavin, Schieman, & Reid, 2011). These burdens are disproportionately shouldered by parents, especially mothers, who experience greater work−family conflict and, as a consequence, deteriorated health (Glavin et al., 2011). In response, many advanced democracies have instituted policies to alleviate family burdens, penalize discriminatory practices, and empower women. These policies provide resources to expand autonomy and freedom of choice, especially for those vulnerable to competing work and family demands (Esping-Andersen, 1990; Gornick & Meyers, 2003, 2008; Hobson, 2011). Yet, the relationship between these policies and reports of conflict requires investigation. An emerging area of research documents that macro-level gender empowerment structures work−family conflict and that policies structure work−family strain (Lyness, Gornick, Stone, & Grotto, 2012; Ruppanner & Huffman, 2014). Yet, an explicit analysis simultaneously weighing policies against gender empowerment is warranted. I expand upon this research to ask: do family-responsive and antidiscriminatory policies and women's political representation at the country-level structure work−family and family−work conflict at the individual-level?

To address this question, I pair individual-level data from the 2002 International Social Survey Program (ISSP) for over 14,000 respondents in 29 nations with country-level measures of family-responsive (public childcare enrollment) and antidiscriminatory (presence of affirmative action legislation) policies and female empowerment (women's parliamentarian representation). This study advances existing research in four important ways. First, it considers a wide range of countries ($n = 29$), expanding existing small sample studies (Crompton & Lyonette, 2006; Ruppanner & Pixley, 2012). Second, it models country-level effects that capture theoretically driven processes − family-responsive and antidiscriminatory policies and female parliamentary representation − to build on previous multilevel research (Lyness et al., 2012). Third, it considers bidirectional conflict, from work−family and family−work, as theory predicts these macro-level measures to have differential effects by direction of conflict. Finally, it models multilevel effects for populations − women, fathers, and mothers − shown to be vulnerable to conflict. The results contribute to a growing body of comparative cross-national work−family research.

THEORIZING CONFLICT AT THE COUNTRY-LEVEL: A CAPABILITIES FRAMEWORK

The capabilities framework identifies the individual, cultural, and structural constraints that limit capability and agency (Sen, 1993). This theory addresses a central question: what would individuals do if completely autonomous and what factors inhibit their capabilities? Indeed, choices are often bound by cultural constraints and desires do not always match actions (Robeyns, 2005). This tension is demonstrated through fertility decisions (Hobson & Olah, 2006) and female work patterns (Damaske, 2011). To disentangle these processes, Sen (1993) identifies individual, structural, and cultural constraints to autonomy. Individual-level constraints include education, age, gender, and socioeconomic status. Structural-level constraints capture physical surroundings and infrastructure. Finally, cultural-level constraints include social norms and legal policies conditioning autonomy.

The application of the capabilities framework to work−family conflict research is established (Hobson, 2011). Specifically, Hobson (2011) investigates how structural- and cultural-level characteristics impact individual-level work−family balance. Structural-level attributes, measured at the firm-level, capture workplace constraints including job quality, organizational culture, flexibility, and autonomy. The impact of the firm-level characteristics on work−family conflict is well theorized, empirically supported, and well-established across a variety of research (Jacobs & Gerson, 2004; Schieman & Young, 2011; Schieman, Glavin, & Milkie, 2009; Voydanoff, 2007). Yet, the relationship between work−family conflict and cultural constraints is less fully understood. An emerging body of research explores these relationships. Specifically, Ruppanner and Huffman (2014) find macro-level gender empowerment structures parents' family−work conflict with important gender differences. Further, Lyness et al. (2012) weigh public policies, economic development, and union coverage on work−family strain and find workers are more strained in more economically developed countries with important gender differences. Collectively, this research highlights the impact of culture on individuals', especially women's, work−family experiences. It is within this macro-level context that this study makes a contribution.

What is more, I model the impact of cultural constraints on the gender and parental gaps in conflict. Constraints are highly gendered imposing different limitations on autonomy and opportunity (Hobson, 2011). For example, women remain disproportionately responsible for housework and childcare even when employed full-time (Bianchi, Milkie, Sayer, & Robinson, 2000; Treas & Drobnic, 2010). Within the labor market, women face additional barriers to advancement explained, partially, by real or perceived competing family responsibilities (Cohen & Huffman, 2003; Lennon, 1994). In response to this inequality, governments enact policies to redistribute work and family responsibilities more equally (Gornick & Meyers, 2003). The effectiveness of these policies on work−family conflict is directly explored here. What is more, I also weigh the impact of one measure, female parliamentary representation, shown to capture gender empowerment more broadly (Ruppanner, 2010). Guided by previous research, specific gender expectations are outlined below.

Childcare Enrollment

Welfare states institute public childcare to provide parents with reliable and cost-effective care, in part, to encourage continuous maternal employment. Indeed, mothers in countries with more expansive childcare are more likely to be employed, experience fewer employment interruptions, and report higher earnings (Leira, 1993; Misra, Budig, & Boeckmann, 2011; Orloff, 1993; Pettit & Hook, 2009). Yet, the increase in maternal employment indicates that more families are juggling work and family, which may exacerbate work−family conflict. This may be compounded by the gender segregation of women in low wage positions (Mandel & Semyonov, 2005; Pettit & Hook, 2009), which may increase strain. As this body of research suggests, expansive childcare policies may contribute to bidirectional conflict as dual-earner families are institutionally supported. On the other hand, public childcare enrollment may reduce parents' conflict in one direction, from family−work, as the state assumes partial responsibility for children's care. Indeed, welfare states enact public childcare measures to buffer workers from competing work and family demands through structured, reliable, and consistent care (Gornick & Meyers, 2003; Grönlund & Öun, 2010). This may in turn alleviate the spillover of family into work life for the intended population − parents of a young child and, in particular, mothers. The models weigh these competing hypotheses.

Affirmative Action

While childcare policies benefit parents, additional government policies, including affirmative, protect all workers from discrimination. Affirmative action policies are most common in liberal welfare states where economic equality is central and individuals are largely responsible for dependent care (Esping-Andersen, 1990; O'Connor, Orloff, Shola, & Shaver, 1999). For working women, this protection is essential for two reasons: (1) women are disproportionately responsible for child, parental, and elder care across the life course (Dautzenberg, Diederiks, Philipsen, & Tan, 1999; Pinquart & Sörensen, 2003); (2) women are often viewed as less serious about work based on real or perceived family demands (Lennon & Rosenfield, 1992). Thus, affirmative action may protect women from work−family conflict when family demands are high. This may function in multiple ways. Employers, based on the threat of lawsuit, may be less punitive of women's family−work conflict. This in turn may reduce female employees' sensitivity to this conflict as its consequences are less severe. Alternatively, women, bolstered by the law, may be better able to deny employers requests to bring work home, thus reducing work–family conflict. Finally, affirmative action policies may signal longer career-paths for women which may encourage women to mitigate the family–work conflict. Given the dearth of research on these relationships, these processes are largely speculative. However, this gap highlights the need to investigate work–family conflict beyond the parent/family policy nexus. Importantly, affirmative action policy captures protection from gender discrimination across the life course for all women. Ultimately, I expect women, protected by affirmative action policies, to report less work–family and family–work conflict.

Female Parliamentary Representation

The above sections outline expected relationships for specific policies. Yet, women's political empowerment more broadly may structure work–family conflict as well. Research shows electing women to legislature has powerful direct and indirect effects for gender empowerment. Directly, women's greater political representation is associated with family- and gender-responsive policy-making, including increased spending on social services (Bolzendahl, 2009, 2010, 2011). This reflects support, including votes, for gender empowering and antidiscriminatory policies (Bratton, 2002; Caiazza, 2004; Carroll, 2001; Chaney, 2006; Reingold, 2000; Swers, 1998, 2002). Thus, female parliamentary representation serves as a proxy for the wider variation in gender-responsive policies than the affirmative action and childcare policies applied here. In addition to legislation, female parliamentarians also serve as role models highlighting the difficulties of balancing work and family demands which may shift cultural dialogues on work–family issues (Campbell & Wolbrecht, 2006). Indeed, female parliamentarians reflect normative cultural messages about gender equality in work and family that may structure individual behavior (Grönlund & Öun, 2010). The link between gender empowerment and individual behavior is well-established in the housework literature. Specifically, men account for a larger share of the housework in countries where women are politically empowered (Batalova & Cohen, 2002; Fuwa, 2004; Geist, 2005; Ruppanner, 2010). These benefits may extend to work–family conflict as men in these contexts assume a larger share of the family demands. What is more, these benefits may be greatest for parents, especially mothers, of a young child whose family demands are greatest. In sum, I expect women, especially mothers, to report less conflict and men to report more in countries where more women are politically empowered.

DATA, MEASURES, AND MODELS

To address these relationships, this study applies data from the 2002 International Social Survey Program on Family and Changing Gender Roles. This is the third wave of this module and includes data from respondents from 29 countries including: Australia, Austria, Brazil, Chile, Cyprus, Czech Republic, Denmark, Finland, Belgium, France, Germany, Great Britain, Hungary, Israel, Japan, Latvia, Mexico, Netherlands, Northern Ireland, Norway, Poland, Portugal, Russia, Slovenia, Slovakian Republic, Spain, Sweden, Switzerland, and the United States. The Philippines and Taiwan are excluded from the sample because they are missing measures for the public childcare measure. Bulgaria, Ireland, and New Zealand are excluded because they are missing for the child under 5 in the home measure. The sample is restricted to those who are aged 25–59, employed, and complete on either the work–family or family–work conflict measures. The effective sample size is 14,396 respondents who reported a family–work conflict score and 14,176 for those with a work–family conflict score.

The data are analyzed using hierarchical linear models (HLM). HLM accounts for the nesting of individuals within macro contexts. Unlike OLS regressions which assume that the standard errors are randomly distributed, HLM estimates clustered standard errors at multiple-levels, in this case individuals within countries. By simultaneously estimating individual and country-level models, I am able to assess whether the policy and participation measures structure individual reports of work–family and family–work conflict net of individual-level controls. In addition, the models estimate cross-level effects for the gender and parents of a child 5 or younger in the home. Unless otherwise noted, I applied multi-item imputation to replace missing data.

Dependent Variables

This study applies two separate dependent measures: family–work and work–family conflict. Family–work conflict is the respondents' mean response to the following statements: (1) "I have found it difficult to concentrate at work because of my family responsibilities"; (2) "I have arrived at work too tired to function well because of the household work I had done" ($r = 0.74$). Those missing on either of these measures were excluded from the sample. Responses are on a four-point scale ranging from never to several times a week with higher values reflecting greater reported family–work conflict.

Work–family conflict is the respondents' mean response to the following statements: (1) "It has been difficult for me to fulfill my family responsibilities because of the amount of time I spend on my job"; (2) "I have come home from work too tired to do the chores which need to be done" ($r = 0.71$). Respondents missing on either of these measures were excluded from the sample. Responses are on a four-point scale ranging from several times a week to never and higher values reflect greater reported family–work conflict

Country-Level Measures: Gender Empowerment and Family-Responsive Policies

The country-level measures are from two sources. The percent of female parliamentarians is from the 2002 United Nations Development Report (UNDR). The UNDR is compiled annually and includes measures of gender empowerment used in previous multilevel research (Batalova & Cohen, 2002; Fuwa, 2004; Ruppanner, 2010). The public childcare and affirmative action measures are compiled by Fuwa and Cohen (2007) who sourced their data from a range of academic and government sources including the United Nations Convention on the Elimination of All forms of Discrimination against Women, Central Bureau of Statistics, Council on the European Union, OECD database, and Gornick and Meyers' (2003) *Families that Work* book. Public childcare is the mean proportion of children under 3 and 3–6 in public childcare to capture average enrollment for children under school age. Affirmative action is dichotomously coded for the presence of programs that give women preferential treatment in hiring and promotion for the sampled country. Table 1 provides the correlations between these macro-level measures. Countries with more female parliamentarians have more children enrolled in public childcare and are more likely to have affirmative action policies, a finding consistent with previous research (Bolzendahl, 2009). The models directly explore the relationship between these measures and conflict.

Table 1. Correlations for Country-Level Measures.

	Female Parliamentarian Representation (%)	Public Childcare Enrollment (%)	Presence of Affirmative Action Legislation (Yes = 1)
Female parliamentarian representation (%)	1	0.408*	0.402*
Public childcare enrollment (0–1)	0.408*	1	0.243
Presence of affirmative action legislation (yes = 1)	0.402*	0.243	1

* Indicates significant at the 0.05 level (two-tailed).

Main Independent Variables: Gender and Presence of a Young Child

To measure the gender gap in work–family and family–work conflict, I include a measure of *gender* dichotomously coded (female = 1). The *presence of a child*, especially a young child, is associated with greater housework and childcare responsibilities (Bianchi et al., 2000; Fuwa, 2004). This is measured dichotomously for the presence of a child 5 or under in the home (value = 1) and a gender interaction term for mothers of a young child (female × child 5 or under present). The cross-level results for this group are presented in the tables.

Individual-Level Controls

Given the focus on the country-level relationships, the individual-level measures are included as controls and thus discussed briefly. These measures are consistent with the job-demands and resources theoretical approach supported in previous research (Schieman et al., 2009) and are consistent with the individual- and firm-level components of the capabilities framework (Hobson, 2011; Sen, 1993). All of these individual-level measures are controlled for but not presented in the multilevel models; the results at the individual-level are consistent with theoretical predictions and previous research (Schieman et al., 2009). *Home stress* reflects the extent to which the respondent finds his/her home life stressful. Responses are on a five-point scale with higher values reflecting greater stress at home. *Home pressure* is respondents' agreement to the following statement: "There are so many things to do at home, I often run out of time before I get them all done." Responses are on a five-point scale ranging from strongly disagree (value = 1) to strongly agree (value = 5). Respondents were asked how satisfied they are with their family lives with higher values reflecting greater *home dissatisfaction*. Finally, I include a measure for strong *attitudinal support for housework equality* to capture housework expectations. Respondents were asked to what extent they agreed with the following statement: "Men ought to do a larger share of the housework than they do now." I recoded the responses dichotomously to reflect strong agreement to this statement (value = 1).

The work demands reflect individual characteristics that contribute to stress at work. *Weekly work hours* are the number of hours the respondent works in a typical week. Job stress, dissatisfaction, and pressure are measured on scale equivalent to home stress, dissatisfaction, and pressure. Briefly, *job stress* reflects agreement to finding one's job stressful. Responses are on a five-point scale with higher values representing greater job stress. *Job dissatisfaction* is the extent to which respondents find their job dissatisfying with higher values reflecting greater job dissatisfaction. Finally, *job pressure* reflects agreement to the following statement: "There are so many things to do at work, I often run out of time before I get them all done." Responses are on a five-point scale ranging from strongly disagree (value = 1) to strongly agree (value = 5).

To capture the availability of help in the home, *partner present* includes those who report living with a cohabiting or married partner dichotomously coded (partner present = 1). Work resources are characteristics that provide the respondent with resources from their job. Respondents reported their current position which was coded based on the ILO/ISCO 1988 4-digit codes. Professional jobs as those with the greatest resources so those currently in a *professional* position (value = 1) are included in the model (Schieman et al., 2009; Voydanoff, 2007). These positions include working as legislators, professionals, or technicians (ILO codes 1 through 3999). *Supervisors* have greater control over the workplace environment and thus are coded dichotomously (value = 1) for those who report supervising employees in their current job. To measure educational resources, I include a dichotomous measure for the *college educated* (completed a college degree or higher = 1). Finally, the *household earnings scale* is used to capture economic variation in total household earnings across countries. Respondents were asked for their total family income in country-specific currency. This measure was standardized across countries on a zero to one scale so that the maximum reported value in each country serves as the cap. Those who are missing or refused to provide their income were deleted from the sample. Finally, I also control for the *presence of a child 6–17* in the home (value = 1). In initial analyses, I explore cross-level effects for this measure but the results were nonsignificant. As such, the presence of an older child serves as an individual-level control.

The models also control for *age* and *age-squared* to account for a nonlinear effect for age. I restricted the models to those aged 25–59 to reflect those in their most productive employment and reproductive years. Consistent with previous research, I expect age to be positively but nonlinearly associated with work–family and family–work conflict (Grzywacz, Almeida, & McDonald, 2002).

RESULTS

Descriptive Overview

Table 2 provides a descriptive overview of the dependent and country-level variables. Respondents in Chile report the highest work–family conflict followed by individuals from the postcommunist bloc (Bulgaria, Slovakia, Poland, Russia, and Hungary). The postcommunist bloc reflects a legacy of long work hour requirements with limited policy support (Panayotova & Brayfield, 1997) which may partially explain their high rates of work–family conflict. By contrast, respondents in Switzerland, Japan, and Austria report the least work–family conflict yet a clear pattern does not emerge for these low work–family conflict countries. For family–work conflict, the Latin-American countries (Chile, Brazil, and Mexico) report the highest conflict. Consistent with reports for work–family conflict, respondents in Switzerland, Japan, and Austria report the least family–work conflict suggesting that on average respondents in these countries report less conflict between work and family.

At the country-level, Belgium has the highest percentage of children in public childcare and Cyprus the lowest. Seven countries have affirmative action policies: Australia, Belgium, Germany, Israel, Netherlands, Norway, Sweden, and the United States. The Nordic countries report the highest and Russia the lowest female parliamentary representation. The Nordic countries cluster as the most gender and family responsive with the highest percentages of childcare enrollment and female parliamentary representation yet the correlation is not perfect. Indeed, many of the countries range

Table 2. Country-Specific Descriptive Statistics (2002 ISSP).

Country	N for Work–Family Conflict Respectively	N for Family–Work Conflict	Mean Work–Family Conflict	Mean Family–Work Conflict	Public Childcare Enrollment (0–1)	Presence of Affirmative Action Policy	Female Parliamentarian Representation (%)
Australia	686	690	2.29	1.55	0.03	Yes	26.5
Austria	877	900	1.85	1.18	0.36	No	25.1
Belgium	681	692	2.30	1.34	0.96	Yes	24.9
Brazil	761	766	2.51	1.90	0.09	No	6.7
Chile	692	699	2.76	2.30	0.07	No	10.1
Cyprus	698	698	2.17	1.56	0.00	No	10.7
Czech Republic	325	326	2.31	1.51	0.40	No	14.2
Denmark	790	793	2.15	1.17	0.90	Yes	38.0
East Germany	190	195	2.13	1.20	0.81	No	31.0
Finland	637	646	2.10	1.32	0.48	No	36.5
France	1,061	1,082	2.33	1.45	0.83	No	10.9
Great Britain	967	1,009	2.30	1.46	0.31	No	17.1
Hungary	385	388	2.52	1.40	0.30	No	8.3
Israel	660	627	2.53	1.71	0.75	Yes	13.3
Japan	554	564	1.85	1.17	0.01	No	10.0
Latvia	613	613	2.38	1.42	0.43	No	17.0
Mexico	714	727	2.37	2.01	0.40	No	15.9

Netherlands	665	695	2.12	1.34	0.39	Yes	32.9
North Ireland	402	422	2.13	1.41	0.31	No	13.7
Norway	855	861	2.21	1.27	0.56	Yes	36.4
Poland	506	507	2.59	1.71	0.10	No	20.7
Portugal	497	515	2.31	1.54	0.14	No	18.7
Russia	855	889	2.54	1.42	0.38	No	6.4
Slovenia	478	493	2.34	1.32	0.64	No	12.2
Slovakia	625	625	2.66	1.70	0.58	No	14.0
Spain	1,094	1,101	2.30	1.51	0.24	Yes	26.6
Sweden	648	664	2.24	1.35	0.84	Yes	42.7
Switzerland	565	590	1.77	1.13	0.52	No	22.4
United States	704	723	2.33	1.56	0.14	Yes	13.8
West Germany	417	430	2.24	1.33	0.31	Yes	31.0

Note: 2002 ISSP data. Individuals nested in 29 countries.

in their distribution across these measures indicating variation in countries' gender and family empowerment and policies.

Multilevel Results

Table 3 presents the HLM results for family−work conflict net of the full set of individual controls. These models address the main research question: do macro-level gender empowerment, childcare policy, and affirmative action structure individual-level conflict reports? Table 3 addresses these relationships by introducing macro-level measures for the overall population (intercept), females (gender gap), and parents with a child 5 or under present (child 5 or under present) by gender (female × child 5 or under present). Initially, it is important to note that all of the models indicate significant differences by gender and parental status net of the full set of individual controls. In order, mothers report the most family−work conflict followed by childless women, fathers, and childless men. Models 1 through 3 introduce the three main macro-level predictors to assess effects for these measures separately. Model 1 includes the childcare enrollment measure which is negative for the entire population (−0.33), for women (−0.09), and for mothers of a young child (−0.33 + −0.09 + −0.17 = −0.59). While I expected childcare enrollment to alleviate mothers' family−work conflict exclusively, the models demonstrate broader benefits to childless men and women. Model 2 includes the presence of affirmative action policy which, consistent with expectations, is negative for women (−0.066) exclusively. Model 3 weighs the impact of female parliamentary representation. Counter to initial hypotheses, the percent of female parliamentarians has a negative effect for the entire population (−0.01) and a larger negative effect for women (−0.01 + −0.003 = −0.013); there is no significant effect for parents of a young child. In other words, female parliamentary representations benefits men as well as women yet has no differential effects by parental status. Collectively, these results support initial hypotheses: gender and family-responsive policy environments, as measured by childcare policy, affirmative action, and female parliamentary representation, alleviate family−work burdens. However, these measures, when modeled simultaneously, may moderate these effects; these results are presented in models 4 through 7.

Model 4 includes female parliamentary representation and childcare enrollment simultaneously. Net of individual controls, childless men (−0.007), and women (−0.007 + −0.003 = −0.010) report lower family−work

Table 3. Macro-Level Results for Hierarchical Linear Models of Family–Work Conflict (2002 ISSP; $n = 14,396$).

	Model 1 Coeff.	Model 2 Coeff.	Model 3 Coeff.	Model 4 Coeff.	Model 5 Coeff.	Model 6 Coeff.	Model 7 Coeff.
Intercept	1.435***	1.457***	1.435***	1.433***	1.438***	1.421***	1.415***
Public childcare enrollment (0–1)	-0.326*	—	—	-0.214	-0.311*	—	-0.220
Presence of affirmative action legislation (yes=1)	—	-0.083	—	—	-0.027	0.034	0.049
Female parliamentarian representation (%)	—	—	-0.010**	-0.007*	—	-0.010**	-0.008+
Female	0.053***	0.073***	0.054***	0.054***	0.070***	0.065***	0.064***
Public childcare enrollment (0–1)	-0.092+	—	—	-0.050	-0.071	—	-0.047
Presence of affirmative action legislation (yes=1)	—	-0.066*	—	—	-0.053+	-0.038	-0.035
Female parliamentarian representation (%)	—	—	-0.003*	-0.003+	—	-0.002	-0.002
Child under five present	0.043***	0.044*	0.043*	0.041***	0.046*	0.048*	0.048*
Public childcare enrollment (0–1)	0.065	—	—	0.057	0.070	—	0.058
Presence of affirmative action legislation (yes=1)	—	0.000	—	—	-0.012	-0.017	-0.021
Female parliamentarian representation (%)	—	—	0.001	0.001	—	0.002	0.001
Female × child under five present	0.073**	0.081**	0.073**	0.078***	0.079***	0.078***	0.080***
Public childcare enrollment (0–1)	-0.169**	—	—	-0.168**	-0.167**	—	-0.163+
Presence of affirmative action legislation (yes=1)	—	-0.037	—	—	-0.012	-0.020	-0.009
Female parliamentarian representation (%)	—	—	-0.002	-0.001	—	-0.002	-0.0005
Variance components							
Intercept	0.046***	0.053***	0.045***	0.043***	0.048***	0.046***	0.045***
Female slope	0.005***	0.005***	0.005***	0.005***	0.005***	0.005***	0.005***
Child under five present slope	0.003	0.002	0.002	0.003	0.003	0.003	0.003
Female × child under five present slope	0.002	0.002	0.002	0.002	0.002	0.002	0.002
Level-1 R	0.341	0.341	0.341	0.341	0.341	0.341	0.341

Notes: Individuals nested in 29 countries. Models include individual-level controls: professional position, supervisor position, work hours, job stress, job pressure, job dissatisfaction, presence of a child 6–17, home stress, home pressure, home dissatisfaction, preference for men's greater housework, partner present, income, college degree, age, and age-squared.
+$p<0.10$; *$p<0.05$; **$p<0.01$; ***$p<0.001$ (two-tailed tests).

conflict in countries where more women are in parliament. For these groups, the negative effect of public childcare loses significance indicating that female parliamentary representation, not childcare enrollment, structures conflict for these groups. This finding indicates that female parliamentary representation benefits all groups net of parental status. Childcare enrollment does play an important role for one group — mothers of a small child — who report significantly less family−work conflict (−0.168) in countries with higher public childcare enrollment. This indicates that this childcare policy and not women's parliamentary representation structures mothers' family−work conflict. As such, childcare enrollment has ameliorating effects for the intended demographic: mothers of a small child. However, these benefits do not extend to fathers of a young child (child under 5 present slope). This may reflect the gendered distribution of childcare among parents and indicates that childcare enrollment strongly benefits women's work−life balance.

Model 5 measures public childcare enrollment net of the presence of affirmative action legislation. Consistent with Model 2, women report less family−work conflict (−.053) in countries with affirmative action legislation. Similarly, childcare enrollment has a negative effect at the intercept (−0.311) and for mothers of a young child (−0.167). In other words, the effects of childcare enrollment and affirmative action policy do not mediate each other but rather have significant net effects. Model 6 assesses affirmative action net of female parliamentary representation. While female parliamentary representation remains negative and significant at the intercept, affirmative action becomes nonsignificant for women. This suggests that women's political representation may serve as a proxy for a variety of gender and family-responsive policies. Indeed, with the addition of childcare enrollment in model 7, the negative effect of female parliamentary representation at the intercept is robust net of macro-level childcare and affirmative action policies suggesting that political empowerment drives these effects. Childcare enrollment also remains negatively associated with family−work conflict for mothers of a young child indicating the robustness of this effect.

Table 4 presents the work−family conflict results net of individual controls. Consistent with the results for family−work conflict, the models indicate significant differences for women (gender slope), parents of a young child (child under 5 present slope) by gender (female × child under 5 present slope). Unlike the other slopes, the effect for mothers is marginal and ultimately loses significance net of affirmative action policy. The patterns of work−family and family−work conflict are consistent with mothers reporting the most work−family conflict followed by childless women, fathers,

Table 4. Macro-Level Results for Hierarchical Linear Models of Work–Family Conflict (2002 ISSP; $n = 14{,}176$).

	Model 1 Coeff.	Model 2 Coeff.	Model 3 Coeff.	Model 4 Coeff.	Model 5 Coeff.	Model 6 Coeff.	Model 7 Coeff.
Intercept	2.172***	2.192***	2.169***	2.170***	2.191***	2.162***	2.164***
Public childcare enrollment (0–1)	−0.060	—	—	0.074	−0.031	—	0.071
Presence of affirmative action legislation (yes=1)	—	−0.069	—	—	−0.062	0.025	0.023
Female parliamentarian representation (%)	—	—	−0.008**	−0.009**	—	−0.008**	−0.009**
Female	0.122***	0.110**	0.122***	0.121***	0.109***	0.115***	0.114***
Public childcare enrollment (0–1)	0.000	—	—	−0.035	−0.015	—	−0.037
Presence of affirmative action legislation (yes=1)	—	0.039	—	—	0.041	0.023	0.022
Female parliamentarian representation (%)	—	—	0.002	0.002	—	0.001	0.002
Child under five present	0.088***	0.117**	0.088**	0.087***	0.110**	0.113**	0.110**
Public childcare enrollment (0–1)	−0.165+	—	—	−0.150	−0.128	—	−0.134
Presence of affirmative action legislation (yes=1)	—	−0.098+	—	—	−0.075	−0.091	−0.084
Female parliamentarian representation (%)	—	—	−0.003	−0.001	—	−0.001	0.001
Female × child under five present	−0.076+	−0.084+	−0.072+	−0.071+	−0.078	−0.096	−0.093
Public childcare enrollment (0–1)	0.097	—	—	0.176	0.087	—	0.160
Presence of affirmative action legislation (yes=1)	—	0.023	—	—	0.007	0.090	0.082
Female parliamentarian representation (%)	—	—	−0.004	−0.006	—	−0.006	−0.008
Variance components							
Intercept	0.030***	0.029***	0.023***	0.023***	0.030***	0.024***	0.024***
Female slope	0.004**	0.004**	0.004*	0.004*	0.004*	0.004*	0.004*
Child under five present slope	0.017***	0.017**	0.019***	0.018***	0.017***	0.018***	0.018***
Female × child under five present slope	0.033**	0.034**	0.031**	0.031***	0.036**	0.031**	0.032**
Level-1 R	0.550	0.550	0.550	0.550	0.550	0.550	0.550

Notes: Individuals nested in 29 countries. Models include individual-level controls: professional position, supervisor position, work hours, job stress, job pressure, job dissatisfaction, presence of a child 6–17, home stress, home pressure, home dissatisfaction, preference for men's greater housework, partner present, income, college degree, age, and age-squared.
+$p<0.10$; *$p<0.05$; **$p<0.01$; ***$p<0.001$ (two-tailed tests).

and childless men. For work−family conflict, gender rather than parenthood status has the largest positive effect. Model 1 includes the proportion of children in publically funded childcare which is negatively associated (−0.165) with parents' work−family conflict, an effect that does not vary by gender. This indicates that parents, regardless of gender, report less work−family conflict in countries with more expansive childcare enrollment. Model 2 includes the presence of affirmative action which is negative and significant for parents of a young child. Model 3 includes the percentage of female parliamentarians which, consistent with expectations, is negatively associated with work−family conflict at the intercept but has no differential effects by gender or parental status. In other words, all respondents, regardless of gender or parental status, report less work−family conflict in countries where women are politically empowered. Collectively, these results indicate that public childcare enrollment, affirmative action, and women's parliamentary representation have distinct effects for specific populations and by direction of conflict (work−family vs. family−work). This supports the claim that these need to be investigated separately.

Models 4 through 7 estimate the effects of the three macro-level measures simultaneously. Consistent with family−work conflict, model 4 shows that living in a country where more women are in parliament is negatively associated with work−family conflict for the entire population but, unlike that for family−work conflict, women's representation does not have differential gender effects. Further, public childcare enrollment loses significance for parents in this model. Given that female parliamentary representation and childcare enrollment are positively correlated (Table 1), I explored an interaction for these terms which, when included, was not significant. Thus, countries with high childcare enrollment and female parliamentary representation are not driving these effects. Model 5 estimates the effect of affirmative action net of childcare enrollment yet neither are significant for any of the groups. In model 6, female parliamentarian representation is negative and significant at the intercept net of affirmative action. The robustness of this effect is further supported in model 7 which includes the full set of macro-level measures.

Fig. 1 graphically presents the family−work conflict results for female parliamentary representation by country. Although the coefficients vary, the pattern of countries is equivalent for work−family conflict and thus only the family−work results are presented. At one end, postcommunist countries − Russia, Hungary, and Slovenia − cluster reflecting the lowest female parliamentary representation and the highest family−work conflict scores. At the other end, the Nordic bloc − Sweden, Denmark, Finland, and

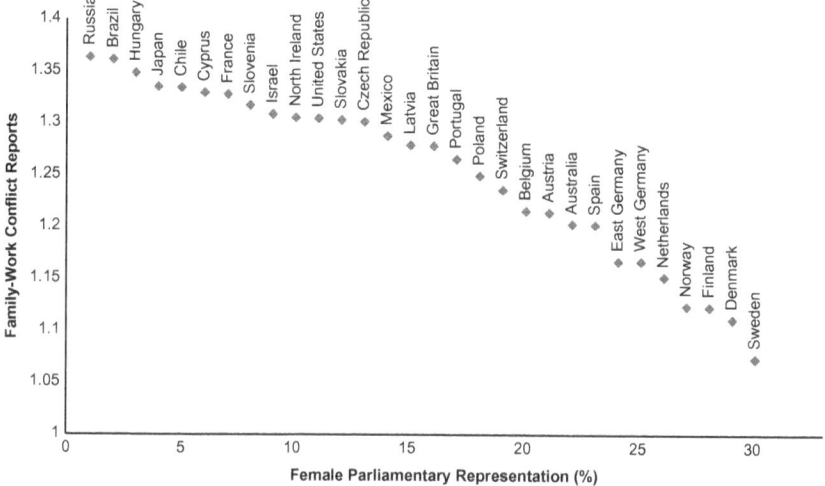

Fig. 1. Hierarchical Linear Model Results for Family–Work Conflict: Distribution of Countries by Female Parliamentary Representation (2002 ISSP).
Note: Minimum value for *y*-intercept is set at 1 to provide clearer distribution of countries. Pattern of countries is equivalent for work–family conflict.

Norway – cluster as the most empowered and lowest conflict scores. Given these clusters, I reran the models with country-level controls for the Nordic bloc (value = 1) and postcommunist countries (value = 1) to test whether these countries are driving the female parliamentary effect. The negative effect for female parliamentary representation on family–work conflict was robust net of these controls; the result was robust for work–family conflict as well. Thus, the pattern observed reflects female political empowerment beyond the clustering of the Nordic and postcommunist countries.

DISCUSSION

This study investigated family–work and work–family conflict in a multilevel perspective and documents that women's parliamentary representation, public childcare enrollment, and affirmative action structure individual-level conflict between work and family. Ultimately, these models highlight two main findings. First, institutional and societal norms structure individual-level conflict between work and family, but these relationships vary by the direction of and group reporting this conflict. This informs the second conclusion: work−family and family−work conflict must be specified directionally especially when investigating macro-contextual influences.

According to the capabilities framework, institutional and social norms bind individual-choice and, as a consequence, well-being. As such, I applied three institutional measures − public childcare, the presence of affirmative action legislation, and female parliamentary representation − which I hypothesized to have equalizing effects for women and mothers. Consistent with expectations, mothers of a young child report less family−work conflict in countries with more expansive public childcare enrollment net of all macro-level controls. This indicates that childcare enrollment buffers mothers from family encroaching on work, a significant finding supporting the policy's aims (Gornick & Meyers, 2003). The results for female parliamentary representation also demonstrate important ameliorating effects. For family−work conflict, I expected female parliamentary representation to have gendered effects; specifically, women would report less but men more family−work and work−family conflict. The models, however, demonstrate negative effects for men and women. When weighed against the childcare measure, female parliamentary representation remains significant for childless men and women. The importance of women's political power is further supported by the affirmative action results. When entered alone, affirmative action benefits the targeted group: women. This effect is robust net of childcare enrollment but loses significance with the inclusion of female parliamentary representation. Indeed, in the final model, only female parliamentary representation is robust at the intercept. This indicates that female parliamentary representation has widespread benefits above and beyond the specific policies explored here.

The importance of women's political power is further supported by the work−family conflict results. Specifically, living in a country where more women are politically empowered is negatively associated with work−family conflict for the entire population. Indeed, this is the only measure that is robust in the final model. What is more, the effect does not vary by gender or parental status indicating that women's political power benefits all citizens, not just parents or women. The results for childcare enrollment are also promising. Parents, regardless of gender, report less work−family conflict in countries with more expansive childcare enrollment. This, in conjunction with the family−work conflict results, indicates that childcare enrollment is an important asset for working parents. Childcare enrollment alleviates mothers' family−work conflict but has broader benefits for both parents' work−family conflict. This suggests that mothers and fathers utilize childcare differently but benefit equally from this policy.

So, what conclusions can be drawn from this research? Across the models, the results indicate that these policies and political empowerment impact how citizens combine work and family. In particular, those in more gender- and family-responsive environments report less family—work and work—family conflict with significant gender effects. Childcare and affirmative action policies directly benefit citizens', and in particular women and mothers', family—work conflict. The models also indicate that female parliamentary representation appears to be the linchpin to a more gender- and family-responsive welfare state. This could function in two ways. Countries with more expansive policies may be more likely to elect female parliamentarians, a process which may be further accelerated by quota systems. Or, female parliamentarians may be more likely to enact gender- and family-responsive policies. Indeed, previous research indicates that female parliamentarians support family- and gender-responsive policies (Bratton, 2002; Caiazza, 2004; Carroll, 2001; Chaney, 2006; Reingold, 2000; Swers, 1998, 2002). As such, female parliamentarians may represent a broader array of family-responsive benefits or may proxy for additional indicators of gender empowerment. A more detailed analysis of country-specific political histories and the application of longitudinal data could sort out the causal relationships for these measures. These types of analyses provide direction for future research.

Macro-level policy and parliamentary representation structure conflict between work and family. This study makes an important contribution by expanding the existing work—family conflict research beyond the individual and situating these experiences within broader social contexts. Future research should further explore these relationships at the macro-level as well as for strategically selected countries. The inclusion of longitudinal data with specific policy implementations would also provide valuable insight for concrete policy recommendations. Yet, the results are clear: gender equality at the country-level structures work—family and family-to-work conflict at the individual-level.

REFERENCES

Allen, T. D., Herst, D. E., Bruck, C. S., & Sutton, M. (2000). Consequences associated with work-to-family conflict: A review and agenda for future research. *Journal of Occupational Health Psychology*, 5(2), 278–308.

Batalova, J. A., & Cohen, P. N. (2002). Premarital cohabitation and housework: Couples in cross-national perspective. *Journal of Marriage and Family*, *64*(3), 743−755.
Bianchi, S. M., Milkie, M. A., Sayer, L. C., & Robinson, J. P. (2000). Is anyone doing the housework? Trends in the gender division of household labor. *Social Forces*, *79*(1), 191−228.
Bolzendahl, C. (2009). Making the implicit explicit: Gender influences on social spending in twelve industrialized democracies, 1980−99. *Social Politics*, *16*, 40−81.
Bolzendahl, C. (2010). Directions of decommodification: Gender and generosity in 12 OECD nations, 1980−2000. *European Sociological Review*, *26*, 125−141.
Bolzendahl, C. (2011). Beyond the big picture: Gender influences on disaggregated and domain-specific measures of social spending, 1980−1999. *Politics & Gender*, *7*, 35−70.
Bratton, K. (2002). The effect of legislative diversity on agenda setting: Evidence from six state legislatures. *American Politics Research*, *30*, 115−142.
Caiazza, A. (2004). Does women's representation in elected office lead to women-friendly policy? Analysis of state-level data. *Women & Politics*, *26*(1), 35−70.
Campbell, D. E., & Wolbrecht, C. (2006). See Jane run: Women politicians as role models for adolescents. *Journal of Politics*, *68*(2), 233−247.
Carroll, S. (2001). *The impact of women in public office*. Bloomington, IN: Indiana University Press.
Chaney, P. (2006). Critical mass, deliberation and the substantive representation of women: Evidence from the UK's devolution programme. *Political Studies*, *54*, 691−714.
Cohen, P. N., & Huffman, M. L. (2003). Occupational segregation and the devaluation of women's work across US labor markets. *Social Forces*, *81*(3), 881−908.
Crompton, R., & Lyonette, C. (2006). Work-life balance in Europe. *Acta Sociologica*, *49*(4), 379−393.
Damaske, S. (2011). *For the family? How class and gender shape women's work*. New York, NY: Oxford University Press.
Dautzenberg, M. G., Diederiks, J. P., Philipsen, H., & Tan, F. E. (1999). Multigenerational caregiving and well-being: Distress of middle-aged daughters providing assistance to elderly parents. *Women & Health*, *29*(4), 57−74.
Esping-Andersen, G. (1990). *Three worlds of welfare capitalism*. Cambridge, UK: Blackwell Publishing.
Fuwa, M. (2004). Macro-level gender inequality and the division of household labor in 22 countries. *American Sociological Review*, *69*(6), 751−767.
Fuwa, M., & Cohen, P. N. (2007). Housework and social policy. *Social Science Research*, *36*(2), 512−530.
Geist, C. (2005). The welfare state and the home: Regime differences in the domestic division of labour. *European Sociological Review*, *21*(1), 23−41.
Glavin, P., Schieman, S., & Reid, S. (2011). Boundary-spanning work demands and their consequences for guilt and psychological distress. *Journal of Health and Social Behavior*, *52*(1), 43−57.
Gornick, J. C., & Meyers, M. K. (2003). *Families that work: Policies for reconciling parenthood and employment*. New York, NY: Russell Sage Foundation.
Gornick, J. C., & Meyers, M. K. (2008). Creating gender egalitarian societies: An agenda for reform. *Politics & Society*, *36*(3), 313−349.
Grönlund, A., & Öun, I. (2010). Rethinking work-family conflict: Dual-earner policies, role conflict and role expansion in Western Europe. *Journal of European Social Policy*, *20*(3), 179−195.

Grzywacz, J. G., Almeida, D. M., & McDonald, D. A. (2002). Work–family spillover and daily reports of work and family stress in the adult labor force. *Family Relations, 51*(1), 28–36.
Hobson, B. (2011). The agency gap in work–life balance: Applying Sen's capabilities framework within European contexts. *Social Politics: International Studies in Gender, State & Society, 18*(2), 147–167.
Hobson, B., & Oláh, L. S. (2006). Birthstrikes? Agency and capabilities in the reconciliation of employment and family. *Marriage and Family Review, 39*(3–4), 197–227.
Jacobs, J. A., & Gerson, K. (2004). *The time divide: Work, family, and gender inequality*. Cambridge, MA: Harvard University Press.
Leira, A. (1993). Mothers, markets and the state: A Scandinavian 'model'? *Journal of Social Policy, 22*(3), 329–347.
Lennon, M. C. (1994). Women, work, and well-being: The importance of work conditions. *Journal of Health and Social Behavior, 35*, 235–247.
Lennon, M. C., & Rosenfield, S. (1992). Women and mental health: The interaction of job and family conditions. *Journal of Health and Social Behavior, 3*, 316–327.
Lyness, K., Gornick, J., Stone, P., & Grotto, A. (2012). It's all about control: Worker control over schedule and hours in cross-national context. *American Sociological Review, 77*(6), 1023–1049.
Mandel, H., & Semyonov, M. (2005). Family policies, wage structures, and gender gaps: Sources of earnings inequality in 20 countries. *American Sociological Review, 70*(6), 949–967.
Misra, J., Budig, M., & Boeckmann, I. (2011). Work-family policies and the effects of children on women's employment hours and wages. *Community, Work & Family, 14*(2), 139–157.
O'Connor, J. S., Orloff, A., Shola, A., & Shaver, S. (1999). *States, markets, families: Gender, liberalism and social policy in Australia, Canada, Great Britain and the United States*. Melbourne: Cambridge University Press.
Orloff, A. S. (1993). Gender and the social rights of citizenship: The comparative analysis of gender relations and welfare states. *American Sociological Review, 58*(3), 303–328.
Panayotova, E., & Brayfield, A. (1997). National context and gender ideology. *Gender & Society, 11*(5), 627–655.
Pettit, B., & Hook, J. (2009). *Gendered tradeoffs: Family, social policy, and economic inequality in twenty-one countries*. New York, NY: Russell Sage.
Pinquart, M., & Sörensen, S. (2003). Associations of stressors and uplifts of caregiving with caregiver burden and depressive mood: A meta-analysis. *The Journals of Gerontology Series B: Psychological Sciences and Social Sciences, 58*(2), 112–128.
Reingold, B. (2000). *Representing women: Sex, gender, and legislative behavior in Arizona and California*. Chapel Hill, NC: University of North Carolina Press.
Robeyns, I. (2005). Selecting capabilities for quality of life measurement. *Social Indicators Research, 74*(1), 191–215.
Ruppanner, L. (2010). Cross-national reports of housework: An investigation of the gender empowerment measure. *Social Science Research, 39*(6), 963–975.
Ruppanner, L., & Huffman, M. (2014). Blurred boundaries: Gender and work-family interference in cross-national context. *Work and Occupations, 41*, 210–236.
Ruppanner, L., & Pixley, J. (2012). Work-to-family and family-to-work spillover: The implications of childcare policy and maximum work-hour legislation. *Journal of Family and Economic Issues, 33*(3), 283–297.

Schieman, S., Glavin, P., & Milkie, M. A. (2009). When work interferes with life: Work-nonwork interference and the influence of work-related demands and resources. *American Sociological Review, 74*(6), 966–988.

Schieman, S., & Young, M. (2011). Economic hardship and family-to-work conflict: The importance of gender and work conditions. *Journal of Family and Economic Issues, 32*(1), 46–61.

Sen, A. (1993). Markets and freedoms: Achievements and limitations of the market mechanism in promoting individual freedoms. *Oxford Economic Papers, 45*(4), 519–541.

Swers, M. (1998). Are women more likely to vote for women's issue bills than their male colleagues? *Legislative Studies Quarterly, 23*, 435–448.

Swers, M. (2002). *The difference women make: The policy impact of women in congress.* Chicago, IL: The University of Chicago Press.

Treas, J., & Drobnic, S. (2010). *Dividing the domestic: Men, women, and household work in cross-national perspective.* Stanford, CA: Stanford University Press.

Voydanoff, P. (2007). *Work, family, and community: Exploring interconnections.* Mahwah, NJ: Lawrence Erlbaum Associates.

DISCUSSING WORK-LIFE FIT: FACTORS THAT PREDICT MANAGERIAL PROMOTION OF FLEXIBLE WORK ARRANGEMENTS

Stephen Sweet, Jacquelyn Boone James and Marcie Pitt-Catsouphes

ABSTRACT

Purpose — *Increased access to flexible work arrangements has the prospect of enhancing work-family reconciliation. Under consideration is extent that managers assumed lead roles in initiating discussions, the overall volume of discussions that occurred, and the outcomes of these discussions.*

Methodology/approach — *A panel analysis of 950 managers over one and a half years examines factors predicting involvement in a change initiative designed to expand flexible work arrangement use in a company in the financial activities supersector.*

Findings — *The overall volume of discussions, and tendencies for managers to initiate discussions, is positively predicted by managers' prior experiences with flexibility, training to promote flexibility, and supervisory responsibilities. Managers were more inclined to promote flexibility when they viewed it as a supervisory responsibility and when they believed that it offered career rewards. An experiment demonstrated that learning of professional standards demonstrated outside of one's own unit increased promotion of flexible work options. Discussions of flexibility led to many more approvals than denials of use, and also increased the likelihood of subsequent discussions occurring, indicating that promoting discussions of flexible work arrangements can be a path toward expanding use.*

Originality — *The study identifies specific factors that can lead managers to support exploration of flexible work arrangement use.*

Keywords: Flexible schedules; telework; supportive supervisor behaviors; alternate work arrangements

Expanding access to flexible work arrangements (FWAs) is perhaps the most often cited means to enhance work-life reconciliation. These arrangements enable workers to reconfigure scheduling, placement, or volume of work outside of traditional on-site full-time standard shifts. However, access to options is unequally distributed among industry sectors, within industry sectors, across work-units within organizations, and among individuals within work-units. As a consequence, the amply documented benefits that flexible work offers in the harmonization of work and family lives can best be characterized as "uneven," with some workers having multiple options to bend work to fit their family and others having few or none. A full understanding of the factors that account for this variation has yet to be developed.

FWAs take many forms, including alternate schedule assignments (variations in starting and ending times, work days, and work weeks), flexible place assignments (adjusting work locations), or reduced work assignments (shorter hours in return for lower pay or job sharing). Manager dispositions can be as important (and in some circumstances more important) than formal policies in determining the conditions in which FWA use is supported or denied (Breaugh & Frye, 2008; McNamara, Pitt-Catsouphes,

Brown, & Matz-Costa, 2012). Managers also have the capacity to provide access to idiosyncratic deals that might not be recognized in formal policy (Rousseau, Ho, & Greenberg, 2006). Almost certainly access to these "I-deals" rests on a manager's willingness to entertain exploration of viabilities. To date, only a limited number of (mostly qualitative) studies have focused on manager discretion in allocating FWAs, but the existing research reveals it to be an important factor in creating access and fostering use (den Dulk, Peper, Sadar, & Lewis, 2012). These observations establish the manager-gatekeeper role as a critical element in shaping both FWA availability and use. Underpinning the orientation of many studies is the question of why some managers are resistant to expanding FWA use. We reframe this question to consider which managers would be most inclined to align their actions with a change initiative by initiating discussions to promote FWA use and if those conversations result in approvals that might not have otherwise occurred.

Our focus is on managers in the US operations of "Company A" (a pseudonym), a large employer in the financial activities supersector. In the case of Company A and its Supervisor-Promoted Flexibility (SPF) program, managers were encouraged to proactively initiate conversations with supervisees after they evaluated the needs of the business unit and the feasibility of each role within their team for a set of FWAs. The SPF program provided managers access to well-developed online training resources (including workshops and a flex resource toolkit) that detailed ways of discussing an extensive range of available work options. In addition, a computer application was developed to determine the viability of proposed arrangements with respect to company policy, thereby easing authorization processes and bolstering managers' confidence in their capacity to grant approvals. The organization also reconfigured workspaces and technological support to facilitate mobile work. Beyond the resources provided, the most innovative aspect of the SPF program was its inversion of discussions concerning flexibility, moving the impetus from the employee to the manager, along with a consistent message (communicated through multiple streams) that flexible work is not simply a means to accommodate workers with special needs, it is something to be encouraged when possible as a strategy for successful business outcomes. For example, communications to all employees illuminated the ways flexible work options enabled Company A to reduce turnover rates, as well as substantially reduce commuting miles and the organization's environmental footprint. One year following the implementation of the SPF program, 66% of the Company A's workforce was able to perform at least some work from home.

Especially important to our analysis is the level of discretion managers had in involving themselves in the SPF program, as they were not explicitly required to participate, nor were they directed to apply the SPF program equally to all of their supervisees. Thus, the success of the SPF program depended upon managers' discretion to become highly engaged, and this discretionary element of participation can explain why organizational change initiatives succeed or fail (Moss Kanter, Stein, & Jick, 1992). The question we consider is which managers were most inclined to do so and what might explain why some were more reluctant than others to align themselves with an initiative intended to promote FWA use. While our interest is primarily in the issue of workplace flexibility, findings can shed light on factors that lead managers to support other types of organizational initiatives.

FACTORS THAT MIGHT INFLUENCE MANAGERS TO BECOME ENGAGED IN A CHANGE INITIATIVE

A largely untested conceptual framing of factors that might influence managers to allocate FWAs is offered by Poelmans and Beham (2008), which includes individual level factors, group level factors, and organizational level features. Drawing on this framework and in concert with an ecological perspective (Voydanoff, 2007), we consider how managerial behavior intersects with contextual circumstances, as well as how those circumstances might change over time as a result of their actions. Our analysis will focus on (1) who the manager is, (2) what the manager's attitudes are, (3) how prior experiences may shape interest in involvement, (4) how training and preparation might lead to action, (5) structural opportunities or barriers that may impede action, and (6) incentives to engage in action.

Managers' Demographics

The characteristics of supervisors, such as their age or gender, may have a significant impact on what is discouraged, tolerated, or promoted. However, existing research does not offer conclusive explanations of the connection between demographic characteristics of supervisors and their responsiveness to work-family concerns. Some studies reveal that organizations with greater proportions of women in leadership positions tend to have enhanced family-friendly policies, but these effects are modest (Bloom, Kretschmer, & Van Reenen, 2010; Galinsky, Bond, Sakai, Kim, & Giuntoli, 2008; Goodstein, 1994; Hutchens & Grace-Martin, 2006; Moshavi & Koch, 2005).

One possible explanation for weak gender effects is that the influence of individual managers is "watered down" in organizational level analyses, as the demographic groups expected to be the most supportive of flexible work also have the lowest representation among managers. This raises a possibility that stronger demographic effects might become evident if analysis shifts from the organization as a whole to the level of individual work units. However, a study of work units within a finance company showed that use of flexible work policies and family leave was substantially lower among employees supervised by women (Blair-Loy & Wharton, 2002, p. 835). This study shows two important things. First, that demographic effects are likely more pronounced when applied to work-unit analyses than when applied to organizations as a whole. Second, that existing organizational level studies might contain an ecological fallacy in that what occurs at the company level does not necessarily reflect what happens at the work unit level.

Supervisor age and generational position might also matter, but predicting which group would be most apt to support flexible work is not clear cut. A life course perspective suggests age might not matter as much as life stage (i.e., whether the supervisor has care-giving responsibilities) (Sweet & Moen, 2006). Managers from more recent generations may have different expectations for the integration of work and family (Gerson, 2009), which might lead them to be more supportive of flexible work. Additionally, although our sample is not restricted to top ranked managers, echelon theory suggests that younger managers are more apt to take risks than older managers, which in turn suggests that younger managers will extend greater support for FWA use (Hambrick, 2007; Hambrick & Mason, 1984).

Attitudinal Disposition

Prevailing cultural attitudes within organizations critically shape access to flexible work (Bailyn, Bookman, Harrington, & Kochan, 2006; Kossek & Lambert, 2005). Again, however, adherence to an overarching culture of tolerance or resistance likely varies remarkably from one work unit to the next. While it is commonly assumed that professionals and managers share similar attitudes with respect to conduct and performance standards, research has shown otherwise (Leicht & Fennel, 2001). Consistent with prior studies (Fried, Kossek, Lee, & MacDermid, 2008), we anticipate that even though Company A established an initiative to enhance access to FWAs, support of the program will not be equal across managers, in part because some managers may view the merits of flexible work (or the program itself) with varying levels of enthusiasm/skepticism.

Prior Experience as Linked to Future Action

FWA use almost inevitably carries risk for managers, as well as has the potential to enhance workplace outcomes (Kelly et al., 2008; Moen, Kelly, & Hill, 2011). So anytime a manager approves FWA use, it opens the prospect that they could create both benefits and costs. The application of conservation of resources suggests that managers will align their efforts so as to maximize returns and minimize potential costs. If the benefits/risk ratio is not known, managers will tend toward conservative courses of action (Hobfoll, 2001). As experience decreases ambiguity and uncertainty, we expect that managers who supported flexibility in the past have had opportunities to more accurately gauge benefits against risks, which in turn will lead them to be more inclined engage in exploration of expansion of FWA use.

Furthermore, if the SPF program design operates as intended, managers will experience gratification resulting from enhanced relationships with supervisees and perhaps in productivity as well. We do not test these assumptions in this chapter. But we do test the extent to which the initial engagement in conversations about flexibility results in approvals and in stimulating future discussions that might create a cycle of expansion in FWA use. If this dynamic is supported, it would suggest that prior support of FWAs and participation in the SPF program is self-affirming and a conclusion that the program's effects are not short term ("tried that") but show prospects for further solidifying the normality FWA use/promotion.

Preparation, Training, and Instruction

Past research indicates that relatively brief instruction can enhance family-supportive behavior among supervisors (Hammer, Kossek, Anger, Bodner, & Zimmerman, 2010). The supervisor, however, must first be aware that flexible work options are available to employees and understand the processes of securing approvals (Casper, Fox, Sitzmann, & Landy, 2004). In the case of Company A, sophisticated online training resources were provided and managers were encouraged (but not required) to access these resources. Managers also had opportunity to attend a limit number of training seminars. Thus, we anticipate that uneven support of flexible work might be due, in part, to differential exposure to training regimens.

Structural Opportunities and Barriers

There is little doubt that access to flexible work options can be linked to the nature of specific types of tasks. Variation can also be influenced by team configurations, where some types of functions require greater amounts of regularity and co-presence, which in turn affects access to flexible work options and managers' capacities to support use (Brewer, 2000). Constraints can take the form of disruptiveness – impinging on the manager's capacity to integrate tasks between workers (Powell & Mainiero, 1999), or dependency – uncompleted tasks in the wake of flexible work use (den Dulk & de Ruijter, 2008; Klein, Berman, & Dickson, 1999; Powell & Mainiero, 1999). Beyond these concerns, other factors can constrain support of change, such as lack of authority or group pressures, legal or policy restrictions, union-contractual agreements, or security concerns (Bacharach, Bamberger, & Sonnenstuhl, 1996; Hutchens & Grace-Martin, 2006; Lauzun, Morganson, Major, & Green, 2010; Muse, 2011; Pitt-Catsouphes, Sano, & Matz-Costa, 2009). In sum, even if managers support flexible work in principle, the nature of the work performed within their units may prevent them from supporting it in practice.

This leads to an expectation that managers who have the fewest constraints with respect to implementation are most apt to encourage exploration of flexible work options. Managers who have more supervisees will potentially have greater structural opportunities not only to engage in conversations with more individuals, but also to experience less disruption as a consequence of expanding flexible work use. On the other hand, a greater volume of supervisees might contribute to work load or present other discouragements to FWA use. Other structural challenges relate to resource management, work processes, client demands, and technological concerns. These constraints would have a negative impact on the extent of managerial support for a change initiative, as managers who believe in the viability of flexible work are more likely to support its implementation

(Lirio, Lee, Williams, Haugen, & Kossek, 2008; Swanberg, James, Werner, & McKechnie, 2008).

Incentives

Economic explanations for variation in the availability of flexible work most commonly focus on the magnitude of benefits organizations receive for implementation, such as improved workplace performance, enhanced talent retention, brand reputation, and shareholder value (Arthur & Cook, 2004; Drago & Hyatt, 2003; Richman, Civian, Shannon, Hill, & Brennan, 2008). An assumption (to our knowledge untested) within the existing research is that managers are swayed by these outcomes (if achieved) to support expansion of FWA use. There is reason to wonder if purposive incentives are as powerful as might be assumed. For example, evidence indicates that even when organizations may benefit from a change initiative, managers may resist participating because they do not view it as being in their own personal interests (Detert & Pollock, 2008; Milliken, Morrison, & Hewlin, 2003). However, managers might support flexibility if they believe that it is not only in the interests of their organization, but also their own careers (Eversole, Venneberg, & Crowder, 2012).

Classic organization theory identifies another type of incentive − social solidarity − as also enhancing prospects for involvement (Clark & Wilson, 1961). Because normative pressures have been shown to affect other aspects of managerial work (Lauer, Rockenbach, & Walgenbach, 2008), we expect that they could influence managers to promote explorations of FWA viabilities. The pressure that we study takes the form of a personalized report (discussed below) that shows each manager's performance relative to that of her/his peers. In this manner, the report demonstrated high levels of involvement, creating a normative pressure that could be especially salient to managers who had yet to engage in conversations with supervisees.

In sum, the existing literature specific to FWA use as coupled with theories of organizational change suggests that managers are not likely to be equally involved in supporting a change initiative to promote FWA use, and that higher levels of involvement may depend on specific contextual concerns. By focusing on Company A's efforts to encourage managers to raise the issue of the viability of FWAs with supervisees, the analysis that follows tests assumptions about the contexts that lead to supportive actions. Are managers inclined to help employees access FWAs? And if so, what contexts lead managers to engage in the greatest levels of support?

METHOD

Sample

Company A is a large employer in the financial activities supersector. It launched the SPF program to its US workforce in November 2011, proximate to the time our research team was recruiting organizations to participate in projects relating to evaluation of time and place management practices. The study design included assessment of work units as they operated in November 2011 (retrospective appraisals) and current conditions with six online surveys conducted in two month intervals beginning in June 2012 and ending in June 2013.

Company A provided contact information to its entire US management staff and recruitment was permitted for the first two survey waves. Of the 4793 managers invited to participate in the baseline survey in June 2012, 1058 completed the entire survey and 192 partially completed the survey. An additional 107 managers entered the study in Wave 2 to perform the baseline instrument, yielding a response rate of 28.3%. The retention rate from Wave 1 (June 2012) to Wave 2 (August 2012) was 61.6% ($N=775$). When wave one participants were combined with new entrants in wave two, the retention rates were as follows: wave three (October 2012) 56.1% ($N=706$), wave four (January 2013) 45.8% ($N=577$), wave five (March 2013) 49.4% ($N=621$), and wave six (June 2013) 47.6% ($N=599$). Participants who skipped any particular wave remained eligible to participate in subsequent waves so long as they continued to work in a supervisory position. At the conclusion of the study, 21.2% of participants completed only the baseline survey, 14.9% completed two waves, 11.5% three waves, 12.4% four waves, 15.2% 5 waves, and 24.8% completed all six survey waves. In this study we restrict analyses to managers who completed the June 2012 baseline survey, who supervised 50 or fewer workers and who reported information on conversation frequencies ($N=950$).

Instrument and Measures

Given the logistics of securing confidentiality agreements with Company A, human subjects research approval, and online survey instrument development, a baseline survey was not fielded until June 2012, approximately seven months after the initiation of the SPF program. To compensate for the lag, the baseline instrument included questions concerning current work arrangements and changes from November 2011 as compared to the current situation. Five subsequent bimonthly follow-up surveys inquired about current conditions and changes that may have occurred since the previous survey. The online survey took approximately 10–15 minutes to complete.

Dependent Variables: Flex Conversations and Initiation Impetus

Our interest is to predict the frequency of conversations concerning potential flexible work options, gauging the number of conversations as marked at each survey wave, as well as the extent to which managers assumed responsibility for initiating these conversations. Thus, analyses of three dependent variables will be presented: (1) a scale measure of the volume of conversations that occurred in any two month period (irrespective of who initiated these conversations), (2) the outcomes of those discussions, and (3) a nominal measure indicating impetus − whether the manager or employees were primarily responsible for raising discussions.

After first identifying their number of supervisees and use of FWAs, participants were asked "Since we last interviewed you (survey date identified, or in the case of the baseline instrument 'Since November 2011') with how many of your supervisees have you had direct discussions about potentially working a flex arrangement? A discussion could be either a short or a long conversation initiated either by you or your supervisee." Subsequent questions probed who initiated each conversation by asking "We would like to ask you just a couple of questions about the nature of these discussions. Thinking about each employee ... was the conversation initiated by you or by the employee? Was the option flexibility option to change only the work location, only the work schedule, or both the work location and the work schedule." In circumstances when managers reported many conversations, they were prompted to only report on the five most recent discussions. Bimonthly approval/denial rates were determined from the question "Of the X# of supervisees with whom you have only discussed changing their work schedules [and in subsequent question 'work locations or work locations in addition to schedule changes'] how many requested no changes, requested changes in that were ultimately approved, or requested changes that were ultimately denied."

Combining information collected across waves allowed for the creation of frequencies within three time ranges: the volume of conversations that occurred between November 2011 and June 2012 (early stage), July 2012 and December 2012 (mid stage, proximate to one half year to a full year subsequent to the SPF launch), and January 2013 and June 2013 (late stage, 1–1½ years following the launch of the program). These three reference points are used to determine whether the same types of factors predict involvement in a new change initiative continue to hold sway after that program has taken further root in the organization.

To create bimonthly averages of the volume of conversations occurring within different time periods, the first wave (report of change from November 2011 to June 2012) was divided by 3. Because subsequent waves occurred in bimonthly intervals, usually the mean score within each wave was used as the estimate of bimonthly conversations. Additional adjustments were made to account for managers who may have missed one or more waves in any given interval. To create the nominal impetus variable (who most frequently initiated conversations) the number of employee-initiated conversations and manager-initiated conversations that occurred within each reference period was summed. These sums were then used to classify responses into three groups within each reference period: (1) no discussions occurred; (2) discussions were primarily initiated by employees (>50%); or (3) discussions were initiated primarily by managers (50%+).

Independent Variables

Specific phrasings of questions summarized below are available from the authors. Demographic characteristics of managers include gender and age. Attitudes toward workplace flexibility are assessed with a 16-item index measuring the extent of agreement with general statements about place and schedule flexibility (e.g., "Place flexibility increases productivity") (alpha .896), as well as an individual item measuring agreement with the SPF program that "supervisors should take a lead in initiating discussions of workplace flexibility." Training is assessed with a dummy coded variable indicating that the manager had either taken a SPF training course or reviewed SPF resources using the online took kit. By anchoring exposure to when training occurred, the analysis offers causal insight on whether instructional resources catalyzed involvement with the promoted activities.

Experiences with flexible work are based on the percentage of employees using location flexibility, schedule flexibility, and compressed work weeks at the time of the launch of the SPF program (November 2011). The change in the number of employees using FWAs reflects the average number using these arrangements within the reference period as compared to November 2011. Structural opportunities included a flex-use barrier scale that was constructed from the extent of agreement with 11 different concerns that the use of FWAs might pose for the manager and her/his team (e.g., client interaction, technology issues, etc.) (alpha .888). Change in this barrier index is assessed from the mean rating within reference period as compared to June 2012. Career incentives were assessed with a single item, the perspective on the extent to which efforts to promote FWAs might affect the participant's performance review in a positive manner.

An experimental element was integrated in the study design at the conclusion of the fourth survey (December 2012). Through random selection, half of the managers were provided an opportunity at the conclusion of their survey to view a customized report that compared their involvement in the SPF program to that of other participants at baseline. The information presented to these managers showed graphs depicting comparisons of their assessments of the SPF program as well as of the extent of their involvement in discussions about flexible work among their employees. These reports were coupled with the information the manager provided in the current survey, revealing to participants the extent that they were meeting the performance standards demonstrated by their peers. Exposure to this report is indicated with a dummy variable included in analysis of the final reference period.

Table 1 shows descriptive characteristics of the sample at the three reference periods. Most important to note in this table is the consistency in the characteristics of the sample across time as reflected in demographics, as well as measures of manager attitudes and use of flexible work. While it is possible that some of these factors may have influenced initial participation in the survey, they did not exert any apparent influence on attrition. However, it is important to note one change that did occur across time, that of movement of managers out of the work units which they were initially located. Because we limited the sample to those supervising the same units between June 2012 and November 2011, 100% of managers were in the same units at the early stage of the study. By the end of the mid stage (December 2012), 77% of managers were in the same positions, and by the end of the late stage (June 2013), only 57% were. In results not shown, we replicated analyses presented below, limiting the sample only to those managers who remained in the same units within any reference survey wave and found comparable results. In the present study, movement to a new work unit is considered a structural opportunity to engage in new conversations with new sets of supervisees, as well as a statistical control.

Table 1. Descriptive Characteristics of the Sample.

	November 2011–June 2012		July 2012–December 2012		January 2013–June 2013	
	Mean/%	SD	Mean/%	SD	Mean/%	SD
Dependent variables						
# of conversations	0.79	1.22	1.38	2.18	1.06	1.89
Conversations manager led mostly	39.94		36.69		34.16	
Conversations employee led mostly	28.80		30.57		25.93	
No conversations in reference period	31.26		32.74		39.91	
Demographics						
% Women	42.94		45.73		45.19	
Age <35	25.17		22.80		20.81	
Age 35–44	39.39		42.17		41.77	
Age 45–54	28.53		28.41		30.28	
Age 55+ (reference)	6.91		6.62		7.14	
Attitudes						
Flexibility acceptance index (June 2012)	3.50	0.54	3.52	0.55	3.51	0.55
Agree with SPF program (June 2012)	65.64		66.88		66.24	
Experiences						
% Emp. using flex place (November 2011)	40.73	41.70	42.06	41.78	42.20	41.44
% Emp. using flex schedule (November 2011)	34.05	45.06	34.66	45.25	35.78	45.95
% Emp. using comp. week (November 2011)	9.53	23.87	10.07	24.52	10.87	25.34
Change in reliance on flex options	0.69	2.04	0.55	4.20	0.30	5.78
# Flex conversations (November 2011–June 2012)			0.77	1.02	0.77	1.14
# Flex conversations (July 2012–December 2012)					1.30	2.00
Training						
Trained in SPF program (November 2011–June 2012)	72.65		73.26		74.88	
Later trained in SPF program			7.97		8.53	

Table 1. (*Continued*)

	November 2011–June 2012		July 2012–December 2012		January 2013–June 2013	
	Mean/%	SD	Mean/%	SD	Mean/%	SD
Structural opportunity						
# Supervisees	4.75	4.79	4.57	4.12	4.42	4.15
Supervising same unit as November 2011	100.00		76.82		56.68	
Flex barrier scale (June 2012)	2.19	0.81	2.15	0.81	2.17	0.79
Change in flex barrier scale			0.01	0.57	−0.05	0.64
Career incentives						
Performance review rewards (June 2012)	35.05		35.80		35.25	
Solidary incentives						
Reviewed personalized report					36.80	
N	950		740		551	

Analysis Strategy

The set of first analyses use OLS regressions to predict the volume of bimonthly flex conversations that occurred within three reference time periods (early, mid, late), as well as the outcomes of those discussions. We are unable to predict the volume of supervisor-promoted discussions in these models because the instrument only requested reports on the impetus for, and outcomes of, the five most recent discussions. Based on these more detailed reports of specific conversations (see Table 1), likely more than half of the total conversation initiations studied in the first analysis can be attributed to managers.

The second set of analyses focuses specifically on the issue of impetus of discussions using multinomial logistic regression, examining which managers tended to initiate flexible work discussions. In these analyses work units are grouped as (1) no conversations occurred within the defined time period, (2) employees initiated greater than half of the conversations, or (3) the manager initiated half or more of the conversations. Odds coefficients reveal the relative likelihood of the manager or employee initiating the greatest volume of conversations that occurred.

In models predicting both the overall frequency of discussions and the most common impetus for discussions, we include baseline information on work unit structures and manager attitudes. In the analyses of midstream involvement the following additional measures are included: the volume of previous conversations, changes in use of FWAs, changes in barriers to implementing flexibility, and changes in supervising responsibilities. In the analysis of late involvement we add an additional measure indicating exposure to the personalized performance report.

FINDINGS

Volume of Conversations and Approval Rates

Table 2 presents information concerning the types of discussions that were initiated and the outcomes of those discussions. Discussions could focus on issues of work scheduling or on work location. However, because work location flexibility most commonly requires discussions of scheduling (e.g., the days of the week that one might work off site), we asked managers to report on the volume of conversations concerning work location fit even

Table 2. Mean Number of Bimonthly Flex Conversations and Outcomes.

	November 2011–June 2012	July–August 2012	September–October 2012	November–December 2012	January–March 2013	April–June 2013
Work schedule only						
Mean frequency	0.19	0.27	0.22	0.21	0.12	0.20
SD	(.79)	(1.04)	(.91)	(1.17)	(.7)	(.79)
% No change requested	27.06	33.48	20.89	27.42	23.82	37.17
SD	(40.6)	(45.17)	(38.84)	(43.25)	(39.65)	(47.07)
% Approved	63.96	57.25	69.52	65.56	62.55	58.00
SD	43.95	46.66	44.51	46.52	45.43	48.14
% Denied	(7.75)	(8.71)	(6.85)	(.21)	(8.55)	(3.23)
SD	24.38	26.53	25.43	1.37	26.83	15.34
Work location or work location coupled with work schedule						
Mean frequency	0.63	0.97	0.98	0.91	0.53	0.89
SD	(1.18)	(2.05)	(2.06)	(2.17)	(1.86)	(2.12)
% No change requested	25.19	31.97	26.86	35.18	30.00	27.91
SD	(38.88)	(43.83)	(41.74)	(46.17)	(43.52)	(42.25)
% Approved	65.69	60.59	64.34	55.22	65.44	67.24
SD	(42.32)	(45.69)	(44.85)	(48.01)	(45.28)	(44.07)
% Denied	6.55	4.88	4.96	4.57	2.85	3.36
SD	(23.35)	(20.05)	(20.32)	(20.61)	(15.46)	(17.08)

Note: Columns do not consistently total to 100% because a limited number of respondents did not report outcomes of all flex conversations that occurred.

if the conversation also included a discussion of schedule fit as well. Table 2 shows that discussions more commonly focused on work location than on work scheduling, and this may be attributed to Company A's focus on expanding reliance on off-site work locations. On average, in any two month interval, .19–.27 conversations occurred concerning work scheduling, and .55–.98 conversations occurred concerning work locations. However, note also that standard deviation statistics are substantial, indicating considerable variation existing among different work units, with averages pulled downwards largely because of a substantial number of work units having no discussions occurring within any given interval.

When discussions occurred, typically two in three resulted in approvals (range 55.2–69.5%) and one in fifteen resulted in denials (range .2–8.2%). It is especially important to note that approximately one in for conversations (range 20.9–37.2%) had the outcome of no change being requested or pursued. While some variation occurred between waves, on the whole conversation frequencies and approval/denial rates remained fairly similar throughout the study duration. An inherent risk in initiating discussions is that denials might have an unintended consequence of making employees feel as if a carrot has been dangled and then withdrawn. The low denial rates suggest that this concern is probably less critical than might be expected.

Predictors of Conversation Frequency

The next analysis concerns the volume of conversations that occurred. As noted above, while the average occurrence of discussions was quite low (approximately one per bimonthly period), some units had no conversations occurring and others much more. What explains this variation? Table 3 presents the regression of the mean number of bimonthly flex conversations that occurred with respect to early, mid, and later stages of the study, testing the factors that are commonly used to explain variation in FWA use and availability.

Women managers were no more likely than men managers to engage in flex conversations. Older managers were as likely as younger managers to be engaged in discussions of flexible work in the months immediately following the launch of the SPF program and midstream, but by the late stage of the study older manager (age 55+) engaged in the greatest volume of conversations as compared to the other three younger age groupings. Contrary to the expectations generated in accordance with echelon theory,

Table 3. Regression of Mean Bimonthly Frequency of Flex Conversations in Three Stages of the Study.

	November 2011–June 2012	July 2012–December 2012	January 2013–June 2013
Constant	.052	−.260	.296
Demographics			
Gender	−.011	.018	−.008
Age < 35	.109	.196	−.554*
Age 35–44	.019	.190	−.600**
Age 45–54	.090	−.038	−.492*
Age 55+ (reference)			
Attitudes			
Flexibility acceptance index (June 2012)	−.082	−.006	.086
Agree with SPF program (June 2012)	.014	−.054	−.011
Experiences			
% Emp. using flex place (November 2011)	.002*	−.001	.000
% Emp. using flex schedule (November 2011)	.001	−.002	0.000
% Emp. using comp. week (November 2011)	.002	−.003	.001
Change in reliance on flex options	.089**	.063**	.014
# Flex conversations (November 2011–June 2012)		.934**	.068
# Flex conversations (July 2012–December 2012)			.415**
Training			
Trained in SPF program (November 2011–June 2012)	.181**	.218	.127
Later trained in SPF program		.433	−.002
Untrained (reference group)			
Structural opportunity			
# Supervisees	.142**	.059**	.015
Supervising same unit as November 2011		.115	−.079
Flex barrier scale (June 2012)	−.030	.155	.071
Change in flex barrier scale		.002	.006
Career incentives			
Performance review rewards (June 2012)	.181**	.080	.056
Solidary incentives			
Reviewed personalized report			.173
N	950	740	551
Adjusted R^2	0.416	.292	0.319

* $p < .05$; ** $p < .01$.

older managers engaged in more conversations concerning flexible work as compared to all of the younger age groups.

While we were not able to gauge attitudes toward workplace flexibility as they existed at the immediate launch of the SPF program, the attitudes registered in June 2012 were not predictive of the volume of conversations in any phases of the study from that point onward. Agreement with the objectives of the SPF program that managers should take a lead role in initiating conversations concerning flexibility was also not predictive of the volume of conversations at any point in the study.

Existing experience with employees using flexible work assignments was predictive of the volume of conversations. The percent of employees who were already working in flexible place arrangements in November 2011 positively predicted the volume of conversations concerning flexibility that occurred from November 2011 to June 2012. Table 2 also shows that an increase in flexible work option use was associated with higher conversation frequency in both the early and mid-stages. Much of this relationship can be explained by results already presented, that conversations tend to lead to approvals for FWAs. In addition, prior experience in engaging in conversations positively predicted engagement in future conversations. As Table 3 shows, managers who engaged in a greater volume of conversations in the early stage reported higher volumes of conversations at mid stage in the study. Likewise, higher volumes of conversations occurring at mid stage positively predicted the volume of conversations occurring in the late stage of the study. These findings suggest support-use spirals that could lead to long term FWA expansion. And because training positively predicted the volume of conversations that occurred (but only in the early stage of the study) this may help expand promotion efforts.

Only one of the variables indicating structural opportunities (number of supervisees) predicted the volume of conversations that occurred. The greater the number of supervisees, the higher the frequency of conversations during the early and midstream phases of the study. No relationships are found for changes in work unit assignments or barriers to implementing flexibility. We caution here that different findings may have emerged, had Company A not already expended considerable effort to remove barriers where possible.

Believing that promoting flexibility would result in a positive impact on one's own performance review was positively associated with the volume of conversations in the early stage, but not midstream or the late stage of the study. Viewing randomly assigned personalized report was not predictive of the frequency of engaging in flex conversations.

In sum, in considering factors that predicted the volume of conversations occurring during the study period, some expectations were partially supported, including the expected impact of training, prior experience with employees using or discussing flexibility, greater numbers of supervisees, and perceiving that supporting flexibility will have a positive impact on performance reviews. Remarkably, the variables included in these models accounted for 42% of the variance in the volume of conversations in the early stage, 29% at midstream, and 32% at the late stage of the study.

Impetus of Conversations

The next analysis considers which factors predicted who most commonly took the lead in initiating discussions in the work units – the supervisees, the manager, or no one. Our primary interest is identifying the contexts that led managers to be lead agents in the discussions and to actively promote FWA use among their supervisees, and to do so at a greater frequency than their supervisees. The odds coefficients presented in Table 4 were generated from multinomial regressions, showing the relative likelihoods associated with specific variables, as compared to work units where no conversations occurred. It is important to remember in interpreting these findings that if a significant result is not present for manager's initiating 50% or more of the discussion, it does not mean that managers did not initiate any discussions. It only means that they did not initiate most of the discussions.

For the most part, when a specific factor predicted supervisor initiations of discussions, it also predicted employee initiations. The reverse scenario, however, is less often true – factors that predicted supervisor initiation did not always also predict employee initiation.

No gender differences were found, and no age differences were observed in the early stage. However at midstream, younger managers (those aged 35–44 and 45–54) were 3 times (odds ratios 2.76 and 3.54) more likely to initiate the majority of discussions as compared to older managers. So while the age-related expectation generated from echelon theory was not supported with respect to the volume of conversations, it was supported with respect to younger managers being more inclined to take a lead role in initiating the conversations that occurred.

Attitudes mattered, but only at the early stage with respect to agreement with the SPF program. Managers who agreed with the program were 1.5 times more likely to take the initiative in the majority of discussions

Table 4. Multinomial Regression Odds Ratios: Primary Initiators of Flex Number of Flex Conversations in Three Stages of the Study (No Initiations Reference Group).

	November 2011–June 2012		July 2012–December 2012		January 2013–June 2013	
	Empl	Mngr	Empl	Mngr	Empl	Mngr
Demographics						
Gender	1.19	0.96	1.08	0.93	1.32	1.13
Age <35	0.64	1.93	1.07	2.76*	1.09	1.80
Age 35–44	0.71	1.28	1.46	3.54**	0.95	0.99
Age 45–54	0.66	1.28	1.12	1.86	1.18	1.09
Age 55 + (reference)						
Attitudes						
Flexibility acceptance index (June 2012)	0.86	0.94	0.69	0.96	0.86	1.42
Agree with SPF program (June 2012)	0.81	1.51*	0.90	1.03	1.33	1.37
Experiences						
% Employees using flex place (November 2011)	1.00	1.00	1.00	1.00	1.00	1.00
% Employees using flex schedule (November 2011)	1.01	1.00	1.00	1.00	1.01**	1.00
% Employees using comp. week (November 2011)	1.01**	1.00	1.00	0.99	1.01	1.00
Change in reliance on flex options	1.66**	1.84**	1.05	1.04	1.03	1.06*
# Flex conversations (November 2011–June 2012)			2.54**	3.30**	1.12	1.13
# Flex conversations (July 2012–December 2012)					1.05	1.81**
Training						
Trained in SPF program (November 2011–June 2012)	1.83**	2.65**	1.47	1.63*	1.67	2.23*
Later trained in SPF program			2.86*	3.07**	1.31	1.92
Untrained (reference group)						

Table 4. (Continued)

	November 2011–June 2012		July 2012–December 2012		January 2013–June 2013	
	Empl	Mngr	Empl	Mngr	Empl	Mngr
Structural opportunity						
# Supervisees	1.04	1.03	0.97	0.93**	1.05	0.97
Supervising same unit as November 2011			0.72	0.63	0.75	1.03
Flex barrier scale (June 2012)	0.95	0.98	0.86	0.98	0.97	0.95
Change in flex barrier scale			0.61*	0.68	1.36	0.95
Career incentives						
Performance review rewards (June 2012)	1.67**	1.82**	1.48	1.17	1.20	1.00
Solidary incentives						
Reviewed personalized report					0.90	1.63*
N	950		740		551	

*$p < .05$; **$p < .01$.

compared to managers who expressed disagreement or neutrality towards the program. So, while the total volume of discussions was not predicted by agreement with the SPF program (Table 3) in the early stages, agreement was an important factor in identifying who assumed responsibility for initiating discussions.

A heavier initial use of flexible work options within units was not related to a heavier reliance on manager-led discussions, but greater initial use of compressed work weeks (at the early stage) and flexible schedules (at the late stage) positively predicted the tendency for employee's to raise discussions more frequently than managers. However, expanded use of flex options positively predicted greater likelihood that managers had taken lead roles, and at the early stage an increase of one flex option nearly doubled the odds (1.84) that a manager was the primary initiator of discussions. Each additional conversation that occurred in the prior reference period could triple (3.30 mid-stage) or double (1.81 late-stage) the odds that a manager was most commonly the lead initiator of discussions in the subsequent reference period. Again, this suggests a self-affirming relationship between the promotion and implementation of FWAs.

Involvement in training also predicted which managers took the lead in initiating the majority of discussions. Managers who trained in the early stages of the SPF program were more than twice as likely (2.65) to take leading roles in discussions compared to those who did not train. Those who were later trained were three times (3.07) as likely to take the lead role compared to those who had not yet trained at all by mid stage. This provides compelling evidence of a causal connection between training and supervisory practices that was not evident in the prior analysis of discussion frequency. Interestingly, the supervisees of managers who were trained were also more likely to initiate discussions compared with supervisees working under untrained managers. One possible explanation is that trained managers were more effective in fostering climates for discussions, regardless of who initiates the conversations.

Contrary to a conclusion that would have been reached solely on the findings presented in Table 3, Table 4 shows that a greater volume of supervisees at mid stage decreased the likelihood that the manager initiated most of the discussions. In other words, while a higher number of supervisees increased the volume of conversations occurring, it appeared to decrease the likelihood that the manager was the initiator of these discussions. No relationship is observed in the early stage or later stage. Greater barriers to implementing flexibility negatively predicted employee's being the primary initiators of discussions at mid stage, perhaps indicating a self-censoring of potential requests. Barriers did not predict which units had managers initiating most of the discussions.

Career incentives positively predicted supervisor initiation of discussions, as managers who believed that promoting flexibility would be appreciated in their performance reviews were nearly twice (1.82) as likely to initiate the majority of discussions compared to those who did not. This effect is only observed at the early stage however. These same managers were more likely to have employees initiate conversations at the early stage as well. The cause for this is not clear, but we suspect that these managers demonstrated openness to discussions of flexibility leading to them being more approachable.

Finally, managers who received a personalized performance report were 1.6 times more likely to lead a majority of discussions in their work units than those who did not. No relationship is found for the employee initiation of discussion, which lends even more support to a conclusion that the receipt of this personalized feedback generated a change in supportive behaviors.

Considering the impact of combinations of contexts, remarkable differences could have emerged. For example, at the early stage of the study, a manager who was trained in the SPF program who believed that their support of flexible work would be rewarded in a performance review was 4.5 times more likely to be a primary initiator of discussions than a manager who had negative or neutral dispositions on those two combined factors.

DISCUSSION

Company A offers a case study of what happens when an organization attempts to expand access to, and use of, flexible work options. By asking managers to initiate discussions about the extent that work performance might be enhanced via FWAs, Company A explored where and how to expand FWA use in a manner that is often advocated for, but seldom witnessed. It is important to note that Company A implemented the SPF program primarily for business goals, but its successes in expanding workplace flexibility likely translated into enhanced work-family harmonization for its employees. Because participation in the SPF program was not mandatory, its success depended upon managers' willingness to participate in training and to talk about flexible work with their supervisees.

This chapter concerned the issue of participation, asking the basic question of which managers were most likely to advance discussions of flexibility and why. Often times attention is directed to the personal characteristics of managers, such as their gender and age. We found no support for the proposition that women managers tended to be more supportive of flexibility than men, as indicated by the volume of conversations that occurred and whether women managers were more likely to initiate discussions. However, age did predict the volume of conversations, with the oldest age group of managers (those aged 55+) engaging in the most discussions. However, older managers were the least likely group to be initiators of the discussions that occurred at one stage of the study. When comparing relationships on the basis of age across different phases of the study, no consistent pattern was observable. We also tested the possible interaction of age and viewing of the personal report and found no significant relationships. Therefore, we are not inclined to suggest that age necessarily matters with respect to the support of FWAs, but do suggest that it remains a variable worth including in future explorations.

Our study demonstrated that manager actions can be understood in an ecological context, and that prospects for a successful launch of – and sustained involvement in – a change initiative can be bolstered considering how managers are situated. Their commitments were shaped by the beliefs in the merits of the change initiative and experiences relevant to that change initiative over time. While not yielding significant results at all stages of the study, prospects for expanding FWA use were explored more often when managers held favorable attitudes toward the change initiative, engaged in training, had greater experience with managing workers in FWAs, perceived that there were career rewards in promoting flexibility, and had an understanding of their own commitment to the initiative relative to that of other managers. More consistent and more dramatic differences were observed in the early phases of the study in comparison to the latest phases of the study, suggesting that direct effects may be more difficult to assess over time as the newness of any change initiative diffuses into the organization's culture.

Central to the ecological perspective is the proposition that individuals respond to their environments and give shape to them as well (Bronfenbrenner, 1979). Our study shows this duality, as managers who tended to have greater engagement in supervising workers in FWAs tended to have more discussions exploring FWA expansion, and these discussions led to far more approvals than denials. And the more discussions managers had at any point in the study increased the likelihood of subsequent discussions. This suggests that the SPF program created a cultural momentum that enhanced long term prospects for workers and managers to continue to initiate and entertain discussions FWAs.

A conventional approach to advocating for increased FWA availability is that it makes business sense. We found no evidence to support a conclusion that this argument leads managers to promote flexibility within their work units, as attitudes toward the merits of FWAs had no effect on the frequency conversations that occurred. However, when managers believed that supporting flexibility was part of their responsibilities, or believed that it would be recognized in their performance reviews, it enhanced the likelihood of them initiating conversations to explore FWA use. This suggests that what really mattered was the perceived impact supporting FWAs might have on the manager's career or reputation. This observation is commonly neglected in much of the existing research that considers the limited availability of FWAs and the focus on the business case for expansion. Our study indicates that career incentives might contribute to more immediate interest in a new change initiative, but perhaps not once that program is up and running. In other words, a career minded manager many view a new change initiative as an opportunity to accelerate career progression, but would be less inclined to view the initiative in the same way once it is no longer new to the organization. The experiment introduced in the study showed that managers might be swayed to participate in an enduring change initiative if they can be shown that they might be lagging relative to their peers.

It is not unusual for studies of managerial behavior to focus on resistance. But in the case of Company A, there was remarkable initial buy-in and there was also sustained involvement over the course of the study. This suggests that managers may not be as dis-favorably inclined to support flexible work as is sometimes asserted, especially when presented with tools for both approving and denying requests. Even so, by the end of the study, some managers remained disinclined to initiate discussions with employees. This reality highlights the need to further inquire into the issue of behavior change, considering the most effective strategies of moving managers from a state of opposition (or limited involvement) to a state of engagement. We hope that the promising results of our experiment on the normative pressures introduced via a personalized report can be tested on its impact on involvement with other initiatives.

This study offered insights relevant to practice that can be directly transferred not only to programs intended to advance workplace flexibility, but also to other initiatives as well. Company A was able to develop an award-winning initiative by first pulling in key stakeholders and gaining their support of the SPF program. It developed a variety of structural supports, including the development of numerous resources that helped managers expedite approvals of flexible work, as well as technological and physical space redesigns. It then developed a rigorous communications strategy and training resources. In short, Company A did not simply make a program that asked managers to perform a requested task. It built momentum for the program, considered and responded to the challenges that might be presented, and aggressively disseminated information designed to convince managers of the need for their involvement. What Company A did not do, which might inform future efforts at expending workplace flexibility, is consider a means of rewarding managers for their efforts in promoting flexible work. Because managers who believed that their efforts would be recognized in their performance reviews were more likely to promote flexibility, this is an important to consider.

Even if Company A's program cannot be replicated in other organizations in its fullest sense, its basic principle of encouraging managers to take a lead in raising the issue of the viability of flexible work options conforms to the general expectations of family supportive supervisory behavior. Even in more modest applications, similar programs can be studied to consider how conversations lead to changed work arrangements; the impact that approvals and denials have on worker commitment; and results in productivity, quality, and team performance. At this point we know that when asked to promote workplace flexibility, managers will do so and continue to do so over an extended period of time, but not necessarily in an equal fashion. In addition, once explorations of FWAs occur, managerial approvals are likely to be much more common than denials – contingent on the organization being prepared to support FWA use when possible. We also know that managers who promoted flexibility tended to remain committed to Company A's SPF program, perhaps for good reason.

REFERENCES

Arthur, M., & Cook, A. (2004). Taking stock of work-family initiatives: How announcements of "family-friendly" human resource decisions affect shareholder value. *Industrial and Labor Relations Review*, 57, 599–613.
Bacharach, S., Bamberger, P., & Sonnenstuhl, W. (1996). The organizational transformation process: The micropolitics of dissonance reduction and the alignment. *Administrative Science Quarterly*, 41, 477–506.

Bailyn, L., Bookman, A., Harrington, M., & Kochan, T. (2006). Work-family interventions and experiments: Workplaces, communities, and society. In M. Pitt-Catsouphes, E. E. Kossek, & S. Sweet (Eds.), *The work and family handbook: Multidisciplinary perspectives, methods, and approaches* (pp. 651–664). Mahwah, NJ: Lawrence Erlbaum Associates.

Blair-Loy, M., & Wharton, A. (2002). Employees' use of work-family policies and the workplace social context. *Social Forces, 80*, 813–845.

Bloom, N., Kretschmer, T., & Van Reenen, J. (2010). Are family-friendly workplace practices a valuable form resource. *Strategic Management Journal, 32*, 343–367.

Breaugh, J., & Frye, K. (2008). Work-family conflict: The importance of family-friendly employment practices and family-supportive supervisors. *Journal of Business Psychology, 22*, 345–353.

Brewer, A. M. (2000). Work design for flexible work scheduling: Barriers and gender implications. *Gender, Work and Organization, 7*, 33–44.

Bronfenbrenner, U. (1979). *The ecology of human development*. Cambridge, MA: Harvard University Press.

Casper, W., Fox, K., Sitzmann, T., & Landy, A. (2004). Supervisor referrals to work-family programs. *Journal of Organizational Health Psychology, 9*, 136–154.

Clark, P., & Wilson, J. (1961). Incentive systems: A theory of organizations. *Administrative Science Quarterly, 6*, 129–166.

den Dulk, L., & de Ruijter, J. (2008). Managing work-life policies: Disruption versus dependency arguments. Explaining managerial attitudes towards employee utilization of work-life policies. *The International Journal of Human Resource Management, 19*, 1222–1236.

den Dulk, L., Peper, B., Sadar, N., & Lewis, S. (2012). Work, family, and managerial attitudes and practices in the European workplace: Comparing Dutch, British, and Slovenian financial sector managers. *Social Politics: International Studies in Gender, State and Society, 18*, 300–329.

Detert, J., & Pollock, T. (2008). Values, interests, and capacity to act: Understanding professionals' response to market-based improvement initiatives in highly institutionalized organizations. *Journal of Applied Behavioral Science, 44*, 186–214.

Drago, R., & Hyatt, D. (2003). Symposium: The effect of work-family policies on employees and employers. *Industrial Relations, 42*, 139–145.

Eversole, B., Venneberg, D., & Crowder, C. (2012). Creating a flexible organizational culture to attract and retain talented workers across generations. *Advances in Developing Human Resources, 14*, 607–625.

Fried, A., Kossek, E. E., Lee, M. D., & MacDermid, S. (2008). Human resource manager insights on creating and successful reduced-load work arrangements. *Human Resource Management, 47*, 707–727.

Galinsky, E., Bond, J., Sakai, K., Kim, S., & Giuntoli, N. (2008). *2008 national study of employers*. New York, NY: Families and Work Institute.

Gerson, K. (2009). *The unfinished revolution: How a new generation is reshaping family, work, and gender in America*. New York, NY: Oxford.

Goodstein, J. (1994). Institutional pressures and strategic responsiveness: Employer involvement in work-family issues. *Academy of Management Journal, 37*, 350–381.

Hambrick, D. (2007). Upper echelons theory: An update. *Academy of Management Journal, 32*, 334–343.

Hambrick, D., & Mason, P. (1984). Upper echelons: The organization as a reflection of its top managers. *Academy of Management Journal, 9*, 193–206.

Hammer, L., Kossek, E. E., Anger, K., Bodner, T., & Zimmerman, K. (2010). Clarifying work-family intervention processes: The roles of work-family conflict and family-supportive supervisor behaviors. *Journal of Applied Psychology, 96*, 134–150.

Hobfoll, S. (2001). The influence of culture, community, and the nested-self in the stress process: Advancing conservation of resources theory. *Applied Psychology: An International Review, 50*, 337–421.

Hutchens, R., & Grace-Martin, K. (2006). Employer willingness to permit phased retirement: Why are some more willing than others. *Industrial and Labor Relations Review, 59*, 525–546.

Kelly, E., Kossek, E. E., Hammer, L., Durham, M., Bray, J., Chermack, K., & Kaskubar, D. (2008). Getting there from here: Research on the effects of work-family initiatives on work-family conflict and business outcomes. In J. Walsh & A. Brief (Eds.), *The academy of management annals* (Vol. 2, pp. 305–349). New York, NY: Academy of Management.

Klein, K., Berman, L., & Dickson, M. (1999). May i work part-time? An exploration of predicted employer responses to employee requests for part-time work. *Journal of Vocational Behavior, 57*, 85–101.

Kossek, E. E., & Lambert, S. (Eds.). (2005). *Work and life integration: Organizational, cultural and individual perspectives*. Mahwah, NJ: Lawrence Erlbaum Associates.

Lauer, T., Rockenbach, B., & Walgenbach, P. (2008). Not just hot air: Normative codes of conduct and cooperative behavior. *Review of Managerial Science, 2*, 183–197.

Lauzun, H., Morganson, V., Major, D., & Green, A. (2010). Seeking work-life balance: Employees' requests, supervisors' responses, and organizational barriers. *The Psychologist-Manager Journal, 13*, 184–205.

Leicht, K., & Fennel, M. (2001). *Professional work: A sociological approach*. New York, NY: Wiley-Blackwell.

Lirio, P., Lee, M. D., Williams, M., Haugen, L., & Kossek, E. E. (2008). The inclusion challenge with reduced-load professionals, the role of the manager. *Human Resource Management, 47*, 443–461.

McNamara, T., Pitt-Catsouphes, M., Brown, M., & Matz-Costa, C. (2012). Access to and utilization of flexible work options. *Industrial Relations, 51*, 936–965.

Milliken, F., Morrison, E., & Hewlin, P. (2003). An exploratory study of employee silence: Issues that employees don't communicate upward and why. *Journal of Management Studies, 40*, 1453–1476.

Moen, P., Kelly, E., & Hill, R. (2011). Does enhancing work-time control and flexibility reduce turnover? A naturally occurring experiment. *Social Problems, 58*, 69–98.

Moshavi, D., & Koch, M. (2005). The adoption of family-friendly practices in family-owned firms. *Community, Work & Family, 8*, 237–249.

Moss Kanter, R., Stein, B., & Jick, T. (1992). *The challenge of organizational change: How companies experience it and leaders guide it*. New York, NY: The Free Press.

Muse, L. (2011). Flexibility implementation to a global workforce: A case study of Merck and company, inc. *Community, Work & Family, 14*, 249–256.

Pitt-Catsouphes, M., Sano, M., & Matz-Costa, C. (2009). Union's responsiveness to the aging of the workforce. *Journal of Workplace Behavioral Health, 24*, 125–146.

Poelmans, S. A. Y., & Beham, B. (2008). The moment of truth: Conceptualizing managerial work-life policy allowance decisions. *Journal of Occupational and Organizational Psychology, 81*, 393–410.

Powell, G., & Mainiero, L. (1999). Managerial decision making regarding alternative work arrangements. *Journal of Occupational and Organizational Psychology, 72*, 41–56.

Richman, A., Civian, J., Shannon, L., Hill, J., & Brennan, R. (2008). The relationship of perceived flexibility, supportive work-life policies, and use of formal flexible arrangements and occasional flexibility to employee engagement and expected retention. *Community, Work & Family, 11*, 183–197.

Rousseau, D., Ho, V., & Greenberg, J. (2006). I-deals: Idiosyncratic terms in employment relationships. *Academy of Management Review, 31*, 977–994.

Swanberg, J., James, J., Werner, M., & McKechnie, S. (2008). Workplace flexibility for hourly lower-wage employees: A strategic business practice within one national retail firm. *The Psychologist-Manager Journal, 11*, 5–29.

Sweet, S., & Moen, P. (2006). Advancing a career focus on work and family: Insights from the life course perspective. In M. Pitt-Catsouphes, E. E. Kossek, & S. Sweet (Eds.), *The work and family handbook: Multi-disciplinary perspectives, methods and approaches* (pp. 189–208). Mahwah, NJ: Lawrence Erlbaum.

Voydanoff, P. (2007). *Work, family, and community: Exploring interconnections.* Mahwah, NJ: Lawrence Erlbaum Associates.

IMPLEMENTING INSTITUTIONAL CHANGE: FLEXIBLE WORK AND TEAM PROCESSES IN A WHITE COLLAR ORGANIZATION

Kelly Chermack, Erin L. Kelly, Phyllis Moen and Samantha K. Ammons

ABSTRACT

Purpose — *The purpose of this chapter was to examine the implementation of a flexible work initiative that attempted to challenge two institutionalized precepts of contemporary white-collar workplaces: the gendered ideal worker norm, with its expectation of the primacy of paid work over family and personal life, and the assumption of managerial control over employees' schedules and work location.*

Methodology/approach — *Using ethnographic and interview data, how the Results Only Work Environment (ROWE) was experienced by employees in four different teams within the Best Buy, Co., Inc. corporate headquarters was explored.*

Findings — *Comparing more and less successful implementation across teams, results suggested that collective institutional work is required for the emergence of new norms, expectations, and legitimated practices. Findings indicated that managers' task-specific knowledge — their deep experience with the tasks that the team is charged with completing — is a structural condition that facilitates managers' trust in employees and encourages team experimentation with new practices.*

Research limitations — *Data for this study was limited to one organization and four teams. Future research should include similar organizational change efforts in other organizations and in larger teams.*

Practical/social implications — *These findings may promote a better understanding, among researchers and practitioners, of the importance of manager knowledge and background and how this appears to be key to achieving institutional change.*

Originality/value — *This research is an example of an innovative approach to workplace flexibility and applies an institutional theory lens to investigate variation in the implementation of organizational change.*

Keywords: Institutional change; flexible work; ideal worker norm; control

INTRODUCTION

U.S. firms have increasingly adopted and implemented flexible work policies that allow employees an amount of freedom in their work hours, structure or schedule, or daily routines. Bond, Galinsky, Kim, and Brownfield (2005), in their national survey of private sector worksites with 100 + employees, found that 68% of companies offered flextime to some workers, 35% allowed telework for some employees, 39% had compressed work week options, 53% had reduced hours options, and 46% had job-sharing programs. These flexible work options are associated with greater productivity, organizational commitment, citizenship, less turnover, and lower absenteeism (Grandey & Cropanzano, 1999; Greenhaus, Allen, & Spector, 2006; Hammer, Bauer, & Grandey, 2003; Lambert, 2000). Flexible work arrangements are also positively associated with employees' health and well-being, and reducing work-family conflict (Allen, 2001; Kelly, Ammons, Chermack, & Moen, 2010; Lewis & Taylor, 1996; Moen, Kelly, Tranby, & Huang, 2011; Thomas & Ganster, 1995), though there is little research that rigorously demonstrates causality (e.g., Kelly et al., 2008).

These policies and initiatives are often seen as a method for retaining productive employees, and are often described as a *tool* by which human resources personnel and organizational leaders can better manage the workforce (Barnett & Hyde, 2001; Drago & Golden, 2006; Konrad & Mangel, 2000; Kossek & Lee, 2005; Lee, MacDermid, & Buck, 2000; Lewis, 1997; Sanders, Lengnick-Hall, Lengnick-Hall, & Steele-Clapp, 1998). Companies find the adoption of these policies beneficial, or at least not harmful, to their image and bottom line. Galinsky and Bond (1998) found that 84% of companies indicated that such flexible work programs were either cost-neutral or a positive investment overall.

It is an open question, however, whether flexible work policies bring substantial changes to the lived experiences and everyday practices of employees, managers, and the institutionalized organizational culture. Most flexible work policies are written in ways that limit employee use of the initiatives; these programs are administered on an individual basis where an employee requests permission and an individual manager has the authority to grant or deny the request (Eaton, 2003; Kelly & Kalev, 2006). Scholars who have studied work-family policies and flexible work arrangements, specifically, note that they seem to leave the broader structure of work unchallenged and may penalize women, who are more likely to use them (Bailyn, 2011; Glass, 2004; Hochschild, 1997; Ryan & Kossek, 2008). Some have advocated for shifting attention away from policies to organizational culture (i.e., Mennino, Rubin, & Brayfield, 2005; Thompson, Beauvais, & Lyness, 1999), but this raises the question of how that would be accomplished and how researchers could even assess whether there had been sufficient change in the institutionalized assumptions, expectations, norms, policies, and practices to say that the structure of work has changed.

In this chapter, we examine the implementation of a flexible work initiative that attempted to challenge two institutionalized precepts of contemporary white-collar workplaces: the gendered ideal worker norm (with its expectation of the primacy of paid work over family and personal life), and the assumption of managerial control over employees' schedules and ability to work off site. Using data collected from 2005 to 2007, we examined how the Results Only Work Environment (ROWE) was experienced by employees in four different teams within the Best Buy, Co., Inc. corporate headquarters. Under ROWE, workers were urged to "do whatever they want, whenever they want, as long as the work gets done" (Ressler & Thompson, 2008, p. 3).

Our initial research questions were: How do teams institutionalize the new norms and practices suggested by the ROWE initiative? What explains why some teams make broader, coordinated changes and others make only individual changes at the margin? This lead us to confront a more conceptual question: What constitutes institutional change? As we describe below, this question has received relatively little attention at the micro-or meso-level of employees embedded in small groups.

THEORY

Institutional Change at the Micro Level

Institutional theorists have investigated organizational structures, policies, and artifacts, and examined extraorganizational catalysts may stimulate changes in a variety of different types of organizations. The central premise of these macroorganizational theories is that organizations are receptive and responsive to their institutional environment (DiMaggio & Powell, 1991; Meyer & Rowan, 1977; Scott, 1994, 2008; Zucker, 1987). Legal pressures, professional organizations' standards, and normative pressures from outside the organization encourage the widespread adoption of legitimated policies and procedures, though decoupling and uneven implementation often mean organizational changes may be only *window dressing* (e.g., Dobbin, Sutton, Meyer, & Scott, 1993; Edelman, Uggen, & Erlanger, 1999; Kelly & Dobbin, 1999).

Recently, scholars have devoted more attention to institutionalization and institutional change at the micro or meso level as part of an effort to gain leverage on how institutional change occurs and to recognize agency within the constraints of institutions. For example, Kellogg (2011, p. 7) argued that "by looking at the macro level, we can understand how and why institutional change is *initiated* − but until we look at the micro level, we cannot explain how and why institutional change is ultimately *accomplished*." Powell and Colyvas (2008) raised a similar point, calling for studies where researchers consider "How do organizational participants maintain or transform the institutional forces that guide daily practice?" (p. 277). This is called institutional work, or "the purposive action of individuals and organizations aimed at creating, maintaining, and disrupting institutions" (Lawrence & Suddaby, 2006, p. 215; see also Bechky, 2011; Hallett & Ventresca, 2006; Lawrence, Suddaby, & Leca, 2010).

Drawing on primarily on Scott (2008), as well as other theorists who have examined institutional change (Barley & Tolbert, 1997), we determined that, specifically for the initiation of institutional change in subgroups within a larger context, institutional change is evident if *new practices, processes, and expectations* develop within a team or organization. These practices must become: (a) *legitimated* – shared and accepted – in that social setting, (b) *enmeshed* within existing practices, processes, and policies, and (c) *binding* rules where members are at risk of sanctions and criticism if they are not enacting the new practices or conveying the new expectations. New and emerging institutions are not necessarily fully taken for granted, however, because the emergent and uneven nature of the change process mean some members of the organization may defend the status quo (e.g., Kellogg, 2009). We applied this conceptualization to assess whether the teams we studied achieved institutional change.

Flexible Work Contradicts Existing Institutions

In the contemporary United States (and other industrialized countries), the *ideal worker norm*, or the prevailing institutional expectations and practices, assumes that committed workers prioritize work over family and other personal needs and that workers are visibly, fully devoted to their (paid) work (Acker, 1990; Albiston, 2010; Bailyn, 1993; Blair-Loy, 2003; Moen & Roehling, 2005; Williams, 2000). This permeating institution of the ideal worker stabilizes relationships in and out of the organization (Meyer & Rowan, 1977); institutions direct the behavior of individual actors, constraining the purported choices that are realistically available to them, as well as the organization as a whole, as it operates within this institutional environment. This institutionalized norm is gendered because women are less likely than men to be able to live up to the prescription for long work hours and prioritizing paid work over family caregiving, and because the cultural scripts for women conflict with this norm: following the ideal worker norm is consistent with middle-class, hegemonic masculinity (Connell & Wood, 2005; Kelly et al., 2010). Employees who violate the ideal worker norm by using flexible work arrangements are often seen as less committed to the organization or not as hardworking as their counterparts, and are subject to career penalties such as being denied promotions or being judged more harshly in performance reviews and pay decisions (e.g., Briscoe & Kellogg, 2011; Glass, 2004; Leslie, Manchester, Park, & Mehng, 2013).

In addition, managerial control over work time is another aspect of power and control that permeates most workplaces, and is institutionalized as to be unnoticed and unquestioned. Employees and managers generally continue to accept and expect that managers both control and can change schedules (Kelliher & Anderson, 2010). Employees' control over their schedule is unevenly distributed. Many professionals have attained a position where they can assume it, but in practice they often continue to abide by dominant cultural discourses that champion the primacy of employment: years of preparing for, and working in a professional capacity lead to internalized mechanisms of control. Lower-status employees, however, are subject to more externalized mechanisms and are much less likely to report being able to set their hours or take time off at will (Galinsky, Sakai, & Wigton, 2011; Golden, 2008). As Bailyn (2011) described, managers of lower-status workers exercise *surveillance* over who uses flexible work practices and monitor work carefully.

These findings suggest that flexible work policies are often *playing about at the margins* (Lewis, 1997) because employees and managers continue to accept and expect that managers both control and can change schedules (Kelliher & Anderson, 2010). Access to nonstandard schedules and permission to work off-site are granted by managers at their discretion, and are given as rewards for high performers or *perks* for especially valued employees. Thus, new work arrangements often continue to be understood as *accommodations* and deviations from a largely unquestioned norm of set schedules and on-site work (Kelly & Kalev, 2006; Kelly & Moen, 2007; Lewis, 1997).

RESULTS ONLY WORK ENVIRONMENT (ROWE): A PROMPT FOR INSTITUTIONAL CHANGE

ROWE was developed in-house by two Best Buy corporate human resource managers in and rolled out beginning in 2005 (see Ressler & Thompson, 2008). It contrasted with other flexible work policies and initiatives in several ways. First, the ROWE initiative challenged the limited availability of flexibility head-on. The decision to embark on the ROWE process was made by senior managers in a department, but employees participating departments and teams were told that everyone had access to new ways of working in ROWE. Second, ROWE addressed the organizational culture directly. Beginning with a critique of the larger work environment, employees were encouraged to reflect critically on expectations of long hours, visible busyness, overlapping meetings, and instant responsiveness to unpredictable work (Kelly et al., 2010). Third, moving to a *ROWE environment* also prescribed a shift from managerial control over schedules and work time to employees assuming more control. With flexible work universal within teams, ROWE reduced managerial control over employees since managers no longer decided who had access to variable schedules and off-site work (e.g., Kelly et al., 2010). We explore whether and when this shift occurred in the analysis below.

DATA AND ANALYTIC APPROACH

ROWE was implemented at Best Buy headquarters through participatory training that lasted about 6 hours over a period of several weeks. In ROWE sessions, workers were encouraged to disrupt old institutionalized expectations and practices present within the organization, and to create a new culture where employees control when and where work was done. For example, sessions challenged employees' judgments of their coworkers arriving *late* to work, or rewarding others who *appear* to work longer hours (e.g., Kelly et al., 2010; Ressler & Thompson, 2008).

By design, there was little prescription for how teams should implement these ideas. The ROWE facilitators avoided introducing best practices and guidelines, arguing that it was essential for each individual and/or team to have the opportunity to determine their own ideal procedures. The ROWE *migration* was described as a period of creative flux, of unrest, with the discomfort and anxiety of this process encouraging employees and managers to create something new, workable, and authentic to their needs and their work. However, as we describe, this open implementation process also encouraged variation with regard to implementation, and substantial institutional work fell to the teams. In short, ROWE opened the door for institutional change.

In this study we employed a comparative case study method, analyzing multiple embedded cases (teams) within a larger case organization (e.g., Yin, 2009). We use paired comparisons of more successful and less successful teams within the same departments. With the help of human resources personnel and the ROWE facilitators, we recruited teams, Gold, Orange, Silver, and Blue (pseudonyms), from among the teams slated to begin ROWE and obtained consent from individuals on the teams as well. Our design held constant top management support for ROWE — which is argued to be a key to successfully implementing flexible work policies.

We conducted interviews with team members, and observed as the teams went through ROWE training sessions. We also conducted daily observations of employees and managers as they went about their daily work, in meetings, and in informal gatherings such as lunches and birthday parties for about 11 months in 2005 and 2006. We also shadowed (participating) employees early in the process for a full workday, to get to know them personally and ask questions about their work tasks and practices. Early on, we concentrated on getting to know the individuals, their work, and the social dynamics of the group. When ROWE sessions occurred, we attended all of the groups' sessions to observe reactions, responses, and dialogue, and watched as teams applied the new concepts and negotiated difficulties and clashes between the traditional culture and the new vision of ROWE. After the sessions, we observed changes that occurred in daily work routines, hours, interactions, processes, as well as team discussions of ROWE and the change process. We also conducted semistructured interviews with all consenting employees and managers in the Orange and Gold teams before and after ROWE training; respondents in Teams Blue and Silver were only interviewed after ROWE training. Interviews lasted approximately 45–75 minutes. Additionally, we collected Microsoft Outlook calendars for teams Orange and Gold, on a weekly basis. We then triangulated our data and constructed case narratives of how these teams implemented ROWE.

FINDINGS

Overview of Organizational Culture before ROWE

The headquarters of Best Buy Co., Inc. had relatively young employees (average age of about 32 years), a large majority of whom were white and college educated. About half of the employees were women. Most employees dressed in business casual attire, and employees often moved around the building's common spaces (i.e., food court, coffee shop, lounge areas) with a cheerful buzz.

Teams Orange, Gold, Blue, and Silver all enjoyed a limited degree of flexibility in their work schedules and work hours prior to ROWE. The workday consisted of arriving on site between 7:00 and 8:00 am, and leaving between 4:00 and 5:00 pm. Their work included (a) collaborative meetings with coworkers and customers, (b) phone calls, and (c) "heads-down" work at their desks. Employees in these teams often walked down to the company cafeteria for lunch and returned to their desks to eat, only occasionally taking a break for lunch. Leaving for a doctor appointment or a child's school conference required special permission from a manager and often the use of a personal or sick day. During this study, in 2005–2006, smartphones were not common except among top executives. Mobile e-mail was not used by these employees, but they typically read and responded to e-mail from home in the evenings.

Change Implementation in Team Orange

Introduction to Team Orange

Team Orange's work involved sourcing one type of merchandise sold in the stores. The team consisted of five employees and one manager who were all between the ages of 25 and 31. Darren, the manager, headed the team, along with Oliver, Lucy, Hank, Doug, and Charity (all names are pseudonyms). Darren had been promoted from within the team just before our researcher was connected with the group. However, he had worked in this team and done this type of work since he was initially hired at Best Buy, right out of college.

Team Orange embodied a masculinized culture of long hours, busied, heroic dedication to work, as well as frequent physical activity, boisterous joking, and some rough-housing in the work space. In our fieldnotes, we repeatedly described instances of ball-throwing, video-game playing, and other sports-related conversations and noted that "caffeine is their lifeblood." Outlook calendars reinforced employees' evident commitment and prioritization of work over personal life through an over-booked, not a moment to spare representation of their workdays. In line with the standards of the institutionalized ideal worker, outside events such as family time or birthday parties, were only occasionally referenced on their calendars (usually Lucy's). Employees on this team worked an average of 40–50 hours per week.

At baseline, Team Orange believed they did not *need* ROWE because they thought they already had a great degree of flexibility in their work practices since they had the ability to take time off if needed (for an emergency or a doctor's appointment). However, as we explain below, their actual calendars and their pre-ROWE interviews revealed only a hint of flexibility in their schedules.

Beginning to ROWE: Early Emergence of Team Cooperation and Manager Clarifying Priorities in Team Orange

The months following the first ROWE training were a heavy work period for Team Orange. Several members traveled internationally and that, combined with planning for seasonal events, resulted in time a crunch. Darren began circulating ROWE Lists that contained weekly goals and objectives for the team and for each team member. He commented:

> ... and I don't necessarily think these things are ROWE-specific, so I think even if the company decided to kill the program, I don't know that I'd stop ... sending out that sheet, because I think it helps them just in general ....

Darren believed that the lists were useful because they "reduced uncertainty" about what he expected of his employees. He claimed that when he, as the manager, clarified and prioritized tasks, then his employees could then work more efficiently.

Early in the ROWE process, Team Orange began collectively talking about and creating new work norms. For example, in a weekly team meeting, Darren announced that Best Buy would not be paying for cell phones but employees could use their personal devices if they wished (recall that this was before cell phones were ubiquitous). A conversation then ensued about how to effectively reach one another. Charity thought that e-mail seemed to be the best way to contact people regardless of the company paying for cell phone service. Oliver suggested codes for e-mail subject lines that would let team members know how urgent the message was. The team then talked more specifically about when to call versus when to e-mail, deciding not to call each other about a minor problem with a computer program or a vendor. They also decided to schedule official Orange Team meetings and other routine meetings on certain days of the week. This set a clear expectation for when team members needed to be physically present in the office. Team Orange also discussed calendars and they came to consensus on how to mark booked times.

Urgent, unplanned tasks — referred to as *firedrills* — were also discussed strategically. These last-minute requests typically came from upper management, with the expectation that they be immediately addressed. In training sessions, ROWE facilitators expected that the frequency of firedrills would change with ROWE due to increased planning on everyone's part as they took more control over their schedules and worked to fit in more personal and family time. But members of team Orange were concerned that if team members began working from home, firedrills would unfairly burden those who happened to be in the office. In response, Darren instructed his team to send all of the firedrills to him and said that he would deal with them, involving others on the team only as needed.

The team also began to share work in ways that facilitated everyone's use of ROWE. Prior to ROWE, one team member was required to be physically present on Fridays to sign off on a time-sensitive document in another department. Team Orange quickly muted this source of frustration by rotating this task between themselves, and ensuring that minimal work was required of whoever signed the document. Hank described the process in his post-ROWE interview:

> Hank: ... So like the past couple Fridays, probably like last Friday Doug and I were both gone. Like as long as one of us is here on the team, we've been really good. Supervisors [Lucy and Oliver] have been really supportive of that, being like "Hey, we really want you guys to be able to like, be able to go. You should haven't to feel [you have to be here] ..." So we do all the leg, a lot of leg work during the week to make sure, to make sure that on Friday that [document] is really close to being done ... So we can be like, yup you know, change this, this, this, and this, and it's that much less work you have to do on Friday ... So it kind of works both ways.
>
> Sam: So just one of you has to be here to sign off ...
>
> Hank: Just one of us has to be here between, between me, Doug, Lucy and Oliver, one of us has to be here.

Team members also worked out backup or coverage on their own. Hank and Doug worked closely with one another and relied on each other to get a part of their work done. Under ROWE, they worked together to assess which meetings were critical and required both of them in attendance. For noncritical meetings, they made sure they had coverage but only one person attended. This strategy for reducing meetings was specifically mentioned in some ROWE sessions. The pair also designed a schedule that worked well for them and could be altered as needed. These changes allowed Hank and Doug to share more job responsibilities between them and, at the same time, be able to work from home or attend to family commitments while getting the work done. Hank also described this situation in his post-ROWE interview:

> Hank: Um, but as far as meetings, I think it's been good where like on a Tuesday or a Friday for ad meetings, there's that flexibility where we know that one of us has to be here. Um, when two of us are there, obviously we both would like to be there. But for [specific task], Doug and I run that.
>
> Sam: Oh, ok.
>
> Hank: He'll be gone, I have no problem filling in. I'll be gone, and neither one us feel like we've missed anything, because we always like, you know, that person will adjust the according documents and communicate that to the rest of the team when it happens.

Their collaboration and strategizing was not an emergency scenario that unfolded once in a while and uprooted their other daily practices. This collaboration had become the daily practice.

The weekly Team Orange meetings continued to be time for ROWE discussions as members' schedules and work practices shifted. The team began to use laptops more frequently and four out of the six members worked from home and other locations; the other two employees said they preferred to leave work at work. Team members also began to vary their start and end times, leave to run errands, work from home and come in as needed, work from home all day, etc. Oliver shared that he had visited his daughter at the on-site daycare during the day, which he and his peers saw as a nice change. In another meeting, Oliver noted that he had mowed the lawn last Wednesday and it had "made my week" because he did not have to do it on the weekend could "spend more time with my family." Oliver also began leading the team discussion about ROWE, on his own volition. This was a clear case of an employee asserting some involvement with the implementation and discussion of ROWE in Team Orange.

Darren supported these team discussions and encouraged them, using the team coordination to manage the change process and his team rather than directing the implementation more explicitly. Charity stated in her post-ROWE interview that, according to Darren, it did not matter what the team did, as long as they did it together:

> [Darren] is very, he doesn't want to leave anything up to chance. He's very ... like he needs to understand the plan, and you know he wanted to make sure we had sat down as a team and talked about it ahead of time. What's going to work for us, you know, how do we want to handle this? We can do WHATEVER, but let's just make sure we all know how we are all, how we are all handling, were all handling it the same way.

Fieldnotes from the time around the last ROWE sessions noted that:

> Darren has a lot of faith in his employees and trusts them to come up with intelligent solutions. He didn't go to the other managers and ask to get continuity at all – he went straight to his team. That seemed to be the only audience he cared about.

Eventually, Darren also stopped preparing the weekly ROWE List handouts.

Team Strategy Development and Changes in Manager Control Continue After Training
The whole team exhibited differences in their use of their calendars and increased integration of work and personal life in the months after ROWE training. They started thinking about Saturday and Sunday as potential

workdays and often scheduled those dates as specifically *family* or *work time*. The same was true of evenings. Some employees now marked that they were working until 9 pm. Prior to ROWE, their work had sometimes continued into evenings and weekends, but was never noted on their work calendars. Under ROWE, the decision to complete work at night or on the weekends was shared explicitly and this freed employees to also denote when they were taking personal time. For example, Lucy told us that she would leave the office even when it was not an emergency. If her husband was sick, she would rather stay home with him, make him lunch, and work from home, whereas she did not feel she could do that before. Overall, we also saw a greater prevalence of family time and events on their work calendars, such as family members' weddings, volunteer work, celebrations with friends, even *out*; *4th of July with family*.

It is important to note that we did not witness changes in the events themselves, as we know from our observations that these employees participated in these family activities prior to ROWE. Instead, we saw Team Orange explicitly representing their time to others in a new way. To us, this signaled that (a) employees were temporally and physically integrating work and life to a greater extent than before ROWE, and (b) they were consciously dismantling the ideal worker standard by making family and personal commitments visible and accepted. As Charity mentions, the team even discussed ways to safeguard nonwork time:

> The team decided "this is the way we're going to handle our calendars" so that ... cause that in of itself is a form of communication, you know, just so the team all knows that if I have it on purple I'm NOT reachable. You know, I'm not here, I've got my responsibilities covered for me, I don't expect to be called, I won't answer emails, that you know ... um so we, you know, they established that ...

ROWE remained an agenda item on the weekly team meeting through the end of our observation period. This was a time when the team could talk about ROWE and their work and personal lives, including what was and was not working for the team. The team was also able to openly discuss obstacles to ROWE, including the challenge of working with non-ROWE teams, and talk through how to handle it.

Through these changes in behaviors, team communication, representations of their time use and level of transparency between work and family, we argue that Team Orange began institutionalizing a new work culture. Lucy's example above about what is now considered acceptable for staying home or working off site, the fact that they have all changed how they represent their time on their calendars, and the new processes that emerged with Hank and Doug are just a few examples of the ways that Team Orange experimented with and enacted ROWE. The team successfully challenged and broke apart expectations and norms associated with the ideal worker, and had crafted new work structures and work processes in their place. Individual-level changes in work hours, schedules, and locations resulted in team member wins, such as more time for errands, exercise, sleep, and quality time with family. Importantly, these changes arose from team-level discussions and collaborations and represented more than just change "in the margins."

Change Implementation in Team Gold

Introduction to Team Gold
Team Gold was located within the same department as Team Orange, reported to the same VP, and worked closely with Team Orange. Their job demands also included long hours, numerous reoccurring meetings, lots of number-crunching, and occasional travel. Although Team Gold and Team Orange worked closely together to make sure that the stores received what they needed, Team Orange had higher status and more visibility within the department, with Team Gold making sure that everything ran smoothly behind the scenes.

Gold was a small team. It consisted of Carol, the manager, and four of her direct reports (Chad, Emily, and Denise; a fourth direct report declined participation in the study). Carol had worked for Best Buy for almost a decade but she had performed a number of jobs throughout the organization. She had only recently been moved to Team Orange, never having worked with these products before, and had not done this type of work for quite some time. In addition to overseeing the work in Team Gold, Carol also managed two other small teams within the larger department. Team Gold's interactions were quieter and calmer than Team Orange, with fewer antics and no ball games in the cubes.

Like Team Orange, Gold employees felt they had a certain measure of freedom, but their actual practices suggested only limited flexibility. Prior to ROWE, members of Team Gold were often jumping from meeting to meeting or double- or triple-booked. Occasionally members of this team would add "workout" to their calendars, but personal appointments and any mention of family were rare. Their work practices and representations of their work time signal conformity to the institutionalized standards of the ideal worker.

The Beginning of ROWE in Team Gold: Early Hesitations and Managerial Control

Initially, Carol approached the change positively, expressing support for flexibility. She commented in her pre-ROWE interview that the managers above her were "really flexible" in "making sure that you [can] take care of things," and "work-family balance is important to Best Buy global." But her employees viewed her reactions to ROWE differently. Chad explained in his pre-ROWE interview:

> I think there's still kind of a fear out there that (pause) that if one of their [Carol and managers above her] employees are gone, then what happens if something comes up. I think that's still kind of maybe an underlying worry (pause) but so far everything's, you know, taken care of itself and people have still gotten their jobs done. It's just one of those (pause) those hurdles in the ROWE environment.

Denise also mentioned Carol's hesitations later on — hesitating herself as she described Carol's expectations of employees:

> S: Okay. Who do you think was least comfortable in the group? Was anybody kind of like …?
>
> D: I think Carol, my manager. So, that's hard but it has, you know … adds a different aspect to it. But yeah.
>
> S: How do you think overall she dealt with the change? Did she do okay with it?
>
> D: I think yeah, she's (pause) pretty good. But … I think it's a slower process for her. Yeah, she definitely still (pause) she of anyone has the hardest time and definitely still wants us to be there (pause) when it's not necessarily … we don't necessarily need to be there, kind of things.

Both of these employees mentioned that they would like their manager to trust that the work is done or, that they did not necessarily *need* to be in the office to complete their work. However, both respondents felt that their manager expected them to work from the office, regardless.

Carol worked with other managers in the department to create guidelines and handouts although they knew this violated the ROWE philosophy. As Carol explained:

> It was hard initially to determine what um, direction to give the team without giving them rules, or without giving them "here's what you can do and here's what you can't do" right? Cause you couldn't do that [according to ROWE facilitators], but we had to have some sort of just guidelines of how we will work together in this environment …

Carol then held a meeting with her team where she passed out these guidelines and commented that "managers," including herself, were getting nervous about the lack of facetime. Fieldnotes from the meeting reveal this anxiety on the part of managers, or at least Carol:

> Carol said that the managers themselves were struggling with feeling like everyone was going to be gone and no one would be here. They had to remind themselves that that was one end of the spectrum and that the other end would be that everyone's here. She told them that "leadership hasn't lived with it" ourselves. Carol told them she had two expectations of them: one, "that their jobs still get done," and, two, "keep everyone informed of what's going on."

During this same meeting, Carol provided employees with other rules and expectations including a new format – with step-by-step instructions – for the routine *touch bases* (meetings between an employee and his/her manager). Carol also directed to the team which meetings they should attend (another violation of ROWE principles) and began to designate backups and schedules for employees.

This handout with the new rules also covered calendar designations (which we later learned no one followed) including the colors that should be used if someone was *not working*, or *out of office but available*. It also instructed Team Gold employees to put their cell phone numbers on their calendars. Carol received some pushback from the team on this, but not in a manner that produced a team dialogue or constructive problem-solving. During this meeting, there were surprised faces, long pauses, and seemingly frustrated employees, but no one openly disagreed with Carol's new policies or provided an alternative. Carol also did not solicit advice from the team. The following week, Carol revisited these handouts in the broader department meeting, and acknowledged that her *rules* appeared to run counter to ROWE but that they were necessary anyway.

Individual Changes, Working around the Manager
Members of Team Gold implemented ROWE as individuals, with some employees making changes to how they worked. However, there was less deliberate coordination or consensus about how to move ROWE forward. For example, Denise described varying her start and end times, being able to run errands during the day, and working remotely much more often than she had done in the past. Others also described feeling more freedom in general, getting more sleep, and spending less time in traffic (e.g., Moen et al., 2011). Carol was able to incorporate personal time into her afternoons as well. However, sometimes Carol tried to limit employees' flexibility, causing frustration and resentment since employees now believed they should be able to have control over when and where they worked. In her post-ROWE

interview, Emily described a time Carol thwarted her plans to take the afternoon off and cook dinner for a friend who had just had a baby:

> E: She didn't ALLOW it to happen. She was like "I know we're on ROWE but you can't leave." Which kind of ...
>
> S: She said that?
>
> E: Yeah. So, that was ... yeah. So, I SHOULD have been able to do that and work around it for somebody else who needed something but ... Well, that was the week that was so bad, those two or three weeks ago that was so bad but ... She wanted us there to wait around in case she had something to tell us after her meeting that she was going to.
>
> S: Okay, so she just made a grand proclamation "everybody stay put?"
>
> E: Yeah.
>
> S: Wow.
>
> E: She said "you'll have to make other arrangements. I know we're on ROWE but it doesn't ...

The ellipses in the quotes indicates Emily's difficulty finishing her thoughts – perhaps because she was uncomfortable criticizing her manager – and the interviewer showed her surprise at Carol's actions, which contradict the ROWE's vision. In the same interview, Emily revealed that she sometimes ignored Carol's requests to work in the office:

> E: But [Carol] *definitely* has not been nice about certain things, embraced ROWE like we should've (laughs). ... She *really* dislikes the fact that none of like to come in on Fridays.
>
> S: Oh, really?
>
> E: But, we usually get sort of a guilt treatment from her, but I don't care ... Because I get my work done.

Emily justified her own actions with ROWE rhetoric, saying that because she gets her work done it is legitimate to ignore her manager's preferences about when and where she works.

Despite these individual changes, we did not see any cohesive new practices emerge regarding calendars or communications at the team level. Some team members included more personal appointments and put evening and weekend activities on their work calendars, while others did not. Although Carol had requested that all team members put their cell phone numbers on their calendars so anyone with access could see it (which would be most Best Buy headquarters' employees), her team resisted this and only shared their cell phone numbers with each other, excluding Carol. Communication increased among the employees in the team, but not with their manager. As Emily explained:

> S: Let's see ... did the communication levels change at all?
>
> E: Uh-huh. Cell phones. We all have each other's cell phones now and we're all totally okay with calling them. Uh ... which is okay. I like that Carol doesn't have our cell phone. It's just the four of us that have each other's cell phones and [other coworker] has our cell phones. I just think we have a *respect* level and we like each other enough that we don't mind being called by them. You know, [coworker] called me at 5:15pm on Friday afternoon and was totally stressed because he still had some stuff to get done but he needed to leave and just that "can you help me out and do something for 15 minutes with me?" It's like, "oh, yeah." You know, we like each other enough where it's not like "oh my gosh!" And we don't *do it* enough where it's like "*oh*! Calling me again!" It's not like they're pushing work off on us. It's like they call when they're in need of something and it's not a big deal at all. And Chad calls my house. I mean, both him and [other coworker] both call my house and it's ... but they're the only ones that have our numbers. So, I think the communication between the four of us has *really* improved a lot ....

Not everyone on the team was pleased with the changes, though. Chad felt that his Team Gold teammates working remotely or "being on ROWE," as he put it, unfairly resulted a greater workload for team members who performed more of their work in the office (including Chad). He believed there was not enough communication or backups in place for those who were not on site or were unavailable at certain times. As ROWE was implemented in this team, individuals changed their own work patterns but team cohesion or planning did not improve overall. Each employee was left to his or her own devices and consensus was not built.

During this period, Team Gold made a major mistake. Carol and others, including members of Team Orange, seemed to blame a lack of communication and coordination – tied to more remote work – for this poor performance. Several meetings between members of Team Orange and Team Gold were needed to correct the problem. In conversations with us, some members of Team Orange indicated that Carol's anxiety and micromanaging leadership were at fault. The lack of communication between Carol, her employees, and others was thought to be related to Carol's insistence that things be done her way because her employees had retreated out of the office in response. It seemed plausible to us that disagreements about how the team should work in ROWE had segmented the team and allowed for problematic gaps in communication.

After this crisis, the team did attempt to problem-solve more as a team and work through coverage issues and schedule details together, with

Implementing Institutional Change 349

input from everyone; in fact, this occurred in joint meetings with the more successful Team Orange. Denise was asked to be on site more, to ease communications, though we would argue that the issue was not Denise's work patterns but the uneven implementation of change and too little collective work to create better communications and accountability. Team Gold also attempted to establish a more routinized pattern of communication with Team Orange, to ensure that deliverables were arriving as scheduled and deadlines were met. Thus, the team was able to address communication, coverage, and process issues after the error and with the help of another team.

Summary and Comparative Conclusions

In Teams Orange and Gold we observed divergent levels of micro institutional change that were tied to different investments in collective institutional work. Both teams were apparently open to the changes and had managers who said they welcomed ROWE. Throughout the ROWE process, Team Orange strategized and planned together to coordinate communication, coverage, and work processes. The individual team members made changes to when and how their work was completed in a way that fit the demands of their lives and their work. We see their group-level ROWE implementation process as collective institutional work. These members were able to collaboratively implement changes, employing their agency to make changes in both the way work was done and what they expected of each other. In Team Gold, we saw limited enmeshment of these policies and no consensus, legitimacy, or bindings of the new ROWE culture.

In addition, beyond the ability to make changes to work hours and locations, Team Orange confronted and dissipated old, institutionalized expectations and practices together and created a new institution together. We see these new practices as meeting our previously outlined description of micro-institutional change in that they have become (a) legitimate, (b) enmeshed with the current system, and (c) binding. These new processes and practices became legitimate in that everyone on Team Orange understood and accepted the new system.

Conversely, Team Gold struggled with their ROWE implementation to a much greater extent. This group's manager had difficulty ceding control over when, where, and how work was performed, as evidenced by her detailed guidelines given to the team. Employees did not contribute to the new rules and some resisted them, leading to some communications and coordination challenges. This lack of collective institutional work toward institutional change initially resulted in a variety of uncoordinated changes and then to a crisis with the work itself. Employees on Team Gold were able to make small, individual-level adjustments to their work hours and work location, but they were unable to garner the type of fluid autonomy and confidence in the legitimacy of those work patterns that ROWE promulgated.

According to our indicators of micro change, Team Gold failed to successfully institutionalize new work patterns. With regard to legitimacy, team members differed as to whether they saw any of the encouraged ROWE behaviors as legitimate in that team. For example, there was no clear, new approach to representing their work time through their calendars, no new standard forms of communication, and no new work coverage norms. Individual changes *did not* produce new practices that became legitimate, binding, or enmeshed with the current organizational procedures.

DISCUSSION

Task-Specific Knowledge, Shifts in Control, and Epistemic Distress

What we see as crucial in Team Orange's success is the shift in control over work time and arrangements between manager and employees. ROWE encouraged a ceding of control on the managers' part and, as that cannot fully happen without employees assuming more control, an increase in responsibility and self-management by employees. When managerial control over work time is institutionalized, it is also acceptable for managers to evaluate work performance negatively if schedules vary or workers are not where they are expected to be, even if the timing or location of the work is not critical to the actual task. These behavior-based, rather than performance-based, evaluations are addressed directly in ROWE but are so accepted as to be unnoticed in many workplaces. In Team Orange, there was an explicit and obvious transfer of control; Darren ceded control at the same time that employees asserted more. These processes imply strategy and agency — collective institutional work — via intentional behaviors that contribute to break down old institutions and lay the foundations for the new. In Team Gold, there was more of a struggle with Carol exerting more control, some employees resisting that, and a lack of consensus as to how these decisions would be made.

ROWE sessions repeatedly emphasized that managers need to *trust* employees to do the work, but what explains differences in managers' ability or willingness to trust? Darren appeared to have very little issue with trusting employees and shifting control to his subordinates, whereas Carol struggled with this immensely. Individual personalities may have contributed to this, but there were also structural conditions that promoted this trust. We argue that managers who have more task-specific knowledge, like Darren, are better prepared to cede control in these ways. Those who have this type of knowledge are able to (a) properly and confidently evaluate the work performance of their subordinates, and (b) step in to help or provide cover of employees' work when needed. This expertise is a type of *insider knowledge* that is more likely to be available to managers who have performed the job(s) that their subordinates hold.

Conversely, Carol had been employed at Best Buy longer than Darren, but her work experience and career path differed. She was familiar with many of the jobs of her subordinates, but had not actually performed that work herself. In addition to this limited familiarity with the actual work tasks, she had recently worked in management positions in two other departments completely unrelated to her current work. Using this same structural explanation, we suggest that Carol did not have the task-specific knowledge to confidently evaluate employees' performance (beyond observing their work time and effort) or to cover for employees if they were unavailable. Her limited stock of task-specific knowledge made it difficult to shift control and trust her employees as they worked whenever, wherever, and however they chose.

We also propose that the manager's task-specific knowledge was effective in buffering epistemic distress in the institutional change process (e.g., Hallett, 2010). Changing work norms and routines prompted what Hallett (2010, p. 53) describes as the "displacement of meaning, certainty, and expectations;" which created anxiety and distress for managers who were not equipped to cope with these changes. Expanding on Hallett (2010), Carol was removed from routine and disturbed by her lack of control (while employees may have been somewhat stressed by the change in routines but experienced ROWE as an increase in control). In addition, the unpredictability of the new system, anxiety and stress prevailed for managers (such as Carol and others) who did not have the experience to create new methods for evaluating their employees' work and demonstrating their own performance.

Supplementary Cases

In addition to the Orange and Gold cases, we analyzed two supplementary cases. Team Blue and Silver were in the same department as each other (but not the same department as Orange and Gold). We observed these teams first, but analyzed them second to confirm or refine the arguments that we developed from our analysis of the primary cases.

Like Carol's Gold Team, Team Blue struggled with making ROWE work. Maggie, the team manager, was less familiar with the team's work — having come another area to this department — and reacted to ROWE by tightening control over her employees. Maggie created her own guidelines, including telling employees to inform her when they would be working off site for more than 4 hours, or totally out of contact for more than 2 hours (these instructions are inconsistent with ROWE training, which does not oppose collective agreements on availability or communication with one's team, but advises against managers preparing new rules rather than the team deliberating on what is needed to get the work done and communicate effectively). There was limited team discussion about breaking down old expectations of managerial control or to building new practices. Individuals made changes to their own work routines and work hours, but did not collaboratively construct new norms.

Also like Team Gold, Team Blue had communication problems that were believed to cause a team performance problem. According to Maggie, team members were taking too much time away from work and team goals were subsequently not being met. Team Blue did not set up sufficient back-ups (to cover time away) and customers were frustrated that they could not locate team members easily. When we left Team Blue, tensions were high and there was no sense that ROWE was being institutionalized successfully.

Team Silver implemented ROWE smoothly and easily. This was a smaller team, with an experienced manager, Ruby, who had been working in this capacity for a decade and in the department even longer. This gave Ruby more task-specific knowledge than either Carol or Maggie, who both had wide-ranging work experiences. Ruby openly prioritized family over her work demands and she encouraged her team members to work off-site and vary their work hours and schedules. Under ROWE, Team Silver members were soon working off-site regularly and collaborated, seemingly easily, to establish backup routines, use e-mail and Instant Messenger, and coordinate days and meeting coverage (similarly to Doug and Hank on Team Orange).

These additional cases exemplify the same processes and outcomes and reinforce the conclusions about the changes as accommodations on the margins. We examined whether the ROWE, which was designed to confront importance of the group engaging in collective institutional work and the link between task-specific knowledge and managers' ceding of control. Because both managers in these cases are women, they also reassure us that the differences between Orange and Gold are not related to male managers' ability to lend legitimacy employees who wish to embrace flexibility, given men's greater power in the workplace (see Blair-Loy & Wharton, 2002).

CONCLUSION

We began with an interest in understanding what and how flexible work initiatives might bring about real changes to the everyday, lived experience of employees and the institutional expectations about work and family, as opposed to allowing individualized both individual behaviors and the organizational culture, would challenge the institutionalized ideal worker norm and assumptions of managerial control in this white-collar organization. Using qualitative data from four teams, we explored variation in the implementation of ROWE and the extent of micro-institutional change. Through collective institutional work, we observed how some teams confronted the old institutions and created new ones, while other teams were spinning their wheels, even though individuals benefited from some changes in their work practices.

This analysis demonstrates that institutional change requires institutional work at the *collective* level, as we saw that teams that initiated a collaborative approach to the implementation of ROWE were more successful in creating new, institutionalized arrangements than teams that failed to construct and foster collaborative efforts. Our argument is that group-targeted changes, such as ROWE, are not fully institutionalized or accomplished, without being implemented as a group in practice.

The teams (Orange and Silver) that made significant institutional change – where these new practices became legitimate within the team, enmeshed with current policies and practices, and the binding rules of operation – collectively discussed the change process and involved both employees and managers in reflecting on old practices and establishing new ones. We view Darren's and Ruby's ability to cede control and allow their employees to step forward and take initiative as directly related to their own task-specific knowledge of their employees' work tasks. Both managers could (a) confidently set expectations and assess performance, and (b) provide coverage in routine or emergency work situations. This meant they were able to *trust* their employees more easily. Task-specific knowledge also mitigated the effects of epistemic distress (e.g., Hallett, 2010) for managers, allowing them to cope with the anxiety of changing routines and facilitate, through their willingness to experiment and enact new processes, the institutionalization of new ways of working.

Teams Gold and Blue experienced less or no collective success. These groups struggled with a lack of coordination and communication. They also failed to successfully challenge time norms around meetings and calendars. With highly directive managers, and no real space to maneuver, Teams Blue and Gold failed to challenge current institutionalized norms, dissipating any hopes to construct a shared new experience even though some individuals did change their practices.

Institutional work by individuals (as evidenced by individual sense-making, actions, and problem-solving) is critical but, in a bureaucratized workplace, this institutional work must be enacted in a coordinated fashion to challenge and change broader institutional forces. As our respondents demonstrated, this work is neither easy nor intuitive. We are hopeful about the possibilities for change since our study took place within an organization that had entrenched ideal worker norms, which champion long hours and the primacy of work. However, despite the numerous positive outcomes associated with ROWE, such as reduced turnover, reduced work-family conflict, and increased health behaviors (Kelly, Moen, & Tranby, 2011; Moen, Kelly, & Hill, 2011; Moen, Kelly, Tranby, & Huang, 2011), in 2013 a new CEO terminated the initiative after taking over what was perceived to be a company in crisis. In press releases explaining his decision, he argued that employees needed to be working on-site. In one swoop, he reasserted the legitimacy of facetime as an indicator of productivity and reinvigorated ideal worker norms (cf. Kelly et al., 2010; Perlow & Kelly, 2014). Although some remnants of ROWE likely remain at the team and/or individual level, the balance has shifted. Clearly, sustaining institutional change is a challenge even after successful implementation of ROWE in many teams in the organization. In this chapter, we have demonstrated the importance of institutional work, team implementation, and manager task-specific knowledge with respect to institutional change in these cases. Future research should expand on these ideas, focusing on examining these aspects of institutional change over the long term and in different organizational settings.

ACKNOWLEDGMENTS

This research was conducted as part of the Work, Family and Health Network (www.workfamilyhealthnetwork.org), funded by a cooperative agreement through the National Institute of Child Health and Human Development (Grant # U01HD051217, U01HD051218, U01HD051256, U01HD051276), National Institute on Aging (Grant # U01AG027669), Office of Behavioral and Science Sciences Research, and National Institute of Occupational Safety and Health (Grant # U010H008788). The contents of this publication are solely the responsibility of the authors and do not necessarily represent the official views of these institutes and offices. Special acknowledgment goes to Extramural Staff Science Collaborator, Rosalind Berkowitz King, Ph.D. (NICHD), and Lynne Casper, Ph.D. (now of the University of Southern California) for design of the initiative. Additional support was provided by the Alfred P. Sloan Foundation (#2002-6-8) and the Institute for Advanced Studies at the University of Minnesota. Thanks to Rachel Magennis for project management and the audience at the Minnesota Sociology workshop for comments. We especially thank the employees who participated in this research, the managers who facilitated our access to the organization, and Jody Thompson and Cali Ressler.

REFERENCES

Acker, J. (1990). Hierarchies, jobs, bodies: A theory of gendered organization. *Gender & Society*, *4*, 139–158. doi:10.1177/089124390004002002

Albiston, C. (2010). *Institutional mobilization of the family and medical leave act: Rights on leave*. New York, NY: Cambridge University Press.

Allen, T. D. (2001). Family-supportive work environments: The role of organizational perceptions. *Journal of Vocational Behavior*, *58*, 414–435. doi:10.1006/jvbe.2000.1774

Bailyn, L. (1993). *Breaking the mold: Women, men, and time in the new corporate world*. New York, NY: Free Press.

Bailyn, L. (2011). Redesigning work for gender equity and work-personal life integration. *Community, Work & Family*, *14*, 97–112. doi:10.1080/13668803.2010.532660

Barley, S. R., & Tolbert, P. S. (1997). Institutionalization and structuration: Studying the links between action and institution. *Organization Studies*, *18*, 93–117. doi:10.1177/017084069701800106

Barnett, R. C., & Hyde, J. S. (2001). Women, men, work, and family: An expansionist theory. *American Psychologist*, *56*, 781–796. doi:10.1037//0003-066X.56.10.781

Bechky, B. A. (2011). Making organizational theory work: Institutions, occupations, and negotiated orders. *Organization Science*, *22*, 1157–1167. doi:10.1287/orsc.1100.0603

Blair-Loy, M. (2003). *Competing devotions: Career and family among women executives.* Cambridge, MA: Harvard University Press.

Blair-Loy, M., & Wharton, A. S. (2002). Employees' use of work-family policies and the workplace social context. *Social Forces, 80,* 813–845. Retrieved from http://sf.oxford journals.org

Bond, J. T., Galinsky, E., Kim, S. S., & Brownfield, E. (2005). *National study of employers.* New York, NY: Families and Work Institute.

Briscoe, F. S., & Kellogg, C. C. (2011). The initial assignment effect: Local employer practices and positive career outcomes for work-family program users. *American Sociological Review, 76*(2), 291–319. doi:10.1177/0003122411401250

Connell, R. W., & Wood, J. (2005). Globalization and business masculinities. *Men and Masculinities, 7,* 347–364. doi:10.1177/1097184X03260969

DiMaggio, P. J., & Powell, W. W. (1991). *The new institutionalism in organizational analysis.* Chicago, IL: University of Chicago Press.

Dobbin, F., Sutton, J. R., Meyer, J. W., & Scott, W. R. (1993). Equal opportunity law and the construction of internal labor markets. *American Journal of Sociology, 99,* 396–427. Retrieved from http://www.press.uchicago.edu/ucp/journals/journal/ajs.html

Drago, R., & Golden, L. (2006). The role of economics in work–family research. In M. Pitt-Catsouphes, E. E. Kossek, & S. Sweet (Eds.), *The work and family handbook* (pp. 267–282). Mahwah, NJ: Erlbaum.

Eaton, S. C. (2003). If you can use them: Flexibility policies, organizational commitment, and perceived performance. *Industrial Relations, 42*(2), 145–167. doi:10.1111/1468-232X.00285

Edelman, L. B., Uggen, C., & Erlanger, H. S. (1999). The endogeneity of legal regulation: Grievance procedures and rational myth. *American Journal of Sociology, 105*(2), 406–454. doi:10.1086/210316

Galinsky, E., Sakai, K., & Wigton, T. (2011). Workplace flexibility: From research to action. *Work and Family, 21*(2), 141–161. Retrieved from http://futureofchildren.org/future ofchildren/publications/docs/21_02_07.pdf

Galinsky, El., & Bond, J. T. (1998). *The 1998 business work-life study: A sourcebook.* New York, NY: Families and Work Institute. Retrieved from http://familiesandwork.org/summary/worklife.pdf

Glass, J. (2004). Blessing or curse? Work-family policies and mother's wage growth over time. *Work and Occupations, 31,* 367–394. doi:10.1177/0730888413515250

Golden, L. (2008). Limited access: Disparities in flexible work schedules and work-at-home. *Journal of Family and Economic Issues, 29,* 68–109. doi:10.1007/s10834-007-9090-7

Grandey, A. A., & Cropanzano, R. (1999). The conservation of resources model applied to work-family conflict and strain. *Journal of Vocational Behavior, 54,* 350–370. Retrieved from http://http://www.idealibrary.com

Greenhaus, J. H., Allen, T. D., & Spector, P. E. (2006). Health consequences of work-family conflict: The dark side of the work-family interface. In L. Perrewe & D. C. Ganster (Eds.), *Research in occupational stress and well-being* (Vol. 6, pp. 171–211). Amsterdam: JAI.

Hallett, T. (2010). The myth incarnate: Recoupling processes, turmoil, and inhabited institutions in an urban elementary school. *American Sociological Review, 75*(1), 52–74. doi:10.1177/0003122409357044

Hallett, T., & Ventresca, M. J. (2006). Inhabited institutions: Social interactions and organizational forms in Gouldner's patterns of industrial bureaucracy. *Theory and Society*, *35*(2), 213–236. doi:10.1007/s11186-006-9003-z

Hammer, L. B., Bauer, T. N., &. Grandey, A. A. (2003). Work-family conflict and work-related withdrawal behaviors. *Journal of Business and Psychology*, *17*(3), 419–436. doi:10.1023/A:1022820609967

Hochschild, A. R. (1997). *The time bind: When work becomes home and home becomes work*. New York, NY: Metropolitan Books.

Kelliher, C., & Anderson, D. (2010). Doing more with less? Flexible working practices and the intensification of work. *Human Relations*, *63*(1), 83–106. doi:10.1177/0018726709349199

Kellogg, K. C. (2009). Operating room: Relational spaces and microinstitutional change in surgery. *American Journal of Sociology*, *115*(3), 657–711. Retrieved from http://www.press.uchicago.edu/ucp/journals/journal/ajs.html

Kellogg, K. C. (2011). *Challenging operations: Medical reform and resistance in surgery*. Chicago, IL: University of Chicago Press.

Kelly, E. L., Ammons, S. K., Chermack, K., & Moen, P. (2010). Gendered challenge, gendered response: Confronting the ideal worker norm in a white-collar organization. *Gender & Society*, *24*(3), 281–303. doi:10.1177/0891243210372073

Kelly, E. L., & Dobbin, F. (1999). Civil rights law at work: Sex discrimination and the rise of maternity leave policies. *American Journal of Sociology*, *105*, 455–492. Retrieved from http://http://www.press.uchicago.edu/ucp/journals/journal/ajs.html

Kelly, E. L., & Kalev, A. (2006). Managing flexible work arrangements in U.S. organizations: Formalized discretion or 'a right to ask'. *Socio-Economic Review*, *4*(3), 379–416. doi:10.1093/ser/mwl001

Kelly, E. L., Kossek, E. E., Hammer, L., Durham, M., Bray, J., Chermack, K., & Murphy, L. (2008). Getting there from here: Research on the effects of work-family initiatives on work-family conflict and business outcomes. *Academy of Management Annals*, *2*, 305–334. doi:10.1080/19416520802211610

Kelly, E. L., & Moen, P. (2007). Rethinking the clock work of work: Why schedule control may pay off at work and at home. *Advances in Developing Human Resources*, *9*(4), 487–506. doi:10.1177/1523422307305489

Kelly, E. L., Moen, P., & Tranby, E. (2011). Changing workplaces to reduce work-family conflict: Schedule control in a white-collar organization. *American Sociological Review*, *76*(2), 265–290. doi:10.1177/0003122411400056

Konrad, A. M., & Mangel, R. (2000). The impact of work-life programs on firm productivity. *Strategic Management Journal*, *21*, 1225–1237. doi:10.1002/1097-0266(200012)21:12<1225::AID-SMJ135>3.0.CO;2-3

Kossek, E. E., & Lee, M. D. (2005). Making flexibility work: What managers have learned about implementing reduced-load work. Summary of Findings from Phase II of Alfred P. Sloan Grant # 2002-6-11. Michigan State University and McGill University.

Lambert, S. J. (2000). Added benefits: The link between work-life benefits and organizational citizenship behavior. *Academy of Management Journal*, *43*, 801–815. doi:10.2307/1556411

Lawrence, T. B., & Suddaby, R. (2006). Institutions and institutional work. In R. Clegg, C. Hardy, T. B. Lawrence, & W. R. Nord (Eds.), *Handbook of organization studies* (2nd ed., pp. 215–254). London: Sage.

Lawrence, T. B., Suddaby, R., & Leca, B. (2010). *Institutional work: Actors and agency in institutional studies of organizations*. Cambridge: Cambridge University Press.

Lee, M. D., MacDermid, S. M., & Buck, M. L. (2000). Organizational paradigms of reduced load work: Accommodation, elaboration, and transformation. *Academy of Management Journal*, *43*, 1211–1226. doi:10.2307/1556346

Leslie, L. M., Manchester, C. F., Park, T. Y., & Mehng, S. A. (2013). Flexible work practices: A source of career premiums or penalties. *Academy of Management Journal*, *55*, 1407–1428. doi:10.5465/amj.2010.0651

Lewis, S. (1997). 'Family friendly' employment policies: A route to changing organizational culture or playing about at the margins? *Gender, Work & Organization*, *4*, 13–23. doi:10.1111/1468-0432.00020

Lewis, S., & Taylor, K. (1996). Evaluating the impact of family-friendly employment policies: A case study. In S. Lewis & J. Lewis (Eds.), *The work-family challenge: Rethinking employment* (pp. 113–128). London: Sage.

Mennino, S. F., Rubin, B. A., & Brayfield, A. (2005). Home-to-job and Job-to-home spillover: The impact of company policies and workplace culture. *The Sociological Quarterly*, *46*, 107–135. Retrieved from http://onlinelibrary.wiley.com/journal/10.1111/(ISSN)1533-8525

Meyer, J. W., & Rowan, B. (1977). Institutionalized organizations: Formal structure as myth and ceremony. *American Journal of Sociology*, *83*, 340–363. Retrieved from http://www.press.uchicago.edu/ucp/journals/journal/ajs.html

Moen, P., Kelly, E. L., & Hill, R. (2011). Does enhancing work-time control and flexibility reduce turnover? A naturally occurring experiment. *Social Problems*, *58*(1), 69–98. doi:10.1525/sp.2011.58.1.69

Moen, P., Kelly, E. L., Tranby, E., & Huang, Q. (2011). Changing work, changing health: Can real work-time flexibility promote health behaviors and well-being? *Journal of Health and Social Behavior*, *52*(4), 404–429. doi:10.1177/0022146511418979

Moen, P., & Roehling, P. (2005). *The career mystique: Cracks in the American dream*. Lanham, MD: Rowman & Littlefield.

Perlow, L. A., & Kelly, E. L. (2014). Toward a model of work redesign for better work and better life. *Work & Occupations*, *41*, 111–134. doi:10.1177/0730888413516473

Powell, W. W., & Colyvas, J. A. (2008). Microfoundations of institutional theory. In R. Greenwood, C. Oliver, K. Sahlin-Andersson, & R. Suddaby (Eds.), *Handbook of organizational institutionalism* (pp. 276–298). London: Sage Publications.

Ressler, C., & Thompson, J. (2008). *Why work sucks and how to fix it: No schedules, no meetings, no joke – The simple changes that can make your job terrific*. New York, NY: Penguin.

Ryan, A. M., & Kossek, E. E. (2008). Work-life policy implementation: Breaking down or creating barriers to inclusiveness? *Human Resource Management*, *47*, 295–310. doi:10.1002/hrm.20213

Sanders, M. M., Lengnick-Hall, M. L., Lengnick-Hall, C. A., & Steele-Clapp, L. (1998). Love and work: Career-family attitudes of new entrants into the labor force. *Journal of Organizational Behavior*, *19*(6), 603–619. doi:10.1002/(SICI)1099-1379(1998110)19:6<603::AID-JOB856>3.0.CO;2-Z

Scott, W. R. (1994). Institutional analysis: Variance and process theory approaches. In W. R. Scott & J. W. Meyer (Eds.), *Institutional environments and organizations: Structural complexity and individualism* (pp. 81–99). Thousand Oaks, CA: Sage Publications.

Scott, W. R. (2008). *Institutions and organizations* (2nd ed.). Thousand Oaks, CA: Sage Publications.
Thomas, L. T., & Ganster, D. C. (1995). Impact of family supportive work variables on work-family conflict and strain: A control perspective. *Journal of Applied Psychology, 80*, 6–15. Retrieved from http://www.apa.org/pubs/journals/apl/
Thompson, C. A., Beauvais, L. L., & Lyness, K. S. (1999). When work–family benefits are not enough: The influence of work–family culture on benefit utilization, organizational attachment, and work–family conflict. *Journal of Vocational Behavior, 54*, 392–415. doi:10.1006/jvbe.1998.1681
Williams, J. C. (2000). *Unbending gender*. New York, NY: Oxford University Press.
Yin, R. K. (2009). *Case study research: Design and methods* (4th ed.). Thousand Oaks, CA: Sage Publications.
Zucker, L. G. (1987). Institutional theories of organizations. *Annual Review of Sociology, 13*, 443–464. doi:10.1146/annurev.so.13.080187.002303